W0230431

Advances in
Information
Systems Science

Volume 9

Contributors

R. C. Gonzalez   *Electrical Engineering Department*
University of Tennessee
Knoxville, Tennessee

Chi-Heng Hu   *Institute of Automation*
Academia Sinica
Beijing, People's Republic of China

Isamu Kobayashi   *SANNO Institute of Business Administration*
School of Management and Informatics
Kanagawa, Japan

Hung Chi Lai   *STC Computer Research Corporation*
Santa Clara, California

Saburo Muroga   *Department of Computer Science*
University of Illinois
Urbana, Illinois

Yoh-Han Pao   *Department of Electrical Engineering and Applied Physics*
Case Western Reserve University
Cleveland, Ohio

M. G. Thompson   *Computer Science Department*
University of Tennessee
Knoxville, Tennessee

A Continuation Order Plan is available for this series. A continuation order will bring delivery of each new volume immediately upon publication. Volumes are billed only upon actual shipment. For further information please contact the publisher.

Volume 9

Advances in

Information

Systems Science

Edited by

Julius T. Tou

Center for Information Research
University of Florida
Gainesville, Florida

PLENUM PRESS · NEW YORK — LONDON

The Library of Congress cataloged the first volume of this title as follows:

Advances in information systems science. v. 1 –

New York, Plenum Press, 1969.
    v. illus. 24 cm.
   Editor v. 1- J. T. Tou.
   1. Information science – Collections. I. Tou, Tsu-lieh. ed.

| Z699.A1A36 | 029.7 | 69-12544 |

ISBN-13: 978-1-4612-9449-8   e-ISBN-13: 978-1-4613-2369-3
DOI: 10.1007/978-1-4613-2369-3

© 1985 Plenum Press, New York

Softcover reprint of the hardcover 1st edition 1985

A Division of Plenum Publishing Corporation
233 Spring Street, New York, N.Y. 10013

All rights reserved

No part of this book may be reproduced, stored in a retrieval system, or transmitted, in any form or by any means, electronic, mechanical, photocopying, microfilming, recording, or otherwise, without written permission from the Publisher

CONTENTS OF EARLIER VOLUMES

Preface

Volume 9 of this series on information systems science presents four timely topics of current interest in this growing field. In each chapter an attempt is made to familiarize the reader with some basic background information on the advances discussed, so that this volume may be used independently or in conjunction with the previous volumes. The emphasis in this volume is on data structures for scene analysis, database management technology, inductive inference in processing pattern-based information, and logic design of MOS networks.

Scene analysis has become a very important aspect in information system design. The process of scene analysis involves sensing, segmentation, recognition, and interpretation. Innovative development of algorithms for these tasks requires the utilization of structural relationship prevalent within the sensed data. In Chapter 1, Thomason and Gonzalez discuss the formulation of data representation techniques and the properties of data structures and databases in scene analysis.

In view of the growing importance of database management, Chapter 2 is devoted to an overview of database management technology. In this chapter Kobayashi covers a variety of current topics. The topics discussed include system design methodology, data structure theory, semantic considerations, calculus-based database operations, database management functions, and the issues of integrity, security, concurrency, and recoverability. This chapter also discusses the end-user languages and several existing database management systems.

Chapters 3 and 4 present a conceptual framework for the processing of pattern-based information. In these two chapters, Pao and Hu discuss inductive inference methods for pattern recognition and artificial intelligence and describe inductive inference transition networks for pattern classification. Chapter 5 is concerned with design automation for MOS networks. Lai and Muroga review the basic properties of negative-gate networks and discuss algorithms for minimizing the number of negative gates, the synthesis of MOS cells, and the design of nonredundant MOS networks.

The editor wishes to express sincere thanks to the authors of this volume for their cooperation and for the timely completion of their manuscripts. In fact, many more of our colleagues contributed to the book than those whose names appear in the contents. Much credit is due to our reviewers of the articles for their invaluable advice and constructive criticism.

Gainesville, Florida   Julius T. Tou
March, 1985

CONTENTS

Chapter 3 **Processing of Pattern-Based Information, Part I:**
Inductive Inference Methods Suitable for use in Pattern
Recognition and Artificial Intelligence

Yoh-Han Pao and Chi-Heng Hu

Chapter 4   Processing of Pattern-Based Information, Part II: Description of Inductive Inference in Terms of Transition Networks

Chi-Heng Hu and Yoh-Han Pao

Chapter 5   Automated Logic Design of MOS Networks

Hung Chi Lai and Saburo Muroga

Chapter 1

DATA STRUCTURES AND DATABASES IN DIGITAL SCENE ANALYSIS

M. G. Thomason

Computer Science Department
University of Tennessee
Knoxville, Tennessee 37916

and

R. C. Gonzalez

Electrical Engineering Department
University of Tennessee
Knoxville, Tennessee 37916

1. INTRODUCTION

Digital scene analysis may be defined as the process of using a digital computer to extract, characterize, and interpret information from images of a three-dimensional world. Interest in scene analysis techniques ranges from industrial automation applications, such as assembly and inspection, to military applications involving autonomous target detection and identification. Regardless of specific applications, however, an essential characteristic of digital scene analysis techniques is the use of a machine for performing "intelligent" tasks, where the standard for intelligent behavior on the part of the machine is established by the capability of a human in performing the same tasks.

The process of digital scene analysis involves four basic steps: (1) sensing, (2) segmentation, (3) recognition, and (4) interpretation. The function of each of these steps is illustrated with the aid of Fig. 1. The *sensing* problem is one of converting a physical scene into a form suitable for computer processing. For example, if the sensor is a TV image digitizer, its output will be a two-dimensional array of discrete numerical quantities, with the value of each element in the array representing the intensity of the scene at a point in the focal plane of the camera lens. *Segmentation* is the

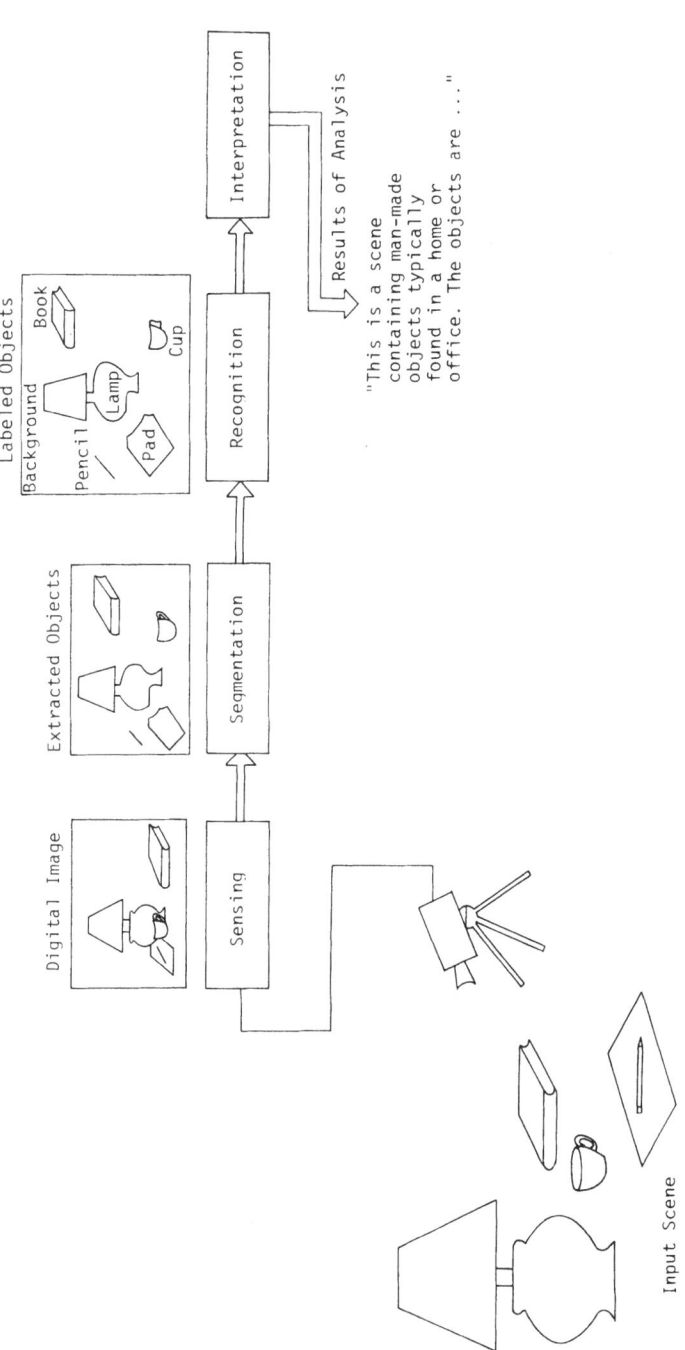

Fig. 1. Basic steps in digital scene analysis.

process that breaks up a sensed scene into its constituent parts or objects. The basic objective of segmentation is to simplify the analysis problem by reducing the scene to a manageable set of components that can be processed independently of one another. *Recognition* is basically a labeling process; that is, the function of recognition algorithms is to identify each segmented object in the scene and to assign a label (e.g., car, building, road, background, etc.) to that object. Finally, *interpretation* is the process that establishes relationships among the labeled objects in a scene in order to produce an analysis of scene composition and meaning.

While the decomposition and analysis of a scene can be relatively simple for a human, a general computer solution to this problem is still open and is an active topic of research in fields such as engineering, computer science, and psychology.† An area of considerable interest in scene analysis recently is the search for techniques suitable for representing and organizing in a systematic way the large amounts of data required for the digital representation of a scene. Innovative development of algorithms for segmentation, recognition, and interpretation involves identifying and exploiting structural relationships prevalent within the sensed data. These requirements lead to the formulation of data representation techniques based on a discrete mathematical framework.

In this chapter, attention is focused on properties of data structures and databases as they apply to problems in scene analysis. There are at least three strong arguments in favor of using standard data structures (such as link lists, stacks, and trees) and standard database organizations (such as relational, hierarchical, and network models) for representing and organizing scene data. First, these standard data representations have a firm mathematical foundation which can be used as a starting point for new algorithm development. Second, they facilitate the evaluation of important algorithm characteristics such as time complexity and computational storage requirements. Finally, consistent data representation techniques allow systematic approaches to scene data documentation, storage, access, and manipulation.

2. DATA STRUCTURES

This section gives some of the important definitions and concepts in data structures (cf. Refs. 3, 18, and 26) and provides several examples of

---

† Much of the present work in scene analysis is carried out using planar (image) views of a three-dimensional scene. This is due both to limitations in three-dimensional sensor technology and to a lack of procedures for segmentation, recognition, and interpretation of three-dimensional data. Spatial relationships of objects in a scene are approximated by using approaches such as stereo image processing or range imaging.

the use of such structures as lists, trees, and graphs in digital scene representation and processing.

2.1. Definitions and Basic Concepts

The *cartesian product* of set A with set B is denoted by $A \times B$ and is the collection of ordered pairs (a, b), a in A and b in B. A subset of $A \times B$, say $R \subseteq A \times B$, is a *binary relation* from A to B.

If $A = B \times C$, then

$$A \times D = \{[(b, c), d] | b \text{ in } B, c \text{ in } C, d \text{ in } D\}$$

Usually, we can view this product as an associative formation of ordered triples and write simply

$$B \times C \times D = \{(b, c, d) | b \text{ in } B, c \text{ in } C, d \text{ in } D\}$$

then $R \subseteq B \times C \times D$ is a *ternary relation*. In general, $R \subseteq A_1 \times A_2 \times \cdots \times A_n$ is an *n-ary relation*, $n \geq 1$.

If $A = B$, then $R \subseteq A \times B = A \times A$ is a *relation on the set A*. For instance, given $A = \{a_1, a_2, a_3\}$ and $A \times A = \{(a_1, a_1),(a_1, a_2),\ (a_1, a_3), (a_2, a_1),\ (a_2, a_2),\ (a_2, a_3),\ (a_3, a_1),\ (a_3, a_2),\ (a_3, a_3)\}$, then $R = \{(a_1, a_1), (a_1, a_2),(a_1, a_3), (a_2, a_2), (a_2, a_3), (a_3, a_3)\}$ is a relation on A. A relation R on a set A is:

   (i) *reflexive* if (a, a) is in R for each a in A;
   (ii) *symmetric* if (a, b) in R implies (b, a) in R;
   (iii) *antisymmetric* if (a, b) and (b, a) in R imply $a = b$; and
   (iv) *transitive* if (a, b) in R and (b, c) in R imply (a, c) in R.

The specific relation R given above on $A = \{a_1, a_2, a_3\}$ is therefore reflexive, antisymmetric, and transitive, but not symmetric.

2.1.1. Lists

A fundamental data structure is one for which the elements of a finite set A are ordered in a list from the first element to the last. Specifically, a *linear list* is a set of elements $A = \{a_1, a_2, \ldots, a_n\}$, $n > 0$, for which there is a relation $R \subseteq A \times A$ that is reflexive, antisymmetric, transitive, and has the additional property that, for any two elements a_i and a_j in A, either (a_1, a_j) is in R or (a_j, a_i) is in R. A relation with these characteristics is called a *linear ordering*. If (a_1, a_j) is in a linear ordering R, we usually write $a_i \leq a_j$. The *first element* in the linear list is that element a_i such that $a_i \leq a_j$

for each a_j in A. The *last element* is that element a_j for which $a_i \leq a_j$ for each a_i in A. When subscripts are used for a linear list of n elements, the standard notation has elements ordered as $a_1 \leq a_2 \leq \cdots \leq a_{n-1} \leq a_n$. The specific relation R on $A = \{a_1, a_2, a_3\}$ given above defines a linear list with the order $a_1 \leq a_2 \leq a_3$.

Often a linear list used as a data structure must be altered during the execution of an algorithm. Special kinds of linear lists are defined by the ways in which operations on them are allowed to be performed. A list is a *stack* if all insertions and deletions of elements are made on one predetermined end. A list is a *queue* if all insertions are made on one end and all deletions are made on the other.

In actual computer storage, a linear list of n elements that is static and fixed in size can have the data value(s) of its elements stored in sequential memory locations according to the natural sequencing of elements from first to last. Other techniques are more appropriate for a nonstatic list that must be changed in size or rearranged at certain times. A *linked list* is created by associating with an element both its data value(s) and a *pointer* or *link* to the first location of the next element in the linear ordering. Insertions and deletions of elements can then be handled by changing the necessary link values, as shown in Figs. 2(a), (b), and (c).

A *circular-linked list* is created by linking the last element to the first in a linear list; this allows all elements to be accessed by tracking through the list, independently of which node is used as the initial entry point. The concept of first and last elements is not always enforced for a circular-linked list, but a unique element is sometimes designated the "head" or starting node for entry into the list, as shown in Fig. 3.

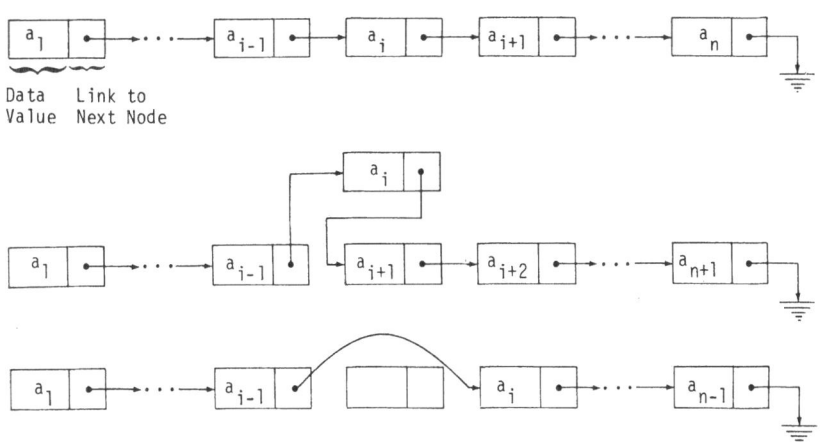

Fig. 2. (a) Linked list; (b) node insertion to expand list; (c) node deletion to shorten list.

Head Node

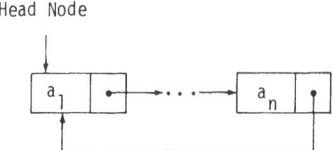

Fig. 3. Circular-linked list.

A *double-linked list* is one in which there is stored for each element (i) its data value(s), (ii) a pointer to its immediate predecessor in the linear ordering, and (iii) a pointer to its immediate successor in the linear ordering. A search or trace in this kind of list structure can move easily in either direction for any entry node.

If a linear list is regarded as a set of items each of which has a single subscript, then a generalization is an *array* of items with multiple subscripts such that any subscript, when taken through all its values in order from first to last while other subscript values are fixed, creates a linear list. For an array, any one of the simple list storage or linking techniques may be used for the individual subscripts; for example, linked lists as shown in Figs. 4(a) and (b).

It is also possible to order a static multidimensional array in a one-dimensional, linear way. One method is to impose a standard sequence for stepping through subscript values, as in the FORTRAN convention. A second method employs a relation between the set of subscript values and the integers. For example, for a two-dimensional array, say $A(x, y)$, with positive integer subscripts, let the relation $R \subseteq (I \times I) \times I$, where I is the set of

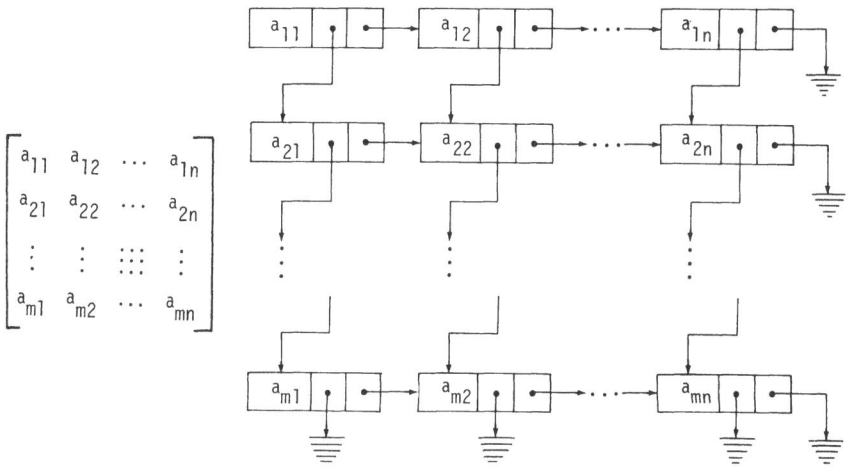

Fig. 4. (a) Two-dimensional array; (b) possible array linkages.

	y			
	1	2	3	...
x 1	1	3	6	...
2	2	5	9	...
3	4	8	13	...
⋮	⋮	⋮	⋮	⋮

Fig. 5. Values of $z = (x + y - 1)(x + y - 2)/(2 + y)$.

positive integers, be defined so that $((x, y), z)$ in R means

$$z = \frac{(x + y - 1)(x + y - 2)}{2} + y$$

It can be shown that, for a given ordered pair (x, y), z is a unique positive integer (see Fig. 5) which can be interpreted as the position of the element $A(x, y)$ in a linear list. This equation can be used recursively for arrays of dimension greater than two.

2.1.2. Trees

A structure more complex than a list is obtained by permitting a node to link to more than one immediate successor. This hierarchical or tree structure occurs frequently in computing. A *tree* T consists of a set of nodes with the properties:

(i) there is a unique node called the *root* of T; and
(ii) the remaining nodes are partitioned into m disjoint subsets $T_1, \ldots, T_m$, each of which is a tree called a *subtree* of T.

It is noted that this is a *recursive definition* in the sense that it cites itself. The convention is to draw a tree from its root downward to its leaves (a *leaf* being a node with no offspring or successors), as illustrated in Fig. 6. Among the characteristics of a tree T is that there is exactly one directed path from the root to any other node in T, so that each complete path from the root to a leaf follows a linear ordering of a subset of the nodes in which the root is the first element and the leaf is the last.

In order physically to represent a tree, we note that two items are required for each element:

(i) information about a node, stored as a set of values for the node; and
(ii) information relating a node to its predecessor and/or offspring, stored as a set of pointers to these nodes.

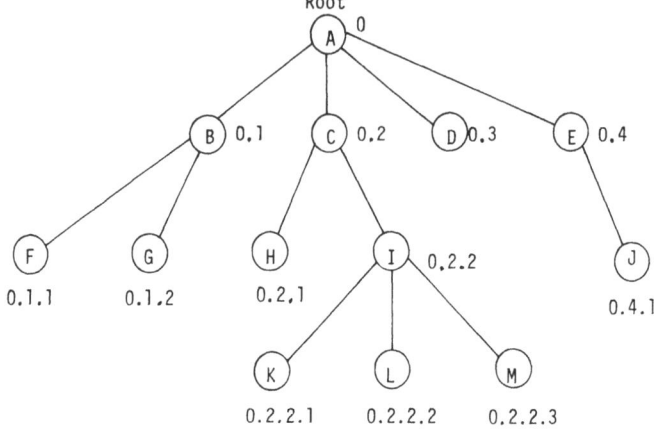

Fig. 6. Tree *T*.

Thus, the pointer techniques described above for lists may also be used for trees.

Although a tree is inherently a two-dimensional structure, it is often necessary to represent a tree as a one-dimensional list of all its nodes obtained in a manner consistent with the way in which nodes of other trees would be listed. The fundamental hierarchy of the tree can be used to obtain either a *left-bracketed* or a *right-bracketed* representation as follows.[2] For the left-bracketed representation, denoted by lrep(*T*):

  (i) If the root is labeled X and has subtrees $T_1, \ldots, T_m$ in left to right order, then

$$\text{lrep}(T) = X[\text{lrep}(T_1), \text{lrep}(T_2), \ldots, \text{lrep}(T_m)].$$

  (ii) If T consists of root X only, then lrep(*T*) = X.

For the right-bracketed representation, rrep(*T*):

  (i) If the root X has subtrees $T_1, \ldots, T_m$ in left to right order, then

$$\text{rrep}(T) = [\text{rrep}(T_1), \ldots, \text{rrep}(T_m)]X.$$

  (ii) If T consists of root X only, then rrep(*T*) = X.

For tree T in Fig. 6, lrep(*T*) = $A(B(F, G), C(H, I(K, L, M)), D, E(J))$ and rrep(*T*) = $((F, G)B, (H, (K, L, M)I)C, D, (J)E)A$. The linear list of nodes that remain when the brackets are deleted from lrep(*T*) is the *preorder* of the elements in T; the linear list obtained by deleting the brackets from rrep(*T*) is the *postorder* of the elements in *T*.

Another representation of the tree hierarchy is obtained by using *Gorn addressing* for the nodes.[16] The indices of T are defined recursively by assigning the index 0 to the root, and if a node with index k has n offspring, they are assigned indices $k \cdot 1, k \cdot 2, \ldots, k \cdot n$ in order from left to right. Given a tree with these indices, there is a *lexicographical ordering relation* $\underset{L}{<}$ defined on T as follows. Let r and s be indices; then $r \underset{L}{<} s$ if

    (i) there is an index c such that $s = r \cdot c$, or

    (ii) $r = c \cdot i \cdot u$ and $s = c \cdot j \cdot v$, where c, u, and v are indices, and i and j are positive integers, with i being less than j.

Condition (i) establishes a top-to-bottom ordering along the descendant paths from the root; condition (ii) establishes a left to right ordering among the descendants of any one node.

Figure 6 includes the Gorn addresses for the nodes in the tree T. The node labeled K with index $s = 0 \cdot 2 \cdot 2 \cdot 1$ is a descendant of node I with index $r = 0 \cdot 2 \cdot 2$ because $s = r \cdot c$ with $r = 0 \cdot 2 \cdot 2$ and $c = 1$. The node labeled H with index $r = 0 \cdot 2 \cdot 1$ is to the left of node I with index $s = 0 \cdot 2 \cdot 2$ because $r = c \cdot i$ and $s = c \cdot j$ with $i < j$.

2.1.3. Graphs

The last discrete mathematical structure we define is a *directed graph* or *digraph G*, which is a set A of nodes and a relation $R \subseteq A \times A$. If (a, b) is in R, then there is an *edge* or *arc* directed from node a to node b. An *acyclic digraph* is one that contains no cycles, i.e., no path along directed edges from a node back to itself; thus, a tree is a special case of an *acyclic digraph*.

An *ordered digraph G* is defined by a pair (A, R) where A is the set of nodes and R is a set of linear lists of arcs, with each list of the general form $((a, b_1), (a, b_2), \ldots, (a, b_n))$ for $a, b_1, \ldots, b_n$ in A. This list, in its digraph interpretation, means that there are n arcs leaving node a, the first going to node b_1, the second going to b_2, and so on through the last going to node b_n. The tree T in Fig. 6, viewed as an ordered digraph, would be defined by the set of nodes $\{A, B, C, D, E, F, G, H, I, J, K, L, M\}$ and the following lists: $((A, B), (A, C), (A, D), (A, E))$; $((B, F), (B, G))$; $((C, H), (C, I))$; $((E, J))$, $((I, K), (I, L), (I, M))$.

2.2. Use of Lists for Scene Representation and Processing

Important tasks in many scene processing systems are the detection and representation of boundaries for the regions in an image view of a scene. A *region* is generally defined to be a subimage of pixels that are connected by transitivity and share a common characteristic or attribute, such as having the same value of gray level. A pixel that has at least one immediate neighbor which belongs to a different region in any of the eight adjacency directions is called a *boundary pixel*; otherwise, a pixel is *interior* to a region. Various algorithms to detect the boundary pixels and to order them as sequences that trace the outlines of the regions may be found in the literature (cf. Refs. 4, 15, 17, 22, 28, and 39). Circular-linked lists are often used to store the sequenced boundary pixels to allow an efficient trace around the outline of any region in a two-dimensional image.

In this section, we illustrate the use of lists for boundary representation and give an example of list processing to compress the boundary representation. An approach developed by Lee[28] uses two words of storage for each node in the sequenced boundary list. The first word stores the location of the boundary pixel as a single value z obtained from its (x, y) coordinates by the equation

$$z = x + (y - 1) * n$$

where n is the dimension of the $n \times n$ image array. The second word is the link that points to the first word of the next node in the boundary sequence. The location value z of a *singular boundary pixel* (that is, a boundary pixel not adjacent to any of its region's interior pixels, as illustrated in Fig. 7) is

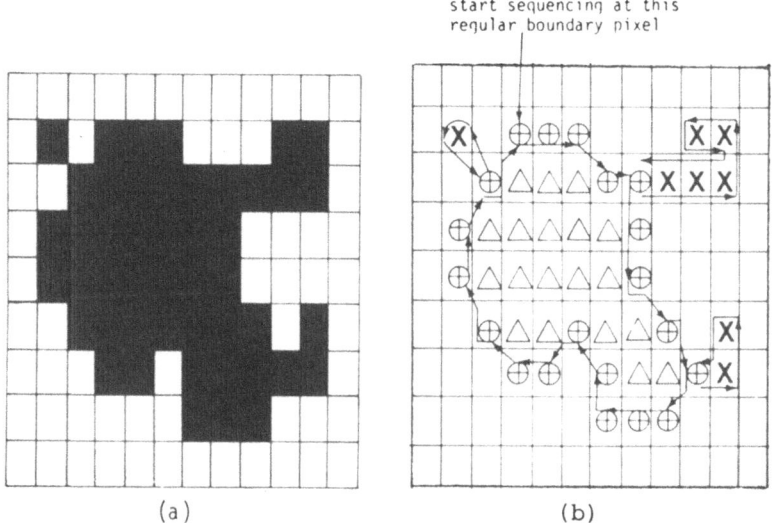

start sequencing at this
regular boundary pixel

(a)   (b)

Fig. 7. (a) Region; (b) classification of region pixels. KEY: $\oplus$, regular boundary pixel; $\times$, singular boundary pixel; $\triangle$, interior pixel; $\rightarrow$, sequencing direction. (From Ref. 28.)

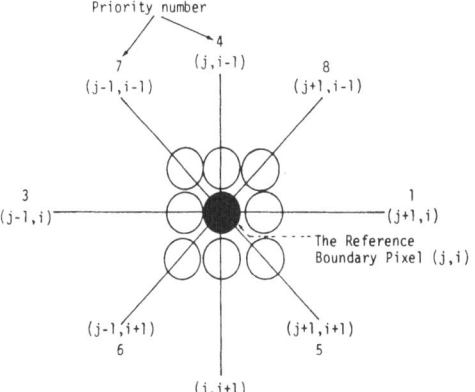

Fig. 8. Sequencing priorities.

made a negative number as a flag. The sequencing priority is shown in Fig. 8 in which a lower number indicates a higher priority.

Figure 9(a) and (b) shows two digitized images. Figure 9(c) and (d) shows segmented and averaged versions of the images, respectively. Figure 9(e) and (f) shows the region boundaries traced and displayed via the circular-linked list representations.

Two methods for compressing the data in the sequenced circular-linked lists for region boundaries have been studied by Lee.[28] Both are based on the eight direction codes[13] corresponding to eight connective descriptions with respect to a reference boundary pixel, as shown in Fig. 10. The codes are assigned pixel by pixel by moving through the circular-linked list from an arbitrarily selected starting pixel, so that every node in the list has a direction code from 0 to 7, except for the starting pixel itself.

The first coding scheme sequentially combines every two successive direction codes into one code by using the coding equation

$$\text{CODE} = (\text{DIRCD1} + 1) * 8 + \text{DIRCD2}$$

where DIRCD1 is the first of the two successive base direction codes and DIRCD2 is the second. CODE is the value of this part of the shape descriptor. If the total number of base direction codes of the boundary is odd, the last direction code cannot be combined into one code using the above equations, so in this case, CODE is just set equal to this last base direction code. Since the value of CODE generated by the equation is always positive, "−128" is used to represent the endmark of the shape descriptor. A segment of a sequenced boundary is shown in Fig. 11; the shape descriptor is "17, 26, 8, 15, 7, −128."

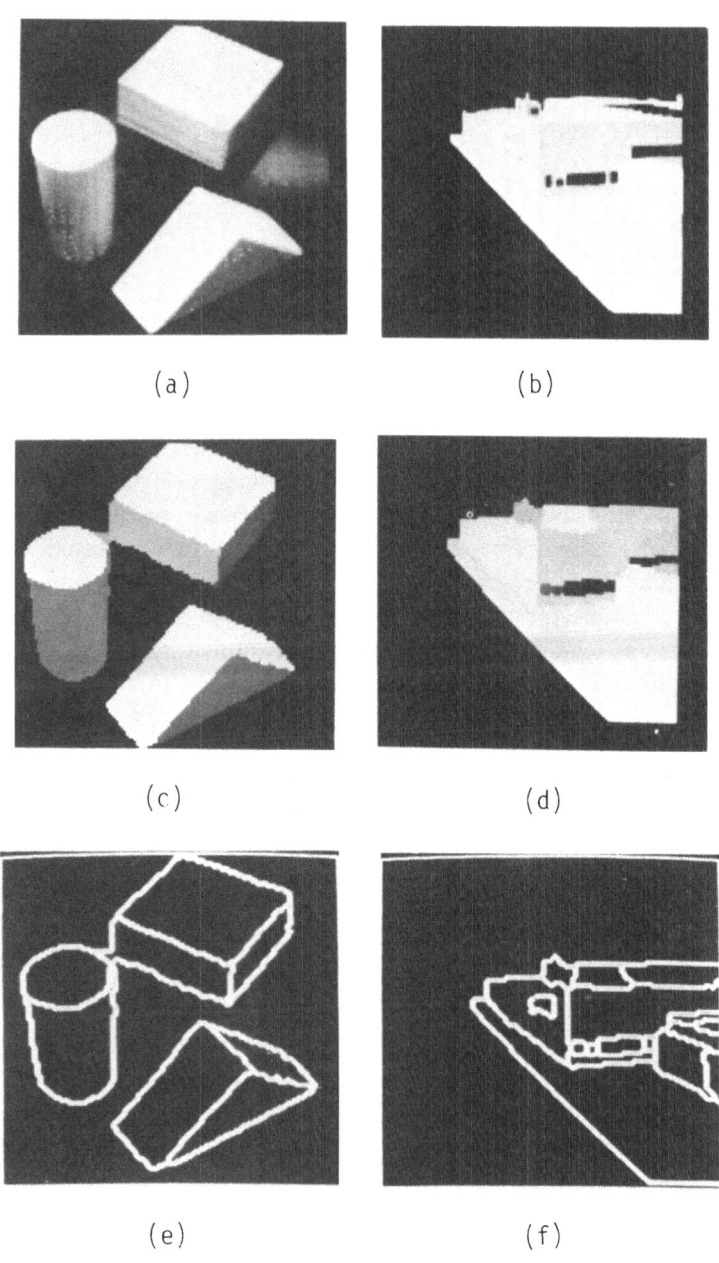

Fig. 9. (a, b) Original images; (c, d) segmented images; (e, f) boundaries from lists of sequenced boundary pixels. (From Ref. 28.)

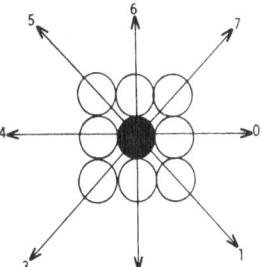

Fig. 10. Base direction codes.

The second coding scheme is basically a run-length coding of the *direction vector*.[15] A direction vector is a section of a boundary in which all pixels have the same base direction codes. The number of the pixels of a direction vector is called its *length*. Since the number represented by a byte for the code ranges from −128 to 127, the eight possible kinds of direction vector are divided into two parts in order to code as long a direction vector as possible. Each direction vector is coded by the corresponding coding equations

$$\text{CODE} = (\text{DIRCOD} * 32) + \text{LENGTH} \qquad \text{for } 0 \le \text{DIRCOD} \le 3$$

and

$$\text{CODE} = -[(\text{DIRCOD} - 4) * 32] + \text{LENGTH} \qquad \text{for } 4 \le \text{DIRCOD} \le 7$$

where DIRCOD represents the base direction code of the direction vector and LENGTH is the length of the direction vector.

The number "0" is used to represent the endmark of the shape descriptor in the second coding scheme. The maximum length of the direction vector is 31 because four different kinds of direction vector with lengths ranging from 1 up to 31 can be represented by the numbers from 1 to 124 (−1 to −124) without exceeding the range from 1 to 127 (−1 to −127). If a direction vector's length exceeds 31, it must be divided into multiple direction vectors;

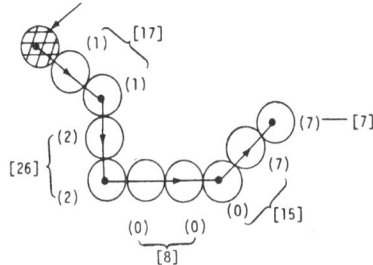

Fig. 11. Shape description using first coding scheme. (*n*) Base direction code. [*m*] Code in shape descriptor. (From Ref. 28.)

for example, if there is a direction vector with length 70, it will be sequentially divided into three direction vectors with lengths 31, 31, and 8. (If the maximum length of the direction vector were allowed to be 32, direction vectors could be coded by the numbers ranging from 0 to 127 and −1 to −128; however, a problem might arise, since no more numbers would be available to represent the endmarks of the shape descriptors.) A segment of a sequenced boundary is shown in Fig. 12; the shape descriptor is "70, 5, −98, 39, −3, 0" using the second coding scheme.

The above compression techniques have been used for processing 128 × 128 images with no more than 256 regions. For the first scheme, two boundary pixels represented by four words in the original list can be represented by 1 byte after compression, giving a compression ratio approaching 16 to 1. The compression ratio in the second scheme is a function of the lengths of the direction vectors in the image. If the boundaries are relatively "regular" and consist of long runs of pixels with the same direction code, the ratio can approach 248 to 1 because up to 31 boundary pixels can be coded into 1 byte. In the worst case, the direction vectors have length 1, in which case the ratio is 8 to 1.

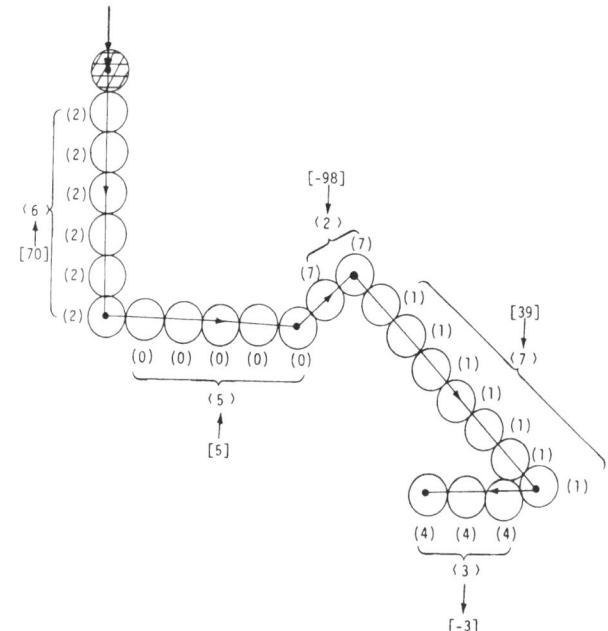

Fig. 12. Shape description using second coding scheme. (*n*) Base direction code. ⟨*m*⟩ Length of direction vector. [*k*] Code in shape descriptor. (From Ref. 28.)

2.3. Use of Quad Trees for Image Representation and Processing

An *n-ary* tree for $n \geq 1$ is a tree in which each node either has n offspring or is a leaf with no offspring; thus, $n = 2$ means a binary tree, $n = 3$ means a ternary tree, and $n = 4$ means a quad tree. Quad trees have been found to be particularly attractive as data structures in certain areas of scene analysis and image processing.

Given an image P as a rectangular array of pixels characterized by quantitative parameters such as gray level or color intensity, we develop a quad tree for P using Gorn addressing in the following way:

(i) The root with index 0 is labeled P.

(ii) P is divided into quarters to make subimages corresponding to tree nodes 0.1, 0.2, 0.3, and 0.4. If the parameter(s) for all pixels in the subimage for node $0 \cdot i$, $1 \leq i \leq 4$, are identical, then node $0 \cdot i$ becomes a leaf labeled with the parameter value(s); if all parameters are not equal, then node $0 \cdot i$ becomes the root of a quad subtree and the subimage $0 \cdot i$ is itself quartered. The test for creating a leaf node is then applied to the subimages $0 \cdot i \cdot j$, $1 \leq j \leq 4$.

(iii) Step (ii) is carried out until all paths terminate on labeled leaves. Ultimately, of course, a leaf could correspond to an individual pixel.

Figure 13 shows the nature of the quad tree hierarchy for an image, and Fig. 14 shows the subimages associated with a polygon. A quad tree is an example of a *regular decomposition* of an image because there is regularity in the shape, size, and parameters of a subimage represented by a given level in the tree. Some of the advantages of a regular decomposition of an image are (i) the creation of subimages convenient for processing if the entire image P is too large for main storage; (ii) rapid access to the representation of any geographical part of the image; (iii) a hierarchical structure suitable for recursive analysis techniques; and (iv) general independence of the structure from the type of image being processed.

To carry out experiments in reduction of quad trees, Klinger and Dyer[24] define the *relative importance* of subimage $i \cdot j$ subimage i as

$$d(i \cdot j, i) = \frac{\text{intensity of } i \cdot j}{\text{intensity of } i}$$

where intensity refers to the average gray level value of the pixels; thus, $0 \leq d(i \cdot j, i) \leq 1.0$. Using two thresholds, w_1 and w_2, a subimage $i \cdot j$ is

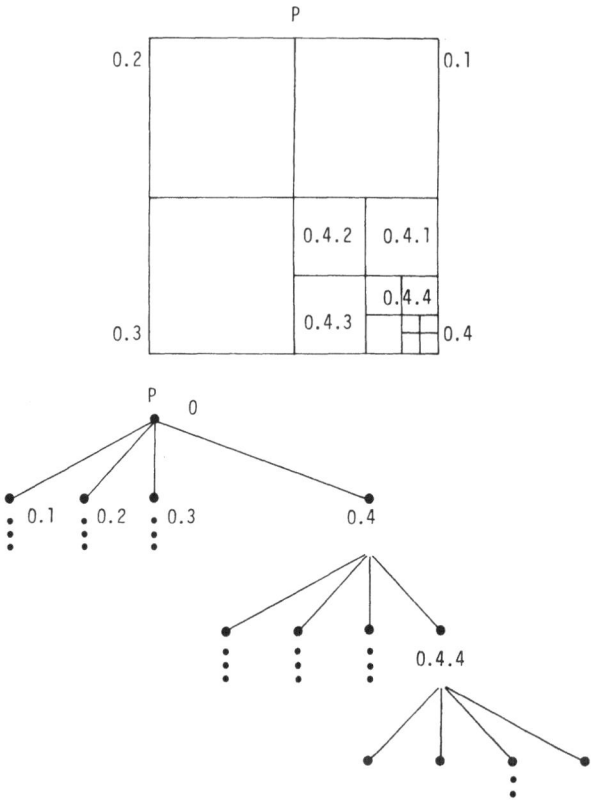

Fig. 13. (a) Quartering of image *P*; (b) quad tree for image *P*.

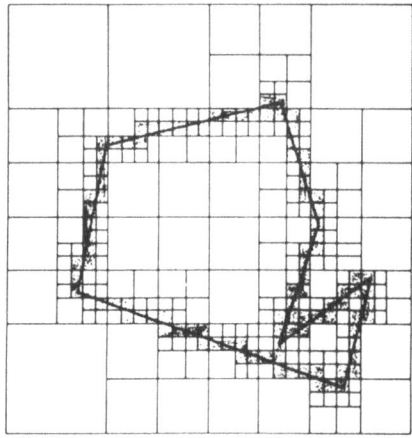

Fig. 14. Quartering for polygon. [From Hunter and Steiglitz (1979).]

TABLE I
Experimental Results for Thresholds $w_1 = 0.10$ and $w_2 = 0.25$

Figure class	% Object area lost	% Picture area deleted
Letters	18.0	75.0
Blocks	10.0	64.0
Polygons	4.0	50.0

called "informative" if $w_2 \leq d(i \cdot j, i) \leq 1.0$, "questionable" or "not sure" if $w_1 \leq (di \cdot j, i) < w_2$, and "noninformative" if $0 \leq d(i \cdot j, i) < w_1$. In building the quad tree for the offspring of node i, the node $i \cdot j$ is made an empty entry if $i \cdot j$ is noninformative, made a single leaf if $i \cdot j$ is informative, and made a nonleaf node (the root of a quad subtree) if $i \cdot j$ is questionable.

Digitized images representing letters, blocks, and polygons in 64×64 and 32×32 arrays of pixels with gray levels ranging from 0 to 9 were processed to obtain quad tree structures for the image objects. Illustrations of the kinds of results obtained in the experiment are given in Table I. Details of the experiment may be found in Klinger and Dyer.[24]

The time and space complexity of a variety of algorithms that perform operations on quad tree representations of images have been investigated by Hunter and Steiglitz.[20] In their model, a picture of image $P = (C, A)$ consists of set C, a finite set of pixel colors, and set A, a square array of pixels. Because of the image- and subimage-quartering property of a quad tree, such a tree T corresponds to P decomposed into a $2^q \times 2^q$ array, $q > 0$; and T has at most $q + 1$ levels.

The algorithms are taken to be executed on a random access machine for which a data transfer to or from memory requires a constant amount of time. Storage size is a fixed number of bits adequate to store, for example, the information labeling a node. Time is measured in executions of constant-time operations on pairs of data words, such as multiplication and comparison of numerical values. The complexity of an algorithm with real-valued inputs $x_1, x_2, \ldots, x_n$ is measured as follows: for real-valued functions f and g, if $f(x_1, \ldots, x_n)$ time or space is required, the algorithm is of *order* $g(x_1, \ldots, x_n)$, denoted by $O(g(x_1, \ldots, x_n))$, iff $f(x_1, \ldots, x_n)$ is not greater than $kg(x_1, \ldots, x_n)$ for some constant k and for all $x_1, \ldots, x_n$ greater than some fixed integer.

As an illustration, a "condensation algorithm" to eliminate any instances in which the four offspring of a node have the same color in a quad tree can be described essentially as a postorder transversal of the nodes. Specifically, we start at the root and recursively traverse the subtree rooted at each offspring. For a root which is itself a leaf, we attach the leaf color to the root; for a root of a nontrivial subtree, if all four offspring have the same color label, we color the root their color and remove them. This algorithm visits each node only once and therefore requires time that is a linear function of the number of nodes in the original tree.

This technique is representative of a large number of efficient tree-processing algorithms that are recursive and perform various operations on a tree (including modifications of its structure) as nodes and subtrees are traversed. Often the specific modifications done at a certain node are determined by the information passed from the frontier upwards to the offspring of the node, that is, the information flows from the bottom upwards through the tree's hierarchy.

A second algorithm described by Hunter and Steiglitz[20] creates an image that is the ordered superposition of N trees representing N pictures of the same size. One color is designated to be transparent to the other colors; otherwise, the nontransparent colors of picture x on top of picture y dominate in the resulting image. Let Super(x, y) be the pairwise superposition of upper tree x on lower tree y. The algorithm traverses both trees x and y in parallel and modifies y wherever necessary to create the new image tree. One of three cases determines the actions taken when a leaf is encountered in either tree:

  (i) The traversal visits leaves in both x and y. If the x leaf is transparent, the y leaf is not changed; if the x leaf is not transparent, its color replaces the color of the y leaf.

  (ii) The traversal visits a leaf in x and an interior node in y. If the x leaf is transparent, nothing is done; otherwise, the y node and its descendants are replaced by the color of the x leaf. The traversal is continued as if the y node's descendants had been explicitly visited.

  (iii) The traversal visits an interior node in x and a leaf in y. In this case, the y leaf is replaced by the subtree rooted at the x node, and all transparent leaves in that subtree are given the color of the y leaf.

If the input and output data for the Super(x, y) algorithm must be transferred to and from memory, then the order of Super(x, y) is O(total number of nodes in x and y).

As a generalization to N trees ordered as N, $N - 1, \ldots, 2, 1$ for super-position, we first compute Super(N, Super($N - 1$, Super($N - 2, \ldots,$ Super(3, Super(2, 1)), $\ldots$))) as a series of pairwise superpositions, then apply the "condensation algorithm" described above to the result. Each computation of Super can be done in time and storage that is linear in the number of nodes of its upper tree; the total computation can be done in time and space linear in the number of nodes in all trees. Other picture combinations (union, intersection, etc.) can be performed by similar techniques on quad trees.

An interesting and effective use of quad trees is in dealing with images containing polygons, as shown in Fig. 14. Basically, a polygon consists of a collection of vertices characterized by pairs of coordinates, with nonintersecting edges as line segments between consecutive vertices. In a quad tree for a picture of a polygon, the nodes are partitioned into three classes: boundary, interior, and exterior.

In order to describe the complexity of quad tree algorithms for polygons, we assume that the picture $P = (C, A)$ is a $2^q \times 2^q$ array of square, colored pixels. The base-2 algorithm of the length of a side of A is q. Let v be the number of vertices in the polygon and p be the smallest integer number of pixel widths not less than the polygon's perimeter. The following results are proved by Hunter and Steiglitz.[20]

(i) There are no more than $O(p + q)$ nodes in the quad tree for a polygon. (The actual bound on the number of nodes is $16q - 11 + 16p$.)

(ii) Time $O(v(p + q))$ is sufficient to construct the quad tree for a polygon, beginning with the original picture $P = (C, A)$.

(iii) Space proportional to the size of the input and output is sufficient to construct the quad tree for a polygon.

Among further results on quad trees, it is shown that there is an algorithm for tree construction for polygons that is asymptotically $O(v)$, and that this is an optimal algorithm in the limit of increasing v when the resolution q is fixed.

A method of image segmentation based on traversal of a quad tree has been proposed by Horowitz and Pavlidis.[19] In a pure "merging" method for segmentation, a large number of small picture regions are merged to form larger regions; in a pure "splitting" method, the picture is recursively divided into smaller regions. This technique attempts a direct two-dimensional segmentation by a combined split-and-merge approach.

Suppose X is the domain of a picture, for example, a square array of pixels. Let $f(x, y)$ be the function assigning values to pixels; here $f(x, y)$ is taken to be the brightness function. For purposes of setting the segmentation criteria, a logic function $P: 2^X \to \{TRUE, FALSE\}$ is defined on the power set of X such that

$$P(S) = \begin{cases} TRUE & \text{if there is a constant } a \text{ such at } |f(x, y) - a| \le e \\ & \text{for all points } (x, y) \text{ in } S \\ FALSE & \text{otherwise} \end{cases}$$

where e is a preset threshold factor. A *segmentation* of X is a partition into subsets S_i, $1 \leq i \leq m$, where, by the definition of a partition,

(a) $X = \bigcup_{i=1}^{m} S_i$
(b) $S_i \cap S_j = \emptyset, i \neq j$

and, in addition

(c) $P(S_i) = \text{TRUE}, 1 \leq i \leq m$
(d) $P(S_i \cup S_j) = \text{FALSE}, i \neq j$

provided that S_i and S_j are adjacent in X. Note that there may be more than one segmentation of picture X for a given P. A merging algorithm would begin with regions satisfying (c) and merge to create regions satisfying (d). A splitting algorithm would begin with regions satisfying (d) and split to achieve (c). The method of Horowitz and Pavlidis begins with a partition that does not necessarily satisfy either (c) or (d) and produces a partition satisfying both.

In the quad tree structure used, each node corresponds to a square picture region. From an arbitrary initial tree, such a region may be merged with its four adjacent neighbors if all have agreement within the error threshold of their pixel brightness values, or a region may be split into four quarters if there is greater variation in the brightness values. These split-and-merge steps must be followed by a grouping procedure to eliminate artificial region boundaries that might arise from the original segmentation; in this grouping step, adjacent nodes with different predecessors and at different levels of the tree may be merged together (and the regions they represent thereby merged together), provided the segmentation criterion P remains satisfied.

The details of this segmentation technique, including the algorithms given in a high-level programming code and some experimental results, may be found in Horowitz and Pavlidis.[19]

Wu *et al.*[49] have discussed threshold selection using quad trees. Samet[40] defines a data structure called QMAT as a quad tree skeleton with a set of distance values. The QMAT, based on a "chessboard distance," partitions an image into a set of nondisjoint squares the sides of which are sums of powers of 2; this representation is convenient for a variety of algorithms and can be a more compact structure than the ordinary quad tree for an image.

3. DATABASES

This section presents some of the important definitions and concepts in contemporary database design and provides several illustrations of the relevance of databases to various aspects of scene data organization and processing. Because a database is generally a high-level organization of large amounts of data, the choice of a database format often implies the designer's own version (or "world model") of the ways in which the information within a scene itself is organized.

3.1. Definitions and Basic Concepts

We can informally define a *database* (DB) to be a large collection of data organized according to some predefined structural model. A *database management system* (DBMS) is a software–hardware organization that permits users to create, access, and/or modify a database. A *data definition* (DD) *language* is a high-level language used to establish a database and to define its entities and the relationships among them. A *data manipulation* (DM) *language* or *query language* is a high-level language used to extract or modify data in an existing database.

The decade of the 1970s was an era of intense study of databases, both in theory seeking unifying concepts and terminology and in practice with various implementations. Generally speaking, a computer system designer expects one or more of the following characteristics to be obtained by an adequate database system (DBS) design[11]:

(i) reduction of redundancy in the data;
(ii) reduction or elimination of inconsistency in the data;
(iii) standard, well-documented procedures for using the data;
(iv) convenient methods for a variety of users to share the data;
(v) maintenance of data integrity, i.e., assurance that only accurate data is available;
(vi) assurance that, in the tradeoffs necessary in any digital system design, the aspects of data storage and manipulation have received direct attention;
(vii) enforcement of data security requirements.

The operating environment in which a DBS is to be used determines the relative weight of each of the above seven considerations. For database design in scene analysis systems, one would virtually always give items (i), (ii), (iii), (v), and (vi) high weights. For a system dedicated to a specific task, item (iv) might not apply; and for a system located in a secure facility, item (vii) might be achieved automatically.

The field of database systems does not as yet have a complete set of accepted nomenclature; however, three areas for concentrated investigation in DBS design have emerged,[11] namely:

(i) the physical and conceptual descriptions of a DBS;

(ii) the three fundamental DB organizations as relational, hierarchical, and network models; and

(iii) the DD and DM languages and other DBMS requirements.

Certainly these areas are not disjoint, nor are they necessarily all-inclusive for each specific set of needs; but in so far as a unified DBS analysis/synthesis procedure can be said to exist today, it exists in dealing with questions arising in the above three areas. We use these areas as a framework to consider database design for image and scene processing systems.

3.1.1. The Physical and Conceptual Descriptions

Figure 15 is a standard block diagram of a general DBS. The *physical database* refers to the actual storage of information as fields, records, files, pages, and perhaps data structures such as lists or trees; thus, it includes characteristics of the storage devices themselves and the stored items such as the organization of memory pages, for example. The *conceptual database* is the user's model of the physical database after a syntax-directed translation has been applied to give an interpretation to the stored items; thus, it could include aspects such as, for instance, "the database is a relational model of an image in which rows are segmented regions for which the third attribute is average gray level." A user might then further interpret the information.

3.1.2. The Relational, Hierarchical, and Network Models

Three models of a DBS provide the general organizational schemes currently available.

In the *relational DB model*, data is organized as a table, the rows of which are the individual DB entries and the columns of which are the attributes of the entries. This model is particularly important in image DB design because it places fundamental emphasis on the concept of relations among image components and lends itself naturally to the representation of those relationships. The format for storage frequently used for a relational

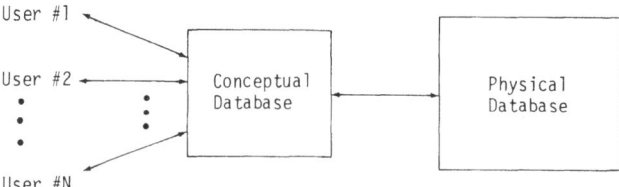

Fig. 15. General DB model.

DB is as a file of fixed-length records in which each record is an individual entry and the fields of the record define the attributes.

Figure 16 is an illustration of a relational DB table containing information about two "snapshot" images, the first image having four identified objects and the second having three. A generic name appears in the third column as an object attribute. The "superposition order" attribute in the fourth column is a nonnegative integer giving an ordering of objects with respect to the relative distance of an object's center of mass from the image sensor. Thus, the data available about image #1 is that it consists of a CHILD, a TREE TRUNK, and a SHADOW embedded in a BACK-GROUND, with the CHILD and the TREE TRUNK at the same distance, and the SHADOW at a different location relative to the sensor.

For the purposes of retrieving data, a *key* for a relational DB is a subset of the columns with the property that values specified for those columns serve to locate a unique row. For instance, in the table in Fig. 16, the set of keys includes [SNAP#, OBJECT#], [SNAP#, OBJECT NAME], and [OBJECT#, OBJECT NAME, SUPERPOSITION ORDER]. A *candidate key* is a key without redundant attributes (SUPERPOSITION ORDER is redundant in the third key just listed because [OBJECT#, OBJECT NAME] is a key). A candidate key selected for use in accessing data is a *primary key*; other keys are called *nonprimary* or *secondary*.

The organization of a relational DB makes it convenient to form logical combinations of keys for queries. For example, to respond to a user's request for all images in Fig. 16 containing a CHILD but not a SHADOW, the DBMS could first find all images without SHADOW as an OBJECT NAME value, then search those images for an occurrence of CHILD as an OBJECT NAME value.

An illustration of using the relational model to advantage is provided by Chang and Fu,[7] who discuss a query by pictorial example (QPE) method for a relational database system for images. In using the "query by example" approach, one inputs to the system an example of a partially completed

SNAP #	OBJECT #	OBJECT NAME	SUPERPOSITION ORDER
1	1	CHILD	1
1	2	TREE TRUNK	1
1	3	SHADOW	2
1	4	BACKGROUND	0
2	1	LADY	1
2	2	CHILD	1
2	3	BACKGROUND	0

Fig. 16. Image relational DB. (From Ref. 20.)

row in a relational table with all the fixed attributed values entered as constants; these are matched in a given table, and the items sought from the matches are displayed or printed. In addition to handling queries in which conventional logical combinations of constants and variables are allowed, QPE has facilities for including spatial relationships in more complex queries concerning image data.

In the *hierarchical DB model*, data is organized as a tree in which the root is the least detailed entry and a leaf on the tree frontier contains the most specific type of information. In this model, an entry takes on its full significance only in the context of its superior and its descendant nodes. This model is most effective for data in which a natural tree hierarchy is known or can be approximated. For example, a hierarchical DB model is the basis for IBM's general Information Management System (IMS).[11,47] Often a hierarchical DB is stored as a file of variable-length records: one record serves for each DB entry, and its record length is determined by its attributes and its links to other entries. Figure 17 is such a model for the tree in Fig. 6.

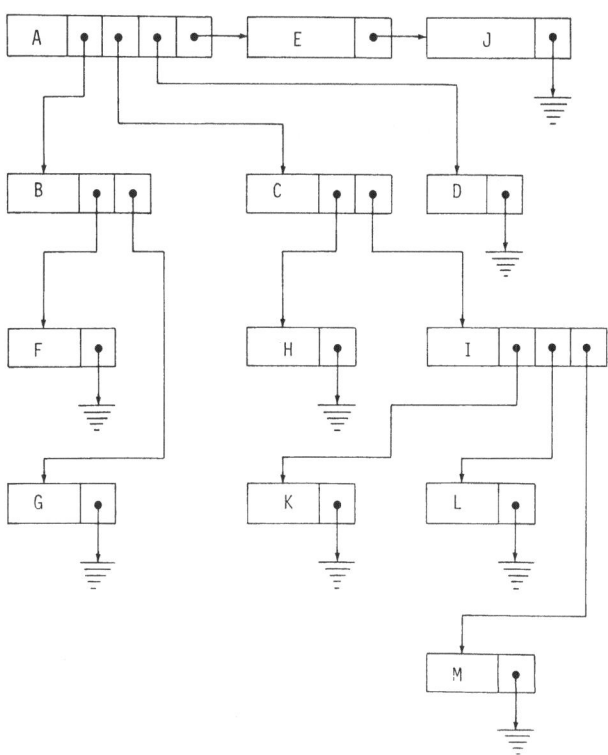

Fig. 17. Linkages for hierarchy of Fig. 6.

Symbolic or semantic models of images, in which generic names are attached to collections of real image pixels determined to be objects or regions of interest, almost always are considered to have a representational hierarchy determined by the level of the primitive components. Thus, those processing systems that support research in scene understanding or knowledge acquisition include a hierarchical DB defined explicitly or implicitly. For example, a picture description DB described by Kunii *et al.*[27] is based on an image or picture hierarchy as follows:

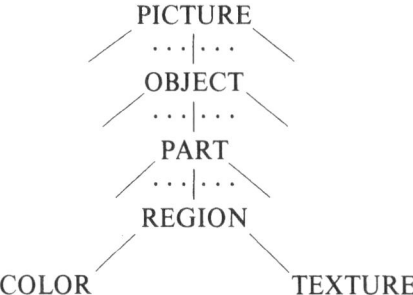

There is also a relational DB associated one-to-one with each level in the hierarchy: the picture-relational DB is a table of all pictures; for each picture, there is a table of objects such as Fig. 16, and so on. Another hierarchy described by McKeoun and Reddy[32] has six levels:

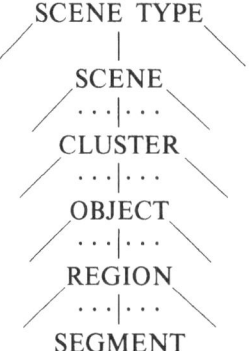

In the *network DB model,* data is essentially organized as a directed graph, the nodes of which are data records and the arcs of which are record-to-record links. As such, it can be considered a generalization of the tree of the hierarchical model for the case in which there is not a unique hierarchical relationship. This is the organization of some proposed general purpose DBSs (cf. Ref. 47). A network DB can be stored as a file of variable-length records. Often used is a multi-list in which each entry's record has as many pointers to other records as the type of entry has links.

With respect to *ease of use* by an applications programmer, the relational model has the advantage that it is conceptually the least complex and requires a user to learn the least number of organizational details. With respect to *efficiency of implementation* (including creation of the DBMS and its expected speed of execution), the two other models perhaps rate higher; in effect, these models often have explicit linkage information that must be inferred in the relational model.

3.1.3. Design of the Database Management System

The DBMS includes the systems software necessary to compile and execute data definition/manipulation commands, as well as any hardware designed specifically to support these tasks. In general, the DBMS consists of the operating system interface, DB language compilers and interpreters, and memory management software. In the case of DB organization for scene analysis and image processing, the commands for the definition, construction, modification, and querying of image DBs must be accepted, translated, and executed by the DBMS. The DBMS should assume the burden of the memory operations for data arrays that are too large to reside simultaneously in the main memory.

The advantages of an adequate DBS design include reduction of redundancy in the data and consistency of format. In addition, data independence can be achieved because the DBMS handles the translation of operations expressed in a language convenient to users into detailed database manipulations; in other words, the details of storage, formatting, file manipulation, and other characteristics of the physical database do not have to be known to users who issue processing commands in a high-level language.

3.2. Hierarchical and Relational Models for Scene Representation and Processing

One of the most fundamental and frequently used approaches for analyzing a scene by computer is to decompose it into simpler elements and to arrange these elements in the form of a hierarchical representation of the scene. This concept is illustrated in Fig. 18 using a simple scene. The highest node in the hierarchy represents the scene itself. At the next level, the scene is composed of several objects: a group of blocks, a pyramid, the wall, and the floor. At the next level, it is shown that the group of blocks is composed of a big block and a little block. The level below this shows

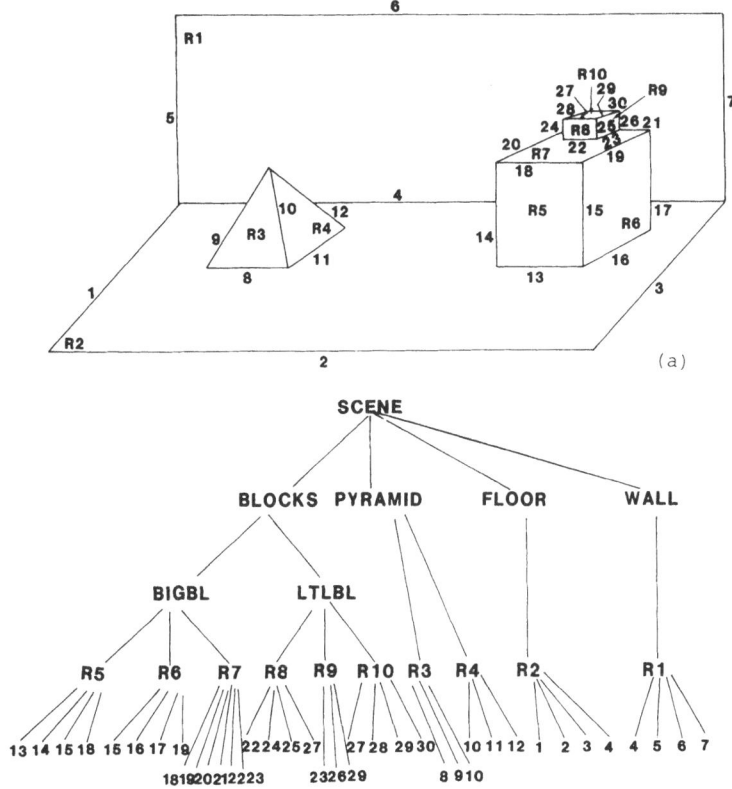

Fig. 18. (a) A simple scene; (b) a hierarchical representation.

that the objects are composed of regions. Finally, in the last level, we see that the regions are composed of edge segments, which are numbered in the figure for easy reference.

As indicated in Section 1, obtaining a decomposition of this type can be fairly simple for a human but is quite complicated for a computer. In practice, most procedures for generating a hierarchical representation start at the bottom with the most primitive elements (e.g., the edges) and attempt to arrive at the top node in a bottom-up manner. The basic approach for implementing this bottom-up procedure may be explained with the aid of Fig. 19. Starting with a digital representation of a scene derived from one or more sensors (e.g., optical and range images), the first problem is to identify and label the primitives in the scene. Examples of commonly used primitives are edges, boundaries, and vertices. It is noted that, in Fig. 19, the process of assigning a label to a primitive is basically a recognition problem. For instance, if edges are being used as primitives, the first step

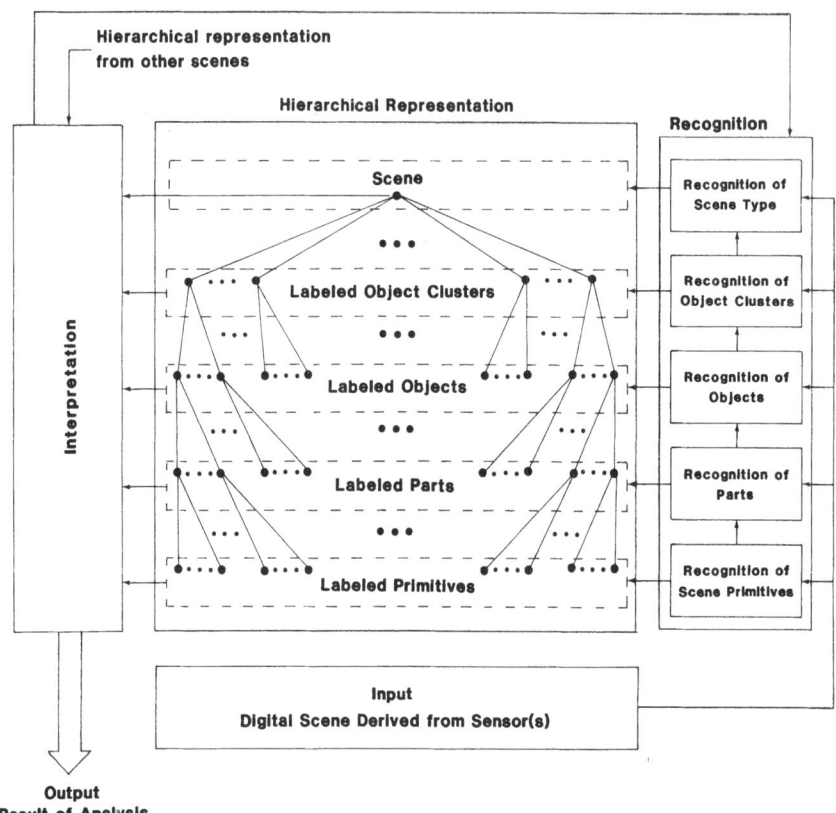

Fig. 19. A model of the scene analysis process.

is to recognize the presence of edges in the scene and to categorize these edges according to type based on descriptors such as length and orientation.

Higher levels in the hierarchy are explained in a similar manner. Labeled parts are obtained by recognition based on the labeled primitives. In turn, these parts are used as inputs to recognition procedures for detecting objects. The resulting labeled objects are classified to form clusters based on some predefined measures of similarity (e.g., man-made objects). The labeled clusters of objects are then recognized as forming a scene of a certain type (e.g., either of military or of nonmilitary interest). Finally, the interpretation stage uses the resulting hierarchical representation, and possibly representations from other scenes, to produce an analysis of the scene.

Figure 19 is consistent with the discussion in Section 1 concerning the four basic processes involved in scene analysis: sensing, segmentation, recognition, and interpretation. In the present model, segmentation techniques are used to extract primitives, parts, and objects from a scene, and

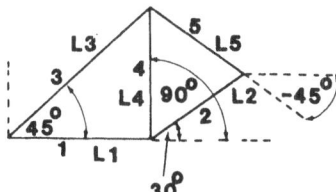

Fig. 20. Characterization of edges in an object.

recognition algorithms are used to identify (label) these elements. Recognition is also used to group these objects into clusters and to identify the type of scene under consideration. Finally, the interpretation stage yields an analysis of scene composition and meaning.

An implementation of the basic scene analysis model shown in Fig. 19 requires that data be organized in a systematic manner at all levels in the hierarchy. The most commonly used method for doing this is to arrange the labeled information at each level in the form of a relational table. A typical structure for these tables contains an identification of each element (for example, by number), a list of attributes for each element, and a list of relationships between all elements in the table.† An example is shown in Fig. 20 and Table II, where the elements in the relational table are edges, the attributes of individual edges are direction and length, and the relationship between edges is "connected." By examining the first row, for instance, we see that edge number 1 is horizontal, has length $L1$, and is connected to edges 2, 3, and 4.

As a more complete illustration of these concepts, consider the scene shown in Fig. 21. In order to simplify the explanation, we have placed a coarse grid on the scene such that every vertex of interest coincides with a grid coordinate. In practice, one would use the finer resolution provided by the digitized scene itself. With reference to the model of Fig. 19, let us assume that the primitives used in the analysis of the scene in Fig. 21 are edges; then the purpose of the lowest-level recognizer is to extract and label these edges. The results of recognition would be organized in a relational table of the form shown in Table 2, in which each row represents a labeled primitive in the hierarchy of Fig. 19.

The next higher level in the hierarchy involves segmentation and recognition of parts. In this example, the parts are geometrical surfaces or regions, and recognition is basically reduced to a shape analysis problem. Assuming for the purpose of illustration that region R_1 is red, region R_2 is white, the pyramid is blue, both cubes are red, and all regions (with the

---

† Formally, the relations between elements are defined by columns in a table in the way that *all* attributes are handled in the relational DB model. However, we identify and label these structural relationships separately in our tables to emphasize their role in scene analysis.

TABLE II
Relational Table for the Edges in Fig. 20

Element number	Attributes		Relationship connected to
	Direction	Length	
1	0°	$L1$	2, 3, 4
2	30°	$L2$	1, 4, 5
3	45°	$L3$	1, 4, 5
4	90°	$L4$	1, 2, 3, 5
5	−45°	$L5$	2, 3, 4

exception of R_7) are smooth, the labeled information extracted at this level would be organized in a relational table of the form shown in Table III, with each row in the table representing a labeled part in the hierarchy of Fig. 19. It is noted that some of the information computed by the previous stage of recognition (such as the location of edges) would be used in the assignment of attributes to each of the scene parts.

The extraction and labeling of objects would use the labeled primitives and parts, as well as other sensor information such as range data, the latter

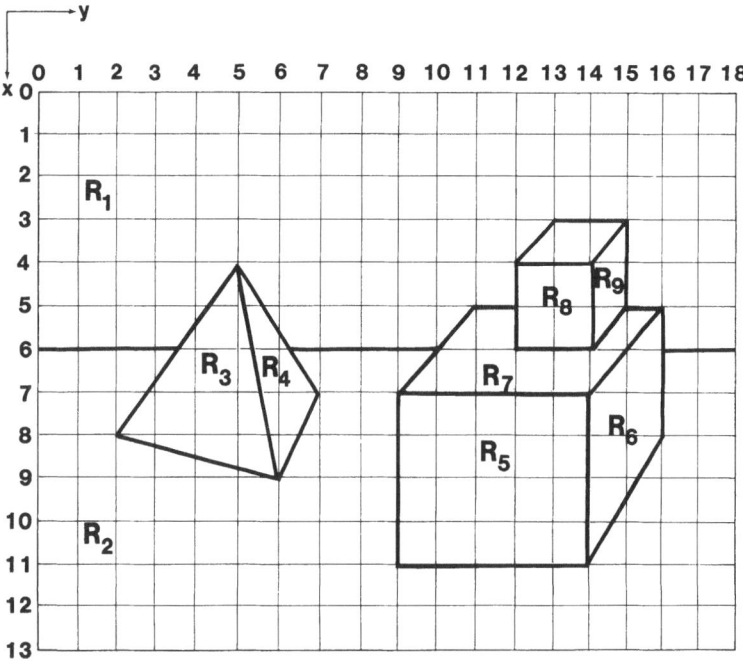

Fig. 21. Scene composed of geometric solids.

TABLE III
Relational Table of Parts for the Scene Shown in Fig. 21

| Element no. | Attributes | | | | Relationship connected to |
	Shape	Color	Texture	Boundary	
1	Rectangle	Black	Smooth	$(0,0) - (0,18) - (6,18) - (6,0)$	2
2	Rectangle	White	Smooth	$(6,0) - (6,18) - (13,18) - (13,0)$	1, 3, 4, 5, 6
3	Triangle	Blue	Smooth	$(4,5) - (9,6) - (8,2)$	2, 4
4	Triangle	Blue	Smooth	$(4,5) - (7,7) - (9,6)$	2, 3
5	Rectangle	Red	Smooth	$(7,9) - (7,14) - (11,14) - (11,9)$	2, 6, 7
6	Rectangle	Red	Smooth	$(5-16) - (8,16) - (11,14) - (7,14)$	2, 5, 7
7	Rectangle	Red	Rough	$(5,11) - (5,16) - (7,14) - (7,9)$	5, 6, 8, 9
8	Rectangle	Red	Smooth	$(4,12) - (4,14) - (6,14) - (6,12)$	7, 9, 10
9	Rectangle	Red	Smooth	$(3,15) - (5,15) - (6,14) - (4,14)$	7, 8, 10
10	Rectangle	Red	Smooth	$(3,13) - (3,15) - (4,14) - (4,12)$	8, 9

being useful for determining the relative three-dimensional location of objects. In this example, the object recognition problem is one of analyzing the shape, properties, and relationships of geometrical volumes. The results would be summarized in a table of the form shown in Table IV. As before, each row in the table represents a labeled object in the hierarchy of Fig. 19.

The next level in the hierarchy involves grouping objects according to some clustering criterion. For the purpose of illustration, suppose that objects are grouped only if they have the same color and geometrical characteristics. These criteria lead to only one group containing the small and medium red blocks. The relational table for this level of the hierarchy is shown in Table V. In this case, information required to group the objects was already available from the previous level in the hierarchy.

As shown in Fig. 19, the highest level in the hierarchy is the scene itself, which is composed of labeled object clusters. This level has only one

TABLE IV
Relational Table of Objects for the Scene Shown in Fig. 21

| Element no. | Attributes | | | | Relationships | | |
	Type	Color	Texture	Size	In front of	Right of	Resting on
1	Rectangle	Black	Smooth	Large			
2	Rectangle	White	Smooth	Large	1		
3	Pyramid	Blue	Smooth	Medium	1		2
4	Cube	Red	Smooth	Medium	1	3	2
5	Cube	Red	Smooth/rough	Small	1	3	4

TABLE V
Relational Table of Object Clusters for the Scene Shown in Fig. 21

Element no.	Attributes				Relationships		
	Type	Color	Texture	Size	In front of	Right of	Resting on
1	Rectangle	Black	Smooth	Large			
2	Rectangle	White	Smooth	Large	1		
3	Pyramid	Blue	Smooth	Medium	1		2
4	Blocks	Red	Smooth/rough	Medium	1	3	2

labeled node, the root of the hierarchical tree. Typically, attributes associated with the root node would include scene type and sensor(s) from which the hierarchical representation was derived. In the present example, the scene is a "block-world" scene and the sensors used in obtaining the information for the hierarchical representation were optical and range sensors.

Although the foregoing example illustrates procedures to analyze a scene using a digital computer, a totally automated implementation of these procedures is still an unsolved problem, as indicated in Section 1. Algorithms have been proposed to carry out machine recognition at all levels in the hierarchy of Fig. 19 in specialized situations, but the only state-of-the-art techniques which are of a general nature and which have exhibited some degrees of success deal with the lowest two levels in that figure.

3.3. Use of Relational Tables for Three-Dimensional Object Location

An important aspect of scene analysis as applied to computer vision is the location of objects and the interpretation of three-dimensional relationships between these objects. In this section, we illustrate how relational tables may be applied to this problem.

A widely used approach for locating an object in three-dimensional space is the *triangulation method*.[12,50] This technique uses two or more image views of the object and, by employing geometric relations and a model of the viewing system (e.g., a TV camera), infers the location in three-dimensional space of corresponding image points. The basic problem is illustrated in Fig. 22. Points O_1 and O_2 are the focal points of two cameras which produce images I_1 and I_2 of the three-dimensional body shown in the figure. Point P_1 in this body is projected as point Q_1 onto image I_1 and as point F_1 onto image I_2. Similarly, point Q_2 and F_2 are the projections of P_2 onto these images. It is noted that any point contained in the ray $O_1P_1S_1$ will be imaged as point Q_1 on I_1. However, by considering triangle $O_1O_2P_1$, we see that this ray will be imaged as line $C_2F_1K_1$ on I_2. Thus,

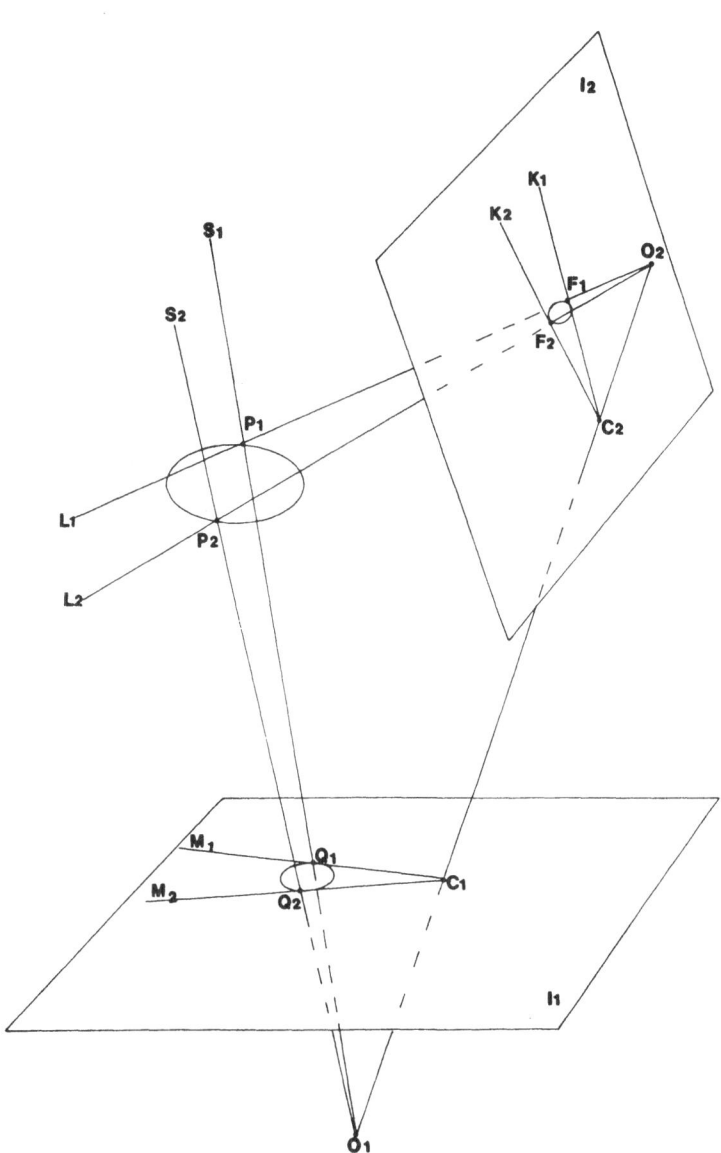

Fig. 22. Two images of a three-dimensional object. (From Ref. 21.)

the point I_2 which corresponds to Q_1 in I_1 will lie on the line $C_2F_1K_1$. Similarly, the point I_1 which corresponds to point F_1 in I_2 will lie on the line $C_1Q_1M_1$. It can be shown[21] that a point I_1 with image coordinates (x_1, y_1), and its corresponding point in I_2 with coordinates (x_2, y_2), satisfy the equation

$$f(x_1, y_1, x_2, y_2, k_1, \ldots, k_9)$$
$$= (k_1x_1 + k_2y_2 + k_3)x_2 + (k_4x_1 + k_5y_1 + k_6)y_2 + (k_7x_1 + k_8y_1 + k_9)$$
$$= 0$$

where the coefficients k_i, $i = 1, 2, \ldots, 9$, are determined from geometrical considerations. Hwang has investigated the use of relational tables in conjunction with the above equation as a tool for determining corresponding points in two images of the same body. Once these corresponding points are known, their three-dimensional coordinates are easily obtained by standard perspective transformations.[33] These results can then be used to locate and describe the object in three-dimensional space. The advantage of this approach is that it uses the structural information in two views to eliminate the need for a camera model in the three-dimensional reconstruction process.

Hwang's approach is based on extracting regions in images I_1 and I_2 and describing the boundaries of these regions by vertices and their interconnecting edges. The general form of the relational table used to tabulate this information is shown in Table VI. The portion of the table above the dashed line represents the information extracted from image I_1, while the bottom section, whose elements are primed, refers to the information from image I_2. The attribute columns are self-explanatory. The entries in the relationship column are made by using the concept of *consistency*, which is defined as follows: Two vertices v_i and v'_j with coordinates (x_1, y_1) and (x_2, y_2) are said to be consistent if

$$|f(x_1, y_1, x_2, y_2, k_1, \ldots, k_9)| < \theta$$

where $|f|$ is the absolute value of f and θ is a positive threshold. Ideally, two matching vertices should yield $f = 0$. The use of a threshold is introduced to allow for distance-based extracting and computer processing.

A pair of consistent vertices in an image define a consistent edge. Two regions R_i and R'_j are said to be *K-consistent* if $K\%$ of their vertices are consistent. In theory, two truly matching regions should have the same number of vertices and every vertex in one region should have a consistent vertex in the other. In practice, the distortions mentioned above often lead

TABLE VI
Relational Table for Object Location

Elements (regions)	Attributes		Relationship "consistent"
	Vertices	Edges	
R_1	$v_{11}, v_{12}, \ldots, v_{1m_1}$	$e_{11}, e_{12}, \ldots, e_{1p_1}$	R'_h or ϕ
R_2	$v_{21}, v_{22}, \ldots, v_{2m_2}$	$e_{21}, e_{22}, \ldots, e_{2p_2}$	R'_j or ϕ
$\vdots$	$\vdots$	$\vdots$	
R_M	$v_{M1}, v_{M2}, \ldots, v_{Mm_M}$	$e_{M1}, e_{M2}, \ldots, e_{Mp_M}$	R'_L or ϕ
R'_1	$v'_{11}, v'_{12}, \ldots, v'_{1n_1}$	$e'_{11}, e'_{12}, \ldots, e'_{1q_1}$	R_k or ϕ
R'_2	$v'_{21}, v'_{22}, \ldots, v'_{2n_2}$	$e'_{21}, e'_{22}, \ldots, e'_{2q_2}$	R_i or ϕ
$\vdots$	$\vdots$	$\vdots$	
R'_N	$v'_{N1}, v'_{N2}, \ldots, v'_{Nn_N}$	$e'_{N1}, e'_{N2}, \ldots, e'_{Nq_N}$	R_K or ϕ

to considering a match of $K\%$ of these vertices as the condition for consistency between two regions. Each of the remaining inconsistent vertices is then merged with the nearest vertex that was found to be consistent.

With reference to the last column in Table VI, and using the concepts just described, a region R_i in image I_1 is said to be related to a region R'_j in I_2 if they are K-consistent. Use of the null set symbol, $\varnothing$, indicates that R_i may not have a consistent region in I_2. The essence of Hwang's approach is to use a relaxation-labeling algorithm[38] with the above equation as a constraint to find consistent regions and merge those regions into an image that was found to be inconsistent. The final result of this procedure is a (usually reduced) relational table all of whose entries are consistent.

Use of the approach described above is illustrated in Fig. 23. Parts (a) and (b) of this figure were obtained by digitizing the images produced by two cameras at different locations and viewing angles with respect to a three-dimensional solid. Figure 23(c) and (d) shows the corresponding results after region extraction, and Fig. 23(e) and (f) are the vertices and edges defining the boundaries of the regions in each image. Figure 23(g) and (h) shows the consistent regions obtained with $\theta = 0.707$ and $K = 95\%$. Note that the interior regions, because of their irregularities, failed to meet the consistency test. These two resulting views were then used to reconstruct the object in three-dimensional space. As an illustration of the accuracy of the reconstruction process, Fig. 23(i) and (j) show the reconstructed object projected back onto the original image planes. The importance of these

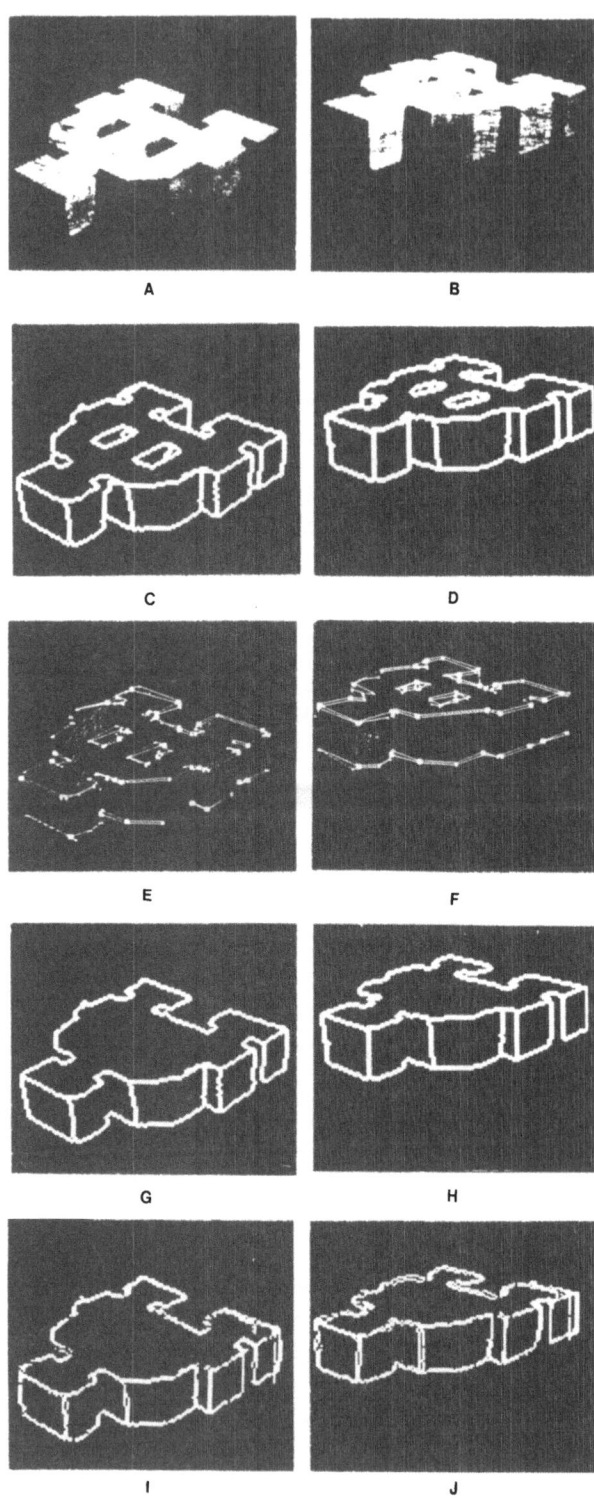

A   B

C   D

E   F

G   H

I   J

results is that they were obtained without using a camera model. As mentioned earlier, once the three-dimensional coordinates of the object in question are known, they can be used to establish its true location with respect to other objects in the scene.

4. EXAMPLES OF EXISTING SYSTEMS

The following illustrate the design goals, hardware–software configurations, and database organizations in two existing systems.

4.1. Multisensor Image Database System (MIDAS)

4.1.1. Design Goals

The design goal of the multisensor image database system (MIDAS)[32] is the development of a research tool for image processing and scene analysis to support research in the following areas:

(i) Performance evaluation of a variety of algorithms at various levels of image representation and abstraction; these levels include real digitized images and hierarchical symbolic descriptions of images.

(ii) Error analysis as an extension of performance evaluation to focus on the nature of erroneous results in automatic extraction of scene descriptions.

(iii) Development of knowledge acquisition techniques for the automated learning of structural and feature descriptions of objects and of symbolic feature primitives.

The MIDAS facility was designed to function in an environment in which there are several hundred images that range from LANDSAT multispectral pictures to electron photomicrographs. The system permits multiple representations of scenes and offers a high degree of data independence in which users explicitly define relationships as needed.

A real image (called the "signal representation" of a scene) is maintained as a collection of reduced images, with the number of reductions by powers of 2 determined by the size of the original. Symbolic representations of an image are stored as relational DBs with object or subobject names attached to collections of real-image picture points; the six levels of

---

Fig. 23. (a, b) Two views of a three-dimensional object; (c, d) segmented region boundaries; (e, f) segmented vertices; (g, h) consistent regions; (i, j) projections onto original planes after three-dimensional reconstruction using consistent vertices. (From Ref. 21.)

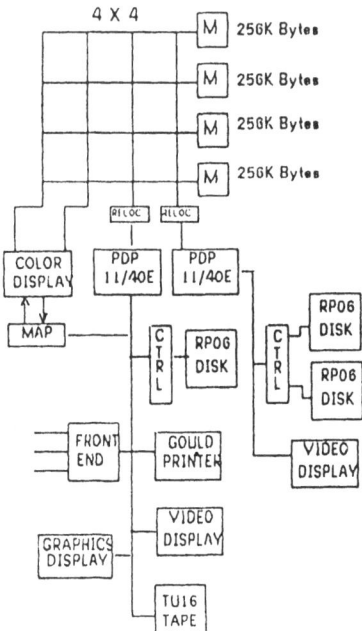

Fig. 24. MIDAS hardware configuration. (From Ref. 32.)

symbolic representation (scene type, scene, cluster, object, region, segment) form a hierarchical model of an image.

4.1.2. Hardware and Software

The MIDAS hardware organization is shown in Fig. 24. The multiprocessor configuration, using the UNIX operating system, is one factor in providing less than a one second response time to database requests.

Interactive software packages provides MIDAS's image DB manipulation capabilities. The software incorporates memory paging to handle large images and provides access to a library of subroutines for image modification, analysis, and display. These subroutines are considered to be "picture processing primitives;" low-level routines control buffer transfers, and higher-level routines exist for operations such as histogram generation, extraction of subimages, and rescaling of pixel data.

4.1.3. Database Organization

For a given image, both the signal and the symbolic representations are hierarchies—the real image according to resolution (reduction) and the symbolic image according to six levels are illustrated as follows:

SCENE DESCRIPTION TREE

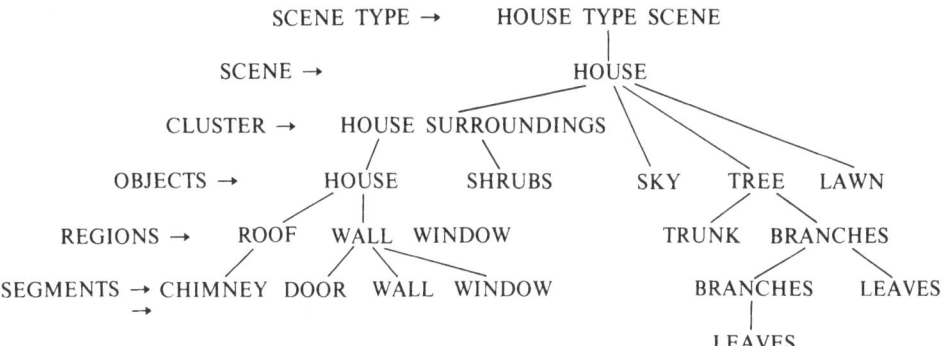

IMAGE DESCRIPTION FILE (IDF)

EXACT SEG
#REG = 19
MCKEOWN
1-14-77
HOUSE = R0
HOUSE SURROUNDINGS = R1
SKY = R2

ROOF = R15
WINDOW = R16

LEAVES = R18
LEAVES = R19

[0] REGION IS HOUSE
    LEVEL = SCENE
    ANCESTOR = −1
    DESCENDANTS = 1 2 3 4
    MBR = 1, 1 : 1, 800 : 600, 800 : 600, 1

[1] REGION IS HOUSE SURROUNDINGS
    LEVEL = CLUSTER

    ANCESTOR = 0
    DESCENDANTS = 15 16 19
    MBR = 57, 94 : 57, 738 : 441, 738 : 441, 94

[16] REGION IS WINDOW
    LEVEL = REGIONS
    ANCESTOR = 5
    DESCENDANTS = −1
    MBR = 244, 621 : 244, 272 : 259, 672 : 259, 621

    The hierarchical symbolic DB is stored as an image description file (IDF) that contains the tree structure along with such general information as the person who generated the segmentation, the number of regions and their reference numbers, and each region's location given by the coordinates of a minimum bounding rectangle (MBR). A typical subset of an IDF appears to the right of the scene tree above. Symbolic representations generally are interactively formed. Vector lists of MBRs are also interactively defined to tie the symbolic representations into subimages in the signal representations.

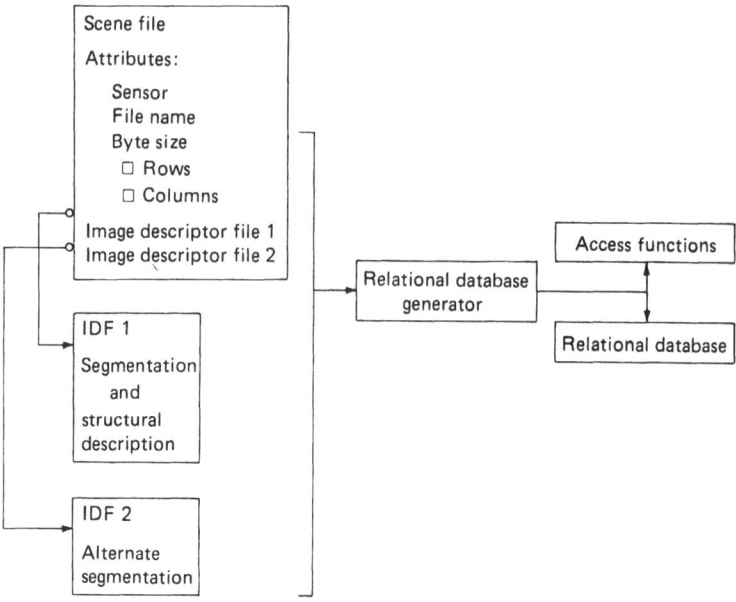

Fig. 25. Scene file, IDFs, and relational DB diagram. (From Ref. 32.)

The overall DB organization is as a text file containing a unique scene file for each image in MIDAS; see Fig. 25. A scene file contains such data as the names of the signal representation files, pixel size, kind of sensor providing the original image, and the number of rows and columns. There are also pointers to the IDFs that have been created for the image. There is provision for a relational DB to be generated automatically for a scene file to afford rapid response to relation-based queries.

4.2. Relational Pictorial Database System

4.2.1. Design Goals

The design goal of the relational pictorial database system[5,6] is the development of an integrated pictorial DBS for efficient representation of physical images and logical pictures. The physical images are digitized real images occupying a separate, paged, image store handled by an Image Store Management System (ISMS). The logical pictures are representations of the physical images as collections of picture objects stored as a set of relational DBs managed by a Relational Algebraic Interpreter (RAIN). Correspondences between physical images and logical pictures are established by a Picture Page Table (PPT), a relational DB that links objects in a logical picture to memory pages (which are essentially rectangular subimages) in a real image.

4.2.2. Hardware–Software

The pictorial analysis system is supported by a Graphics-Oriented Relational Algebraic Interpreter (GRAIN), as shown in Fig. 26. User interaction is accomplished via a touch-panel plasma display. The host machine is a PDP-11/40 with a UNIX operating system. System software is written in the C language, a high-level UNIX-supported language.

4.2.3. Database Organization

The ISMS interprets host commands for the image store processor. These commands are essentially independent of the physical image hardware, and some concurrent operations are possible. Two versions of an image are defined in the ISMS:

(i) A contour picture describes a line drawing for a logical picture object as a minimum enclosing rectangle (MER). Five formats for contour representation, including chain codes or (x, y) coordinates with a directory, are allowed.

(ii) A digitized image defines a rectangle of arbitrary size and orientation with respect to a Cartesian coordinate system. Each pixel in a rectangle is addressed by its (x, y) coordinates and has an associated nonnegative integer value with gray-level information.

A picture object contained in a MER must be partitioned into rectangular picture pages to be accessed from the image store; the page size is not fixed but must not exceed an upper limit determined by memory buffer constraints.

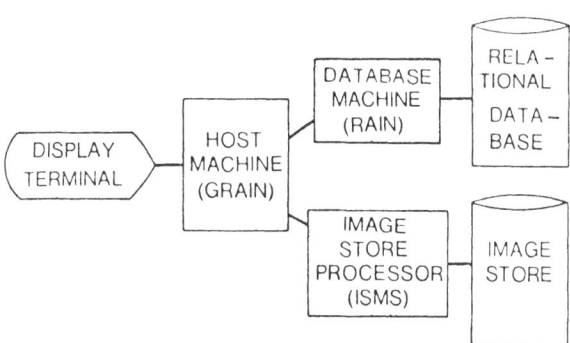

Fig. 26. GRAIN system. (From Ref. 6.)

The paging is guided by a user-specified cost function which, for instance, could reflect that a minimum number of pages is desired or that minimum total area coverage by the rectangular subimages is desired.

A logical picture is represented as three relational DBs:

(i) The Picture Object Table (POT) has individual objects as its rows. The columns for an object row give a labeling position, the name of the picture object of which the row object is a component, a tilting angle to define the object's orientation with respect to the object of which it is a part, and a number of additional attributes as necessary to complete the characterization. In the position label, the entry $(-1, -1)$ flags a composite object; otherwise, the object has a contour description in a contour table (PCT).

(ii) The Picture Contour Table (PCT) contains contour information about objects in the POT. The contour is defined by one of the formats shared with the image store contour picture and may reside in the image store itself or be a part of the PCT.

(iii) The PPT mentioned above specifies which of the image store picture pages correspond to a given object in logical picture.

Figure 27 is an example of a POT for objects A, B, C, and D with the following hierarchy:

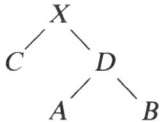

The remaining columns for object A, for example, give $(x - y$ angle) positional information and specify that A possesses attribute A_1. Figure 28 is an associated PCT in which object A is designated type 4 in contour format (which here means encoded as chain codes) and PIC.A is a reference name for a corresponding file as an image store contour table. Figure 29 is an associated PPT showing, for example, that objects A and B each occupy one picture page whereas object C occupies two pages. Figure 30 is a

NAME	ONAME	LABEL		ANGLE	ATTRIBUTES			
		X	Y		A_1	A_2	A_3	A_4
A	D	0	4	0	1	0	0	0
B	D	4	4	0	0	1	1	1
C	X	1	1	0	0	0	1	1
D	X	-1	-1	0	0	0	0	0

Fig. 27. Picture object table (POT). (From Ref. 6.)

NAME	TYPE	UNAME	CONTOUR CODES
A	4	PIC.A	$((0,4),(2,4))$ $((2,4),(2,6))$ $((2,6),(0,6))$ $((0,6),(0,4))$
B	4	PIC.B	$((4,4),(6,4))$ $((6,4),(6,6))$ $((6,6),(4,6))$ $((4,6),(4,4))$
C	4	PIC.C	$((1,1),(5,1))$ $((5,1),(5,3))$ $((5,3),(1,3))$ $((1,3),(1,1))$

Fig. 28. Picture contour table (PCT). (From Ref. 6.)

representation of the logical picture showing where objects *A*, *B*, and *C* are located.

5. SUMMARY

This chapter has dealt mainly with concepts of data structures and databases as they apply to digital scene analysis and image processing. As indicated in Section 1, these concepts play an important role in the representation of structural information in a scene.

The area of data structures is concerned with the details of the storage and linking of information. The principal data structures used in contemporary computer systems are lists, trees, and graphs. These data structures were defined and several illustrations of linked lists and quad trees were given in the context of scene analysis and image processing applications.

NAME	NPAGE	LOCATION		ANGLE	PAGE SIZE	
		X_p	Y_p		I_x	I_y
A	0	0	4	0	2	2
A	1	0	4	0	2	2
B	0	4	4	0	2	2
B	1	4	4	0	2	2
C	0	1	1	0	4	2
C	1	1	1	0	2	2
C	2	3	1	0	2	2

Fig. 29. Picture page table (PPT). (From Ref. 6.)

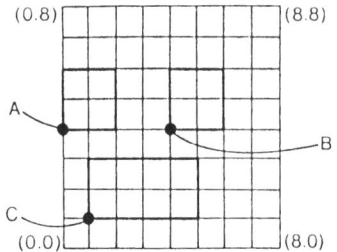

Fig. 30. Location of objects in logical picture. (From Ref. 6.)

The area of databases is concerned with the representation of information at a level higher than that afforded by data structures. In particular, databases allow explicit utilization of relationships between primitives of a scene at various levels. The principal database approaches used in scene analysis are based on hierarchical and relational models. The use of these models is motivated by the fundamental structural relationships that exist among elements of a scene. As indicated in Section 4, database organizations have received considerable attention in the design of state-of-the-art scene analysis and image processing systems.

It is of interest to note that an explicit definition of a relational database did not exist before 1970, and that the application of these concepts to

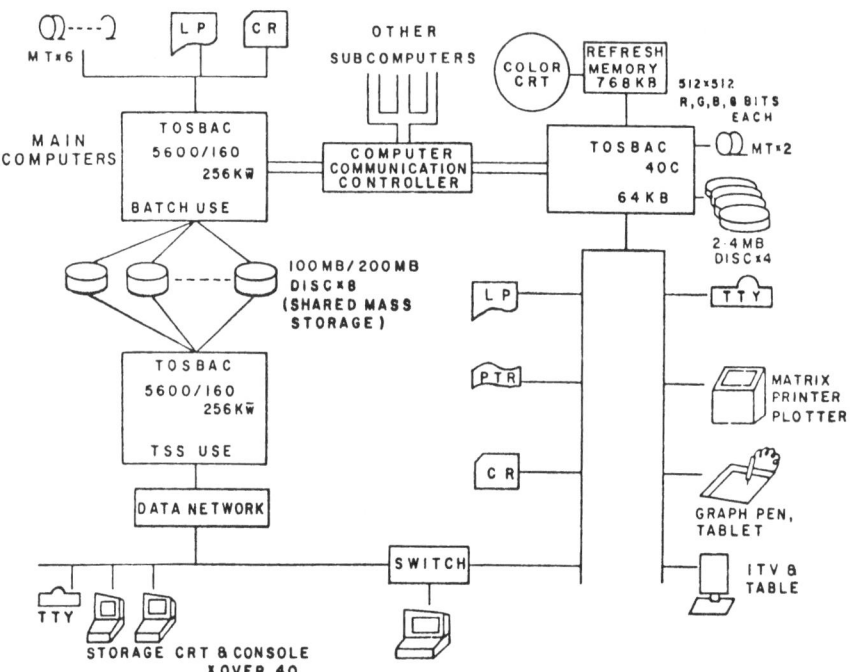

Fig. 31. Electrotechnical Laboratory image processing facilities. (From Ref. 45.)

scene analysis is even more recent. The extensive research that is presently being carried out in the theory and applications of data structures and databases reflects their importance in the development of computer techniques for handling problems whose solution requires the systematic organization of large amounts of data.

REFERENCES

1. A. V. Aho, J. E. Hopcroft, and J. D. Ullman, *The Design and Analysis of Computer Algorithms*, Addison-Wesley, Reading, MA (1974).
2. A. V. Aho, and J. D. Ullman, *The Theory of Parsing, Translation, and Compiling*, vol. 1, Prentice-Hall, Englewood Cliffs, NJ (1972).
3. A. V. Aho, J. E. Hopcroft, and J. D. Ullman, *Data Structures and Algorithms*, Addison-Wesley, Reading, MA (1983).
4. C. R. Brice, and C. L. Fennema, Scene analysis using regions, *Artif. Intell.* **1**, 205–226 (1970).
5. S. K. Chang, N. Donato, J. Reuss, R. Rocchetti, and B. H. McCormick, An integrated relational database system for pictures, *Proc. IEEE Workshop on Picture Data Description and Management*, April, pp. 142–149 (1977).
6. S. K. Chang, J. Reuss, and B. H. McCormick, Design considerations of a pictorial database system, *Policy Anal. Info. Sys.* **1**(2), 49–70 (1978).
7. S. K. Chang, and K. S. Fu, *Pictorial Information Systems*, Springer-Verlag, Berlin (1980).
8. Digital image archiving in medicine, *Computer* **16**(8), 14–56 (1983).
9. E. F. Codd, A relational model of data for large shared data banks, *CACM* **13**(6), 377–387 (1970).
10. A. Klinger, K. S. Fu, and T. L. Kunii, eds., *Data Structures, Computer Graphics, and Pattern Recognition*, Academic Press, NY (1977).
11. C. J. Date, *An Introduction to Database Systems*, Addison-Wesley, Reading, MA (1977).
12. R. O. Duda, and P. E. Hart, *Pattern Classification and Scene Analysis*, Wiley-Interscience, NY (1973).
13. H. Freeman, On the encoding of arbitrary geometric configurations, *IRE Trans. Electron. Comput.* **EC-10**, 260–268 (1961).
14. W. K. Giloi, *Interactive Computer Graphics: Data Structures, Algorithms, Languages*, Prentice-Hall, Englewood Cliffs, NJ (1978).
15. R. C. Gonzalez, and P. A. Wintz, *Digital Image Processing*, Addison-Wesley, Reading, MA (1977).
16. S. Gorn, Explicit definitions and linguistic dominoes, in *Systems and Computer Science* (J. F. Hart and S. Takasu, eds.), University of Toronto Press, Toronto, Canada (1967).
17. E. L. Hall, *Computer Image Processing and Recognition*, Academic Press, NY (1979).
18. E. Horowitz, and S. Sahni, *Fundamentals of Data Structures*, Computer Science Press, Potomac, MD (1977).
19. S. L. Horowitz, and T. Pavlidis, Picture segmentation by a tree traversal algorithm, *J. ACM* **23**(2), 368–388 (1976).
20. G. M. Hunter, and K. Steiglitz, Operations on images using quad trees, *IEEE Trans. Pat. Anal. Mach. Intell.* **PAMI-1**(2), 145–153 (1979).
21. J. J. Hwang, Computer stereo vision for three-dimensional object location, Ph.D. dissertation, University of Tennessee, Knoxville (1980).

22. J. J. Hwang, C. C. Lee, and E. L. Hall, Segmentation of solid objects using global local edge coincidence, *Proceedings of the IEEE Conference on Pattern Recognition and Image Processing*, August, pp. 114–121 (1979).

23. W. Kim, Relational database systems, *Comp. Surveys* **11**(3), 185–211 (1979).

24. A. Klinger, and C. R. Dyer, Experiments on picture representation using regular decomposition, *Comput. Graphics Image Processing* **5**, 68–105 (1976).

25. A. Klinger, M. L. Rhodes, and V. T. To, Accessing image data, *Policy Anal. Info. Sys.* **1**(2), 171–190 (1978).

26. D. E. Knuth, *The Art of Computer Programming: Fundamental Algorithms*, Addison-Wesley, Reading, MA (1968).

27. T. Kunii, S. Weyl, and J. M. Tenenbaum, A relational database scheme for describing complex pictures with color and textures, *Policy Anal. Info. Sys.* **1**(2), 127–142 (1978).

28. C. C. Lee, Boundary adjacency tracing and its application to database compression, M.S. thesis, Computer Science Dept., University of Tennessee, Knoxville (1979).

29. C. C. Lee, J. H. Hwang, E. L. Hall, and M. G. Thomason, Boundary direction vector coding for scene description, *Proc. IEEE Region 3 Conf.*, April, pp. 95–102 (1980).

30. Y. E. Lien, and R. Schroff, An interactive query language for an image database, *Policy Anal. Info. Sys.* **1**(2), 91–112 (1978).

31. Y. E. Lien, and D. F. Utter, Jr., Design of an image database, *Proc. IEEE Workshop on Picture Data Description and Management*, April, pp. 131–136 (1977).

32. D. McKeoun, Jr., and R. Reddy, A hierarchical symbolic representation for an image data base, *Proc. IEEE Workshop on Picture Data Description and Management*, April, pp. 40–44 (1977).

33. W. M. Newman, and R. F. Sproul, *Principles of Interactive Computer Graphics*, McGraw-Hill, New York, NY (1979).

34. F. Palermo, and D. Weller, Picture building system, *Proc. IEEE Spring Compcon*, San Francisco, pp. 235–237 (1979).

35. T. Pavlidis, A minimum storage boundary tracing algorithm and its applications to automatic inspection, *IEEE Trans. Syst. Man Cybern.* **SMC-8**(1), 66–69 (1978).

36. T. Pavlidis, *Structural Pattern Recognition*, Springer-Verlag, Berlin (1977).

37. A. Rosenfeld, *Picture Languages: Formal Models for Picture Recognition*, Academic Press, NY (1979).

38. A. Rosenfeld, R. A. Hummel, and S. Zucker, Scene labeling by relaxation operations, *IEEE Trans. Syst. Man Cybern.* **SMC-6**, 420–433 (1976).

39. A. Rosenfeld, and A. C. Kak, *Digital Picture Processing*, Academic Press, NY (1976).

40. H. Samet, A quadtree medial axis transform, *CACM* **26**(9), 680–693 (1983).

41. M. E. Senko, Data structures and data accessing in database systems, past, present, future, *IBM Sys. J.* **16**(3), 208–257 (1977).

42. L. G. Shapiro, Data structures for picture processing: a survey, *Comput. Graphics Image Processing* **11**, 162–184 (1979).

43. Special section on pattern recognition software, *IEEE Trans. Software Eng.* **SE-3**(2), 160–190 (1977).

44. H. Tamura, and S. Mori, A data management system for manipulating large images, *Proc. IEEE Workshop on Picture Data Description and Management*, April, pp. 45–54 (1977).

45. H. Tamura, S. Mori, and T. Shimada, Data management for manipulating partitioned large images, *Policy Anal. Info. Sys.* **1**(2), 143–170 (1978).

46. S. L. Tanimoto, Pictorial feature distortion in a pyramid, *Comput. Graphics Images Processing* **5**(3), 333–352 (1976).

47. J. D. Ullman, *Principles of Database Systems*, Computer Science Press, Potomac, MD (1980).

48. D. Weller, and F. Palermo, Database requirements for graphics, *Proc. IEEE Spring Compcon*, San Francisco, pp. 231–233 (1979).

49. A. Y. Wu, T. H. Hong, and A. Rosenfeld, Threshold selection using quad trees, *IEEE Trans Pat. Anal. Mach. Intell.* **PAMI-4**(1), 90–94 (1982).

50. Y. Yakimovsky, and R. Cunningham, A system for extracting three-dimensional measurements from a stereo pair of TV cameras, *Comput. Graphics Image Processing* **7**, 195–210 (1978).

Chapter 2

AN OVERVIEW OF DATABASE MANAGEMENT TECHNOLOGY

Isamu Kobayashi

SANNO Institute of Business Administration
School of Management and Informatics
Kamikasuya 1573, Isehara, Kanagawa 259-11
Japan

1. INTRODUCTION

Today, *database* is a fashionable word. A number of generalized database management systems are available that can be used as the foundation for various kinds of information systems. They are considered just as basic as programming language translators and operating systems. Many people want to introduce and use these generalized database management systems even before their needs have been established. As a result, they constitute several of the best-selling software packages.

The philosophy behind database technology is not always well understood because most database management system users are not aware of the goals of these systems. Consequently, database management systems are very often misused. We can find many incorrect applications that have brought unnecessarily bad performances into the information processing systems.

Meanwhile, much effort is being devoted to establishing a concrete foundation for database technology. A number of researchers are engaged in developing data models, data processing models, physical database representations, advanced database languages, database machines, and so forth. Much space in conference proceedings and technical journals is usually occupied by papers on related topics. This situation probably arose because database technology has been considered as no more than a synthesis of existing computer technologies.

However, most of these works are too heavily concentrated on specific topics, and sometimes the significance of these works appears to be misunderstood even by their authors. Hence, they are not always well received by information systems designers.

In this chapter, the author would like to clarify the motivations that triggered the development of current database technology, and describe the correct usage of generalized database management systems. Two different systems design methods, the traditional *output-oriented* approach and the new *database-oriented* approach, are explained, and the latter method is extensively studied. The author also presents applications to which database technology should be applied, design procedures which the systems designer should employ in implementing a database system, and selection criteria which the user should adopt for choosing a database management system for his applications.

Technical discussions on data structure, database operations, and other requirements are made in relation to the database design procedures. In this way, the author provides a global view of database technology for both information systems designers and database researchers.

The rest of this chapter is composed of ten sections. In Section 2, several different motivations for the development of database technology are described. Database as a new systems design methodology is briefly discussed in Section 3. A theoretical discussion of data structure is given in Section 4 with emphasis placed on the various semantic constraints holding in database relations. Section 5 describes elementary database operations. A calculus-based operation is presented first with various algebra-based operations described as special cases, and then tuple-by-tuple operations are introduced. Other requirements regarding integrity, security, concurrency, recoverability, and so on are discussed in Section 6. Section 7 is devoted to physical database representations. Section 8 deals with basic database management functions, which must be implemented in the database management system. In Section 9, several existing database management systems are described and compared. Section 10 discusses the end-user languages. Finally, several topics designated for future research are described in Section 11.

2. MOTIVATIONS

A database can be defined as a collection of data files which can represent *complicated data structures*, are equipped with *various access paths*, and can be used for *various purposes* by *many users*. Operational considerations in database management design include *data independence, security, integrity, concurrency* and *recoverability*.

The motivations for the development of database management technology have included the rapid development of computer hardware and software, the rapid change in the society of which enterprises are a part, and the necessity for man–computer systems in solving large problems.

2.1. Large Shared Files

Due to the rapid increase of computer capabilities, the construction of fairly large information processing systems has become possible. In particular, development of various large-volume direct-access storage devices has enabled the construction of large-scale integrated systems. Multipurpose shared files to be equipped in these systems must be able to represent complicated data structures and must be provided with a variety of access paths. The file technology that has been developed in the past has not been good enough to conform with these requirements.

During the development of large programs, defects in past programming methods which resembled those in handicrafts have gradually been recognized, and "software crisis" has been declared. Starting from Dijkstra's structured programming, *software engineering* has begun to focus on the modernization of programming methodology and is attracting keen interest in the computer community. Database technology is one of the most important topics in software engineering, as it is now required for the design and implementation of large-scale information processing systems.

It is very hard to design and implement large-scale information processing systems with a clear view of all the requirements. In particular, optimal design of files that are to be shared by various processing programs in the system is a very difficult task. In addition to the importance of producing an explicit program structure as emphasized in the structured programming, it is essential to make the data structure as explicit as possible. Database technology presents several distinct levels of *data abstraction* and an extended set of standard database procedures.

2.2. Rapid Social Change

Several years ago, the United States abrogated the gold standard and the whole world was confronted with "dollar shock." We also encountered the oil crisis that has caused international suffering from the petroleum shortage. Such events cause great changes in society. It can be said that we meet with mini-dollar shock every year, with a mini-oil crisis every month, and a micro-dollar shock and micro-oil crisis every day.

Such rapid social changes necessitate changes in the organization of enterprises and management decision-making processes. These changes in turn necessitate redesign and reconstruction of the information systems which form the core of computers usage. Since the redesign and reconstruction of such information systems are very time- and money-consuming tasks, a new methodology which can reduce these costs is very desirable. As social changes tend to occur more and more rapidly, such a methodology is sought more and more eagerly.

Database technology presents a method of modularly constructing information systems, in which we can minimize the effort needed to redesign and reconstruct the system according to the changes in the social mechanism and the reorganization of the enterprises.

2.3. Man–Computer Cooperation

Historically, computers were first used as calculating machines. They were first used for several engineering problems in military applications and then became widely applied to business problems with huge volumes of data. If, and only if, a designated *algorithm* was given in the form of a computer program, could a computer solve the problem. The computer was, therefore, a closed system for problem solving. With the emancipation of human beings from mechanical computing tasks due to the computer's high speed and accuracy, the computer became a tool for economizing human brainwork.

In various problem areas, many algorithms have been devised, such as various mathematical and statistical methods, and operations research and management control techniques. On the other hand, the mathematical theory of computation clarified the ranges of problems for which algorithms can be devised, using the beautiful theory of recursive functions.

We know that humans do not always deal with problems using an algorithm. For example, we do not confront problems like manipulating natural languages, proving theorems, and playing games *algorithmically*. With an optimistic expectation that such problems might also be handled well by the computer, much research was made under the flag of artificial intelligence. However, mechanisms such as trial and error, learning and self-organization have not been fully understood, and researchers are now rather pessimistic about progress in this area. These mechanisms seem to be closely related to human mental activities, especially to the mechanism of *cognition,* and they are not likely to be embodied by the computer without elucidating the cognition mechanism physiologically.

Let us call these capabilities, whose mechanisms are unknown, *heuristics.* In a narrow sense, heuristics are finite processes by which a problem might be solved. These differ from algorithms that always lead to the solution because there are no guarantees of obtaining a solution using heuristics.

Sometimes a heuristic process can be embodied in the form of a computer program. Here we use the term heuristics in a wider sense that include processes of learning, self-organizing, and inventing algorithms.

Some heuristics, which computers can simulate only poorly, are indispensable in various problem-solving tasks. Consequently, man–computer systems are being constructed in which the computer takes charge of the algorithmic part and the human controls the heuristic part. Concepts such as time-sharing, computer graphics, and management information systems can be seen as directed at such man–computer systems. The man–computer systems constructed in this way can expand the problem areas that can be dealt with.

The major functions that should be integrated into such man–computer systems are a man–machine interface, a collection of established algorithms, and a database. Since man, who is an important component of the system, asks the computer a variety of nonpredetermined questions during the problem-solving process, the database must have a flexible mechanism executing a wide range of commands. Therefore, we should provide a multipurpose database with a complicated data structure and various access paths.

3. DATABASE AS A NEW SYSTEMS DESIGN METHODOLOGY

Different motivations for the development of database technology result in different types of implemented systems. In fact, several distinct types of database management systems have been developed for distinct purposes. We will first study a new systems design methodology, which can be used to construct all these types of systems. This is the *database-oriented* approach which differs greatly from the traditional *output-oriented* approach.

3.1. Output-Oriented Approach

In traditional systems design, the designer first thoroughly analyzed the users' demands and then determined the system's outputs. The outputs were designed so that there was nothing lacking that was necessary and nothing redundant. The designer then planned the system's inputs which were necessary for producing the outputs. Timing considerations for inputs arrival and outputs generation were important. The third task was to design the computational processes that transformed the inputs into the outputs. Files were designed in parallel with processing programs in order to minimize the input data and improve the processing efficiency.

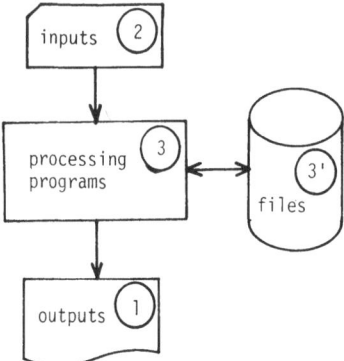

Fig. 1. Output-oriented design approach.

Such a traditional output-oriented design approach was certainly appropriate for constructing a system producing several predetermined outputs. Routine applications such as payroll, accounts payable and receivable, and various other billing jobs, have been designed in this manner and will henceforth be designed in the same manner. The computer is used as a production machine in a computing factory where performance is the most important criterion.

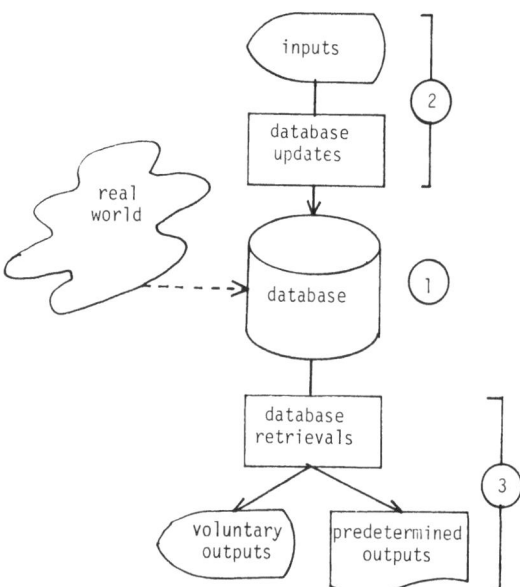

Fig. 2. Database-oriented design approach.

In an output-oriented approach, however, the larger a system becomes, the more difficult the system design procedure grows. In addition, even if the system has been well implemented, it becomes an *inflexible* system in the sense that it would require expensive redesign and reconstruction when requests for unexpected outputs are made. The society of which enterprises are a part is changing very rapidly and large-scale systems are strongly affected by these changes. Very often, some of the reports that have been produced become unnecessary and new reports are requested. These considerations call for a new design method that enables construction of a *flexible* system.

In designing information systems that support planning tasks, in particular, it is very hard or even impossible to completely predetermine a system's outputs. Such an information system must be designed as a man-machine system in which the computer capabilities in managing and processing data according to the given programs is combined with the human capabilities that the computer cannot substitute. Such a system is constructed in order to expand the problem-solving faculty. Man asks the computer various questions. What problems he will have to solve and what questions he will ask are hardly predictable, so the output-oriented design approach is difficult to adopt in this case.

3.2. Database-Oriented Approach

Recent development of database management technology has enabled a quite different information systems design methodology. The first step is designing a database. The database is what represents things in the real world, which become the objects to be monitored and/or managed by the information system users. The output requirements are not explicitly considered in this step. After the database design has been completed inputs are determined so that they are the devices by which changes in the real world are reflected on database updates. Outputs are obtained by retrieval from the database. Usually two distinct types of outputs, predetermined and voluntary, are produced. The former should be generated at a predetermined time in a predetermined format, while the latter should be created on demand in a format requested at that time.

The new design methodology is superior to the traditional one in several respects. First, the system designed in this manner becomes *flexible* enough to conform with changes in the requirements because it does not assume any specific output requirements. Any output that can be extracted from the database or generated from the data stored in the database is available to the users. Second, the systems design procedures become much easier by attaching importance to clarifying *static* data structure rather than to clarifying *dynamic* processing program structure. Third, the systems inputs are regarded as database updates, while the systems outputs are regarded as database retrievals, and hence the inputs and outputs design are completely separated. This enables a modular systems design procedure and a modular systems construction.

Systems designed in this manner are not as efficient as those designed using the traditional output-oriented design approach when both are requested to produce the same predetermined outputs. In fact, the former systems store not only the data that are required in the present but also the data that will be required in the future, and are equipped also with general purpose data manipulating functions to cope with a wide range of the users' requirements.

Not all the systems can be designed with the database-oriented approach. In fact, most information processing systems must still be designed and implemented with the output-oriented approach. With the currently available hardware and software technology, imprudent application of the database-oriented design approach can be harmful. The cases in which the database-oriented design approach is definitely effective include:

(i) when there are a variety of application programs giving access to shared files. In this case, the data structure becomes fairly complicated and various access paths must be implemented. The system might be built with the traditional output-oriented approach but the system development and maintenance cost could become very high. Some types of real-time applications may fall into this category. The use of database management systems will greatly reduce the system development and maintenance cost.

(ii) when a system is required for planning. The heuristic capabilities possessed by the human brain must be combined with the algorithmic power possessed by the computer in order to expand the problem-solving faculty. Information systems such as management information systems, medical information systems, engineering information systems, and regional information systems fall into this category. In these systems, planning through man–computer interactions is mandatory.

(iii) when reports of varying format are frequently required. In the past, report program generators were used to create such reports, and most statistical reports still must be produced in this manner. Processing is usually carried out in batch mode.

Now that computer hardware is becoming less and less expensive, the systems design and implementation are becoming more and more expensive. This situation will justify adoption of the new database-oriented design approach in many more cases.

3.3. Design Procedure

The database-oriented design approach is usually composed of three major phases; the logical database design, the physical database design, and the end-user language design.

In the logical database design phase, we must identify the objects in the real world that are to be represented in the database. Then the attributes that accurately describe these objects are selected. Next we must aggregate the elementary data manipulating operations that can be invoked by the users. Several quantitative considerations must be used to determine physical database organization in the later phase. Finally, additional requirements for the processing environment must be clarified.

The logical database structure must be a precise reflection of the real world. There are, however, a diversity of views of the real world. Some of the existing data models may provide us with an appropriate guide for designing the logical database structure and data manipulations which will operate on them.

In the physical database design phase, we should determine the physical representations of the logically defined objects. Again, there are a variety of possible representations and it is a difficult task to find an optimal one. Various file organizations and index provisions must be examined and compared.

Next, the database management functions necessary for managing the created database must be implemented. These include a database definition function, a collection of database access routines, a binding function, and various utility processors to be used by database administrators.

The above phase can be omitted if we find a generalized database management system that possesses sufficient functions for our applications.

The final phase is the actual implementation of the information system and its expansion. We must define the database structure using the given data description language. Some subroutines necessary for the applications must be integrated into the system and then one or more problem-oriented languages must be implemented for different types of end-users.

In the remainder of this chapter, the database-oriented design procedure is described in detail, together with theoretical discussions of various design stages.

4. LOGICAL DATABASE STRUCTURE

The first step of the database-oriented design procedure is the selection of the objects to be represented in the database. The database is a reflection of the real world which contains a number of objects, some of which are visible while others are invisible. Since we can only use a limited amount of data storage, only that data relevant to the users' universe of discourse can be represented in the database. Therefore, we confront the problem of selecting the objects to be represented.

We cannot store the objects themselves in the computer storage and the database should store a model that reflects the real world. Therefore, a specific data model into which objects in the real world can be mapped must be constructed. There exists diverse views of the real world, but we will begin our discussion with a relational view.

4.1. Relational View of the Real World

We may regard the real world as a collection of *primitives*, each being recognized as a unit, plus various *facts*, each being described as a relationship among these primitives. We use natural languages to express these facts. One way to formally represent sentences that express facts of a specific type in a natural language is to transcribe these sentences into an *atomic predicate* in formal logic of the form

$$p(a_1, a_2, \ldots, a_n)$$

where p is the predicate symbol and each a_k $(k = 1, 2, \ldots, n)$ is a primitive in our universe of discourse.

For example, "Fernão is a professor" can be represented by a unary predicate

professor(Fernão)

"Fernão is Monica's father" by a binary predicate

father(Fernão, Monica)

and "Fernão gives Monica a book" by a ternary predicate

give(Fernão, Monica, a book)

A fact can be expressed by many distinct verbal expressions. We have no means of choosing a specific expression as the only correct one. In fact, the second sentence in the examples above can be rewritten as "Monica is Fernão's daughter," and the third sentence in a passive form as "Monica is given a book by Fernão" or "A book is given to Monica by Fernão." In addition, there is more than one predicate representation of the same verbal expression. The first and second sentence can be rewritten respectively as

$$be(\text{Fernão, professor})$$

and

$$be([\text{Fernão, Monica}], \text{father})$$

while the third sentence can be rewritten as

$$give([\text{Fernão, Monica}], \text{a book})$$

Note that "professor" and "father" are now regarded as primitives instead of predicate types and that [Fernão, Monica] is regarded as a primitive instead of a pair of primitives. The distinction between different predicate representations can be considered a reflection of *semantic differences* between predicate types.

A much more complex situation exists in transcribing a compound sentence into the predicate expression. For example, "Fernão has a daughter who is 17 years old and whose name is Monica" can be regarded as a combination of two facts, "Fernão is Monica's father" and "Monica is female and 17 years old." A straightforward transcription may be

$$father(\text{Fernão, [Monica, female, 17]})$$

but one may alternatively transcribe this sentence into a pair of predicates

$$father(\text{Fernão, Monica})$$

and

$$person(\text{Monica, female, 17})$$

In the latter representation, the compound primitive [Monica, female, 17] has been eliminated. The last predicate may be further decomposed into two binary predicates

$$sex(\text{Monica, female})$$

and

$$age(\text{Monica, 17})$$

"Fernão has two daughters, Monica who is 17 years old and Carla who is 15 years old" is a slightly more complicated sentence. It can be transcribed as

father(Fernão, [[Monica, female, 17], [Carla, female, 15]])

This can be decomposed into three predicates:

father(Fernão, [Monica, Carla])

person(Monica, female, 17)

person(Carla, female, 15)

The first predicate can be further decomposed into two predicates

father(Fernão, Monica)

father(Fernão, Carla)

to eliminate the compound primitive [Monica, Carla].

In order to examine the fine structure of sentences and to express their semantics, devices like Case Grammar and Semantic Net were contrived. Given a finite number of binary predicate types, these models transcribe a natural language sentence into one or more binary predicates. Some data models such as Data Semantics,[1] DIAM,[81] Binary Logical Association,[13] and Extensible Semantic Model,[44] are based on binary predicates.

Such binary models may be suitable for obtaining a unique representation as a predicate; however, they do not seem to fit fully the database management environment. Therefore, we will assume that we are given a collection of n-ary $(n \geq 1)$ predicates representing facts in the real world. Primitives may be either simple or compound.

There exist several data models based on n-ary predicates. Although it was not a model developed for database technology, Information Algebra[23] can be regarded as an n-ary data model. The Relational Model[26] is the most popular n-ary data model. Extended Set Theory[19] and the Infological Model[89] also fall into this category. In the following discussion, we will conform with the terminology used in the Relational Model.

An n-ary predicate with n primitives (a proposition) is evaluated to be either "true" or "false" with reference to the state of the real world at a given time τ. A set

$$R_p^\tau = \{(a_1, a_2, \ldots, a_n) \mid p(a_1, a_2, \ldots, a_n) = \text{"true" at } \tau\}$$

is called a *relation* (instance). Its member

$$t = (a_1, a_2, \ldots, a_n)$$

is called a *tuple*, and a_k is called the kth *attribute value* of tuple t, which is denoted by

$$a_k = A_k(t)$$

(We use this notation because attribute A_k can be regarded as a function of tuples.)

Since the state of the real world is constantly changing, the relation is time-varying. Let $\mathcal{R}_p(\mathcal{A})$ be the set of possible relations with a specific predicate symbol p, where

$$\mathcal{A} = \{A_1, A_2, \ldots, A_n\}$$

$\mathcal{R}_p(\mathcal{A})$ is called the *relation schema* of type p. Several relation schemata of distinct types compose a *database schema*, which is a set of databases (instances), each realizable at a certain time. For example, we may have a database schema composed of three relation schemata

$$\mathcal{R}_{\text{father}}(\{\text{father name, child name}\}),$$

$$\mathcal{R}_{\text{mother}}(\{\text{mother name, child name}\})$$

$$\mathcal{R}_{\text{person}}(\{\text{name, sex, age}\})$$

At a specific time τ, the database is composed of three relations

$$R_{\text{father}}^{\tau} = \{(\text{Fernão, Monica}), (\text{Fernão, Carla})\}$$

$$R_{\text{mother}}^{\tau} = \{(\text{Maria, Monica}), (\text{Maria, Carla})\}$$

$$R_{\text{person}}^{\tau} = \{(\text{Fernão, male, 47}), (\text{Maria, female, 43}),$$
$$(\text{Monica, female, 17}), (\text{Carla, female, 15})\}$$

Since a variety of verbal expressions and predicate representations can express the very same fact, it would be desirable to establish a standard way to derive a unique predicate representation. Unfortunately, this uniqueness is not obtainable. However, several normal forms have been presented to make the predicate representation as unique as possible. They will be discussed later in relation to various semantic constraints.

There exists another category of data models that distinguish relationship relations from entity relations. These two types of relations are treated differently in these models according to their semantic differences. They will also be discussed later in relation to the relationship constraint.

4.2. Geometric Representation of Relations

A relation has been defined as a mathematical relation, that is, a subset of a Cartesian product of several sets. An *n*-ary relation, therefore, is regarded as a subset of *n*-dimensional space, each of whose coordinate axes corresponds to an attribute.

In Information Algebra,[23] every attribute can take a special value Ω which means that the attribute value is "undefined." By this means we can consider a space of a sufficiently large dimension, which is called the *property space*. In an appropriate property space, any relation is a subset of a subspace. A relation schema is a family of realizable relations in a subspace.

A tuple representing a fact in the real world is alternatively called a *point* because it is mapped onto a point in a property space. An ordered set of points is called a *line* although it is different from a geometric line. A subset of a property space is called an *area*. A relation is a special area in a property space.

Many other concepts in the database theory can be interpreted into certain concepts regarding the property space. For example, the *union*, *intersection*, and *difference* operations in the information algebra, which are described later in Section 5, are those operating in the property space. Also,

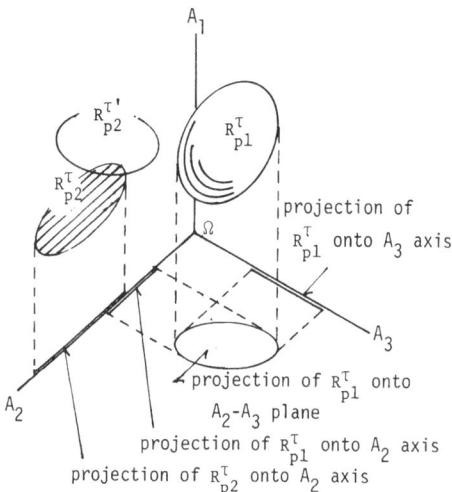

Fig. 3. Property space.

the *projection* operation is nothing more than geometric projection in the property space.

We will use such geometric interpretations when they are convenient.

4.3. Semantic Constraints

In addition to the various facts that can be represented by n-ary predicates with n primitives (constants), we may have some facts that can only be expressed by sentences with one or more bound variables. Some of them are *inductively* found from various states of the real world, while others are *deductively* given by the basic properties of the real-world objects.

For example, we know that "every person is less than 150 years old," "sex is either male or female," and "there are males and females." These facts are based on historical observations.

Let us denote the fact "a (name) is b (sex) and c (years old)" and "d (integer) is less than 150" respectively by a ternary predicate

$$\text{person}(a, b, c)$$

and a special unary predicate

$$d < 150$$

The first fact can then be represented by

$$(\forall z)((\exists x)(\exists y)\text{person}(x, y, z) \to z < 150)$$

which is a first-order sentence whose universe is the set of primitives in the real world. It has three bound variables, of which one is universally quantified and the others are existentially quantified.

If we have a relation schema

$$\mathscr{R}_{\text{person}}(\{\text{name, sex, age}\})$$

representing predicates of the form $\text{person}(a, b, c)$, the same fact can be represented by a sentence of another form

$$(\forall \tau)(\forall x / R^{\tau}_{\text{person}})\text{age}(x) < 150$$

in which x is a tuple variable quantified over a relation R^{τ}_{person} belonging to the $\mathscr{R}_{\text{person}}$. Since the latter form of sentences conforms with the database environment better than the former form, we will use the latter form in the remainder of this chapter.

Similarly, the second and third facts in the example can be represented respectively by

$$(\forall \tau)(\forall x / R^\tau_{person})(sex(x) = male \vee sex(x) = female)$$

and

$$(\forall \tau)((\exists x_1 / R^\tau_{person})sex(x_1) = male \wedge (\exists x_2 / R^\tau_{person})sex(x_2) = female)$$

Facts such as "all fathers are male" are deduced from the basic property of the "father" concept. If we have a relation schema

$$\mathscr{R}_{father}(\{father\ name,\ child\ name\})$$

in addition to the relation schema $\mathscr{R}_{person}$, this fact can be represented by

$$(\forall \tau)(\forall x / R^\tau_{father})(\forall y / R^\tau_{person})(father\ name(x) = name(y) \rightarrow sex(y) = male)$$

which has two universally quantified tuple variables, one quantified over R^τ_{father} and the other over R^τ_{person} belonging respectively to $\mathscr{R}_{father}$ and $\mathscr{R}_{person}$.

For the "ancestor" concept, we have "father is an ancestor," "mother is an ancestor," and "ancestor's ancestor is an ancestor." If we have two more relation schemata

$$\mathscr{R}_{mother}(\{mother\ name,\ child\ name\})$$

$$\mathscr{R}_{ancestor}(\{ancestor\ name,\ descendant\ name\})$$

these three facts can be represented respectively by

$$(\forall \tau)(\forall x / R^\tau_{father})(\exists y / R^\tau_{ancestor})(father\ name(x) = ancestor\ name(y))$$

$$(\forall \tau)(\forall x / R^\tau_{mother})(\exists y / R^\tau_{ancestor})(mother\ name(x) = ancestor\ name(y))$$

and

$$(\forall \tau)(\forall x_1 / R^\tau_{ancestor})(\forall x_2 / R^\tau_{ancestor})(\exists x_3 / R^\tau_{ancestor})(descendant\ name(x_1)$$

$$= ancestor\ name(x_2) \rightarrow (ancestor\ name(x_1)$$

$$= ancestor\ name(x_3) \rightarrow descendant\ name(x_2)$$

$$= descendant\ name(x_3)))$$

The last implies the binary predicate "ancestor" is *transitive*.

Sentences can include some tuple variables that are bound by some means other than quantification. For example, if $\mathcal{R}_{person}$ has one more attribute "number of children," that is, if we have a relation schema

$$\mathcal{R}_{person}(\{name, sex, age, number\ of\ children\})$$

then

$$((\forall \tau)(\forall x/R^{\tau}_{person})(number\ of\ children(x)$$

$$= \sum_{(y \in R^{\tau}_{father} \wedge father\ name(y)=name(x))} count(y)$$

$$+ \sum_{(y \in R^{\tau}_{mother} \wedge mother\ name(y)=name(x))} count(y))$$

holds. Here $count(y)$ is a constant function that assigns value 1 to every value of the tuple variable y. The variable y is said to be bound in the scope of an aggregate function $\sum$.

All the above examples are *static* in the sense that they concern one or more relations in only one database (instance). There also are *dynamic* facts that concern more than one databases (instances) belonging to a database schema. For example, a fact that "the age does not decrease" can be represented by

$$(\forall \tau)(\forall \tau')(\tau < \tau' \rightarrow (\forall x/R^{\tau}_{person})(\forall x'/R^{\tau'}_{person})$$

$$(name(x) = name(x') \rightarrow age(x) \leq age(x')))$$

There can be other facts that are only represented by second-order predicates with predicate variables or higher-order predicates. However, we will not discuss these in this chapter.

The facts described by predicates with one or more tuple variables are called *semantic constraints* because they are considered as adding semantics to data. As already shown, there are static and dynamic semantic constraints. In contrast to the database relations which are time-varying, these semantic constraints are basically not time-varying. A collection of semantic constraints can be stored and maintained in computer storage as well as a database (instance) which is a collection of relations. The former is sometimes called an *intension database*, while the latter is called an *extension database*. These terms are used because the latter can be regarded as a part of extension corresponding to the intension stored in the former.

The semantic constraints, when they are recorded in a certain form, are called *assertions*. The assertions do not have to be proven, as they must be given *a priori* like axioms. As an axiom system, assertions must be mutually consistent. Sometimes it is desirable for them to be irredundant. Various sets of assertions that are logically equivalent to each other exist; hence, problems arise such as determining whether a given set of assertions is consistent, determining whether a given set of assertions is irredundant, and obtaining a consistent and irredundant set which is minimal in a certain sense. However, these problems are in most cases *recursively undecidable* and have been solved only for some sets of relatively simple assertions.

One of the major functions of the assertions is regulating database update operations. A database (instance) is said to be *consistent* if it does not conflict with any static assertions. A database update is said to be *proper* if it transforms a consistent database into another consistent database without violating any dynamic assertion.

Assertions can also be used as a basis of the *deduction* by which some facts that are not explicitly represented in the (extension) database are inferred from some other facts currently represented in the database. More generally, assertions together with all the tuples in a database can be regarded as constituting an axiom system and many theorems can be proven from this axiom system. If such a theorem-proving function is implemented, we can retrieve not only simple facts represented by some tuples but also facts represented by some sentences with tuple variables, which are inferred from the axiom system.

By the way, static constraints of some special forms play very important roles in logical database design. Next we will survey such semantic constraints.

In general, static constraints can be written in their prenex normal form as

$$(\forall \tau) Q'_1 Q'_2 \cdots Q'_\mu \lambda(x_1, x_2, \ldots, x_\mu, x_{\mu+1}, x_{\mu+2}, \ldots, x_{\mu+\nu})$$

where Q'_k is either $(\forall x_k / R^\tau_k)$ or $(\exists x_k / R^\tau_k)$, and λ is a predicate in which tuple variables $x_1, x_2, \ldots, x_\mu$ ($\mu \geq 0$) are free and $x_{\mu+1}, x_{\mu+2}, \ldots, x_{\mu+\nu}$ ($\nu \geq 0$) are bound by some means other than quantifications. For simplicity, we omit the $(\forall \tau)$ part and replace R^τ_k with $\mathcal{R}_k$, that is, we write

$$Q_1 Q_2 \cdots Q_\mu \lambda(x_1, x_2, \ldots, x_{\mu+\nu})$$

with Q_k being either $(\forall x_k / \mathcal{R}_k)$ or $(\exists x_k / \mathcal{R}_k)$. We call this form a *schema calculus.* Since the schema calculus is a sentence regarding one or more relation schemata in a database schema, it must be distinguished from the relational calculus,[28] which is a sentence regarding one or more relations in a database (instance).

4.4. Tuple Constraints

A static semantic constraint is called a *tuple constraint* if it has only one tuple variable and this variable is universally quantified. Tuple constraints are so named because they are semantic constraints imposed on each tuple in any relation belonging to the relation schema over which the tuple variable is bound. Tuple constraints regarding a relations schema determine a framework of relations belonging to this relation schema.

4.4.1. Domain Constraints

A tuple constraint described in terms of only one attribute is called a *domain constraint*.[96] Schema calculi of the form

$$(\forall x / \mathcal{R}_p) A_k(x) \in D_k$$

where $A_k(x) \in D_k$ is a monadic (unary predicate) that becomes "true" iff $A_k(x)$ belongs to the value set D_k, are simple domain constraints. For example, we have

$$(\forall x / \mathcal{R}_{\text{person}}) \text{sex}(x) \in \{\text{male, female}\}$$

and

$$(\forall x / \mathcal{R}_{\text{person}}) \text{age}(x) \in \{0, 1, \ldots, 149\}$$

The D_k is called A_k's *domain*. Any relation in a relation schema is a subset of a Cartesian product of n domains because of the existence of n such simple domain constraints.

Domain constraints can be registered as assertions by means of devices such as the *type* statement in PASCAL.[49] Domains can be simple scalar type such as *integer, real, boolean,* and *char*; a subrange type that specifies a subset of a predetermined value set; or a structured type such as *array, record,* and (power) *set.*

For example, given an arbitrary value set V, compound domains such as

V^m: a set of fixed-length arrays (vector, matrix, etc.)
$\bigcup_{k=1}^{\infty} V^k$: a set of variable-length arrays (linear list, stack, etc.)
$\mathcal{P}(V)$: a power set
$\{x \cup y \mid x \subset V \wedge y \subset x^2\}$: a set of directed graphs

and so forth can be generated. Some sets must be defined recursively. For example, the set L of nested lists is defined by

$$T_1 = \bigcup_{i=1}^{\infty} V^i$$

$$T_{k+1} = \bigcup_{j=1}^{\infty} T_k^j$$

and $L = T_{\infty}$. Given m value sets $V_1, V_2, \ldots, V_m$, we can generate

$$V_1 \times V_2 \times \cdots \times V_m: \quad \text{a Cartesian product (record)}$$

and

$$\mathscr{P}(V_1 \times V_2 \times \cdots \times V_m): \quad \text{a power set of a Cartesian product}$$
$$\text{(repeating group)}$$

Sometimes it is necessary to combine an additional term $C(x)$ containing the tuple variable x conjunctively with the matrix part of a simple domain constraint as

$$(\forall x/\mathscr{R}_p)(A_k(x) \in D_k \wedge C(x))$$

to further restrict the A_k's domain. For example,

$$(\forall x/\mathscr{R}_p)(A_k(x) \in V^2 \wedge c_1(A_k(x)) < c_2(A_k(x)))$$

where c_i is an operator extracting the ith component of the value of $A_k(x)$, restricts the form of two-dimensional vectors that can become a value of $A_k(x)$. Given a vocabulary, we can generate sentences that obey a certain grammar. Such a grammar can be regarded as introducing an additional, and in this case very complicated, term $c(x)$. When the domain is a Cartesian product or a power set of a Cartesian product, there usually are some additional restrictions described in terms of components of the attribute value. These restrictions are discussed later in connection with the first normal form.

An important aspect is that a set of operators is associated with each value set. For example, arithmetic operators are defined on the set of numbers, logical operators on the set of truth values, and string operators on the set of symbol strings. Different sets of operators can be provided for the very same set. For example, the same set of variable-length arrays can be either a linear list or a push-down stack, according to the operators defined on it. Such operators can be extended to operators defined on the set of functions of tuples.

We have three kinds of basic function of tuples: constants, attributes, and logical functions judging whether a given tuple belongs to a specified relation. We can generate compound functions of tuples by combining these basic functions using the above-mentioned extended operators. In describing semantic constraints, such functions of tuples are used. Functions of tuples are discussed later in Section 5.

4.4.2. Interdomain Constraints

There may be tuple constraints that can be described in terms of more than one attribute; that is,

$$(\forall x/\mathcal{R}_p)\lambda(A_{k_1}(x), A_{k_2}(x), \ldots, A_{k_m}(x))$$

where

$$\{k_1, k_2, \ldots, k_m\} \subset \{1, 2, \ldots, n\}$$

and λ is a logical function of tuples defined in terms of m attributes. Such a constraint specifies a subset of $D_{k_1} \times D_{k_2} \times \cdots \times D_{k_m}$ and is called an *interdomain* constraint. For example,

$$(\forall x/\mathcal{R}_p)A_1(x) < A_2(x)$$

imposes a restriction on the $A_1(x)$ and $A_2(x)$ value of tuples in any relation belonging to $\mathcal{R}_p$. Constraints of the form

$$(\forall x/\mathcal{R}_p)A_{k_1}(x)\theta A_{k_2}(x)$$

where θ is an arbitrary relational operator, are called *theta dependencies* and have been studied extensively by Weber.[94]

In particular, interdomain constraints of the form

$$(\forall x/\mathcal{R}_p)A_{k_1}(x) = f(A_{k_2}(x), A_{k_3}(x), \ldots, A_{k_m}(x))$$

where f is an arbitrary function of tuples defined in terms of $A_{k_2}(x)$, $A_{k_3}(x), \ldots, A_{k_m}(x)$, are called *permanent functional dependencies* since they are special cases of functional dependencies which we mention later. If a permanent functional dependency exists, attribute A_{k_1} is usually excluded from the relation schema $\mathcal{R}_p$ and its value becomes an item to be calculated from other attribute values accommodated in the relation in $\mathcal{R}_p$.

4.5. Dependencies

If a schema calculus includes more than one tuple variable quantified over the same relation, and if the first quantification in its prenex normal form is universal, then we call it a *dependency*. Thanks to many researchers, several splendid theories have been constructed for various sets of dependencies taken as axiom systems. We will briefly review and comment on some of the important results in these theories.

4.5.1. Functional Dependencies

Let $\mathcal{A}_1$ and $\mathcal{A}_2$ be two subsets of attribute set $\mathcal{A}$ constituting a relation schema $\mathcal{R}_p(\mathcal{A})$. Let $\mathcal{A}_1(x)$ and $\mathcal{A}_2(x)$ be concatenations of values of attributes in $\mathcal{A}_1$ and those in $\mathcal{A}_2$, respectively. The schema calculus

$$(\forall x_1/\mathcal{R}_p)(\forall x_2/\mathcal{R}_p)(\mathcal{A}_1(x_1) = \mathcal{A}_1(x_2) \to \mathcal{A}_2(x_1) = \mathcal{A}_2(x_2))$$

is called a *functional dependency*[26] from $\mathcal{A}_1$ to $\mathcal{A}_2$ and is denoted simply by

$$\mathcal{A}_1 \to \mathcal{A}_2$$

We say "attributes in $\mathcal{A}_1$ determine attributes in $\mathcal{A}_2$," or simply "$\mathcal{A}_2$ is functionally dependent on $\mathcal{A}_1$."

In contrast to tuple constraints, functional dependencies specify neither a Cartesian product of domains nor a subset of such a product. At every moment τ the $\mathcal{A}_2(x)$ value is determined by the $\mathcal{A}_1(x)$ value for any tuple x. However, the function form itself can be time-varying. Permanent functional dependencies are special functional dependencies of which the function form is not time-varying.

There may be more than one functional dependency in a relation schema and some of them can be deduced from others. The following three properties of functional dependency can be directly obtained from the above definition of functional dependency:

(F1) If $\mathcal{A}_2 \subset \mathcal{A}_1 \subset \mathcal{A}$, then $\mathcal{A}_1 \to \mathcal{A}_2$ holds in $\mathcal{R}_p(\mathcal{A})$.

(F2) If $\mathcal{A}_1 \to \mathcal{A}_2$ holds in $\mathcal{R}_p(\mathcal{A})$, then $\mathcal{A}_1 \cup \mathcal{A}_3 \to \mathcal{A}_2 \cup \mathcal{A}_3$ holds in $\mathcal{R}_p(\mathcal{A})$ for any subset $\mathcal{A}_3$ of $\mathcal{A}$.

(F3) If both $\mathcal{A}_1 \to \mathcal{A}_2$ and $\mathcal{A}_2 \to \mathcal{A}_3$ hold in $\mathcal{R}_p(\mathcal{A})$, then $\mathcal{A}_1 \to \mathcal{A}_3$ holds in $\mathcal{R}_p(\mathcal{A})$.

Given a set $\mathcal{F}$ of functional dependencies, we can deduce some other functional dependencies using the above three properties as deductive rules. As deductive rules to infer other functional dependencies, these three are *sound* and *complete*. The set of all the functional dependencies deduced from $\mathscr{F}$ is called the *closure* of $\mathscr{F}$ and denoted by $\mathscr{F}^+$. Since any set of functional dependencies is a subset of its closure, two sets $\mathscr{F}_1$ and $\mathscr{F}_2$ of functional dependencies can be said to be equivalent if $\mathscr{F}_1^+ = \mathscr{F}_2^+$.

A set $\mathscr{F}$ of functional dependencies whose right-hand side consists of a single attribute is said to be *minimal* if for any functional dependency $\mathscr{A}_1 \to \mathscr{A}_2$ in $\mathscr{F}$, $\mathscr{A}_1' \to \mathscr{A}_2$ does not hold for any proper subset $\mathscr{A}_1'$ of $\mathscr{A}_1$, and if $\mathscr{F}'^+ \neq \mathscr{F}^+$ for any proper subset $\mathscr{F}'$ of $\mathscr{F}$. When we are given a set $\mathscr{F}$ of functional dependencies, we can obtain a minimal set $\mathscr{F}'$ equivalent to $\mathscr{F}$, that is, $\mathscr{F}'^+ = \mathscr{F}^+$. The algorithm for obtaining a minimal set equivalent to a given set corresponds to the algorithm for obtaining a minimal cover of switching functions.[37] It is known that there may be more than one minimal set equivalent to a given set of functional dependencies.

If $\mathscr{A}_1 \to \mathscr{A}$ holds in $\mathscr{R}_p(\mathscr{A})$, and for any proper subset $\mathscr{A}_1'$ of $\mathscr{A}_1$, $\mathscr{A}_1' \to \mathscr{A}$ does not hold, then $\mathscr{A}_1$ is called a *candidate key* (set) of relation schema $\mathscr{R}_p(\mathscr{A})$. Since $\mathscr{A} \to \mathscr{A}$ holds in any case, there exists at least one candidate key for every relation schema. Usually one of the candidate keys is selected as the *primary key* for each relation schema.

Functional dependency $(\mathscr{A}_r \to \mathscr{A} - \mathscr{A}_r)$ regarding a candidate key is called a *key dependency*.

A functional dependency is said to be *proper* if the right-hand side consists of a single attribute that is not contained in the left-hand side. Proper functional dependencies in $\mathscr{R}_p(\mathscr{A})$ can be classified into the following four types with respect to a key dependency $\mathscr{A}_r \to \mathscr{A} - \mathscr{A}_r$ in $\mathscr{R}_p(\mathscr{A})$:

1. If $\mathscr{A}_1 = \mathscr{A}_r$, then $\mathscr{A}_1 \to \{A_k\}$ is called a *prime dependency*.
2. If $\mathscr{A}_1 \subset \mathscr{A} - \mathscr{A}_r$ and $\mathscr{A}_k \in \mathscr{A} - \mathscr{A}_r$, then $\mathscr{A}_1 \to \{A_k\}$ is called a *transitive dependency*.
3. If $\mathscr{A}_1 \neq \mathscr{A}_r$, $\mathscr{A}_1 \cap \mathscr{A}_r \neq \varnothing$, and $A_k \in \mathscr{A} - \mathscr{A}_r$, then $\mathscr{A}_1 \to \{A_k\}$ is called a *pseudopartial dependency*. In particular, if $\mathscr{A}_1$ is a proper subset of $\mathscr{A}_r$, then $\mathscr{A}_1 \to \{A_k\}$ is called a *partial dependency*.
4. If $A_k \in \mathscr{A}_r$, then $\mathscr{A}_1 \to \{A_k\}$ is called a *pseudoreflexive dependency*. In particular, if $\mathscr{A}_1 \subset \mathscr{A} - \mathscr{A}_r$, then $\mathscr{A}_1 \to \{A_k\}$ is called a *reflexive dependency*.

There are no other proper functional dependencies in $\mathscr{R}_p(\mathscr{A})$ with respect to the given key dependency. It is easy to see that if $\mathscr{A}_1 \to \{A_k\}$ is a pseudoreflexive dependency, then

$$\mathscr{A}_r' = \mathscr{A}_r - \{A_k\} \cup \mathscr{A}_1$$

is another candidate key. In particular, if $\mathscr{A}_r = \{A_1, A_2, \ldots, A_m\}$ and $\mathscr{A}_1 \to \{A_k\}$ holds for $k = 1, 2, \ldots, m$, then $\mathscr{A}_1$ itself is another candidate key.

4.5.2. Normal Forms Regarding Functional Dependencies

Let R be a relation in $\mathcal{R}_p(\mathcal{A})$ where

$$\mathcal{A} = \{A_1, A_2, \ldots, A_n\}$$

and let

$$\mathcal{A}' = \{A_{k_1}, A_{k_2}, \ldots, A_{k_m}\}$$

be a subset of $\mathcal{A}$. We omit the τ designation of the relation because the following discussion is valid for an arbitrarily fixed time. We also omit the p designation of the relation for simplicity. The set defined by

$$\mathsf{p}[\mathcal{A}'](R) = \{t \mid t \in D_{k_1} \times D_{k_2} \times \cdots \times D_{k_m} \wedge (\exists x/R)\mathcal{A}'(t) = \mathcal{A}'(x)\}$$

where D_{k_j} is the domain of attribute A_{k_j}, is called the *projection* of relation R by $\mathcal{A}'$. Some examples of projection are illustrated in Fig. 3.

Let R_1 and R_2 be two relations belonging to relation schemata $\mathcal{R}_{p_1}(\mathcal{A}_1)$ and $\mathcal{R}_{p_2}(\mathcal{A}_2)$, respectively, where

$$\mathcal{A}_1 \cup \mathcal{A}_2 = \mathcal{A} = \{A_1, A_2, \ldots, A_n\}$$

The set defined by

$$\mathsf{j}_n[\mathcal{A}_1 \cap \mathcal{A}_2](R_1, R_2) = \{t \mid t \in D_1 \times D_2 \times \cdots \times D_n \wedge (\exists x_1/R_1)\mathcal{A}_1(t)$$
$$= \mathcal{A}_1(x_1) \wedge (\exists x_2/R_2)\mathcal{A}_2(t) = \mathcal{A}_2(x_2)\}$$

is called the *natural join* of relations R_1 and R_2 by $\mathcal{A}_1 \cap \mathcal{A}_2$. Although it is not so comprehensive as examples of projection, an example of natural join is illustrated in Fig. 4. If $\mathcal{A}_1 \cap \mathcal{A}_2 = \mathcal{A}_1 = \mathcal{A}_2$, the natural join is the intersection of R_1 and R_2, while if $\mathcal{A}_1 \cap \mathcal{A}_2 = \varnothing$, it is the Cartesian product of R_1 and R_2.

The projection and natural join will be defined in another way as set operations later in Section 5.

For any tuple t in R, there exists a tuple t_1 in $\mathsf{p}[\mathcal{A}_1](R)$ for which $\mathcal{A}_1(t) = \mathcal{A}_1(t_1)$, and a tuple t_2 in $\mathsf{p}[\mathcal{A}_2](R)$ for which $\mathcal{A}_2(t) = \mathcal{A}_2(t_2)$. Therefore, t belongs to $\mathsf{j}_n[\mathcal{A}_1 \cap \mathcal{A}_2](\mathsf{p}[\mathcal{A}_1](R), \mathsf{p}[\mathcal{A}_2](R))$. This implies

$$R \subset \mathsf{j}_n[\mathcal{A}_1 \cap \mathcal{A}_2](\mathsf{p}[\mathcal{A}_1](R), \mathsf{p}[\mathcal{A}_2](R))$$

However, generally,

$$R \supset \mathsf{j}_n[\mathcal{A}_1 \cap \mathcal{A}_2](\mathsf{p}[\mathcal{A}_1](R), \mathsf{p}[\mathcal{A}_2](R))$$

does not hold, as shown in Fig. 5.

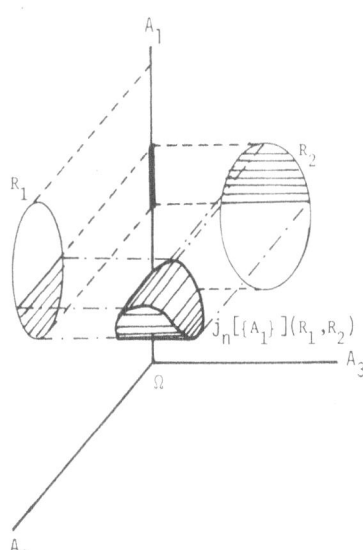

Fig. 4. Natural join.

The following theorem is very important:

Theorem 1:

$$R \supset j_n[\mathscr{A}_1 \cap \mathscr{A}_2](p[\mathscr{A}_1](R), p[\mathscr{A}_2](R))$$

holds for any relation R in $\mathscr{R}_p(\mathscr{A})$, where $\mathscr{A} = \mathscr{A}_1 \cup \mathscr{A}_2$, if one of functional

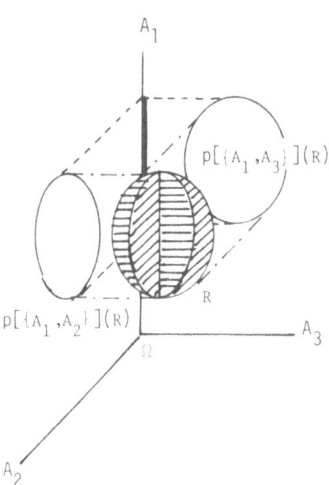

Fig. 5. A case in which $R \neq j_n[\mathscr{A}_1 \cap \mathscr{A}_2](p[\mathscr{A}_1](R), p[\mathscr{A}_2](R))$.

dependencies

$$\mathcal{A}_1 \cap \mathcal{A}_2 \to \mathcal{A}_1 - \mathcal{A}_2$$

or

$$\mathcal{A}_1 \cap \mathcal{A}_2 \to \mathcal{A}_2 - \mathcal{A}_1$$

holds in $\mathcal{R}_p(\mathcal{A})$.[76]

Proof: Assume that

$$R \supset j_n[\mathcal{A}_1 \cap \mathcal{A}_2](p[\mathcal{A}_1](R), p[\mathcal{A}_2](R))$$

does not hold. Then there exists at least one tuple t in

$$j_n[\mathcal{A}_1 \cap \mathcal{A}_2](p[\mathcal{A}_1](R), p[\mathcal{A}_2](R))$$

which does not belong to R. For this tuple t, there exist a tuple t_1 in $p[\mathcal{A}_1](R)$, for which $\mathcal{A}_1(t) = \mathcal{A}_1(t_1)$, and a tuple t_2 in $p[\mathcal{A}_2](R)$, for which $\mathcal{A}_2(t) = \mathcal{A}_2(t_2)$. Since t does not belong to R, there exist at least one tuple t_1' and at least one tuple t_2', both in R, for which

$$(\mathcal{A}_1 \cap \mathcal{A}_2)(t_1') = (\mathcal{A}_1 \cap \mathcal{A}_2)(t_1) = (\mathcal{A}_1 \cap \mathcal{A}_2)(t)$$
$$= (\mathcal{A}_1 \cap \mathcal{A}_2)(t_2) = (\mathcal{A}_1 \cap \mathcal{A}_2)(t_2')$$

but

$$(\mathcal{A}_2 - \mathcal{A}_1)(t_1') \neq (\mathcal{A}_2 - \mathcal{A}_1)(t_2) = (\mathcal{A}_2 - \mathcal{A}_1)(t_2')$$

and

$$(\mathcal{A}_1 - \mathcal{A}_2)(t_2') \neq (\mathcal{A}_1 - \mathcal{A}_2)(t_1) = (\mathcal{A}_1 - \mathcal{A}_2)(t_1')$$

This implies neither $\mathcal{A}_1 \cap \mathcal{A}_2 \to \mathcal{A}_1 - \mathcal{A}_2$ nor $\mathcal{A}_1 \cap \mathcal{A}_2 \to \mathcal{A}_1 - \mathcal{A}_2$ holds in $\mathcal{R}_p(\mathcal{A})$. Therefore, if $\mathcal{A}_1 \cap \mathcal{A}_2 \to \mathcal{A}_1 - \mathcal{A}_2$ or $\mathcal{A}_1 \cap \mathcal{A}_2 \to \mathcal{A}_1 - \mathcal{A}_2$ holds in $\mathcal{R}_p(\mathcal{A})$, then

$$R \supset j_n[\mathcal{A}_1 \cap \mathcal{A}_2](p[\mathcal{A}_1](R), p[\mathcal{A}_2](R))$$

holds for any relation in $\mathcal{R}_p(\mathcal{A})$.   □

Theorem 1 insists that if $\mathcal{A}_1' \cup \mathcal{A}_2'$ is a proper subset of $\mathcal{A}$ and a functional dependency $\mathcal{A}_1' \to \mathcal{A}_2'$ holds in $\mathcal{R}_p(\mathcal{A})$, then any relation R

belonging to $\mathscr{R}_p(\mathscr{A})$ can be decomposed into

$$R_1 = p[\mathscr{A} - \mathscr{A}_2'](R)$$

and

$$R_2 = p[\mathscr{A}_1' \cup \mathscr{A}_2'](R)$$

from which R can be reconstructed by applying a natural join by $\mathscr{A}_1'$ to them, that is,

$$R = j_n[\mathscr{A}_1'](R_1, R_2)$$

This is shown by letting $\mathscr{A}_1 \cap \mathscr{A}_2$ be $\mathscr{A}_1'$ and $\mathscr{A}_1 - \mathscr{A}_2$ be $\mathscr{A}_2'$. In other words, $\mathscr{R}_p(\mathscr{A})$ can be decomposed into two relation schemata $\mathscr{R}_{p_1}(\mathscr{A} - \mathscr{A}_2')$ and $\mathscr{R}_{p_2}(\mathscr{A}_1' \cup \mathscr{A}_2')$ without loss of any information. (This is not correct in a precise sense, as is mentioned later in Section 4.6.1.)

If a relation schema $\mathscr{R}_p$ is decomposed into two relation schemata $\mathscr{R}_{p_1}$ and $\mathscr{R}_{p_2}$, and if any relation R in $\mathscr{R}_p$ can be reconstructed by a certain operation using two relations R_1 in $\mathscr{R}_{p_1}$ and R_2 in $\mathscr{R}_{p_2}$, both obtained from R by a certain operation, this decomposition is said to be *lossless*. The above decomposition uses a natural join in reconstructing R and, therefore, is called a lossless join decomposition. Theorem 1 gives a sufficient condition for a lossless join decomposition of a relation schema. Note that it does not give any necessary condition. Figure 7 shows an example in which a lossless join decomposition is possible without functional dependencies. It is based on a multivalued dependency, which will be defined later.

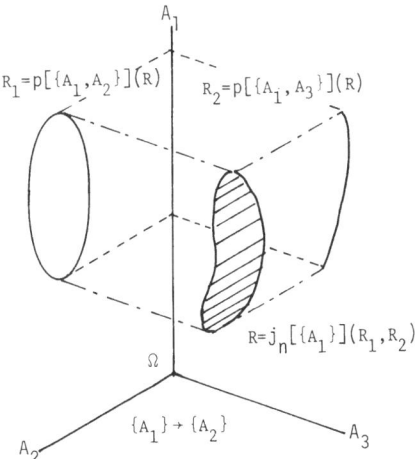

Fig. 6. Lossless join decomposition using a functional dependency.

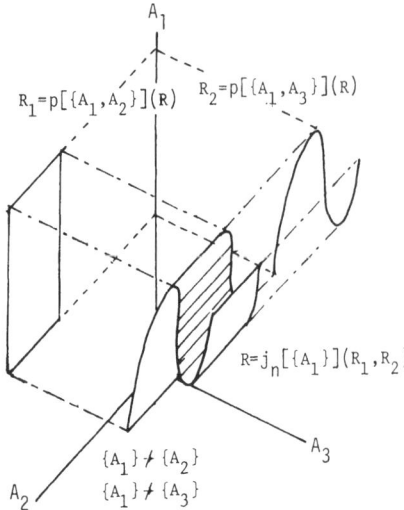

Fig. 7. Lossless join decomposition without functional dependencies.

Let $\mathscr{R}_{p_1}(\mathscr{A} - \mathscr{A}_2)$ and $\mathscr{R}_{p_2}(\mathscr{A}_1 \cup \mathscr{A}_2)$ be two relation schemata obtained by decomposing $\mathscr{R}_p(\mathscr{A})$ using a functional dependency $\mathscr{A}_1 \to \mathscr{A}_2$ for which $\mathscr{A}_1 \cup \mathscr{A}_2$ is a proper subset of $\mathscr{A}$. Functional dependencies $\mathscr{A}'_1 \to \mathscr{A}'_2$ in $\mathscr{R}_p(\mathscr{A})$ can be classified into the following four types with respect to the functional dependency $\mathscr{A}_1 \to \mathscr{A}_2$:

1. $\mathscr{A}'_1 \cup \mathscr{A}'_2 \subset \mathscr{A}_1 \cup \mathscr{A}_2$.
2. $\mathscr{A}'_1 \cup \mathscr{A}'_2 \subset \mathscr{A} - \mathscr{A}_2$.
3. Functional dependencies that can be deduced from functional dependencies of the first and second type.
4. All other cases.

Functional dependencies of the first type can be regarded as those in $\mathscr{R}_{p_1}$, while functional dependencies of the second type as those in $\mathscr{R}_{p_2}$.

Let $\mathscr{F}$ be a set of functional dependencies in $\mathscr{R}_p$, $\mathscr{F}_1$ be the set of functional dependencies of the first type in $\mathscr{F}$, and $\mathscr{F}_2$ be the set of functional dependencies of the second type in $\mathscr{F}$, both with respect to $\mathscr{A}_1 \to \mathscr{A}_2$. If $\mathscr{F} \subset (\mathscr{F}_1 \cup \mathscr{F}_2)^+$ for any set $\mathscr{F}$ of functional dependencies in $\mathscr{R}_p$, that is, if there are no functional dependencies of the fourth type, then the decomposition is said to be *dependency preserving*.

A lossless join decomposition using a functional dependency is not always dependency preserving. For example, if in $\mathscr{R}_p(\{A_1, A_2, A_3\})$ there exist functional dependencies $\{A_1\} \to \{A_2\}$, $\{A_1\} \to \{A_3\}$ and $\{A_2\} \to \{A_3\}$ (the second one can be deduced from the other two), we can decompose $\mathscr{R}_p$ either into $\mathscr{R}_{p_1}(\{A_1, A_3\})$ and $\mathscr{R}_{p_2}(\{A_1, A_2\})$ using $\{A_1\} \to \{A_2\}$ or $\{A_1\} \to \{A_3\}$ or into $\mathscr{R}'_{p_1}(\{A_1, A_2\})$ and $\mathscr{R}'_{p_2}(\{A_2, A_3\})$ using $\{A_2\} \to \{A_3\}$. The former decomposition is not, but the latter *is* dependency-preserving. It will be obvious that if every member of a minimal set of functional dependencies equivalent to the given set of functional dependencies holds in at least one of the relations in the result of decomposition, this decomposition is dependency preserving.

A relation schema $\mathcal{R}_p(\mathcal{A})$ is said to be in *weak second normal form* if there exist no partial dependencies with respect to any candidate key. A relation schema $\mathcal{R}_p(\mathcal{A})$ in weak second normal form is said to be in *weak third normal form*[27] if for any candidate key $\mathcal{A}_r$, whenever a transitive dependency $\mathcal{A}_1 \to \{A_k\}$ with respect to $\mathcal{A}_r$ exists, $\mathcal{A}_1 \to \mathcal{A}_r$ holds in $\mathcal{R}_p(\mathcal{A})$. The term *weak* is used because these normal forms do not assume the first normal form condition, which will be described later.

Given a relation schema $\mathcal{R}_p(\mathcal{A})$ and a set $\mathcal{F}$ of functional dependencies in $\mathcal{R}_p(\mathcal{A})$, we can obtain a set of relation schemata, all in weak third normal form, by repeatedly applying the lossless join decomposition based on a partial dependency, or a transitive dependency whose left-hand side does not determine the candidate key. For example, given a relation schema $\mathcal{R}_p(\{A_1, A_2, A_3, A_4, A_5\})$ and functional dependencies

$$\{A_1, A_2\} \to \{A_3, A_4, A_5\}: \quad \text{key dependency}$$

$$\{A_1\} \to \{A_3\}: \quad \text{partial dependency}$$

$$\{A_4\} \to \{A_5\}: \quad \text{transitive dependency}$$

we first decompose $\mathcal{R}_p$ into $\mathcal{R}'_{p_1}(\{A_1, A_2, A_4, A_5\})$ and $\mathcal{R}_{p_3}(\{A_1, A_3\})$ using $\{A_1\} \to \{A_3\}$ and then decompose $\mathcal{R}'_{p_1}$ further into $\mathcal{R}_{p_1}(\{A_1, A_2, A_4\})$ and $\mathcal{R}_{p_2}(\{A_4, A_5\})$ using $\{A_4\} \to \{A_5\}$. In this case, there is only one (key) dependency in each of the three resultant relation schema; therefore, all these three are in weak third normal form. This decomposition is dependency preserving because $\{A_1, A_2\} \to \{A_3, A_4, A_5\}$ can be deduced from $\{A_1, A_2\} \to \{A_4\}$ in $\mathcal{R}_{p_1}$, $\{A_4\} \to \{A_5\}$ in $\mathcal{R}_{p_2}$, and $\{A_1\} \to \{A_3\}$ in $\mathcal{R}_{p_3}$.

An anomalous case exists in which the above decomposition procedure is not dependency preserving. If there are more than one partial dependencies with a common right-hand side with respect to the same key dependency, the decomposition using one of them is not dependency preserving. For example, given a relation schema $\mathcal{R}_p(\{A_1, A_2, A_3\})$ and functional dependencies

$$\{A_1, A_2\} \to \{A_3\}: \quad \text{key dependency}$$

$$\{A_1\} \to \{A_3\}: \quad \text{partial dependency}$$

$$\{A_2\} \to \{A_3\}: \quad \text{partial dependency}$$

we can decompose $\mathcal{R}_p$ into $\mathcal{R}_{p_1}(\{A_1, A_2\})$ and $\mathcal{R}_{p_2}(\{A_1, A_3\})$ using $\{A_1\} \rightarrow \{A_3\}$. This is a lossless join decomposition but it is not dependency preserving. In fact, $\mathcal{R}_{p_1}$ has only a trivial functional dependency $\{A_1, A_2\} \rightarrow \varnothing$, while $\mathcal{R}_{p_2}$ has $\{A_1\} \rightarrow \{A_3\}$; however, $\{A_2\} \rightarrow \{A_3\}$ cannot be deduced from these two.

We have another way to obtain weak third normal form relation schemata. Given a relation schema $\mathcal{R}_p(\mathcal{A})$ and a set $\mathcal{F}$ of functional dependencies, we can obtain a minimal set of functional dependencies which is equivalent to $\mathcal{F}$. For each member $\mathcal{A}_k \rightarrow \{A_k\}$ of this minimal set, we create a relation schema $\mathcal{R}_{p_k}(\mathcal{A}_k \cup \{A_k\})$, which is obviously in weak third normal form. Then we obtain a dependency preserving decomposition. If there are two or more members in the minimal set having a common left-hand side, we can combine the relation schemata corresponding to them to form a single weak third normal form relation schema.

In the above-mentioned anomalous case, we obtain a different result, that is, $\mathcal{R}'_{p_1}(\{A_1, A_3\})$ with $\{A_1\} \rightarrow \{A_3\}$ and $\mathcal{R}'_{p_2}(\{A_2, A_3\})$ with $\{A_2\} \rightarrow \{A_3\}$. This is a dependency preserving, but not a lossless join decomposition.

A relation schema $\mathcal{R}_p(\mathcal{A})$ is said to be in *weak Boyce-Codd normal form*[31] if whenever a functional dependency $\mathcal{A}_1 \rightarrow \{A_k\}$ holds, then $\mathcal{A}_1 \rightarrow \mathcal{A} - \mathcal{A}_1$ also holds, that is, $\mathcal{A}_1$ is a candidate key. This condition excludes any partial dependency and any transitive dependency whose left-hand side is not another candidate key. Therefore, a weak Boyce-Codd normal form relation schema is in weak third normal form. However, the weak Boyce-Codd normal form condition also excludes any pseudopartial dependency whose left-hand side is not completely included in any candidate key, and any pseudoreflexive dependency whose left-hand side is another candidate key, both of which the weak third normal form does not exclude. Therefore, a weak third normal form relation schema is not always in weak Boyce-Codd normal form. If such a pseudopartial dependency or pseudoreflexive dependency exists, dependency preserving decomposition into weak Boyce-Codd normal form relation schemata is impossible. For example, a relation schema $\mathcal{R}_p(\{A_1, A_2, A_3, A_4\})$ with functional dependencies

$$\{A_1, A_2\} \rightarrow \{A_3, A_4\}: \quad \text{key dependency}$$

and

$$\{A_2, A_3\} \rightarrow \{A_4\}: \quad \text{pseudopartial dependency}$$

is in weak third normal form but not in weak Boyce-Codd normal form. If we decompose $\mathcal{R}_p$ using the second functional dependency, we obtain $\mathcal{R}_{p_1}(\{A_1, A_2, A_3\})$ with $\{A_1, A_2\} \rightarrow \{A_3\}$ and $\mathcal{R}_{p_2}(\{A_2, A_3, A_4\})$ with

$\{A_2, A_3\} \rightarrow \{A_4\}$. Then $\{A_1, A_2\} \rightarrow \{A_4\}$, which is a prime dependency in $\mathscr{R}_p$, cannot be deduced from these two functional dependencies in $\mathscr{R}_{p_1}$ and $\mathscr{R}_{p_2}$. Also a relation schema $\mathscr{R}'_p(\{A'_1, A'_2, A'_3\})$ with functional dependencies

$$\{A'_1, A'_2\} \rightarrow \{A'_3\}: \quad \text{key dependency}$$

$$\{A'_3\} \rightarrow \{A'_1\}: \quad \text{reflexive dependency}$$

is in weak third normal form but not in weak Boyce–Codd normal form. If we decompose $\mathscr{R}'_p$ using the second functional dependency, we obtain $\mathscr{R}'_{p_1}(\{A'_2, A'_3\})$ with $\{A'_2, A'_3\} \rightarrow \varnothing$ and $\mathscr{R}'_{p_2}(\{A'_3, A'_1\})$ with $\{A'_3\} \rightarrow \{A'_1\}$. Then $\{A'_1, A'_2\} \rightarrow \{A'_3\}$ in $\mathscr{R}_p$ cannot be deduced from these two functional dependencies in $\mathscr{R}'_{p_1}$ and $\mathscr{R}'_{p_2}$.

4.5.3. Attribute with a Power-Set-Type Domain

The Relational Model assumes that every relation schema is in first normal form. Although the definition of the first normal form given by Codd[26] was ambiguous, Codd apparently intended to exclude any Cartesian product-type or power-set-type domain.

Exclusion of Cartesian product-type domains (such as record-type in PASCAL) does not generate additional problems in the logical database design. In fact, if an attribute A_k has a Cartesian product-type domain

$$D_k = V_1 \times V_2 \times \cdots \times V_m$$

then A_k can be decomposed into m attributes $A_{k_1}, A_{k_2}, \ldots, A_{k_m}$ with A_{k_j}'s domain being V_{k_j}. There often exists a dependencylike constraint that when conjunctively combined with a domain constraint imposes an additional restriction on possible A_k values, that is,

$$(\forall x_1/\mathscr{R}_p)(\forall x_2/\mathscr{R}_p)([c_i(A_k)|I_1](x_1) = [c_i(A_k)|I_1](x_2) \rightarrow [c_i(A_k)|I_2](x_1)$$
$$= [c_i(A_k)|I_2](x_2))$$

where c_i is an operator extracting the ith component of the A_k value, and $[c_i(A_k)|I]$ indicates the concatenation of $c_i(A_k)$ values for $i \in I$. After the attribute A_k has been decomposed into the m attributes, this constraint is transformed into a functional dependency

$$\{A_{k_j}|j \in I_1\} \rightarrow \{A_{k_j}|j \in I_2\}$$

On the other hand, exclusion of power set-type domains is not a trivial matter. If an attribute A_k has a power set-type domain

$$D_k = \mathscr{P}(V_k)$$

then for each tuple

$$t = (A_1(t), A_2(t), \ldots, A_n(t))$$

in a relation R in $\mathscr{R}_p(\{A_1, A_2, \ldots, A_n\})$, for which

$$A_k(t) = (a_1, a_2, \ldots, a_m)$$

we generate m tuples

$$t_1 = (A_1(t), A_2(t), \ldots, A_{k-1}(t), a_1, A_{k+1}(t), \ldots, A_n(t))$$

$$t_2 = (A_1(t), A_2(t), \ldots, A_{k-1}(t), a_2, A_{k+1}(t), \ldots, A_n(t))$$

....

$$t_m = (A_1(t), A_2(t), \ldots, A_{k-1}(t), a_m, A_{k+2}(t), \ldots, A_n(t))$$

Then we obtain a relation R' by collecting all these generated tuples, which can be regarded as a member of another relation schema

$$\mathscr{R}'_p(\{A_1, A_2, \ldots, A_{k-1}, A'_k, A_{k+1}, \ldots, A_n\})$$

in which A_k's domain is V_k. If V_k itself is a Cartesian product, we can decompose it further into several attributes, each with a simple domain.

Although the Relational Model assumes the above transformation, it is not always appropriate to do so. For example, in most document-processing applications, each document record (tuple) must have a keyword list indicating the content of a corresponding document, which is an attribute whose domain is the power set of a keyword set. Sometimes certain pattern matching techniques are used to retrieve documents relevant to a given query.[80] A similar situation occurs in medical applications. Each disease record must have a list of symptoms, signs, clinical laboratory tests, and pathological data.[90] In such cases this transformation makes pattern matching much more difficult.

Another case in which this transformation is not appropriate is when a functional dependency from an attribute with a power set-type domain exists. For example, a set of symptoms determines the medicines to be given to the patient. Such a functional dependency is not preserved by the above transformation.

An empty set, which is surely a member of the power set, may cause another problem. What tuples must be generated in R' when the $A_k(t) = \varnothing$ for tuple t in R? We must introduce an unnatural *null* value.

Removal of the power set-type domains must be made only when these problems do not exist. When any attribute with a Cartesian product- or power set-type domain does not exist in it, a relation schema is said to be in *first normal form*. A weak second normal form relation schema, a weak third normal form relation schema, and a weak Boyce-Codd normal form relation schema are said to be, respectively, in *second normal form*, in *third normal form*, and in *Boyce-Codd normal form* if they are in first normal form.

As the result of the first normal form transformation

$$\mathcal{A}_1 \rightarrow \{A_k\}$$

where A_k has a power set-type domain, is transformed into a dependency

$$(\forall x_1/\mathcal{R}_p)(\forall x_2/\mathcal{R}_p)(\exists x_3/\mathcal{R}_p)(\mathcal{A}_1(x_1) = \mathcal{A}_1(x_2) \rightarrow ((\mathcal{A}_1 \cup \{A_k'\})(x_1)$$

$$= (\mathcal{A}_1 \cup \{A_k'\})(x_3) \wedge (\mathcal{A} - \{A_k'\})(x_2)$$

$$= (\mathcal{A} - \{A_k'\})(x_3))$$

In general, a dependency of the form

$$(\forall x_1/\mathcal{R}_p)(\forall x_2/\mathcal{R}_p)(\exists x_3/\mathcal{R}_p)(\mathcal{A}_1(x_1) = \mathcal{A}_1(x_2) \rightarrow ((\mathcal{A}_1 \cup \mathcal{A}_2)(x_1)$$

$$= (\mathcal{A}_1 \cup \mathcal{A}_2)(x_3) \wedge (\mathcal{A} - \mathcal{A}_2)(x_2)$$

$$= (\mathcal{A} - \mathcal{A}_2)(x_3))$$

is called a *multivalued dependency*,[40] and is denoted by

$$\mathcal{A}_1 \twoheadrightarrow \mathcal{A}_2$$

The following four properties of multivalued dependencies can be directly deduced from the definition:

(M1) If $\mathcal{A}_2 \subset \mathcal{A}_1 \subset \mathcal{A}$, then $\mathcal{A}_1 \twoheadrightarrow \mathcal{A}_2$ holds in $\mathcal{R}_p(\mathcal{A})$.

(M2) If $\mathcal{A}_1 \twoheadrightarrow \mathcal{A}_2$ holds in $\mathcal{R}_p(\mathcal{A})$ and $\mathcal{A}_4 \subset \mathcal{A}_3 \subset \mathcal{A}$, then $\mathcal{A}_1 \cup \mathcal{A}_3 \twoheadrightarrow \mathcal{A}_2 \cup \mathcal{A}_4$ holds in $\mathcal{R}_p(\mathcal{A})$.

(M3) If $\mathcal{A}_1 \twoheadrightarrow \mathcal{A}_2$ and $\mathcal{A}_2 \twoheadrightarrow \mathcal{A}_3$ holds in $\mathcal{R}_p(\mathcal{A})$, then $\mathcal{A}_1 \twoheadrightarrow \mathcal{A}_3 - \mathcal{A}_2$ holds in $\mathcal{R}_p(\mathcal{A})$.

(M4) If $\mathcal{A}_1 \twoheadrightarrow \mathcal{A}_2$ holds in $\mathcal{R}_p(\mathcal{A})$, then $\mathcal{A}_1 \twoheadrightarrow \mathcal{A} - \mathcal{A}_2$ holds in $\mathcal{R}_p(\mathcal{A})$.

The last property implies that the notion of multivalued dependency is *symmetric* with respect to $\mathcal{A}_2$ and $\mathcal{A} - \mathcal{A}_2$. Hence we sometimes write a multivalued dependency as

$$\mathcal{A}_1 \twoheadrightarrow \mathcal{A}_2 | \mathcal{A} - \mathcal{A}_2$$

Obviously a functional dependency is a multivalued dependency; that is, we have

(FM1)   If $\mathcal{A}_1 \rightarrow \mathcal{A}_2$ holds, then $\mathcal{A}_1 \twoheadrightarrow \mathcal{A}_2$ holds in $\mathcal{R}_p(\mathcal{A})$.

In addition, we have

(FM2) If $\mathcal{A}_1 \twoheadrightarrow \mathcal{A}_2$ holds in $\mathcal{R}_p(\mathcal{A})$, $\mathcal{A}_3 \subset \mathcal{A}_2$, and for some $\mathcal{A}_4$ for which $\mathcal{A}_2 \cap \mathcal{A}_4 = \varnothing$, $\mathcal{A}_4 \rightarrow \mathcal{A}_3$ holds, then $\mathcal{A}_1 \rightarrow \mathcal{A}_3$ holds in $\mathcal{R}_p(\mathcal{A})$.

(F1)-(F3) and (M2)-(M4), together with (FM1) and (FM2), can be used as a set of deductive rules, by which we can obtain a closure $\mathcal{M}^+$ of a set of functional and multivalued dependencies when $\mathcal{M}$ is given. The set of these eight rules is sound and complete.

Existence of a multivalued dependency is the necessary and sufficient condition for a lossless join decomposition; that is, we have

Theorem 2:

$$R \supset j_n[\mathcal{A}_1 \cap \mathcal{A}_2](p[\mathcal{A}_1](R), p[\mathcal{A}_2](R))$$

holds for any relation R in $\mathcal{R}_p(\mathcal{A})$, where $\mathcal{A} = \mathcal{A}_1 \cup \mathcal{A}_2$, iff a multivalued dependency

$$\mathcal{A}_1 \cap \mathcal{A}_2 \twoheadrightarrow \mathcal{A}_1 - \mathcal{A}_2$$

holds in $\mathcal{R}_p(\mathcal{A})$.[2,76]

Proof: Assume that

$$R \supset j_n[\mathcal{A}_1 \cap \mathcal{A}_2](p[\mathcal{A}_1](R), p[\mathcal{A}_2](R))$$

does not hold. Then there exists at least one tuple t in

$$j_n[\mathcal{A}_1 \cap \mathcal{A}_2](p[\mathcal{A}_1](R), p[\mathcal{A}_2](R))$$

which does not belong to R. For this tuple t, there exists a tuple t_1 in $p[\mathscr{A}_1](R)$ for which $\mathscr{A}_1(t) = \mathscr{A}_1(t_1)$ and a tuple t_2 in $p[\mathscr{A}_2](R)$ for which $\mathscr{A}_2(t) = \mathscr{A}_2(t_2)$. Since t does not belong to R, there exists at least one tuple t_1' and one tuple t_2', both in R, for which

$$(\mathscr{A}_1 \cap \mathscr{A}_2)(t_1') = (\mathscr{A}_1 \cap \mathscr{A}_2)(t_1) = (\mathscr{A}_1 \cap \mathscr{A}_2)(t) = (\mathscr{A}_1 \cap \mathscr{A}_2)(t_2)$$
$$= (\mathscr{A}_1 \cap \mathscr{A}_2)(t_2')$$

However, according to the assumption, the tuple t for which

$$\mathscr{A}_1(t) = \mathscr{A}_1(t_1) = \mathscr{A}_1(t_1')$$

and

$$\mathscr{A}_2(t) = \mathscr{A}_2(t_2) = \mathscr{A}_2(t_2')$$

is not in R. Since $\mathscr{A}_1 = (\mathscr{A}_1 \cap \mathscr{A}_2) \cup (\mathscr{A}_1 - \mathscr{A}_2)$ and $\mathscr{A}_2 = (\mathscr{A}_1 \cup \mathscr{A}_2) - (\mathscr{A}_1 - \mathscr{A}_2)$, the above implies that $\mathscr{A}_1 \cap \mathscr{A}_2 \twoheadrightarrow \mathscr{A}_1 - \mathscr{A}_2$ does not hold. Therefore, if $\mathscr{A}_1 \cap \mathscr{A}_2 \twoheadrightarrow \mathscr{A}_1 - \mathscr{A}_2$ holds, then

$$R \supset j_n[\mathscr{A}_1 \cap \mathscr{A}_2](p[\mathscr{A}_1](R), p[\mathscr{A}_2](R))$$

holds.

Conversely, let t_1' and t_2' be two tuples in R for which

$$(\mathscr{A}_1 \cap \mathscr{A}_2)(t_1') = (\mathscr{A}_1 \cap \mathscr{A}_2)(t_2')$$

but

$$(\mathscr{A}_1 - \mathscr{A}_2)(t_1') \neq (\mathscr{A}_1 - \mathscr{A}_2)(t_2')$$

and

$$(\mathscr{A}_2 - \mathscr{A}_1)(t_1') \neq (\mathscr{A}_2 - \mathscr{A}_1)(t_2')$$

A tuple t for which $\mathscr{A}_1(t) = \mathscr{A}_1(t_1')$ and $\mathscr{A}_2(t) = \mathscr{A}_2(t_2')$ belongs to

$$j_n[\mathscr{A}_1 \cap \mathscr{A}_2](p[\mathscr{A}_1](R), p[\mathscr{A}_2](R))$$

However, t does not necessarily belong to R if $\mathscr{A}_1 \cap \mathscr{A}_2 \twoheadrightarrow \mathscr{A}_1 - \mathscr{A}_2$ does not hold in $\mathscr{R}_p(\mathscr{A})$. Therefore, if

$$R \supset j_n[\mathscr{A}_1 \cap \mathscr{A}_2](p[\mathscr{A}_1](R), p[\mathscr{A}_2](R))$$

then $\mathscr{A}_1 \cap \mathscr{A}_2 \twoheadrightarrow \mathscr{A}_1 - \mathscr{A}_2$ holds in $\mathscr{R}_p(\mathscr{A})$. $\square$

In a manner similar to the lossless join decomposition using a functional dependency, a lossless join decomposition of $\mathscr{R}_p(\mathscr{A})$ into

$$p_1(\mathscr{A} - \mathscr{A}_2')$$

and

$$p_2(\mathscr{A}_1' \cup \mathscr{A}_2')$$

is possible if $\mathscr{A}_1' \cup \mathscr{A}_2'$ is a proper subset of $\mathscr{A}$ and a multivalued dependency $\mathscr{A}_1' \twoheadrightarrow \mathscr{A}_2'$ holds in $\mathscr{R}_p(\mathscr{A})$. Hence, we can make a decomposition of a first normal form relation schema into several relation schemata in an extended version of third or Boyce-Codd normal form defined somehow in terms of multivalued dependencies. However, it is easier to define these normal forms as those obtained by applying decompositions into weak third or Boyce-Codd normal form relation schemata with multivalued dependencies being regarded as functional dependencies whose right-hand sides are attributes with power set-type domains, followed by applying transformations into first normal form relation schemata.

$\mathscr{R}_p(\mathscr{A})$ is decomposed into

$$\mathscr{R}_{p_1}(\mathscr{A} - \mathscr{A}_2)$$

and

$$\mathscr{R}_{p_2}(\mathscr{A}_1 \cup \mathscr{A}_2)$$

using the multivalued dependency

$$\mathscr{A}_1 \twoheadrightarrow \mathscr{A}_2$$

then this multivalued dependency becomes a trivial multivalued dependency

$$\mathscr{A}_1 \twoheadrightarrow \mathscr{A}_2 | \varnothing$$

It may be possible to define a fourth normal form relation schema as a third normal form relation schema in which any nontrivial multivalued dependency is a functional dependency.

This definition is different from Fagin's definition, in which a relation schema $\mathscr{R}_p(\mathscr{A})$ is said to be in fourth normal form if $\mathscr{A}_1 \rightarrow \mathscr{A} - \mathscr{A}_1$ whenever a multivalued dependency $\mathscr{A}_1 \twoheadrightarrow \mathscr{A}_2$ holds in $\mathscr{R}_p(\mathscr{A})$ where $\mathscr{A}_2 \neq \varnothing$ and $\mathscr{A}_1 \cup \mathscr{A}_2 \neq \mathscr{A}$. This implies that a fourth normal form relation schema is in Boyce-Codd normal form. Here we did not assume the Boyce-Codd normal form condition in defining the fourth normal form. Sometimes it will be desirable to define relations in the fourth normal form in our sense but not in Boyce–Codd normal form.

4.5.4. Example of Normal Form Decomposition

Here we will present a simple example of stepwise normal form decomposition. Let us consider a relation schema

$$\mathscr{R}_{professor}(\{name, sex, age, institute, location, [(course, unit)]\})$$

where brackets are used to specify a repeating-group attribute. The only candidate key is "name," that is, we have a key dependency

$$\{name\} \rightarrow \{sex, age, institute, location, [(course, unit)]\}$$

As we have a transitive dependency

$$\{institute\} \rightarrow \{location\}$$

we can decompose $\mathscr{R}_{professor}$ into two weak third (and Boyce–Codd) normal form relation schemata

$$\mathscr{R}'_{professor}(\{name, sex, age, institute, [(course, unit)]\})$$

$$\mathscr{R}_{institute}(\{institute, location\})$$

Since a multivalued dependency

$$\{name\} \twoheadrightarrow \{course, unit\}$$

holds in $\mathscr{R}'_{professor}$, we can decompose it into two fourth normal form relation schemata

$$\mathscr{R}''_{professor}(\{name, sex, age, institute\})$$

$$\mathscr{R}'''_{professor}(\{name, course, unit\})$$

Finally, as we have a functional dependency

$$\{course\} \rightarrow \{unit\}$$

$\mathscr{R}'''_{\text{professor}}$ can be decomposed into third (and Boyce–Codd) and fourth normal form relation schemata

$$\mathscr{R}''''_{\text{professor}}(\{\text{name, course}\})$$

and

$$\mathscr{R}_{\text{course}}(\{\text{course, unit}\})$$

When we are given a relation (instance)

$$R_{\text{professor}} = \{(\text{Fernão, male, 47, Ciências Matématicas,}\\ \text{São Carlos, [(math, 8), (soft eng, 4)]})\}$$

in $\mathscr{R}_{\text{professor}}$, it is decomposed into four relations

$$R''_{\text{professor}} = \{(\text{Fernão, male, 47, Ciências Matématicas})\} \quad \text{in } \mathscr{R}''_{\text{professor}}$$

$$R''''_{\text{professor}} = \{(\text{Fernão, math}), (\text{Fernão, soft eng})\} \quad \text{in } \mathscr{R}''''_{\text{professor}}$$

$$R_{\text{institute}} = \{(\text{Ciências Matématicas, São Carlos})\} \quad \text{in } \mathscr{R}_{\text{institute}}$$

$$R_{\text{course}} = \{(\text{math, 8}), (\text{soft eng, 4})\} \quad \text{in } \mathscr{R}_{\text{course}}$$

In most cases, such a straightforward decomposition is possible. Sometimes some intermediate form is more desirable than the final one, as mentioned previously.

4.5.5. Other Dependencies

Many researchers have studied various other dependencies such as embedded multivalued dependencies, mutual dependencies, embedded mutual dependencies, generalized mutual dependencies, join dependencies, and subset dependencies. All of these are dependencies of the form

$$(\forall x_1/\mathscr{R}_p)(\forall x_2/\mathscr{R}_p) \cdots (\forall x_{m-1}/\mathscr{R}_p)(\exists x_m/\mathscr{R}_p)\lambda(x_1, x_2, \ldots, x_m)$$

where λ is a logical function of $x_1, x_2, \ldots, x_m$, of some specific form defined in terms of attributes of $\mathscr{R}_p$.

Such dependencies (including multivalued dependencies) are collectively called *template dependencies*.[17] They have been studied theoretically, but their application to practical database design have not yet been evaluated.

4.6. Interrelation Constraints

Tuple constraints and dependencies are *intrarelation constraints* which are defined on a single-relation schema. All the tuple variables appearing in the schema calculus are quantified over the same relation schema. There are *interrelation constraints* which are defined over more than one relation schema: that is, there are more than one tuple variables in the schema calculus that are quantified over different relation schemata.

Next we will discuss some interrelation constraints that play important roles in logical database design.

4.6.1. Into and Onto Constraints

Assume that we are given relation schemata

$$\mathscr{R}_{p_1}(\{\text{name, sex, age, institute}\})$$

$$\mathscr{R}_{p_2}(\{\text{name, course}\})$$

$$\mathscr{R}_{p_3}(\{\text{institute, location}\})$$

each in third (and Boyce-Codd) and fourth normal form, respectively, with key dependencies

$$\{\text{name}\} \to \{\text{sex, age, institute}\}$$

$$\{\text{name, course}\} \to \varnothing$$

and

$$\{\text{institute, course}\} \to \varnothing$$

and

$$\{\text{institute}\} \to \{\text{location}\}$$

Examining the meanings of these relation schemata carefully, we may find semantic constraints such as

$$(\forall x/\mathscr{R}_{p_1})(\exists z/\mathscr{R}_{p_3})\text{institute}(x) = \text{institute}(y)$$

and

$$(\forall y/\mathscr{R}_{p_2})(\exists x/\mathscr{R}_{p_1})\text{name}(y) = \text{name}(x)$$

These are interrelation constraints, both defined over two relation schemata.

In general, if $\mathscr{A}_f$ is a subset of a candidate key (set) of $\mathscr{R}'_{p_2}$, a semantic constraint of the form

$$(\forall x/\mathscr{R}'_{p_1})(\exists y/\mathscr{R}'_{p_2})\mathscr{A}_f(x) = \mathscr{A}_f(y)$$

is called an *into constraint* from $\mathscr{R}'_{p_1}$ to $\mathscr{R}'_{p_2}$. The above two examples are into constraints from $\mathscr{R}_{p_1}$ to $\mathscr{R}_{p_3}$ and from $\mathscr{R}_{p_2}$ to $\mathscr{R}_{p_1}$, respectively.

Sometimes, semantic constraints hold such as

$$(\forall z/\mathscr{R}_{p_3})(\exists x/\mathscr{R}_{p_1})\text{institute}(z) = \text{institute}(x)$$

and

$$(\forall x/\mathscr{R}_{p_1})(\exists y/\mathscr{R}_{p_2})\text{name}(x) = \text{name}(y)$$

in addition to the into constraints.

In general, if $\mathscr{A}_f$ is a subset of a candidate key (set) of $\mathscr{R}'_{p_2}$, a semantic constraint of the form

$$(\forall y/\mathscr{R}'_{p_2})(\exists x/\mathscr{R}'_{p_1})\mathscr{A}_f(y) = \mathscr{A}_f(x)$$

is called an *onto constraint* from $\mathscr{R}'_{p_1}$ to $\mathscr{R}'_{p_2}$. The above two examples are onto constraints from $\mathscr{R}_{p_1}$ to $\mathscr{R}_{p_3}$ and from $\mathscr{R}_{p_2}$ to $\mathscr{R}_{p_1}$, respectively. The $\mathscr{A}_f$ is sometimes called a *foreign key* in $\mathscr{A}'_{p_1}$.

The existence of an into constraint from $\mathscr{R}_{p_1}$ to $\mathscr{R}_{p_2}$ implies the existence of a correspondence from R_1^τ in $\mathscr{R}_{p_1}$ *into* R_2^τ in $\mathscr{R}_{p_2}$ at any time τ, while the existence of an onto constraint from $\mathscr{R}_{p_1}$ to $\mathscr{R}_{p_2}$ implies that this correspondence is from R_1^τ *onto* R_2^τ. If $\mathscr{A}_f$ itself is a candidate key of $\mathscr{R}_{p_2}$, then the correspondence is *many-to-one*. If $\mathscr{A}_f$ is a proper subset of a candidate key of $\mathscr{R}_{p_2}$, then it becomes *many-to-many*.

Now assume that we have decomposed a relation schema $\mathscr{R}_p(\mathscr{A})$ into

$$\mathscr{R}_{p_1}(\mathscr{A} - \mathscr{A}_2)$$

and

$$\mathscr{R}_{p_2}(\mathscr{A}_1 \cup \mathscr{A}_2)$$

using a functional dependency $\mathscr{A}_1 \rightarrow \mathscr{A}_2$, where $\mathscr{A}_1 \cup \mathscr{A}_2$ does not cover all the attributes in $\mathscr{A}$. Then any relation R in $\mathscr{R}_p$ is decomposed into two relations R_1 in $\mathscr{R}_{p_1}$ and R_2 in $\mathscr{R}_{p_2}$; that is,

$$R_1 = \text{p}[\mathscr{A} - \mathscr{A}_2](R)$$

and

$$R_2 = \mathsf{p}[\mathscr{A}_1 \cup \mathscr{A}_2](R)$$

Obviously, we have

$$\mathsf{p}[\mathscr{A}_1](R_1) = \mathsf{p}[\mathscr{A}_1](R_2)$$

which implies both

$$(\forall x/\mathscr{R}_{p_1})(\exists y/\mathscr{R}_{p_2})\mathscr{A}_1(x) = \mathscr{A}_1(y)$$

and

$$(\forall y/\mathscr{R}_{p_2})(\exists x/\mathscr{R}_{p_1})\mathscr{A}_1(y) = \mathscr{A}_1(x)$$

These two are an into constraint and an onto constraint, respectively, from $\mathscr{R}_{p_1}$ to $\mathscr{R}_{p_2}$.

If the $\mathscr{R}_p(\mathscr{A})$ is a *semantically correct* relation schema, these two interrelation constraints must be held over $\mathscr{R}_{p_1}(\mathscr{A} - \mathscr{A}_2)$ and $\mathscr{R}_{p_2}(\mathscr{A}_1 \cup \mathscr{A}_2)$. In most cases, the onto constraint does not necessarily hold; that is, tuples in R_2 in $\mathscr{R}_{p_2}$ can exist regardless of the existence of corresponding tuples in R_1 in $\mathscr{R}_{p_1}$. However, if this is the case, $\mathscr{R}_p$ itself is not semantically correct.

The same situation exists when we make a lossless join decomposition using a multivalued dependency. The difference is that $\mathscr{A}_f = \mathscr{A}_1$ is a candidate key of $\mathscr{R}_{p_2}$ for the decomposition based on a functional dependency, while it is not for that based on a multivalued dependency.

In short, normal form decompositions can be lossless and dependency preserving; however, they are not constraint preserving unless we add newly generated into and onto constraints.

4.6.2. Relationship Constraints

A conjunct of more than one into constraints of the form

$$(\forall x/\mathscr{R}_p)(\exists y_1/\mathscr{R}_{p_1})(\exists y_2/\mathscr{R}_{p_2}) \cdots (\exists y_m/\mathscr{R}_{p_m}) \bigwedge_{k=1}^{m} (\mathscr{A}_k(x) = \mathscr{A}_k(y_k))$$

is called a *relationship constraint* if every $\mathscr{A}_k$ is a candidate key of $\mathscr{R}_{p_k}$. In particular, binary relationship constraints of the form

$$(\forall x/\mathscr{R}_p)(\exists y_1/\mathscr{R}_{p_1})(\exists y_2/\mathscr{R}_{p_2})(\mathscr{A}_1(x) = \mathscr{A}_1(y_1) \wedge \mathscr{A}_2(x) = \mathscr{A}_2(y_2))$$

are important.

A relation belonging to a relation schema $\mathcal{R}_p$ with the above m-ary ($m \geq 2$) relationship constraint is called a *relationship relation*. A relation belonging to a relation schema without such relationship constraints is sometimes called an *entity relation* in order to distinguish it from relationship relations.

The Entity–Relationship Model[16] is the model that determines a special treatment for the relationship relations. Entity relations are used for representing real-world objects, each recognized as an individual, while relationship relations are used for representing relationships among these objects. This view of the real world seems to be more intuitive than the relational view of the real world in most cases. The notion of relationship constraints bridges the gap between the Relational Model and the Entity–Relationship Model.

4.6.3. Relationship Normal Form

In Section 4.5.1 we introduced the notion of foreign keys. The foreign key is distinguished from other attributes because it represents a function of tuples whose value is a tuple in contrast to other attributes with simple values (not tuples). We can deal with such a function as a correspondence among tuples. This correspondence can be represented more explicitly by a binary relationship relation.

Let $\mathcal{A}_f$ be a foreign key in $\mathcal{R}_{p_1}(\mathcal{A})$, that is, we have an into constraint

$$(\forall x / \mathcal{R}_{p_1})(\exists y / \mathcal{R}_{p_2})\mathcal{A}_f(x) = \mathcal{A}_f(y)$$

where $\mathcal{A}_f$ is a part of a candidate key $\mathcal{A}_2$ of $\mathcal{R}_{p_2}(\mathcal{A}')$. Let us decompose $\mathcal{R}_{p_1}(\mathcal{A})$ into

$$\mathcal{R}'_{p_1}(\mathcal{A} - \mathcal{A}_f)$$

and

$$\mathcal{R}_p(\mathcal{A}_1 \cup \mathcal{A}_f)$$

using a functional dependency $\mathcal{A}_1 \rightarrow \mathcal{A}_f$ from a candidate key $\mathcal{A}_1$ of $\mathcal{R}_{p_1}(\mathcal{A})$. Then $\mathcal{R}'_{p_1}$ does not have the foreign key $\mathcal{A}_f$, while $\mathcal{R}_p$ has two foreign keys $\mathcal{A}_1$ and $\mathcal{A}_f$; that is, we have a constraint

$$(\forall x / \mathcal{R}_p)(\exists y_1 / \mathcal{R}'_{p_1})(\exists y_2 / \mathcal{R}_{p_2})(\mathcal{A}_1(x) = \mathcal{A}_1(y_1) \wedge \mathcal{A}_f(x) = \mathcal{A}_f(y_2))$$

This is a binary relationship constraint if $\mathcal{A}_f = \mathcal{A}_2$. If not, we replace $\mathcal{A}_f$

by $\mathscr{A}'_f$ defined for tuples t in R in $\mathscr{R}_p$ by

$$\mathscr{A}'_f(t) = \{\mathscr{A}_2(t')|\mathscr{A}_f(t) = \mathscr{A}_f(t')\}$$

for tuples t' in R_2 in $\mathscr{R}_{p_2}$. Then $\mathscr{A}'_f$ is an attribute with a power set-type domain. We apply the first normal form transformation to

$$\mathscr{R}'_p(\mathscr{A}_1 \cup \mathscr{A}'_f)$$

The resultant relation schema

$$\mathscr{R}''_p(\mathscr{A}_1 \cup \mathscr{A}_2)$$

is then accompanied by a binary relationship constraint

$$(\forall x/\mathscr{R}''_p)(\exists y_1/\mathscr{R}'_{p_1})(\exists y_2/\mathscr{R}_{p_2})(\mathscr{A}_1(x) = \mathscr{A}_1(y_1) \wedge \mathscr{A}_2(x) = \mathscr{A}_2(y_2))$$

A relation in $\mathscr{R}_p$ (or in $\mathscr{R}''_p$ if $\mathscr{A}_f \neq \mathscr{A}_2$) is a binary relationship relation that directly represents the correspondence from $\mathscr{R}'_{p_1}$ to $\mathscr{R}_{p_2}$. The correspondence can be one-to-one, one-to-many, many-to-one, or many-to-many. It can be an into and/or onto correspondence. Such a classification will be described later in Section 4.6.4.

An m-ary relationship relation schema $\mathscr{R}_p(\mathscr{A})$ with a constraint

$$(\forall x/\mathscr{R}_p)(\exists y_1/\mathscr{R}_{p_1})(\exists y_2/\mathscr{R}_{p_2}) \cdots (\exists y_m/\mathscr{R}_{p_m}) \bigwedge_{k=1}^{m} (\mathscr{A}_k(x) = \mathscr{A}_k(y_k))$$

can be decomposed into an entity relation schema and m relationship relation schemata as follows. Let $\mathscr{A}_r$ be an arbitrary candidate key of $\mathscr{R}_p$. Then, using $\mathscr{A}_r \rightarrow \mathscr{A}_k$, we can decompose $\mathscr{R}_p(\mathscr{A})$ into

$$\mathscr{R}'_p\left(\mathscr{A} - \left(\bigcup_{k=1}^{m} \mathscr{A}_k\right)\right) \cup \mathscr{A}_r$$

and

$$\mathscr{R}'_{p_k}(\mathscr{A}_r \cup \mathscr{A}_k)$$

for $k = 1, 2, \ldots, m$. Each $\mathscr{R}'_{p_k}(\mathscr{A}_r \cup \mathscr{A}_k)$ is now accompanied by a binary relationship constraint

$$(\forall x/\mathscr{R}'_{p_k})(\exists y_1/\mathscr{R}'_p)(\exists y_2/\mathscr{R}_{p_k})(\mathscr{A}_r(x) = \mathscr{A}_r(y_1) \wedge \mathscr{A}_k(x) = \mathscr{A}_k(y_2))$$

The above considerations lead us to another normal form. A relation schema $\mathscr{R}_p(\mathscr{A})$ is said to be in *relationship normal form* if it has no foreign key (i.e., it is accompanied by no into constraints), or it has exactly two foreign keys (i.e., it is accompanied by one and only one binary relationship constraint). The Information Space Model[55] assumes that all the relation schemata are in relationship normal form.

In the example shown in Section 4.5.4, we obtained four relation schemata as the result of decomposing

$$\mathscr{R}_{\text{professor}}(\{\text{name}, \text{sex}, \text{age}, \text{institute}, [(\text{course}, \text{unit})]\})$$

Let them be

$$\mathscr{R}_{p_1}(\{\underline{\text{name}}, \text{sex}, \text{age}, \text{institute}\})$$

$$\mathscr{R}_{p_2}(\{\underline{\text{name}}, \underline{\text{course}}\})$$

$$\mathscr{R}_{p_3}(\{\underline{\text{institute}}, \text{location}\})$$

$$\mathscr{R}_{p_4}(\{\underline{\text{course}}, \text{unit}\})$$

Attributes constituting a candidate key are underlined. Among them, $\mathscr{R}_{p_2}$, $\mathscr{R}_{p_3}$, and $\mathscr{R}_{p_4}$ are in relationship normal form. In fact, $\mathscr{R}_{p_2}$ is a binary relationship relation schema, while the other two are entity relation schemata (accompanied with no relationship constraints). However, $\mathscr{R}_{p_1}$ is not in relationship normal form because it has a single foreign key, "institute." To obtain relationship normal form schemata, we must decompose it into

$$\mathscr{R}_{p_5}(\{\underline{\text{name}}, \text{sex}, \text{age}\})$$

which is an entity relation schema and

$$\mathscr{R}_{p_6}(\{\underline{\text{name}}, \text{institute}\})$$

which is a binary relationship relation schema.

A relation in $\mathscr{R}_{p_2}$ is a many-to-many correspondence, while a relation in $\mathscr{R}_{p_6}$ is a many-to-one correspondence.

4.6.4. Classifications of Binary Relationship Relation Schemata

Binary relationship relation schemata can be classified in various aspects.

A binary relationship relation schema $\mathcal{R}_p(\mathcal{A})$ accompanied by a binary relationship constraint

$$(\forall x/\mathcal{R}_p)(\exists y_1/\mathcal{R}_{p_1})(\exists y_2/\mathcal{R}_{p_2})(\mathcal{A}'_1(x) = \mathcal{A}_1(y_1) \wedge \mathcal{A}'_2(x) = \mathcal{A}_2(y_2))$$

is said to be *recursive* if $\mathcal{R}_{p_1} = \mathcal{R}_{p_2}$; that is, $\mathcal{R}_p(\mathcal{A})$ is accompanied by

$$(\forall x/\mathcal{R}_p)(\exists y_1/\mathcal{R}_{p_1})(\exists y_2/\mathcal{R}_{p_2})(\mathcal{A}'_1(x) = \mathcal{A}_1(y_1) \wedge \mathcal{A}'_2(x) = \mathcal{A}_1(y_2))$$

In this case, we have to distinguish foreign keys in $\mathcal{R}_p$ from a candidate keys in $\mathcal{R}_{p_1}$. (In a precise sense, foreign keys must be distinguished from candidate keys in any case. However, we use the same notation when the distinction is obvious.) If $\mathcal{R}_{p_1} \neq \mathcal{R}_{p_2}$, we say that the binary relationship relation schema is *irrecursive*.

A binary relationship schema $\mathcal{R}_p(\mathcal{A})$ is said to be $\mathcal{R}_{p_1}$ *into* $\mathcal{R}_{p_2}$ if an onto constraint

$$(\forall y_1/\mathcal{R}_{p_1})(\exists x/\mathcal{R}_p)\mathcal{A}'_1(x) = \mathcal{A}_1(y_1)$$

holds. It is said to be $\mathcal{R}_{p_1}$ *onto* $\mathcal{R}_{p_2}$ if an onto constraint

$$(\forall y_2/\mathcal{R}_{p_2})(\exists x/\mathcal{R}_p)\mathcal{A}'_2(x) = \mathcal{A}_2(y_1)$$

holds.

The following are constraints that determine the *cardinality* of the correspondence. The first two are functional dependencies

$$\mathcal{A}'_1 \rightarrow \mathcal{A}'_2$$

$$\mathcal{A}'_2 \rightarrow \mathcal{A}'_1$$

which we call the *forward dependency* and the *backward dependency*, respectively. The existence of the forward dependency implies that the correspondence is many-to-one, while that of the backward dependency implies that the correspondence is one-to-many.

The forward and backward dependencies can also be described using an aggregate function $\sum$ and a function count (see Section 4.3). The forward dependency is described as

$$(\forall x/\mathcal{R}_p) \sum_{x' \in \mathcal{R}_p \wedge \mathcal{A}'_1(x) = \mathcal{A}'_1(x')} \text{count}(x') = 1$$

while the backward dependency is described as

$$(\forall x/\mathcal{R}_p) \sum_{x' \in \mathcal{R}_p \wedge \mathcal{A}_2'(x) = \mathcal{A}_2'(x')} \text{count}(x') = 1$$

More generally, we may have constraints such as

$$(\forall x/\mathcal{R}_p)\left(\mu \leq \sum_{x' \in \mathcal{R}_p \wedge \mathcal{A}_1'(x) = \mathcal{A}_1'(x')} \text{count}(x') \leq \nu\right)$$

and

$$(\forall x/\mathcal{R}_p)\left(\mu \leq \sum_{x' \in \mathcal{R}_p \wedge \mathcal{A}_2'(x) = \mathcal{A}_2'(x')} \text{count}(x') \leq \nu\right)$$

where $0 \leq \mu \leq \nu$, which specify the maximum and minimum cardinality of the correspondence.

A relation is a recursive relationship schema $\mathcal{R}_p$ which represents a correspondence from a relation in $\mathcal{R}_{p_1}$ to itself. It can also be regarded as the set of arcs in a directed graph whose set of nodes is a relation in $\mathcal{R}_{p_1}$; that is, a tuple in a relation R in $\mathcal{R}_p$ is an arc, and a tuple in a relation R_1 in $\mathcal{R}_{p_1}$ is a node. Two additional constraints are used for classifying such graphs. One is the *acyclicness constraint*

$$(\forall x/\mathcal{R}_p) \sim (x \in S(x))$$

where $S(t)$ is the *successor* of the tuple t defined recursively by

$$S_1(t) = \{t' | \mathcal{A}_1'(t') = \mathcal{A}_2'(t)\}$$

$$S_{k+1}(t) = \{t'' | t' \in S_k(t) \wedge \mathcal{A}_1'(t'') = \mathcal{A}_2'(t')\}$$

and

$$S(t) = \bigcup_k S_k(t)$$

The union is made from $k = 1$ up to $k = K$, for which

$$\bigcup_{k=1}^{K} S_k(t) = \bigcup_{k=1}^{K+1} S_k(t)$$

This constraint excludes any circuit; that is, the graph is *acyclic*.

The other important constraint is the *connectedness constraint*

$$(\forall x/\mathcal{R}_p)(\forall x'/\mathcal{A}_p)x' \in C(x)$$

where $C(t)$ is the *connection* of the tuple t defined recursively by

$$C_1(t) = \{t'|\mathcal{A}_1'(t') = \mathcal{A}_1'(t) \vee \mathcal{A}_1'(t')$$

$$= \mathcal{A}_2'(t) \vee \mathcal{A}_2'(t') = \mathcal{A}_1'(t) \vee \mathcal{A}_2'(t') = \mathcal{A}_2'(t)\}$$

$$C_{k+1}(t) = \{t''|t' \in C_k(t) \wedge (\mathcal{A}_1'(t'') = \mathcal{A}_1'(t') \vee \mathcal{A}_1'(t'')$$

$$= \mathcal{A}_2'(t') \vee \mathcal{A}_2'(t'') = \mathcal{A}_1'(t') \vee \mathcal{A}_2'(t'') = \mathcal{A}_2'(t'))\}$$

and

$$C(t) = \bigcup_k C_k(t)$$

The union is made from $k = 1$ up to $k = K$, for which

$$\bigcup_{k=1}^{K} C_k(t) = \bigcup_{k=1}^{K+1} C_k(t)$$

If these constraints hold, then the graph is *connected.*

Various terms regarding relationship relation types can be defined precisely in terms of these constraints. A *sequence* is a relation in a recursive relationship relation schema in which all the forward dependencies, backward dependencies, acyclicness constraints, and connectedness constraints hold. A *quasi sequence*, which is a relation in a recursive relationship relation

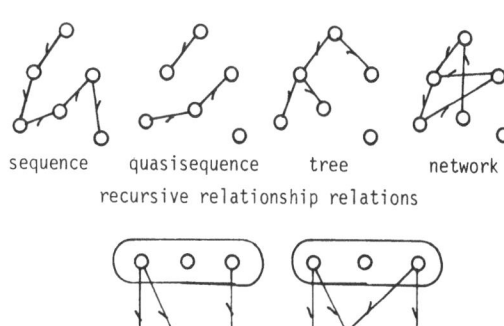

sequence   quasisequence   tree   network

recursive relationship relations

Fig. 8. Binary relationship relation types.

irrecursive tree   irrecursive network

schema with the forward dependency, backward dependency, and circuit constraint, but without the connection constraint, plays some important role in many cases.

A *tree* (sometimes called a *forest*) is a relation in a (recursive or irrecursive) relationship relation schema in which both the backward dependency and acyclicness constraint hold. A *backward tree* is defined by replacing the backward dependency by the forward dependency. It can be converted into a tree by interchanging $\mathscr{R}_{p_1}$ and $\mathscr{R}_{p_2}$.

A *network* (sometimes called a *plex*) is a relation in a (recursive or irrecursive) relationship relation schema, which assumes neither the forward nor backward dependency. Recursive trees and networks are *connected* if their relation schemata assume the connectedness constraint. Recursive networks are *oriented* if their relation schemata assume the acyclicness constraint.

4.6.5. Hierarchies and Hierarchical Normal Form

An irrecursive tree is called a (single-level) *hierarchy* if its relation schema $\mathscr{R}_p(\mathscr{A})$ is accompanied by the onto constraint from $\mathscr{R}_p$ to $\mathscr{R}_{p_2}$. (The onto constraint from $\mathscr{R}_p$ to $\mathscr{R}_{p_1}$ is not necessarily assumed.) A hierarchy R in $\mathscr{R}_p$ can be regarded as a one-to-many correspondence from R_1 in $\mathscr{R}_{p_1}$ onto R_2 in $\mathscr{R}_{p_2}$.

Hierarchies are of special importance because in some cases we may assume another normal form which is defined in terms of hierarchies. Given a recursive relationship relation schema $\mathscr{R}_p(\mathscr{A})$ accompanied by a binary relationship constraint

$$(\forall x/\mathscr{R}_p)(\exists y_1/\mathscr{R}_{p_1})(\exists y_2/\mathscr{R}_{p_2})(\mathscr{A}_1'(x) = \mathscr{A}_1(y_1) \wedge \mathscr{A}_2'(x) = \mathscr{A}_1(y_2))$$

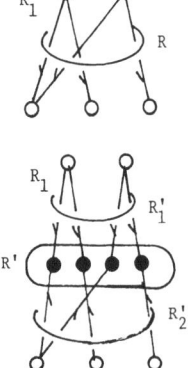

Fig. 9. Decomposition of a recursive relationship relation into hierarchies.

we decompose $\mathcal{R}_p$ into

$$\mathcal{R}'_p(\mathcal{A} - \mathcal{A}'_1 - \mathcal{A}'_2 \cup \mathcal{A}_r)$$

where $\mathcal{A}_r$ is an arbitrary candidate key of $\mathcal{R}_p$

$$\mathcal{R}'_{p_1}(\mathcal{A}_r \cup \mathcal{A}'_1)$$

and

$$\mathcal{R}'_{p_2}(\mathcal{A}_r \cup \mathcal{A}'_2)$$

using functional dependencies $\mathcal{A}_r \to \mathcal{A}'_1$ and $\mathcal{A}_r \to \mathcal{A}'_2$. Both $\mathcal{R}'_{p_1}$ and $\mathcal{R}'_{p_2}$ become hierarchical relationship relation schemata from $\mathcal{R}_{p_1}$ to $\mathcal{R}'_p$; that is, we have

$$(\forall y'_1 / \mathcal{R}'_{p_1})(\exists y_1 / \mathcal{R}_{p_1})(\exists x' / \mathcal{R}'_p)(\mathcal{A}'_1(y'_1) = \mathcal{A}_1(y_1) \wedge \mathcal{A}_r(y'_1) = \mathcal{A}_r(x'))$$

$$(\forall y'_2 / \mathcal{R}'_{p_2})(\exists y_2 / \mathcal{R}_{p_1})(\exists x' / \mathcal{R}'_p)(\mathcal{A}'_2(y'_2) = \mathcal{A}_1(y_2) \wedge \mathcal{A}_r(y'_2) = \mathcal{A}_r(x'))$$

$$\mathcal{A}_r \to \mathcal{A}'_1$$

$$\mathcal{A}_r \to \mathcal{A}'_2$$

$$(\forall x' / \mathcal{R}'_p)(\exists y'_1 / \mathcal{R}'_{p_1})\mathcal{A}_r(x') = \mathcal{A}_r(y'_1)$$

and

$$(\forall x' / \mathcal{R}'_p)(\exists y'_2 / \mathcal{R}'_{p_2})\mathcal{A}_r(x') = \mathcal{A}_r(y'_2)$$

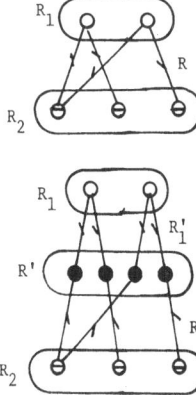

Fig. 10. Decomposition of an irrecursive relationship relation into hierarchies.

In particular, if $\mathcal{R}_p$ is a relationship relation schema for trees, then $\mathcal{R}'_{p_2}$ becomes a relationship relation schema that gives a one-to-one correspondence.

A similar decomposition can be applied to an irrecursive relationship relation schema $\mathcal{R}_p(\mathcal{A})$ with a binary relationship constraint

$$(\forall x/\mathcal{R}_p)(\exists y_1/\mathcal{R}_{p_1})(\exists y_2/\mathcal{R}_{p_2})(\mathcal{A}'_1(x) = \mathcal{A}_1(y_1) \wedge \mathcal{A}'_2(x) = \mathcal{A}_2(y_2))$$

using functional dependencies $\mathcal{A}_r \to \mathcal{A}'_1$ and $\mathcal{A}_r \to \mathcal{A}'_2$. In this case, $\mathcal{R}'_{p_1}$ becomes a hierarchical relationship relation schema from $\mathcal{R}_{p_1}$ to $\mathcal{R}'_p$, while $\mathcal{R}'_{p_2}$ becomes a hierarchical relationship relation schema from $\mathcal{R}_{p_2}$ to $\mathcal{R}_p$.

A binary relationship relation schema in relationship normal form is said to be in *hierarchical normal form* if it is a quasi sequence or a hierarchy. The Network Model[7] (or Coset Model[70]) assumes that all the relationship relation schemata are in hierarchical normal form. We have discussed decompositions for obtaining hierarchical normal form relationship relation schemata.

Several hierarchies may compose a multilevel hierarchy. Let $\bar{\mathcal{R}}$ be a set of m hierarchical relationship relation schemata $\mathcal{R}_{p_1}, \mathcal{R}_{p_2}, \ldots, \mathcal{R}_{p_m}$ where $\mathcal{R}_{p_k}$ is defined as being between $\mathcal{R}_{u_k}$ and $\mathcal{R}_{l_k}$. Then $\bar{\mathcal{R}}$ can be regarded as a recursive relationship relation defined on

$$\bar{\mathcal{R}}' = \{\mathcal{R}_{u_1}, \mathcal{R}_{u_2}, \ldots, \mathcal{R}_{u_m}, \mathcal{R}_{l_1}, \mathcal{R}_{l_2}, \ldots, \mathcal{R}_{l_m}\}$$

The $\bar{\mathcal{R}}$ is called the *skeleton* of a multilevel hierarchy if

(i)

$$(\forall \mathcal{R}_{p_i}/\bar{\mathcal{R}})(\forall \mathcal{R}_{p_j}/\bar{\mathcal{R}})(\mathcal{R}_{l_i} = \mathcal{R}_{l_j} \to \mathcal{R}_{u_i} = \mathcal{R}_{u_j})$$

(ii)

$$(\forall \mathcal{R}_{p_i}/\bar{\mathcal{R}}) \sim (\mathcal{R}_{p_i} \in \bar{S}(\mathcal{R}_{p_i}))$$

where $\bar{S}(\mathcal{R}_{p_i})$ is defined recursively by

$$\bar{S}_1(\mathcal{R}_{p_i}) = \{\mathcal{R}_{p_j}|\mathcal{R}_{u_j} = \mathcal{R}_{l_i}\}$$

$$\bar{S}_{\nu+1}(\mathcal{R}_{p_i}) = \{\mathcal{R}_{p_k}|\mathcal{R}_{p_i} \in \bar{S}_\nu(\mathcal{R}_{p_i}) \wedge \mathcal{R}_{u_k} = \mathcal{R}_{l_i}\}$$

and

$$\bar{S}(\mathcal{R}_{p_i}) = \bigcup_{\nu=1}^{m} \bar{S}(\mathcal{R}_{p_i})$$

(iii)

$$(\forall \mathcal{R}_{p_i}/\bar{\mathcal{R}})(\forall \mathcal{R}_{p_j}/\bar{\mathcal{R}})\mathcal{R}_{p_j} \in C(\mathcal{R}_{p_i})$$

where $\bar{C}(\mathcal{R}_{p_i})$ is defined recursively by

$$\bar{C}_1(\mathcal{R}_{p_i}) = \{\mathcal{R}_{p_j} | \mathcal{R}_{u_j} = \mathcal{R}_{u_i} \vee \mathcal{R}_{u_j} = \mathcal{R}_{l_i} \vee \mathcal{R}_{l_j} = \mathcal{R}_{u_i} \vee \mathcal{R}_{l_j} = \mathcal{R}_{l_i}\}$$

$$\bar{C}_{\nu+1}(\mathcal{R}_{p_i}) = \{\mathcal{R}_{p_k} | \mathcal{R}_{p_j} \in \bar{C}_\nu(\mathcal{R}_{p_i})$$

$$\wedge (\mathcal{R}_{u_k} = \mathcal{R}_{u_j} \vee \mathcal{R}_{u_k} = \mathcal{R}_{l_j} \vee \mathcal{R}_{l_k} = \mathcal{R}_{u_j} \vee \mathcal{R}_{l_k} = \mathcal{R}_{l_j})\}$$

and

$$\bar{C}(\mathcal{R}_{p_i}) = \bigcup_{\nu=1}^{m} \bar{C}(\mathcal{R}_{p_i})$$

hold in $\bar{\mathcal{R}}$. In other words, the skeleton is a connected tree. The union of hierarchies in each of $\mathcal{R}_{p_1}, \mathcal{R}_{p_2}, \ldots, \mathcal{R}_{p_m}$, is called a *multilevel hierarchy*. The Hierarchical Model[92] deals with multilevel hierarchies.

It is obvious from this definition that a multilevel hierarchy can be decomposed into several (single-level) hierarchies.

4.6.6. Transformation of a Tree into Two Quasi Sequences

One more important transformation can be applied to trees. Let $\mathcal{R}_p(\mathcal{A})$ be a relationship relation schema for trees with two foreign keys $\mathcal{A}_1$ and

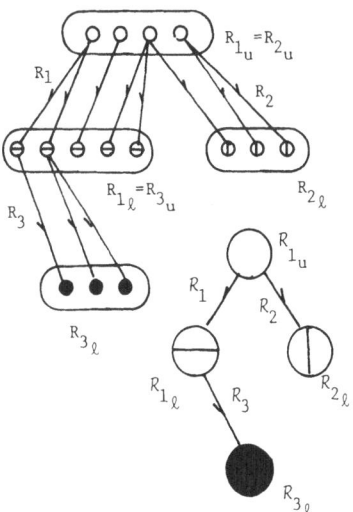

Fig. 11. A multilevel hierarchy and its skeleton.

$\mathcal{A}_2$, which are candidate keys of $\mathcal{R}_{p_1}$ and $\mathcal{R}_{p_2}$, respectively. Let R, R_1, and R_2 be relations in $\mathcal{R}_p$, $\mathcal{R}_{p_1}$, and $\mathcal{R}_{p_2}$, respectively, at a given time. For a tuple t_1 in R_1

$$E(t_1) = \{t | t \in R \wedge \mathcal{A}_1(t) = \mathcal{A}_1(t_1)\}$$

is called the *elementary tree* belonging to t_1, and

$$T(t_1) = \{t_2 | t_2 \in R_2 \wedge t \in E(t_1) \mathcal{A}_2(t_2) = \mathcal{A}_2(t)\}$$

is called the *terminal set* belonging to t_1.

Let $S(t_1)$ be a sequence defined on the terminal set $T(t_1)$. This sequence can be that which already exists, or it can be an arbitrarily defined one. The union

$$R^* = \bigcup_{t_1 \in R_1} S(t_1)$$

is a quasi sequence defined on R_2, which can be regarded as a relation in a relationship relation schema $\mathcal{R}^*_{s_2}$ defined on $\mathcal{R}_{p_2}$.

For each sequence $S(t_1)$, there exists exactly one *apex* t_a in $T(t_1)$, that is, a tuple for which

$$(\forall x / S(t_1)) \mathcal{A}'_1(x) \neq \mathcal{A}_2(t_a)$$

holds, where $\mathcal{A}'_1$ is the first foreign key in $\mathcal{R}^*_{s_2}$. For this apex t_a, there exists exactly one tuple t_b in $E(t_1)$ for which

$$\mathcal{A}_2(t_b) = \mathcal{A}_2(t_a)$$

Let R' be the set of all such tuples, each in each $E(t_1)$. Obviously, R' is a quasi sequence defined on $R_1 \cup R_2$, which can be regarded as a relation in a relationship relation schema $\mathcal{R}_{p_1} \cup \mathcal{R}_{p_2}$, that is, the set of possible instances of $R_1 \cup R_2$. The R' is regarded as a relation in a relationship

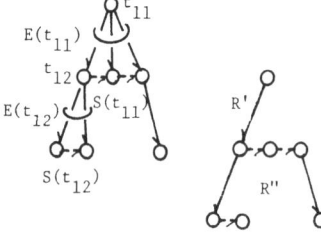

Fig. 12. Transformation of a tree into two quasisequences.

relation schema $\mathcal{R}_{s_1}$ defined on $\mathcal{R}_{p_1} \cup \mathcal{R}_{p_2}$. (Here $\mathcal{R}_{p_1} \cup \mathcal{R}_{p_2}$ is regarded as a single-relation schema though $\mathcal{R}_{p_1}$ and $\mathcal{R}_{p_2}$ have different sets of attributes if $\mathcal{R}_{p_1} \neq \mathcal{R}_{p_2}$. This particular union is called the *extended union*. It must be distinguished from the join union, which will be defined later.)

If $\mathcal{A} - \mathcal{A}_1 - \mathcal{A}_2 = \mathcal{A}_3 \neq \varnothing$, we must add $\mathcal{A}_3$ to the relationship relation schema $\mathcal{R}_{s_2}^*$; that is, we must use $\mathcal{R}_{s_2}(\mathcal{A}' \cup \mathcal{A}_3)$. The $\mathcal{A}_3(t)$ value for the tuple t, which is in R but not in R', must be transferred to $\mathcal{A}_3(t')$ value for the tuple t' in R'' in $\mathcal{R}_{s_2}$, for which $\mathcal{A}_2(t) = \mathcal{A}_1'(t')$.

It is easy to see that we can reconstruct the original R using R' and R''. Given a tuple t' in R'' we can find a tuple t_b in R' such that

$$(\exists t_1'/R'')(\exists t_2'/R'') \cdots (\exists t_m'/R'')(\mathcal{A}_2(t_b) = \mathcal{A}_1'(t_1') \wedge \mathcal{A}_2'(t_1')$$

$$= \mathcal{A}_1'(t_2') \wedge \mathcal{A}_2'(t_2') = \mathcal{A}_1'(t_3') \wedge \cdots \wedge \mathcal{A}_2'(t_{m-1}')$$

$$= \mathcal{A}_1'(t_m') \wedge \mathcal{A}_2'(t_m') = \mathcal{A}_1'(t'))$$

holds. We then generate a tuple t for which $\mathcal{A}_1(t) = \mathcal{A}_1(t_b)$, $\mathcal{A}_2(t) = \mathcal{A}_2'(t)$ and $\mathcal{A}_3(t) = \mathcal{A}_3'(t)$. Adding all such tuples to R', we obtain the original R. (The R^*, if necessary, can be obtained by simply dropping $\mathcal{A}_3$ values from all tuples in R''.)

We will denote such equivalence relation between $\{R, R^*\}$ and $\{R', R''\}$ by

$$\{R, R^*\} \simeq \{R', R''\}$$

The above transformation and reconstruction can be made for either a recursive or an irrecursive tree. In short, we have

Theorem 3: If R is a tree defined between R_1 and R_2 ($R_1 = R_2$ if R is recursive), and if there is a sequence $S(t_1)$ defined on the terminal set $T(t_1)$ belonging to each tuple t_1 in R_1, then there exist two quasi sequences, R' defined on $R_1 \cup R_2$ and R'' defined on R_2, such that

$$\left\{R, \bigcup_{t_1 \in R_1} S(t_1)\right\} \simeq \{R', R''\}$$

Two quasi sequences R' and R'' are called the *vertical relation* and the *horizontal relation*, respectively.

Let R' be in $\mathcal{R}_{s_1}(\mathcal{A}_1 \cup \mathcal{A}_2 \cup \mathcal{A}_3)$ where $\mathcal{A}_1$ and $\mathcal{A}_2$ are foreign keys, and let R'' be in $\mathcal{R}_{s_2}(\mathcal{A}_1' \cup \mathcal{A}_2' \cup \mathcal{A}_3')$ where $\mathcal{A}_1'$ and $\mathcal{A}_2'$ are foreign keys. Two relation schemata can be combined into a relation schema $\mathcal{R}_s(\mathcal{A}_1 \cup \mathcal{A}_2 \cup \mathcal{A}_3 \cup \mathcal{A}_3')$ by identifying $\mathcal{A}_1'$ with $\mathcal{A}_1$ and $\mathcal{A}_2'$ with $\mathcal{A}_2$, and by giving an "undefined" value to attributes $\mathscr{A}_3'$ of tuples in R' in $\mathscr{R}_{s_1}$, and to attributes $\mathscr{A}_3$ of tuples in R'' in $\mathscr{R}_{s_2}$. This procedure is called the *generalization* of relation schemata. $R' \cup R''$ as well as R' and R'' then becomes a relation in $\mathscr{R}_s$. This union is called the *join union.*

If R is an irrecursive tree (which can be hierarchy) then $R° = R' \cup R''$ for R' and R'', which are obtained by transforming R as mentioned in Theorem 3, also becomes a quasi sequence. This is because there are no two tuples in $R°$ having a common $\mathscr{A}_1$ value. We can reconstruct the original R using this $R°$. Given a quasi sequence $R°$, we generate

$$R' = \{t \mid t \in R° \wedge (\forall t/R°)\mathscr{A}_1(t) = \mathscr{A}_2(t')\}$$

and

$$R'' = R° - R$$

from which R can be reconstructed as described previously. Hence we have:

Theorem 4: If R is an irrecursive tree defined as being between R_1 and R_2, and if there is a sequence $S(t_1)$ defined on the terminal set $T(t_1)$ belonging to each tuple t_1 in R_1, then there exists a quasi sequence $R°$ defined on $R_1 \cup R_2$ such that

$$\left\{ R, \bigcup_{t_1 \in R_1} S(t_1) \right\} = \{R°\}$$

The $R°$ can be regarded as a relation in a relationship relation schema $\mathscr{R}°$ defined on $\mathscr{R}_{p_1} \cup \mathscr{R}_{p_2}$ (extended union).

The above transformation can be extended to that of multilevel hierarchies. A multilevel hierarchy R can be decomposed into (single-level) hierarchies $R_1, R_2, \ldots, R_m$, and each R_k can be transformed into two quasi sequences R_k' and R_k'' if a sequence is defined on each terminal set. Then both

$$R^* = \bigcup_{k=1}^{m} R_k'$$

and

$$R^{**} = \bigcup_{k=1}^{m} R_k''$$

(both being the join union) become quasi sequences. However, in this case, $R^* \cup R^{**}$ (join union) is not a quasi sequence because there can be pairs of tuples in $R^* \cup R^{**}$ having a common $\mathscr{A}_1$ value. We can obtain a quasi sequence from R^* and R^{**} by the following procedure. If there is a tuple t_1 in R^* and a tuple t_2 in R^{**} for which $\mathscr{A}_1(t_1) = \mathscr{A}_1(t_2)$, then we find a tuple t in R^* such that

$$(\exists t_1'/R^*)(\exists t_2'/R^*) \cdots (\exists t_m'/R^*)$$

$$(\mathscr{A}_1(t_1') = \mathscr{A}_2(t_1) \wedge \mathscr{A}_1(t_2') = \mathscr{A}_2(t_1') \wedge \mathscr{A}_1(t_3')$$

$$= \mathscr{A}_2(t_2') \wedge \cdots \wedge \mathscr{A}_1(t_m') = \mathscr{A}_2(t_{m-1}') \wedge \mathscr{A}_1(t) = \mathscr{A}_2(t_m))$$

and

$$(\forall x/R^*)\mathscr{A}_1(x) \neq \mathscr{A}_2(t)$$

We then remove t_2 from R^{**} instead we add a tuple t' to R^{**}, for which $\mathscr{A}_1(t') = \mathscr{A}_2(t)$, $\mathscr{A}_2(t') = \mathscr{A}_2(t_2)$ and all other attribute values are those of t_2. Now $R^\circ = R^* \cup R^{**}$ becomes a quasi sequence.

We can reconstruct the original multilevel hierarchy R from R° but only when the skeleton $\bar{\mathscr{R}}$ of this multilevel hierarchy is known. In fact, when we are given a tuple t in R°, we have three cases

1. $\mathscr{A}_1(t)$ belongs to a relation one level higher than the relation to which $\mathscr{A}_2(t)$ belongs.
2. $\mathscr{A}_1(t)$ belongs to a relation in the same level as that of the relation to which $\mathscr{A}_2(t)$ belongs.
3. $\mathscr{A}_1(t)$ belong to a relation one or more levels lower than the relation to which $\mathscr{A}_2(t)$ belongs.

In the first case, t is to be in R^*, while in the second case, t is to be in R^{**}. However, in the third case, we must generate a tuple t' to be added to R^{**} by the following procedure. We find a tuple t'' in R° for which $\mathscr{A}_2(t)$

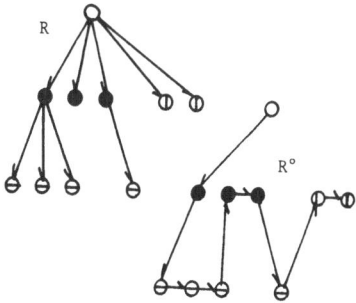

Fig. *13.* Transformation of a multilevel hierarchy into a quasisequence.

and $\mathcal{A}_2(t'')$ belong to relations of the same level, and

$$(\exists t_1/R°)(\exists t_2/R°) \cdots (\exists t_m/R°)$$

$$(\mathcal{A}_1(t_1) = \mathcal{A}_2(t'') \wedge \mathcal{A}_1(t_2) = \mathcal{A}_2(t_1) \wedge \mathcal{A}_1(t_3)$$

$$= \mathcal{A}_2(t_2) \wedge \cdots \wedge \mathcal{A}_1(t_m) = \mathcal{A}_2(t_{m-1}) \wedge \mathcal{A}_1(t) = \mathcal{A}_2(t_m))$$

holds. Then we add a tuple t' to R^{**}, for which $\mathcal{A}_1(t') = \mathcal{A}_2(t'')$, $\mathcal{A}_2(t') = \mathcal{A}_2(t)$, and all other attributes, are copied from those of t. Then we can reconstruct R using R^* and R^{**} according to Theorem 3. Note that the level of a relation can be determined only with reference to the hierarchical skeleton $\bar{\mathcal{R}}$. Hence we have

Theorem 5: If R is a multilevel hierarchy defined on $R_1, R_2, \ldots, R_m$, and if there is a sequence $S(t_1)$ defined on the terminal set $T(t_1)$ belonging to each tuple t_1 in $R_1, R_2, \ldots, R_m$, then there exists a quasi sequence $R°$ defined on $R_1, R_2, \ldots, R_m$ such that

$$\left\{ R, \bigcup_{t_1 \in R^*} S(t_1) \right\} \simeq \{R°, \bar{\mathcal{R}}\}$$

where

$$R^* = \bigcup_{k=1}^{m} R_k$$

and $\bar{\mathcal{R}}$ is the skeleton of multilevel hierarchy R.

The three equivalence theorems we have discussed can be regarded as presenting a kind of lossless transformation. In contrast to other normal form transformations (except the first normal form transformation), they neither use projections in the transformation nor simple natural joins in the reconstruction.

4.7. Other Static Constraints

So far we have reviewed several static constraints that play important roles in database design, but there are other types of intrarelation and interrelation constraints. Of these, we will discuss the following two special cases.

4.7.1. Existential Constraints

In all the schema calculi we have discussed, the first quantification is always universal when written in prenex normal form. We will call them *universal constraints.* There can be *existential constraints* whose first quantification in prenex normal form is *existential.* For example,

$$(\exists x/\mathcal{R}_p)\mathcal{A}_k(x) = C$$

is an intrarelation existential constraint, and

$$(\exists x_1/\mathcal{R}_{p_1})(\forall x_2/\mathcal{R}_{p_2})\mathcal{A}_1(x_1) \leq \mathcal{A}_2(x_2)$$

is an interrelation existential constraint.

A major difference between universal constraints and existential constraints is that the former hold in any empty relation, while the latter do not. This necessitates a special treatment for the empty relation when its relation schema is accompanied by at least one existential constraint. Also, unlike tuple constraints, which are the constraints with only one universally quantified tuple variable and are regarded as constraints imposed on each tuple, existential constraints are the constraints imposed on the whole relation even if they have only one existentially quantified tuple variable. This difference results in different integrity preservation mechanisms when they are used for regulating database update operations.

4.7.2. Aggregate Constraints

Sometimes the schema calculi do not include any quantified variables. All the tuple variables are bound by some other means. If they are bound in the scope of an aggregate function, they are called *aggregate constraints.* For example,

$$\sum_{(x\in\mathcal{R}_p)} \text{count} \leq C$$

is an intrarelation aggregate constraint, and

$$\min_{x_1\in\mathcal{R}_{p_1}} \mathcal{A}_1(x_1) \geq \max_{x_2\in\mathcal{R}_{p_2}} \mathcal{A}_2(x_2)$$

is an interrelation aggregate constraint.

4.8. Definition of Logical Database Structure

In order to define the logical database structure, we must first select the objects to be represented in the database. Next we must select the attributes to express these objects. Finally, we must enumerate various semantic constraints to hold in the database, some of which are to be registered as assertions.

As described previously, many data models have been presented to provide database designers a guide for logical database design. They can be classified into three categories: binary models, *n*-ary models, and models distinguishing relationship relations from entity relations. Data models in the first category might be useful, for example, in dealing with natural language question answering. However, they are not suitable for use in an early stage of database design.

Models in the second category provide a very simple database structure, which proves to be superior, particularly as the basis for theoretical discussions of database structure and data manipulation on it. However, they are not always intuitive for database designers. In particular, when we need fairly complicated database structure, it is not convenient for database designers to use such models.

Models in the third category are superior in the sense that in many cases they provide database designers with a much more intuitive view of the real world. Most of the existing database management systems have been developed to support this type of view of the real world.

We have discussed the relational view of the real world; however, we have also formally clarified the difference between entity relations and relationship relations. To support an intuitive view of the real world, we will hereafter employ the entity–relationship view as a tool of the first stage of logical database design.

4.8.1. Selection of the Objects to be Represented

All data models in the third category provide some sort of diagrams to express entities and relationships in the real world. Chen's entity-relationship diagram[16] can express any number of entity sets and any number of *n*-ary ($n \geq 2$) relationship sets. Bachman's diagram[7] assumes each relationship set to be in hierarchical normal form. Therefore, it can express any number of entity sets and any number of hierarchies. Here the author would like to present a diagram based on the relationship normal form; that is, a diagram assuming that each relationship relation is in relationship normal form. We call this diagram the DAVID (data analysis-based very intuitive design) diagram.

Entities are objects in the real world, each perceived as an individual. In an enterprise, for example, employees, departments, and projects, are entities in this sense. Hence, we have entity sets EMP, DPT, and PRJ, which are the set of employees, the set of departments, and the set of projects, respectively.

There are various relationships among entities. For example, an employee belongs to a department, an employee engages in one or more projects, and an employee manages several other employees. These are relationships among entities. Hence, we have relationship sets BELONG-TO, ENGAGE-IN, and MANAGE. BELONG-TO is a relationship set defined as being between two entity sets EMP and DPT. ENGAGE-IN is a relationship set defined as being between EMP and PRJ. Unlike these two, MANAGE is a relationship set defined on an entity set EMP.

Figure 14 is a DAVID diagram expressing these three entity sets and three relationship sets. As a correspondence, a relationship set can be one-to-one, many-to-one, one-to-many, or many-to-many. The cardinality of the correspondence can also be specified in the DAVID diagram. In our example, ENGAGE-IN is a many-to-one correspondence if no employee engages in more than one project. Otherwise it is a many-to-many correspondence. Similarly, BELONG-TO is a many-to-one correspondence if no employee belongs to more than one department. MANAGE is a one-to-many correspondence if an employee reports to only one manager.

A much more complicated DAVID diagram is shown in Fig. 15. It is devised to express cartographic data to be used in a regional information system. P represents a set of geographical points, L_k represents a set of poligonal lines of level k, and A_k represents a set of geographical areas of level k. They are entity sets. Various relationship sets exist, which represent various incidence relations among points, lines, and areas. Several relationship sets are defined on other relationship sets. In this example, S(X) is a quasi sequence defined on a relationship set X. Such a cartographic database is discussed extensively by Kobayashi.[58]

If necessary, it is easy to convert a DAVID diagram into a Bachman's diagram. This conversion corresponds to the hierarchical normal form

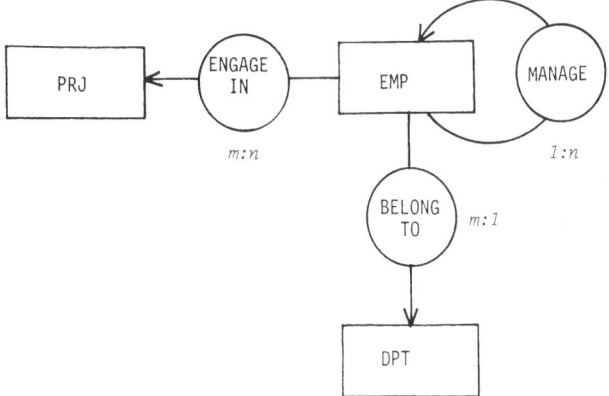

Fig. 14. A DAVID diagram.

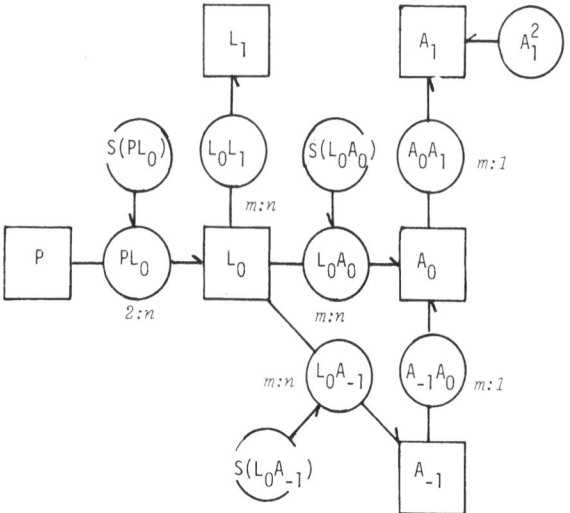

Fig. 15. A DAVID diagram for a cartographic database.

transformation. Figure 16 is the Bachman's diagram which is obtained by converting the DAVID diagram shown in Fig. 14. Each arrow in the Bachman's diagram represents a one-to-many onto correspondence. We have five such correspondences in this example. Two of them are obtained by decomposing ENGAGE-IN, another two by decomposing MANAGE. These two decompositions also generate entity sets ENGAGE-IN' and MANAGE'. The other correspondence is derived from BELONG-TO, which is a many-to-one correspondence.

Each rectangular box in a DAVID diagram can be regarded as an entity relation schema, while each circle in it as a relationship relation schema. (As for a Bachman's diagram, each rectangular box can be regarded as an entity relation schema and each arrow as a hierarchical relationship relation schema.)

Note that up to this stage we are neither concerned with the attributes to be attached to each relation schema nor with domains of these attributes;

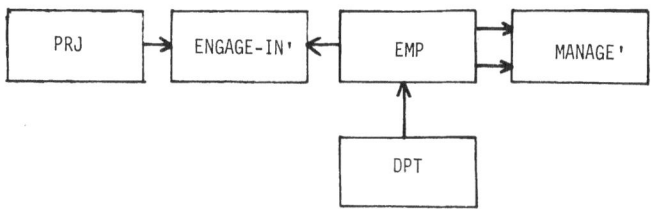

Fig. 16. Bachman's diagram.

that is, there are no restrictions on the attribute domains. This differs from the design procedure based on the Relational Model, which assumes the first normal form condition at a very early stage of logical database design.

On the other hand, the entity is defined as an object in the real world that can be perceived as an individual. This almost an equivalent assumption to the second and third normal form condition.

One more important note is that, in practice, it is not necessary or even harmful to count all kinds of relationships as DAVID relationship sets. Only relationships of certain strength must be defined as relationship sets. The strength of relationship sets is evaluated with regard to somewhat deeper semantics. In fact, the definition of relationship sets is significant only when navigations, which will be described in the next section, along these relationship sets are frequently invoked. In this sense, the relationship normal form condition is sometimes too strong. We may weaken this condition so that it allows entity relation schemata with one or more foreign keys.

After selecting the entity sets and relationship sets to be represented in the database, we should estimate the number of elements in each entity set and in each relationship set as these estimates are useful for achieving better physical organization.

4.8.2. Selection of Attributes to be Included in Relation Schemata

Next, we have to specify the attributes to be attached to the objects already selected. In traditional data processing applications, it is a rather easy task to choose attributes (fields or items) to be included in tuples (logical records). In fact, only the attributes that are necessary to generate the predetermined outputs need to be selected and represented in data files. However, in the database-oriented design approach no such criteria exist. We must select the attributes to be represented in the database somehow by weighing the cost of gathering and storing the attribute values against the potential profit that may be obtained by using the stored attribute values in the balance. This process resembles feature extraction in pattern recognition. A set of attributes, by whose values each entity and each relationship can be well represented, must be chosen. In practice, the selection is done with the expected applications in mind. However, the outputs requirements can be much less concrete than those in traditional design approach. Instead it is desirable for database designers to make an effort in creating a database that is easily modified when it becomes inconvenient.

Entities may have as many attributes as required. There are no restrictions on attribute domains in this stage. On the other hand, relationships always have two attributes specifying the *origin* and *destination*. Both the origin and destination are entities (or other relationships). Relationships may have some other attributes in addition to the origin and destination. For example, an employee may engage in Project A three days a week and in Project B two days a week. Such information can be given as attributes of relationships in ENGAGE-IN.

After the attributes to be represented are selected, we can write the relation schemata corresponding to entity sets and relationship sets in terms of schema and attribute names.

4.8.3. Enumeration of Semantic Constraints

Next, we must think over various semantic constraints which hold in the real world. When objects in the real world are represented by relations in various relation schemata, these semantic constraints are regarded as being imposed on these relation schemata. We know that there are static constraints and dynamic constraints and that the former can be described using schema calculi.

Semantic constraints are usually used for regulating database updates. Since such an integrity preservation procedure is always an expensive task, not all the semantic constraints can be registered as assertions.

Domain constraints, which determine attribute domains of relation schemata, are the most simple but the most basic constraints. Some attributes may have compound domains. In some cases it is desirable to eliminate such compound domains by transforming the subject relation schema into a first normal form relation schema. However, in other cases it is better to treat attributes with compound domains as they are. In these cases, attribute values must be represented physically by variable-length field values.

Domain constraints can be described as schema calculi; however, they can be described also by the data definition part of most existing programming languages. We may use COBOL picture, FORTRAN type, format and dimension, or whatever linguistic devices we think convenient. PASCAL has a richer repertoire. An attribute domain can be of a simple scalar type such as integer, real, Boolean, and char; it can be of a subrange type, which specifies a subset of a predefined value set; it can be of a structured type such as array, record, and (power) set. The extensible data type is powerful for describing compound attribute domains. Sometimes it is desirable to describe the *operation cluster* together with the value set on which it operates.

As for foreign keys, two different treatments are possible. If the connection between two tuples is weak (in the sense that navigations between these two tuples are not so frequent), the foreign key can be treated as an attribute with a simple domain (the set of foreign key values). If the connection is fairly strong, a relationship normal form transformation is mandatory.

Among the functional dependencies holding in a relation schema, the key dependency regarding the selected primary key is of special importance. It can be described by underlining the primary key attributes. If partial or transitive dependencies exist, we may apply to the subject relation schema a decomposition into (weak or strong) third or Boyce–Codd normal form relation schemata. This decomposition is, however, not absolutely necessary. The decomposition is very desirable when a new relation schema obtained by the decomposition can be regarded as corresponding to a kind of individual in the real world.

Into constraints can be registered by declaring attributes as being foreign keys. In particular, relationship constraints can be registered by distinguishing relationship relation schemata from entity relation schemata. Constraints classifying relationship relation types can be registered by specifying the types in relationship relation schemata declarations. Other semantic constraints may be described as schema calculi or specified by some other means.

In the future advanced information systems will have the capability of inferring some facts that are implicit in the given database from other facts that are explicit in it. It is desirable for such systems to keep all the semantic constraints described in a general format such as predicate calculus.

Integrity preservation mechanisms using assertions will be discussed in Section 6, while inference execution using semantic constraints as inference rules will be discussed in Section 11.

5. DATABASE OPERATIONS

An (extension) database is a collection of relations, each representing simple facts of a specific type in the real world. For retrievals and updates of the database, we must prepare various database-manipulating operations. Some of them are relatively simple, but others are very complicated.

In the database-oriented approach, systems output are not concretely predetermined and, therefore, we cannot predetermine the data manipulation requirements completely. In this area, we will take a somewhat bottom-up approach rather than the top-down approach that is a principle in software engineering.

It is desirable for the system to have a finite set of database operations by whose combinations we can achieve any desired database manipulation. Hence, we would like to clarify what the essential operations are. Several different levels of database abstractions can be devised.

As described in Section 4.4.1, we have a set of operations defined on one or more attribute domains. These domains and their operations form the basis of database operations.

5.1. Functions of Tuples

A function whose domain is a Cartesian product of m relations

$$\lambda: R_1 \times R_2 \times \cdots \times R_m \to V$$

is called a *function of lines* of *span* m regardless of what its range is. In particular, λ is called a *function of points* if its span is 1. A function whose domain is the power set of a relation

$$\mu: \mathcal{P}(R) \to V$$

is called a *function of areas* regardless of what its range is. Functions of lines and function of areas are collectively called *functions of tuples.*

For example, "overtime charge" is a function of points defined on a relation R_{emp} if both "overtime rate" and "overtime" are R_{emp}'s attributes. In this case

$$\text{overtime charge}(x) \equiv \text{overtime rate}(x) \times \text{overtime}(x)$$

for $x \in R_{emp}$. We may write the right-hand side simply as

$$(\text{overtime rate} \times \text{overtime})(x)$$

If the "overtime rate" is R_{emp}'s attribute, but the "overtime" is an attribute of another relation R_{trans}, then the "overtime charge" becomes a function of lines of span 2 defined on $R_{emp} \times R_{trans}$, that is,

$$\text{overtime charge}(x_1, x_2) \equiv \text{overtime rate}(x_1) \times \text{overtime}(x_2)$$

for $x_1 \in R_{emp}$ and $x_2 \in R_{trans}$. Only when there is no danger of confusion, we write the right-hand side as

$$(\text{overtime rate} \times \text{overtime})(x_1, x_2)$$

The "salary total" of a department is a function of areas defined on the power set of R_{emp} if "salary" is one of R_{emp}'s attributes. For a subset

S of R_{emp}, this function can be defined

$$\text{salary total}(S) \equiv \sum_{x \in S} \text{salary}(S)$$

using an aggregate function $\sum$.

The following three types of functions of points are called *basic functions of points*, since they are the only available data that are directly obtained from database relations:

1. $\lambda(x) \equiv \text{const}$
2. $\lambda(x) \equiv A_k(x)$: the kth attribute value of the tuple t
3. $\lambda(x) \equiv x \in R$: a monadic whose value is "true" iff the tuple t belongs to the relation R.

From the set B of the basic functions of points, we can generate various functions of tuples. Operators defined on various value sets are extended to operators combining functions of tuples. If an operator

$$f: V_1 \times V_2 \times \cdots \times V_m \to V_f$$

is defined on the Cartesian product of m value sets, then f can be extended to an operator

$$f': F_1 \times F_2 \times \cdots \times F_m \to F_f$$

where each F_k is a set of functions of tuples whose range is V_k and F_f is a set of functions of tuples whose range is V_f. The extension is defined *homomorphically* by

$$f'(\zeta_1, \zeta_2, \ldots, \zeta_m)(z) \equiv f(\zeta_1(z_1), \zeta_2(z_2), \ldots, \zeta_m(z_m))$$

where z is a tuple (point), an ordered set of tuples (line), or a set of tuples (area); and each z_k is a point, a line, or an area, which as a set of points is a subset of z. The previously mentioned overtime examples concur with this definition.

An aggregate operator

$$\alpha: \mathscr{P}(V) \to V_\alpha$$

defined on a value set V can be extended to an aggregate operator

$$\alpha': \Pi \to M$$

where Π is a set of functions of points whose range is V and M_α is a set of functions of areas whose range is V_α. The extension is defined by

$$\alpha'(\lambda)(S) = \alpha_{x \in S}\lambda(x)$$

for $\lambda \in \Pi$ and $S \in \mathscr{P}(R)$. Our salary total example agrees with this definition.

Two types of functions of tuples play important roles in database manipulation. One is the set of logical functions of lines

$$\lambda : R_1 \times R_2 \times \cdots \times R_m \to \{\text{"true"}, \text{"false"}\}$$

which can be regarded as predicates with m free tuple variables. The function λ can include bound tuple variables in addition to these free tuple variables. In prenex normal form, λ can be written as

$$\lambda(x_1, x_2, \ldots, x_m) \equiv Q_1 Q_2 \cdots Q_\mu \lambda'(x_1, x_2, \ldots, x_m, x_{m+1}, x_{m+2}, \ldots, x_{m+\mu+\nu})$$

where x_k is a free tuple variable for $1 \le k \le m$, a quantified tuple variable for $m + 1 \le k \le m + \mu$, and another bound tuple variable for $m + \mu + 1 \le k \le m + \mu + \nu$. Each Q_k is either $(\forall x_{m+k}/R_{m+k})$ or $(\exists x_{m+k}/R_{m+k})$.

For example, in

$$\lambda(x_1) \equiv (\forall x_2/R_2)(A_1(x_1) = A_1(x_2) \wedge A_2(x_1) = \sum_{x_3 \in R_3 \wedge A_3(x_1) = A_3(x_3)} A_2(x_3))$$

defined for $x_1 \in R_1$, x_1 is a free variable, x_2 is an existentially quantified variable, and x_3 is a variable bound in the scope of an aggregate function $\sum$.

As a special case, we may have predicates without free variables (which are called *closed sentences* in formal logic), that is, $m = 0$. They are no longer logical function of lines; instead, they can be considered as statements regarding the whole database.

We will call the logical functions of lines we have so far defined the *extended relational calculus*. As for Codd's relational calculus[28] the matrix part $\lambda'(x_1, x_2, \ldots, x_{m+\mu+\nu})$ of the predicate must be a logical combination of diadics composed of an attribute value and another attribute or a constant combined by one of relational operators $=$, $\neq$, $>$, $<$, $\ge$, and $\le$. Such a restriction is not imposed on our extended relational calculus. For example, all

$$A_1(x) < 3 \times A_3(x),$$

$$A_1(x_1) = A_2(x_2) + A_2(x)$$

$$\sin(A_1(x)) + 3 \times \cos(A_2(x)) < 1/2$$

and

$$\frac{(A_1(x), q)}{|A_1(x)||q|} > 0.75$$

are not relational calculi but extended relational calculi. The last formula is a well-known pattern matching condition, in which $A_1(x)$ and q are vector-type values, $(A_1(x), q)$ is their inner product, and $|A_1(x)|$ and $|q|$ are the norms of $A_1(x)$ and q, respectively.

The other important type of functions of tuples is defined as an ordered set of n functions of tuples, that is,

$$(\zeta_1, \zeta_2, \ldots, \zeta_n)(z) \equiv (\zeta_1(z), \zeta_2(z), \ldots, \zeta_n(z))$$

where z is a point, a line, or an area. For a given z, this function of tuples generates a tuple (point). Hence, we will call such a function of tuples a *tuple-generating function.*

Generation of functions of tuples from the set B of basic functions of points agrees with a certain generative grammar. Let G be the set of productions in this grammar, and Φ be the set of operators combining functions of tuples, quantifiers, and other symbols such as parentheses controlling the operator precedence. We have a set $F(B, \Phi, G)$ of all the functions of tuples that can be generated from B according to G using Φ. This set represents the computational capability possessed by the given system.

5.2. Alpha Operation

Information processing can be seen, in general, as a transformation from m input relations into m' output relations as shown in Fig. 17. Obviously, this transformation is a combination of m' transformations, each of which transforms m input relations into one output relation. Each component transformation can be regarded as an m-ary set operation

$$T(R_1, R_2, \ldots, R_m) = R$$

There are a variety of transformations to be applied to the database, and they cannot be classified into a finite number of patterns. Therefore, we cannot provide all patterns as basic database operations.

However, if we could select a relatively small number of elementary set operations on the database, and if we could describe any data processing pattern as a single elementary set operation or a procedural combination of several elementary set operations, they would become a good abstraction

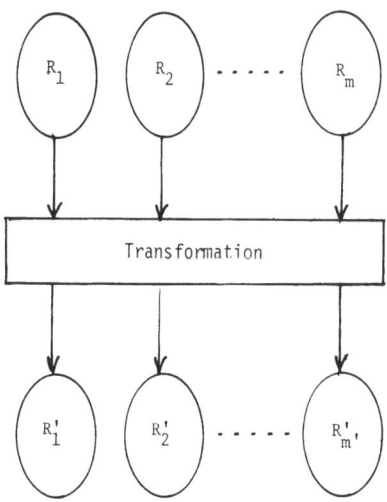

Fig. 17. Data processing as a set operation.

of database manipulation. Several attempts to find such a collection of elementary set operations have been made. Information Algebra provided five set operations;[23] Codd's Relational Algebra provided eight set operations;[30] and Childs' Extended Set Theory provided about twenty set operations.[18] Here, however, we will consider a collection composed of only one elementary set operation, which we will call the *alpha operation* after Codd's ALPHA Sublanguage.[28]

An alpha operation is the set operation which extracts all the lines (ordered sets of tuples) satisfying a logical function λ of lines from a Cartesian product of m relations, and for each qualified line generates a point (tuple) using a tuple-generating function β of lines. It is defined by

$$a[\beta : \lambda](R_1, R_2, \ldots, R_m) = \{\beta(l) | l \in s[\lambda](R_1, R_2, \ldots, R_m)\}$$

where

$$s[\lambda](R_1, R_2, \ldots, R_m) = \{l | l \in R_1 \times R_2 \times \cdots \times R_m \wedge \lambda(l)\}$$

The operation s defined above is called a *search*. In particular, if $m = 1$, the search operation

$$s[\lambda](R) = \{x | x \in R \wedge \lambda(x)\}$$

is called a *retrieval*. If $m \geq 2$, the search operation is an abstraction of a collation applied to m files.

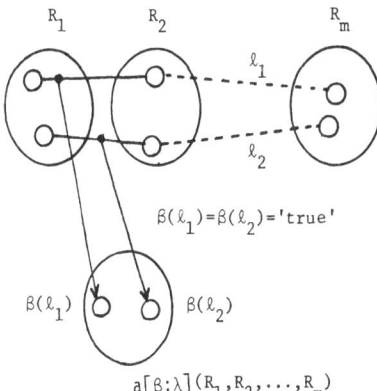

Fig. 18. Alpha operation. $a[\beta:\lambda](R_1, R_2, \ldots, R_m)$

The alpha operation, therefore, must be specified by two arguments: a pair of a logical function of lines λ and a tuple generating function of lines β both defined on $R_1 \times R_2 \times \cdots \times R_m$, and an ordered set of m relations. In Codd's terminology, $\beta:\lambda$ is called an Alpha expression, of which β is called the target list and λ is called the relational calculus. (Our alpha operation uses an extended relational calculus instead of a relational calculus.) In Information Algebra, an alpha operation is called a bundling operation, in which λ is called the function of bundles, and β is called the bundling function. (These two functions were defined in a very conventional manner in Information Algebra.[23])

Figure 18 illustrates an alpha operation. Any n-ary set operation transforming m input relations into one output relation can be expressed by an alpha operation or a procedural combination of several alpha operations.

5.3. Relational Algebra

It is certain that the alpha operation is powerful enough for expressing data processing operations on the database. However, since the predicate calculus is neither widely used nor always convenient in describing search conditions, the alpha operation is sometimes inconvenient for some classes of users.

The relational algebra[30] is a collection of eight elementary set operations which are comprehensive for some classes of users. All the relational algebra operations can be defined in terms of the alpha operation. Among the eight elementary set operation, the following five are basic. The first two are binary set operations whose operands are two relations with a common attribute set:

$$\mathcal{A} = \{A_1, A_2, \ldots, A_n\}$$

1. *Difference* is defined by

$$d(R_1, R_2) = a[\beta:\lambda](R_1)$$

with

$$\lambda(x_1) \equiv (\forall x_2/R_2)(\mathcal{A}(x_1) \neq \mathcal{A}(x_2))$$

and

$$\beta(x_1) \equiv x_1$$

2. *Union* is defined by

$$u(R_1, R_2) = \begin{cases} R_1 & (\text{if } R_2 = \varnothing) \\ R_2 & (\text{if } R_1 = \varnothing \vee d(R_1, R_2) = \varnothing) \\ a[\beta: T](R_1, R_2, d(R_1, R_2)) & (\text{otherwise}) \end{cases}$$

where T is a function of lines that assigns the value "true" to every line (t_1, t_2, t_3) in $R_1 \times R_2 \times d(R_1, R_2)$, and

$$\beta(x_1, x_2, x_3) \equiv \begin{cases} x_1 & \text{if } \mathcal{A}(x_1) = \mathcal{A}(x_2) \text{ or } \mathcal{A}(x_1) \neq \mathcal{A}(x_2) \wedge \mathcal{A}(x_1) = \mathcal{A}(x_3) \\ x_2 & \text{if } \mathcal{A}(x_1) \neq \mathcal{A}(x_2) \wedge \mathcal{A}(x_1) \neq \mathcal{A}(x_3) \end{cases}$$

The above definition implies a procedural combination of two alpha operations. It may generate a number of duplicate elements; however, these are eliminated according to the definition of the alpha operation.

The next two operations are unary set operations. Let R be a relation with attribute set $\mathcal{A}$.

3. *Selection* is defined by

$$s[\lambda](R) = a[\beta:\lambda](R)$$

with

$$\beta(x) \equiv x$$

Here λ is an arbitrary logical function of points defined on R. This is just the retrieval operation defined previously, and so we use the same notation s. Note that the selection defined above is a little more general than the selection (restriction) defined by Codd. The λ in Codd's selection must be a diadic composed of an attribute and another attribute or a constant combined by a relational operator. The λ can be an arbitrary logical function of points in our selection.

4. *Projection* is defined by

$$p[\mathscr{A}'](R) = a[\beta : T](R)$$

where

$$\beta(x) \equiv (A_{k_1}(x), A_{k_2}(x), \ldots, A_{k_m}(x))$$

with

$$\mathscr{A}' = \{A_{k_1}, A_{k_2}, \ldots, A_{k_m}\}$$

This operation also includes the elimination of duplicate elements. It is obvious that the projection defined above coincides with the projection defined in Section 4.5.2.

The last operation is a binary set operation whose operand relations do not necessarily have a common attribute set. Let R_1 and R_2 be two relations with attribute sets

$$\mathscr{A}_1 = \{A_1, A_2, \ldots, A_i\}$$

$$\mathscr{A}_2 = \{A_{i+1}, A_{i+2}, \ldots, A_j\}$$

respectively.

5. *Multiplication* is defined by

$$m(R_1, R_2) = a[\beta : T](R_1, R_2)$$

with

$$\beta(x_1, x_2) \equiv (A_1(x_1), A_2(x_1), \ldots, A_i(x_1), A_{i+1}(x_2), A_{i+2}(x_2), \ldots, A_j(x_2))$$

The multiplication resembles the construction of the Cartesian product of two relations; however, it generates a relation instead of a set of pairs of tuples. In this sense, the two must be distinguished.

The following three operations are those in which Codd originally presented in addition to the above five operations. They are, however, described as procedural combinations of some of the basic five. The first is a binary operation applied to two relations with a common attribute set.

6. *Intersection* is defined by

$$i(R_1, R_2) = d(R_1, d(R_1, R_2))$$

The second is also a binary operation, but the two operand relations do not necessarily have a common attribute set.

7. *Join* is defined as

$$j[\lambda](R_1, R_2) \equiv a[\lambda'](m(R_1, R_2))$$

where λ is an arbitrary logical function of lines of span 2 defined on $R_1 \times R_2$, and λ' is a logical function of point defined on $m(R_1, R_2)$, which is equivalent to λ. For example,

$$\lambda(x_1, x_2) \equiv A_1(x_1) = A_2(x_2)$$

defined on $R_1 \times R_2$ is equivalent to

$$\lambda'(x) \equiv A_1(x) = A_2(x)$$

defined on $m(R_1, R_2)$. The join defined above is a more general operation than Codd's join because the former uses an extended relational calculus.

In particular, if λ is of the form

$$\lambda(x_1, x_2) \equiv \mathscr{A}_1'(x_1) = \mathscr{A}_2'(x_2)$$

where $\mathscr{A}_1'$ is a subset of the attribute set $\mathscr{A}_1$ of relation R_1 and $\mathscr{A}_2'$ is a subset of the attribute set $\mathscr{A}_2$ of relation R_2, the join

$$j_e[\mathscr{A}_1', \mathscr{A}_2'](R_1, R_2) = j[\lambda](R_1, R_2)$$

is called an *equijoin*.

The operation defined by

$$j_n[\mathscr{A}_1', \mathscr{A}_2'](R_1, R_2) = p[\mathscr{A}_1 \cup \mathscr{A}_2 - \mathscr{A}_2'](j_e[\mathscr{A}_1', \mathscr{A}_2'](R_1, R_2))$$

is called a *natural join*. This agrees with the natural join defined in Section 4.5.2 (where $\mathscr{A}_2'$ is identified to $\mathscr{A}_1'$).

An alpha operation with two operand relations can be written as

$$a[\beta:\lambda](R_1, R_2) = \{\beta'(x) | x \in j[\lambda](R_1, R_2)\}$$

where β' is a tuple-generating function of points defined on $m(R_1, R_2)$, which is equivalent to β defined on $R_1 \times R_2$. Although Codd did not count such an alpha operation in his Relational Algebra, it is sometimes called a *computed join*.

The last operation is a binary set operation for which the attribute set $\mathscr{A}_1$ of the first operand relation R_1 must include the attribute set $\mathscr{A}_2$ of the second operand relation R_2.

8. *Division* is defined by

$$v(R_1, R_2) = d(p[\mathscr{A}_1 - \mathscr{A}_2](R_1), p[\mathscr{A}_1 - \mathscr{A}_2]$$

$$(d(m(p[\mathscr{A}_1 - \mathscr{A}_2](R_1), R_2), R_1)))$$

Since the above definition is somewhat cumbersome, another definition of division stated directly in terms of alpha operation is given:

$$v(R_1, R_2) = a[\beta : \lambda](p[\mathscr{A}_1 - \mathscr{A}_2](R_1))$$

where

$$\lambda(x) \equiv (\forall x_2'/R_2)(\exists x_1'/R_1)(\mathscr{A}_2(x_1') = \mathscr{A}_2(x_2') \wedge (\mathscr{A}_1 - \mathscr{A}_2)(x_1')$$

$$= (\mathscr{A}_1 - \mathscr{A}_2)(x))$$

and

$$\beta(x) \equiv x$$

The division was originally introduced for processing universal quantifiers. For example, given a relation

$$R_1 = \{(a_1, b_1), (a_1, b_2), (a_1, b_3), (a_2, b_1), (a_2, b_3), (a_3, b_1), (a_4, b_2), (a_4, b_3),$$

$$(a_5, b_1), (a_5, b_2), (a_5, b_3)\}$$

and

$$R_2 = \{(b_1), (b_2), (b_3)\}$$

we have

$$v(R_1, R_2) = \{(a_1), (a_5)\}$$

The division is so named because it can be regarded as the inverse of multiplication. In the above example, we have

$$R_1 = u(m(R_2, v(R_1, R_2)), R_3)$$

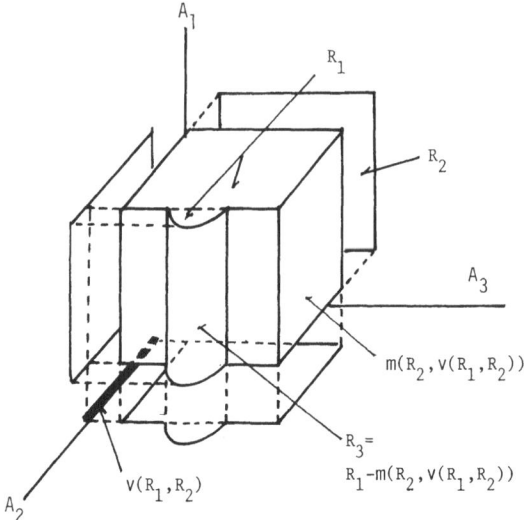

Fig. 19. Multiplication and division.

where the result of division $v(R_1, R_2)$ corresponds to the quotient, while

$$R_3 = \{(a_2, b_1), (a_2, b_3), (a_3, b_1), (a_4, b_2), (a_4, b_3)\}$$

corresponds to the remainder. Figure 19 shows the multiplication and division.

The relational algebra is significant in the following three points:

1. Each of eight set operations in the relational algebra can certainly be described as an alpha operation or a procedural combination of more than one alpha operation. However, they can be implemented much easier than the alpha operation of a general form. Such an implementation produces better performance when we need data manipulations which can be expressed by relational algebra operations.

2. As seen in Section 4, the projection and natural join are closely related to various normal form decompositions based on functional dependencies and multivalued dependencies. The two are used, respectively, in decomposing a given relation and in reconstructing it from the relations obtained by the decomposition.

3. It is obvious that the search $s[\lambda](R_1, R_2, \ldots, R_m)$, can be achieved by a procedural combination of several multiplications (used for combining relations), selections (used for selecting qualified tuples), projections (used for processing existential quantifiers), and divisions (used for processing universal quantifiers). In this sense, the relational algebra is equivalent in

expressive power to the search operation with an extended relational calculus as its argument. [As for Codd's Relational Algebra, the union and intersection are necessary to be equivalent in expressive power to the search operation with a relational calculus as its argument.[30] The difference operation is used for processing a conjunct of two monadics, $x \in R$ and $\sim(x \in R')$.]

Note that the relational algebra has less expressive power than the alpha operation, for the relational algebra can process only tuple-generating functions of a very limited form (if it does not include the computed join). In fact, the tuple-generating function β used in defining relational algebra operations in terms of the alpha operation is an identity function or a function that extracts some attribute values from the given tuples. To make relational algebra equally expressive, we must provide an additional operation.

9. *Transformation* is defined by

$$t[\beta](R) = a[\beta: T](R)$$

where β is an arbitrary tuple-generating function of points.

Practically, the relational algebra is convenient for use by casual users who sit down in front of terminal machines and ask the computer various questions which have arisen during some sort of planning. Queries and the expected answers are not so complicated.

5.5. Information Algebra

A database may be manipulated by casual users as well as by others. Some users may want to retrieve and update the database in batch mode. For *parameter users* who want to operate a file maintenance or report writing process using a collection of elementary set operations, we may provide some collection other than the relational algebra. Information Algebra[23] was not developed for database management, but it seems to be valuable as one of such collections.

We may define the information algebra as a collection of the following five elementary set operations. The first two are (1) *difference* and (2) *union*, which we have already defined in the relational algebra. The next is (3) *extraction*, defined by

$$e(R'_k, s[\lambda](R_1, R_2, \ldots, R_m)) = i(R'_k, t[\beta](s[\lambda](R_1, R_2, \ldots, R_m))$$

where $R'_k \subset R_k$, and

$$\beta(x_1, x_2, \ldots, x_m) \equiv x_m$$

The extraction operation is called the intersection in Information Algebra. (4) The fourth operation is *alpha operation*. As mentioned previously, the alpha operation is called the bundling operation in Information Algebra presented by CODASYL. As functions of tuples were defined in a very conventional manner in Information Algebra, very few people recognized that the bundling operation was equivalent to the alpha operation. However, the essentials of the bundling operation are the same as those of the alpha operation.

The last operation is called the "glumping" in Information Algebra. (5) *Summary* is defined by

$$g[\gamma:\lambda](R) = a[\beta:T](a[\beta':T](R))$$

where λ is a function of points defined on R, and γ is a pair

$$\gamma \equiv (\alpha_1, \alpha_2, \ldots, \alpha_n; \lambda_1, \lambda_2, \ldots, \lambda_n)$$

composed of a list of n aggregate functions, $\alpha_1, \alpha_2, \ldots, \alpha_n$, and a list of n functions of points, $\lambda_1, \lambda_2, \ldots, \lambda_n$. Two tuple-generating functions β' and β are defined, respectively, by

$$\beta'(x) \equiv (\lambda(x))$$

which means a tuple composed of only one attribute λ, and

$$\beta(x') \equiv (a_1, a_2, \ldots, a_n)$$

where

$$a_k = \alpha_{k_{(x \in R \wedge \lambda(x) = \lambda(x'))}} \lambda_k(x)$$

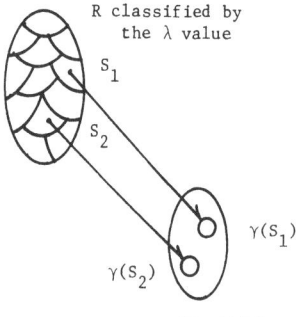

g[γ:λ](R)   *Fig. 20.* A summary operation.

This operation classifies R according to the λ (usually called the control break) value, and then generates a (summary) tuple for each class according to the β.

Although the summary can be defined as a procedural combination of two alpha operations, it can be implemented directly and much more efficiently using a sequential process (in the sequence of the λ value) applied to R. A summary operation is illustrated in Fig. 20.

5.6. Imaginary Tuples

If we would like to integrate database retrievals and updates in batch mode into the system by providing an appropriate alpha operation, we should encounter a difficulty that might occur in various file maintenance and report writing operations. In the file maintenance operation involving one master (relation) to be updated and one or more transactions (relations) to be used in updating the master, collating the master and transactions with a matching condition

$$\lambda(x_1, x_2, \ldots, x_m) \equiv \bigwedge_{k=1}^{m} (\mathscr{A}_p(x_1) = \mathscr{A}_p(x_k))$$

where $\mathscr{A}_p$ is a common primary key, is a basic procedure. A similar situation may occur in some report writing operations. The matching condition is certainly a relational calculus, and can be processed by an alpha operation.

However, in many applications there frequently occur the cases where a match is found except for some relations. For example, let R_{mst}, R_{whs}, and R_{dlv} be three relations representing an inventory master, a warehousing transaction, and a delivery transaction, respectively, in an inventory control application. Tuples in these relations are to be matched by a common primary key "part no." In this case, we must consider seven different matches, each specified by one of the following conditions:

1. For $R_{mst} \times R_{whs} \times R_{dlv}$:

$$\lambda_1(x_1, x_2, x_3) \equiv \text{part no}(x_1) = \text{part no}(x_2) \wedge \text{part no}(x_1) = \text{part no}(x_3)$$

2. For $R_{mst} \times R_{whs}$:

$$\lambda_2(x_1, x_2) \equiv \text{part no}(x_1) = \text{part no}(x_2) \wedge (\forall x_3/R_{dlv})\text{part no}(x_1)$$

$$\neq \text{part no}(x_3)$$

3. For $R_{mst} \times R_{dlv}$:

$$\lambda_3(x_1, x_3) \equiv \text{part no}(x_1) = \text{part no}(x_3) \wedge (\forall x_2/R_{whs})\text{part no}(x_1)$$

$$\neq \text{part no}(x_2)$$

4. For $R_{whs} \times R_{dlv}$:

$$\lambda_4(x_2, x_3) \equiv \text{part no}(x_2) = \text{part no}(x_3) \wedge (\forall x_1/R_{mst})\text{part no}(x_1)$$

$$\neq \text{part no}(x_2)$$

5. For R_{mst}:

$$\lambda_5(x_1) \equiv (\forall x_2/R_{whs})(\forall x/R_{dlv})$$

$$(\text{part no}(x_1) \neq \text{part no}(x_2) \wedge \text{part no}(x_1) \neq \text{part no}(x_3))$$

6. For R_{whs}:

$$\lambda_6(x_2) \equiv (\forall x_1/R_{mst})(\forall x_3/R_{dlv})$$

$$(\text{part no}(x_1) \neq \text{part no}(x_2) \wedge \text{part no}(x_2) \neq \text{part no}(x_3))$$

7. For R_{dlv}:

$$\lambda_7(x_3) \equiv (\forall x_1/R_{mst})(\forall x_2/R_{whs})$$

$$(\text{part no}(x_1) \neq \text{part no}(x_3) \wedge \text{part no}(x_2) \neq \text{part no}(x_3))$$

Figure 21 illustrates these seven matches. To generate a new tuple when a match is found (a tuple indicating an error sometimes having been found), a proper tuple-generating function of span 1, 2, or 3 must be assigned to

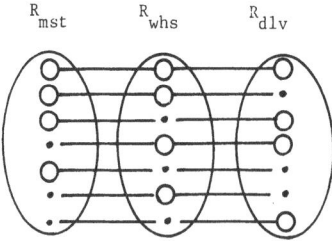

Fig. 21. Seven different matches.

each of the above seven matches. The new inventory master can be obtained by seven separate alpha operations corresponding to the seven cases above, followed by union operations combining their results; that is,

$$u(a[\beta_1 : \lambda_1](R_{mst}, R_{whs}, R_{dlv})$$

$$u(a[\beta_2 : \lambda_2](R_{mst}, R_{whs}), u(a[\beta_3 : \lambda_3](R_{mst}, R_{dlv}), u(a[\beta_4 : \lambda_4](R_{whs}, R_{dlv})$$

$$u(a[\beta_5 : \lambda_5](R_{mst}), u(a[\beta_6 : \lambda_6](R_{whs}), a[\beta_7 : \lambda_7](R_{dlv})))))))$$

where β_1, β_2, β_3, β_4, β_5, β_6, and β_7 are tuple-generating functions of lines defined on $R_{mst} \times R_{whs} \times R_{dlv}$, $R_{mst} \times R_{whs}$, $R_{mst} \times R_{dlv}$, $R_{whs} \times R_{dlv}$, R_{mst}, R_{whs}, and R_{dlv}, respectively. In particular,

$$\beta_5(x_1) \equiv x_1$$

This awkward description can be avoided if we add imaginary tuples as defined below to the relations to be collated. The *imaginary tuple* $\bar{\imath}_k$ of relation R_k is a tuple that is to be added to R_k. It acts as an existing tuple with appropriate attribute values when the λ value is evaluated, but it acts as a *null* tuple when the β value is calculated. An imaginary tuple $\bar{\imath}_k$, for which

$$\mathscr{A}_p(\bar{\imath}_k) = C$$

is activated when there exists a value C such that

1. $(\exists x_1 / R_1)(\exists x_2 / R_2) \cdots (\exists x_{k-1} / R_{k-1})(\exists x_{k+1} / R_{k+1}) \cdots (\exists x_m / R_m)$

$$\left(\bigwedge_{i=1}^{k-1} (\mathscr{A}_p(x_i) = C) \wedge \bigwedge_{i=k+1}^{m} (\mathscr{A}_p(x_i) = C) \right)$$

2. $(\forall x_k / R_k)(\mathscr{A}_p(x_k) \neq C)$

The tuple-generating function assigned to this case does not involve the variable x_k; that is,

$$\beta(t_1, t_2, \ldots, t_{k-1}, \bar{\imath}_k, t_{k+1}, \ldots, t_m) \equiv \beta_k(t_1, t_2, \ldots, t_{k-1}, t_{k+1}, \ldots, t_m)$$

Under the above condition for activating the imaginary tuple $\bar{\imath}_k$, other tuples in $R_1, R_2, \ldots, R_{k-1}, R_{k+1}, \ldots, R_m$, can also be imaginary. However, at least one of them must be an existing tuple. Let us denote $R_k \cup \{\bar{\imath}_k\}$ by $\bar{R}_k$.

When an imaginary tuple has been introduced into each of R_{mst}, R_{whs}, and R_{dlv}, the operation of obtaining the new inventory master can be described simply as

$$a[\beta : \lambda](\bar{R}_{mst}, \bar{R}_{whs}, \bar{R}_{dlv})$$

with

$$\lambda(x_1, x_2, x_3) \equiv \text{part no}(x_1) = \text{part no}(x_2) \wedge \text{part no}(x_1) = \text{part no}(x_3)$$

and

$$\beta(x_1, x_2, x_3) \equiv \begin{cases} \beta_1(x_1, x_2, x_3) & \text{if } x_1 \neq \bar{t}_1 \wedge x_2 \neq \bar{t}_2 \wedge x_3 \neq \bar{t}_3 \\ \beta_2(x_1, x_2) & \text{if } x_1 \neq \bar{t}_1 \wedge x_2 \neq \bar{t}_2 \wedge x_2 = \bar{t}_3 \\ \beta_3(x_1, x_3) & \text{if } x_1 \neq \bar{t}_1 \wedge x_2 = \bar{t}_2 \wedge x_3 \neq \bar{t}_3 \\ \beta_4(x_2, x_3) & \text{if } x_1 = \bar{t}_1 \wedge x_2 \neq \bar{t}_2 \wedge x_3 \neq \bar{t}_3 \\ x_1 & \text{if } x_1 \neq \bar{t}_1 \wedge x_2 = \bar{t}_2 \wedge x_3 = \bar{t}_3 \\ \beta_6(x_2) & \text{if } x_1 = \bar{t}_1 \wedge x_2 \neq \bar{t}_2 \wedge x_3 = \bar{t}_3 \\ \beta_7(x_3) & \text{if } x_1 = \bar{t}_1 \wedge x_2 = \bar{t}_2 \wedge x_3 \neq \bar{t}_3 \end{cases}$$

Introduction of the imaginary tuples allows not only a simple description of some traditional data processing operations but also an efficient implementation of operations to which a sequential collation is applicable.[59]

5.7. Navigations

When we distinguish relationship relations from entity relations, special alpha operations called· the *navigations* become important. In fact, the distinction between relationship relations and entity relations is significant only when we provide navigations.

Let R be a relationship relation with the attribute set $\mathscr{A}$ defined between an (entity or relationship) relation R_1 with the attribute set $\mathscr{A}_1$ and an (entity or relationship) relation R_2 with the attribute set $\mathscr{A}_2$. Assume that

$$\mathscr{A} = \mathscr{A}_{1r} \cup \mathscr{A}_{2r} \cup \mathscr{A}_o, \quad \mathscr{A}_{1r} \cap \mathscr{A}_o = \varnothing \quad \text{and} \quad \mathscr{A}_{2r} \cap \mathscr{A}_o = \varnothing$$

where $\mathscr{A}_{1r}$ and $\mathscr{A}_{2r}$ are a candidate key (set) of R_1 and that of R_2, respectively. Also assume that

$$\mathscr{A}_o = \{A_1, A_2, \ldots, A_h\}$$

$$\mathscr{A}_1 = \{A_{h+1}, A_{h+2}, \ldots, A_i\}$$

$$\mathscr{A}_2 = \{A_{i+1}, A_{i+2}, \ldots, A_j\}$$

Four kinds of navigations are defined as follows:

1. *Forward navigation* is defined by

$$n_f(t_1, R_2, R) = a[\beta:\lambda](R_2, R)$$

with

$$\lambda(x_2, x) \equiv \mathscr{A}_{1r}(x) = \mathscr{A}_{1r}(t_1) \wedge \mathscr{A}_{2r}(x) = \mathscr{A}_{2r}(x_2)$$

and

$$\beta(x_2, x) \equiv (A_1(x), A_2(x), \ldots, A_h(x), A_{i+1}(x_2), A_{i+2}(x_2), \ldots, A_j(x_2))$$

2. *Backward navigation* is defined by

$$n_b(R_1, t_2, R) = a[\beta:\lambda](R_1, R)$$

with

$$\lambda(x_1, x) \equiv \mathscr{A}_{1r}(x) = \mathscr{A}_{1r}(x_1) \wedge \mathscr{A}_{2r}(x) = \mathscr{A}_{2r}(t_2)$$

and

$$\beta(x_1, x) \equiv (A_1(x), A_2(x), \ldots, A_h(x), A_{h+1}(x_1), A_{h+2}(x_1), \ldots, A_i(x_1))$$

3. *Apices navigation* is defined by

$$n_a(R_2, R) = a[\beta:\lambda](R_2)$$

with

$$\lambda(x_2) \equiv (\forall x/R)\mathscr{A}_{2r}(x) \neq \mathscr{A}_{2r}(x_2)$$

and

$$\beta(x_2) \equiv x_2$$

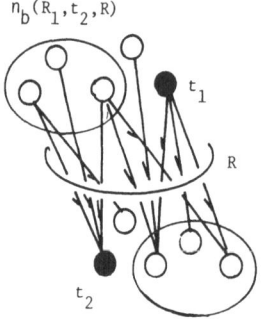

$n_f(t_1, R_2, R)$ *Fig. 22.* Forward and backward navigations.

4. *Terminals navigation* is defined by

$$n_t(R_1, R) = a[\beta : \lambda](R_1)$$

with

$$\lambda(x_1) \equiv (\forall x/R)\mathcal{A}_{1r}(x) \neq \mathcal{A}_{1r}(x_1)$$

and

$$\beta(x_1) \equiv x_1$$

The forward and backward navigation retrieve all the tuples that are connected, respectively, to t_1 and t_2 by some tuples in a relationship relation R. The apices navigation and the terminals navigation retrieve all the *apex* and *terminal* tuples, respectively, with respect to a relationship relation R. Note that the R_1 and R_2 can be the same relation. By these four kinds of navigations we can traverse the relationship relation R. Figure 22 illustrates a forward and a backward navigation.

Navigations are certainly special cases of the alpha operation; however, they can be implemented directly in more efficient ways, in particular, when the binary relationship relation is physically represented in some way different from the representation of entity relations.

Navigations in most cases are considered as lower level operations than other algebraic operations. However, in the system that distinguishes relationships from entities, navigations are as basic as other algebraic operations.

5.8. Disadvantages of Set Operations

So far we have obtained two levels of abstract database operations: (i) the alpha operation, and (ii) various algebraic operations, each being written as a special alpha operation or a procedural combination of two or more alpha operations. Operations in both levels are set operations. Both provide an excellent abstraction because they are powerful enough for describing a wealth of data processing operations. Given a data processing operation, we can describe it as a set operations or a procedural combination of more than one set operation.

However, if a given data processing operation is to be executed by a procedural execution of more than one set operation, we suffer two major difficulties. One is the malperformance caused mainly by redundant data transfers among a hierarchy of storage devices, and the other is the difficulty in checking integrity and security constraints.

Assume that the summary operation is not implemented as an independent operation and is to be executed procedurally by two alpha operations (see Section 5.5). Let us consider a simple summary operation

$$g[\gamma:\lambda](R_{emp}) = a[\beta:T](a[\beta':T](R_{emp}))$$

with

$$\beta'(x) \equiv (dept(x))$$

and

$$\beta(x') \equiv \left(dept(x'), \sum_{x \in R_{emp} \wedge dept(x)=dept(x')} salary(x) \right)$$

for $x' \in a[\beta':T](R_{emp})$

Then this summary operation can be achieved by a program like

$$begin\ TMP:=a[\beta':T](EMP);$$

$$SUM:=a[\beta:T](TMP)\ end;$$

Since the second arguments of the first and second statements are T (assigning the value "true" to all tuples), both statements fetch all tuples in R_{emp}. On the other hand, we know that the same summary operation can be achieved in one sequential read operation applied to R_{emp} if tuples in R_{emp} are physically arranged in the sequence of values of "dept."

Also assume that the imaginary tuples are not integrated in the process of alpha operations, and that the file maintenance must be achieved by a procedural execution of several alpha operations. Let us consider a simple file maintenance operation with one master and one transaction; that is,

$$u(a[\beta_1:\lambda_1](R_{mst}, R_{trs}), u(a[\beta_2:\lambda_2](R_{mst}), a[\beta_3:\lambda_3](R_{trs})))$$

with

$$\lambda_1(x_1, x_2) \equiv id(x_1) = id(x_2)$$

$$\lambda_2(x_1) \equiv (\forall x_2/R_{trs})id(x_1) \neq id(x_2)$$

and

$$\lambda_3(x_2) \equiv (\forall x_1/R_{mst})id(x_1) \neq id(x_2)$$

This operation can be achieved by a program like

$$\text{begin TMP1} := a[\beta_1:\lambda_1](\text{MST, TRS});$$

$$\text{TMP2} := a[\beta_2:\lambda_2](\text{MST});$$

$$\text{TMP3} := a[\beta_3:\lambda_3](\text{TRS});$$

$$\text{TMP4} := u(\text{TMP2, TMP3});$$

$$\text{MST} := u(\text{TMP1, TMP4}) \text{ end};$$

The last statement implies that the relation R_{emp} is to be replaced with the result of this operation. The first statement fetches all tuples in both R_{emp} and R_{tras}; the second statement fetches all tuples in R_{mst}; and the third statement fetches all tuples in R_{trs}. The results of these three operations are newly created relations, which are to be kept in appropriate storage areas. They are R_{tmp1}, R_{tmp2} and R_{tmp3}. All tuples in R_{tmp2} and R_{tmp3} are fetched again by the fourth statement, a new relation R_{tmp4} is created, and it is kept in an appropriate storage area. Finally, all tuples in R_{tmp1} and R_{tmp4} are fetched by the fifth statement, and R_{mst} is replaced with the result of this operation. We know that the same file maintenance can be achieved by one sequential read/write operation applied to R_{mst} and R_{trs} (read only), if tuples in both relations are physically arranged in the sequence of values of "id."

For the second example, which updates the relation R_{mst}, one more difficulty exists in the integrity and security mechanisms. As the result of updating R_{mst}, some tuples are added to R_{mst}, some tuples are deleted from R_{mst} (this happens when the tuple-generating function of lines generates a null tuple), and some tuples in R_{mst} are modified. Integrity and security checking must be made separately for each of these three cases. However, in the above program each of the first four statements generates a new relation, and the last statement replaces an old relation completely with a newly generated relation. It is extremely difficult to make the desired integrity and security checking during the execution of such a program.

The first example can be achieved by a single statement

$$SUM := g[\gamma : \lambda](EMP)$$

if the summary operation is implemented as an independent operation. Also the second example can be achieved by a single statement

$$MST := a[\beta : \lambda](\overline{MST}, \overline{TRS})$$

if the imaginary tuples are integrated in the process of alpha operations. If the given data processing can be achieved by a single set operation, we need not be concerned with these two difficulties. This is because such a single statement does not direct any specific execution sequence of more elementary operations, which are necessary to achieve this operation.

We might implement any data processing patterns as an independent operation when it becomes necesary; however, the number of such patterns are not finite, and hence we must achieve the given data processing by a procedural execution of more than one set operation, very frequently.

5.9. Tuple-by-Tuple Operations

To reduce the number of data transfers, we may decompose the alpha operations into *tuple-by-tuple operations*. These tuple-by-tuple operations can then be combined in the appropriate sequence needed to achieve the required data manipulation. By arranging these operations in a proper sequence, we can remove redundant data transfers that were unavoidable in a procedural execution of set operations. The difficulty in integrity and security mechanisms can also be removed if we use these tuple-by-tuple operations.

Three classes of tuple-by-tuple operations are obtained by decomposing the alpha operation. The first class includes data transfers from database relations (usually stored in some external storage devices) to main storage. Every program loaded in main storage is provided with a *workspace* for each relation to which the program has access. A workspace can accommodate a tuple at a time. Operations in this class, which we call the *read class*, fetch a tuple from a relation into the workspace provided for this relation. A read class operation may fetch a line (an ordered set of tuples) and send

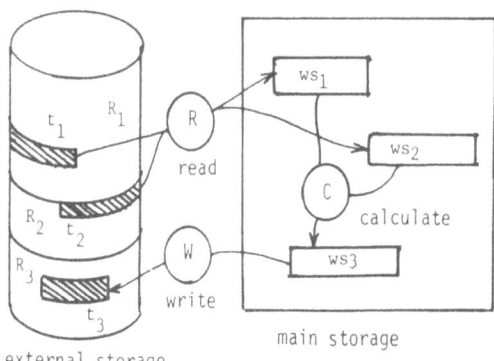

main storage   *Fig. 23. Tuple-by-tuple operations.*

each component tuple (point) to the workspace for the relation to which it belongs.

The second class includes operations generating a new tuple from one or more tuples in the workspaces. The generated tuple is stored in an appropriate workspace. This class is called the *calculate class.* The calculate class also includes some control transfer operations, which determine the operation to be executed next with reference to the value of a certain function of tuples.

The last class, which we call the *write class,* is composed of update operations. These add, delete, or replace a tuple in a relation with reference to a tuple currently in a specific workspace.

These three classes of tuple-by-tuple operations (called the piped mode operations by Codd[28]) are illustrated in Fig. 23.

5.9.1. Read Class Operations

Let $a[\lambda](R_1, R_2, \ldots, R_m)$ be composed of k lines, $l_1, l_2, \ldots, l_k$, where

$$l_i = (t_{i1}, t_{i2}, \ldots, t_{im})$$

and $t_{ij} \in R_j$. We assume that these k lines are arranged in the order of values of a specified function λ' of lines defined on $R_1 \times R_2 \times \cdots \times R_m$, that is,

$$\lambda'(l_1) \le \lambda'(l_2) \le \cdots \le \lambda'(l_k)$$

Let ws_j be the workspace assigned to R_j, and c_j be the *cursor* for R_j. The cursor is a temporary storage area that can accommodate a primary key value (which can be replaced by the record address when tuples are represented by physical records in the physical database) of a tuple in R_j. The contents of a cursor indicate the tuple that was most recently fetched into the workspace.

Decomposing this search operation, we obtain the following two read class operations:

1. *Get first* (qualified line)

$$G_f(R_1, R_2, \ldots, R_m; \lambda, \lambda'; c_1, c_2, \ldots, c_m)$$

which fetches t_{1j} into ws_j, and stores its primary key in c_j, for $j = 1, 2, \ldots, m$.

2. *Get next* (qualified line)

$$G_n(R_1, R_2, \ldots, R_m; \lambda, \lambda'; c_1, c_2, \ldots, c_m)$$

which, provided that each c_j contains the primary key of t_{ij}, fetches $t_{(i+1)j}$ into ws_j, and stores its primary key in c_j for $j = 1, 2, \ldots, m$.

Any R_j can be extended to $\bar{R}_j$, which includes an imaginary tuple $\bar{t}_j$. Note that the λ can be T, which is a function of lines that assigns the value "true" to every line in $R_1 \times R_2 \times \cdots \times R_m$. If $\lambda \equiv T$ and $m = 1$, then G_f and G_n execute a sort operation with sort key λ'.

Although navigations are special alpha operations, many applications use them frequently. Hence, we should decompose navigations into tuple-by-tuple operations separately. Since relationship relations are very often physically represented in a somewhat different manner from that in which entity relations are represented, navigations are usually implemented differently from other search operations.

Let $n_f(t, R_2, R)$ be composed of k tuples, $t_1, t_2, \ldots, t_k$. We assume that these tuples are arranged in the order of values of a specified function λ' of points defined on $n_f(t, R_2, R)$, that is,

$$\lambda'(t_1) \leq \lambda'(t_2) \leq \cdots \leq \lambda'(t_k)$$

Let ws_2 and ws be two workspaces assigned to R_2 and R, respectively. The workspace ws becomes necessary only when R has some attributes other than its origin $\mathscr{A}_{1r}$ and destination $\mathscr{A}_{2r}$, that is, $\mathscr{A}_o \neq \varnothing$ (see Section 5.7). We must have two cursors c_1 and c_2 for R_1 and R_2, respectively. The cursor c_1 is that which was used when t was fetched into the workspace for R_1 by some other read class operation. Then we obtain the following two read class operations:

3. *Get first child* (with respect to λ')

$$G_{fc}(R_1, R_2, R; \lambda'; c_1, c_2)$$

which, provided that c_1 contains the primary key of t, fetches t_1 into ws_2 (values of attributes in $\mathcal{A}_o$ are fetched into ws if $\mathcal{A}_o \neq \varnothing$) and stores its primary key in c_2.

4. *Get next child* (with respect to λ')

$$G_{nc}(R_1, R_2, R; \lambda'; c_1, c_2)$$

which, provided that c_1 contains the primary key of t and c_2 contains the primary key of t_i, fetches t_{i+1} into ws_2 (values of attributes in $\mathcal{A}_o$ are fetched into ws if $\mathcal{A}_o \neq \varnothing$) and stores its primary key in c_2.

In some systems a sequence can be predefined in $n_f(t, R_2, R)$ for every t in R_1 (DBTG proposed such a system[22]). In this case, we can have:

3a. *Get first child* (with respect to the predefined sequence)

$$G'_{fc}(R_1, R_2, R; c_1, c_2)$$

4a. *Get next child* (with respect to the predefined sequence)

$$G'_{nc}(R_1, R_2, R; c_1, c_2)$$

In addition to these two operations, we may have:

3b. *Get last child* (with respect to the predefined sequence)

$$G'_{lc}(R_1, R_2, R; c_1, c_2)$$

4b. *Get previous child* (with respect to the predefined sequence)

$$G'_{pc}(R_1, R_2, R; c_1, c_2)$$

Operations G_{nc}, G'_{nc}, and G'_{pc} are necessary only when R is a tree or a network. The argument c_1 is not necessarily specified for G_{nc}, G'_{nc}, and G'_{pc} unless R is a network.

In a similar way, assuming

$$n_b(R_1, t, R) = \{t_1, t_2, \ldots, t_k\}$$

with

$$\lambda'(t_1) \leq \lambda'(t_2) \leq \cdots \leq \lambda'(t_k)$$

we obtain:

5. *Get first parent* (with respect to λ')

$$G_{fp}(R_1, R_2, R; \lambda'; c_1, c_2)$$

which, provided that c_2 contains the primary key of t, fetches t_1 into ws_1 (values of attributes in $\mathcal{A}_o$ are fetched into ws if $\mathcal{A}_o \neq \varnothing$) and stores its primary key in c_1.

6. *Get next parent* (with respect to λ')

$$G_{np}(R_1, R_2, R; \lambda'; c_1, c_2)$$

which, provided that c_2 contains the primary key of t and c_1 contains the primary key of t_i, fetches t_{i+1} into ws_1 (values of attributes in $\mathcal{A}_o$ are fetched into ws if $\mathcal{A}_o \neq \varnothing$) and stores its primary key in c_1.

If a sequence is predefined in $n_b(R_1, t, R)$ for every t in R_2, we may have:

5a. *Get first parent* (with respect to the predefined sequence)

$$G'_{fp}(R_1, R_2, R; c_1, c_2)$$

6a. *Get next parent* (with respect to the predefined sequence)

$$G'_{np}(R_1, R_2, R; c_1, c_2)$$

5b. *Get last parent* (with respect to the predefined sequence)

$$G'_{lp}(R_1, R_2, R; c_1, c_2)$$

6b. *Get previous parent* (with respect to the predefined sequence)

$$G'_{pp}(R_1, R_2, R; c_1, c_2)$$

Operations G_{np}, G'_{np}, and G'_{pp} are necessary only when R is a backward tree or a network. The argument c_2 is not necessarily specified for G_{np}, G'_{np}, and G'_{pp} unless R is a network.

Let $n_a(R_2, R)$ be composed of k tuples, $t_1, t_2, \ldots, t_k$, where

$$\lambda'(t_1) \le \lambda'(t_2) \le \cdots \le \lambda'(t_k)$$

for a specified function λ' of points defined on $n_a(R_2, R)$. Then by decomposing this apices navigation, we obtain:

7. *Get first apex* (with respect to λ')

$$G_{fa}(R_2, R; \lambda'; c_2)$$

which fetches t_1 into ws_2 and stores its primary key in c_2.

8. *Get next apex* (with respect to λ')

$$G_{na}(R_2, R; \lambda'; c_2)$$

which, provided that c_2 contains the primary key of t_i, fetches t_{i+1} into ws_2 and stores its primary key in c_2.

In a similar way, assuming

$$n_t(R_1, R) = \{t_1, t_2, \ldots, t_k\}$$

with

$$\lambda'(t_1) \le \lambda'(t_2) \le \cdots \le \lambda'(t_k)$$

we obtain:

9. *Get first terminal* (with respect to λ')

$$G_{ft}(R_1, R; \lambda'; c_1)$$

which fetches t_1 into ws_1 and stores its primary key in c_1.

10. *Get next terminal* (with respect to λ')

$$G_{nt}(R_1, R; \lambda'; c_1)$$

which, provided that c_1 contains the primary key of t_i, fetches t_{i+1} into ws_1 and stores its primary key in c_1.

We can traverse any relationship relation in any direction using G_{fa}, G_{na}, G_{ft}, G_{nt}, G_{fc}, G_{nc}, G_{fp}, and G_{np}. Sometimes it is convenient to use G'_{fc}, G'_{nc}, G'_{lc}, G'_{pc}, G'_{fp}, G'_{np}, G'_{lp}, and G'_{pp} instead of G_{fc}, G_{nc}, G_{fp}, and G_{np}.

When a read class operation is invoked but there are no tuples or lines to be fetched into workspaces, the read class operation must fill the workspaces with special tuples Δ telling no more qualified tuples or lines exist.

5.9.2. Calculate Class Operations

Operations in the calculate class generate a new tuple in a specified workspace with reference to one or more tuples in some other workspaces. This implies calculation of a tuple-generating function. This class also contains control transfer operations which beocme necessary for selecting the tuple-by-tuple operation to be executed next with reference to a given or a calculated value. Operations in this class can be effectively described by most existing programming languages (host languages).

If an aggregation becomes necessary for making a (summary) tuple, we must define three tuple-generating functions of lines. The first function is a tuple-generating function of points that specifies the initialization procedure; the second is a tuple-generating function of lines of span 2 that specifies the accumulation procedure; and the third is a tuple-generating function of points that specifies the finalization procedure. For example, if we would like to generate a summary tuple for each subset of tuples with a common value of attribute A_1 by accumulating values of attribute A_2, we define three tuple-generating functions of lines

$$\beta_I(x) \equiv (A_1(x), A_2(x))$$

$$\beta_A(x', x) \equiv (A_1(x'), A_2(x') + A_2(x))$$

and

$$\beta_F(x') \equiv x'$$

Tuples x in R are fetched into the workspace for R one by one. To generate a summary tuple, we provide another workspace in which x' is to be stored. By fetching tuples in R in the order of values of A_1, we can generate the summary tuples using these three tuple-generating functions.

5.9.3. Write Class Operations

We need the following two operations for generating and updating database relations.

    1. *Add*

$$U_a(R)$$

which adds the tuple currently in the workspace for R to R.

2. *Delete*

$$U_d(c)$$

which deletes the tuple pointed to by the cursor c from R.

A new relation can be generated by adding tuples to an empty relation. However, an empty relation is inconsistent if an existential constraint is imposed on its relation schema. In this case, a certain special treatment must be made.

3. *Replace*

$$U_r(R, c)$$

which replaces the tuple pointed by the cursor c with the tuple currently in the workspace for R.

Although it can be written as a combination of a delete and an add operation, replace is convenient. This is because it is desirable to assign the address which has been occupied by the deleted tuple to the tuple to be added.

According to the assertions regarding the relation R, some other update operations with somewhat different semantics can be devised. For example, whenever a tuple in a relation R is deleted, any tuple whose origin or destination is the deleted tuple must also be deleted. We may have various update operations regarding various types of relationship relations.

5.9.4. Procedural Execution of Tuple-by-Tuple Operations

We will here describe the two examples presented in Section 5.8 in terms of tuple-by-tuple operations. The first example can be described as

```
begin Gf(EMP;T,dept;c);
    while not EMP↑=Δ do
  begin temp:=dept(EMP↑); SUM↑:=(dept(EMP↑),salary(EMP↑));
        Gn(EMP;T,dept;c);
        while temp=dept(EMP↑) do
    begin SUM↑:=(dept(SUM↑),salary(SUM↑)+salary(EMP↑));
          Gn(EMP;T,dept;c)
    end;
        Ua(SUM)
  end
end;
```

where EMP↑ and SUM↑ are the workspaces for EMP and SUM, respectively. In the third line of this program

$$\text{SUM}{\uparrow} := (\text{dept}(\text{EMP}{\uparrow}), \text{salary}(\text{EMP}{\uparrow}))$$

specifies β_I (see Section 5.9.2), while in the sixth line

$$\text{SUM}{\uparrow} := (\text{dept}(\text{SUM}{\uparrow}), \text{salary}(\text{SUM}{\uparrow}) + \text{salary}(\text{EMP}{\uparrow}))$$

specifies β_A. Since β_F is in this case an identity function, we used SUM↑ also for accumulating. It is easy to see that this program produces much better performance than a procedural combination of alpha operations does.

The second example can be described as

```
begin Gf(MST,TRS;lambda,id;c1,c2);
      while not MST↑=Δ do
    begin if not TRS↑=Ω then
      begin temp:=id(MST↑); MST↑:=beta(MST↑,TRS↑);
            if temp=Ω then Ua(MST) else if MST↑=Ω then Ud(c1)
            else Ur(MST,c1)
      end;
            Gn(MST,TRS;lambda,id;c1,c2)
    end
end;
```

where Ω is a special value indicating an imaginary tuple or a null tuple. The lambda and beta must be defined elsewhere as function subprograms.

The alpha operations as well as other algebraic operations defined in terms of alpha operations can be implemented efficiently using these tuple-by-tuple operations.

5.10. Data Manipulation Requirements

After the logical data structure that reflects the real world of interest has been determined, we must clarify our data manipulation requirements. We will consider this for each class of tuple-by-tuple operations.

We have two types of operations in the read class; those obtained by decomposing $s[\lambda](R_1, R_2, \ldots, R_m)$, and those obtained by decomposing $n_f(t_1, R_2, R)$, $n_b(R_1, t_2, R)$, $n_a(R_2, R)$ and $n_t(R_1, R)$.

For the tuple-by-tuple search operations, the complexity of the search condition must be examined. We know that the search condition, in general, is a logical function of lines $\lambda(x_1, x_2, \ldots, x_m)$, with m free tuple variables, $x_1, x_2, \ldots, x_m$. The function λ can contain some other variables, each bound by a universal or existential quantifier or by some other means.

The simplest search condition is of the form

$$\lambda(x) \equiv \mathscr{A}_p(x) = \text{const}$$

defined on a single relation whose primary key is $\mathscr{A}_p$. The tuple-by-tuple operation with a search condition of this form is just the direct-access operation.

On the other hand, the most complicated search condition is an extended relational calculus with more than one free variable and one or more bound variables.

Between the above two extremes we have search conditions of various complexity. The following are examples of such complexity levels:

(1) $\lambda(x) \equiv \mathscr{A}_p = \text{const}$;
(2) $\lambda(x) \equiv A_k = \text{const}$ (for an arbitrary attribute A_k);
(3) $\lambda(x) \equiv A_k(x)\ \theta\ \text{const}$ (for an arbitrary relational operator θ);
(4) a logical combination of conditions in level (3);
(5) an arbitrary logical function defined on R (for example $A_i(x) \times 3 < A_j(x)$);
(6) $\lambda(x_1, x_2) \equiv \lambda_1(x_1)\theta\lambda_2(x_2)$ (for arbitrary functions λ_1 and λ_2 of points defined respectively on R_1 and R_2);
(7) an arbitrary logical function of lines of span 2 defined on $R_1 \times R_2$ without bound variables;
(8) an arbitrary logical function of lines of span m defined on $R_1 \times R_2 \times \cdots \times R_m$ without bound variables;
(9) an arbitrary logical function of lines of span m defined on $R_1 \times R_2 \times \cdots \times R_m$ with one or more bound variables.

It is very desirable for the later design stage to estimate which levels of search conditions will become necessary and how frequently they will be requested. Also, the frequency of each attribute (or function of points to be calculated from basic functions of points) appearing in the requested search conditions, if it can be predicted, is helpful for determining which attributes (or functions of points) are to be indexed.

As for the tuple-by-tuple navigation, we must examine which relationship relations will be traversed and how frequently. In most cases, not all eight types of tuple-by-tuple navigations are required. Relationship relations are usually represented in a manner different from the representation of entity relations. The above information can be used to select a specific physical representation of each relationship relation from several different methods.

Since most existing basic programming languages have an adequate capability for describing the calculate class operations, we can employ one or more of them for describing operations in this class. The selected basic programming languages are called *host languages*. Selection can be made according to the type of application; for example, COBOL seems suitable for implementing a management information system, while FORTRAN can be used for implementing an engineering information system. In this chapter, a PASCAL-like language is used as an example of the host language.

The three write class operations—add, delete, and replace—can describe any update of database relations. However, it must be noted that a single write class operation does not always preserve assertions imposed on the database. If it violates one or more assertions, a write class operation produces an inconsistent state of the database. To restore the database to a consistent state, one or more other write class operations must be executed. It is sometimes desirable to provide collective update operations which makes several updates collectively and thereby preserves assertions.

In particular, when a relationship relation is defined over one or more other relations, tuples in this relationship relation must be updated whenever a tuple is added to, or deleted from, a relation on which the relationship relation is defined. For example, as mentioned previously, a tuple in a relationship relation must be deleted whenever its origin or destination tuple is deleted. This is due to the relationship constraint (Section 4.6.2). If a sequence is defined on a relation, an add or a delete operation applied to this relation always results in one or more updates applied to the sequence (a recursive relationship relation). This is due to the relationship constraint and the constraints defining the sequence (see Section 4.6.4). If there is a multilevel hierarchy defined over several relations, deletion of a tuple in one of these relations triggers a cascaded deletion of all the descendant tuples with respect to this multilevel hierarchy. This is due to the relationship constraints and the constraints defining the multilevel hierarchy (see Section 4.6.5).

The update frequency as well as the search (including navigation) frequency affects the physical database design. In general, there is a trade-off between search performance and update performance. The physical representation of database relations may vary according to the ratio between the frequency of read class and write class operations.

We should estimate how frequently write class operations will be requested, and which, and how frequently, collective update operations will be requested.

6. OTHER REQUIREMENTS

Up to this point, we have clarified both the logical data structure to be represented in the database and the basic manipulating operations to be applied to the database. In addition to these basic requirements, we need to consider and determine other factors such as integrity, security, concurrency, recoverability, and database distribution.

6.1. Integrity

As described in Section 4, there may be various semantic constraints on the database relation schemata, some of which must be registered as assertions.

Assertions can be registered in the (intention) database in several different ways. Domain constraints are usually registered by specifying the domain for each attribute. For each relation schema, the key dependency regarding the selected primary key can be registered by underlining attributes constituting the primary key. Relationship constraints can be registered by defining entity relations and relationship relations separately. Semantic constraints classifying relationship relations can be registered by specifying the relationship relation type when defining a relationship relation. All these are integrated in the database description and must be preserved by the system when the database is updated. To preserve assertions, improper (with respect to assertions) updates must be rejected (see Section 4.3).

If we could register assertions in predicate calculus form, and if the system were able to automatically preserve these assertions when the database was updated, the programming effort might be greatly reduced. Such a feature would be very desirable since the registered assertions themselves could also become the objects to be retrieved or used as deductive rules in advanced question answering functions (see Section 11).

An automatic integrity preservation mechanism based on assertions registered in predicate calculus form is used in INGRES.[87] It deals with assertions without existentially quantified variables. Here we will consider integrity preservation for an arbitrary assertion.

Static constraints can be described by schema calculi of the form

$$Q_1' Q_2' \cdots Q_m' \lambda (x_1, x_2, \ldots, x_m)$$

where Q_k' is either $(\forall x_k / \mathcal{R}_{p_k})$ or $(\exists x_k / \mathcal{R}_{p_k})$. At any time τ, we can examine whether or not the database is consistent by examining whether

$$Q_1 Q_2 \cdots Q_k \lambda (x_1, x_2, \ldots, x_m)$$

where

$$Q_k \equiv (\forall x_k / R_k^\tau) \qquad \text{if } Q_k' \text{ is } (\forall x_k / \mathscr{R}_{p_k})$$

or

$$Q_k \equiv (\exists x_k / R_k^\tau) \qquad \text{if } Q_k' \text{ is } (\exists x_k / \mathscr{R}_{p_k})$$

is "true" or not for all the static constraints registered as assertions. The latter form is an extended relational calculus. As will be mentioned later, we can devise a general algorithm to process given extended relational calculi with or without free variables. It is an algorithm of searching a tuple or an ordered set of tuples that satisfies the given extended relational calculus. If the given calculus has no free variables, the search result is "true" or "false." Therefore, we can use this algorithm for examining whether or not the database at a given time is consistent.

If an update has been executed and the database is still consistent, the update can be *proper*. (It can be *improper* because it might violate some dynamic constraints.) If the database becomes inconsistent after the update, the update is *improper*. In the latter case, the database must be restored, and the update must be rejected. However, examining the consistency of the database using a general search algorithm is in most cases unnecessarily time-consuming. We usually can devise a more efficient validation procedure.

In an update operation, each tuple to be updated may be from a relation over whose relation schema one or more tuple variables are quantified in some assertions. In an assertion such a tuple variable is called an *update-relevant variables*. We will first consider *unit updates* in which only one tuple is to be updated.

If the update-relevant variable is universally quantified in the first quantification of an assertion and all other update-relevant variables are universally quantified, this assertion can be written as

$$(\forall x_1 / \mathscr{R}_{p_k}) \lambda'(x_1)$$

where x_1 is a free variable in $\lambda'(x_1)$. The calculus $\lambda'(x_1)$ has now $m - 1$ ($m \geq 1$) quantified variables. Then the update can be validated as follows.

If the update involves adding a tuple t or replacing a tuple t' by t, examine the $\lambda'(t)$ value. If it is "true," the update is proper (with regard to this assertion). If it is "false," the update is improper and must be rejected. If the update involves deleting a tuple t', then it is always proper (with regard to this assertion). This procedure is certainly more efficient than validating this assertion using the universal search algorithm. In fact, this procedure eliminates evaluation of the universal quantifier that binds variable x_1, which is a time-consuming task if the search result is not empty.

If an update-relevant variable is existentially quantified in the first quantification of an assertion and all other update-relevant variables are existentially quantified, this assertion can be written as

$$(\exists x_1/\mathscr{R}_{p_k})\lambda'(x_1)$$

where x_1 is a free variable in $\lambda'(x_1)$. Then the update can be validated as follows.

If the update involves adding a tuple t, the update is always proper (with regard to this assertion). If the update involves replacing a tuple t' by t, a procedure is required that is a little complicated. If value of $\lambda'(t')$ is "false," the update is proper (with regard to this assertion). If it is "true," examine the $\lambda'(t)$ value; if it is "true," the update is also "proper" (with regard to this assertion); if it is "false," a search with $\lambda'(x_1)$ as the search condition must be applied to R_1. If at least one tuple t'' for which $\lambda'(t'')$ is "true" is found, the update is proper (with regard to this assertion). Otherwise, the update is improper, and must be rejected. Finally, if the update involves deleting a tuple t', examine the value of $\lambda'(t')$; if it is "false," the update is proper (with regard to this assertion); if it is "true," a search with $\lambda'(x_1)$ as the search condition must be applied to R_1. If at least one tuple t'' is found for which $\lambda'(t'')$ is "true," the update is proper (with regard to this assertion). Otherwise, it is improper and must be rejected. In both cases, validity can be assured before actual execution of the update. This makes the database restoration procedure unnecessary.

If the update-relevant variable is not the first quantified variable, the above procedure is not applicable. However, since two adjacent universal quantifications as well as two adjacent existential quantifications are interchangeable, we can, in some cases, move the quantification of the update-relevant variable into the first position.

Tuple constraint can be assured easily using the above procedure. The $\lambda'(x_1)$ part includes no bound variables in this case. For other universal constraints, the $\lambda'(x_1)$ part includes one or more bound variables, and hence, in general, a search must be made to examine whether this part is "true" or "false" for the given tuple (t or t') if the update involves adding a tuple t or replacing a tuple t' by t.

However, the key dependency regarding the selected primary key can be assured in a manner that is a little simpler. If the update involves modification of some nonkey attribute values of an existing tuple, this update is always proper (with regard to the key dependency). Only when a tuple is to be added or key attribute values of an existing tuple is to be modified must we assure the key dependency by testing to see that no tuples have the primary key value equal to that of the tuple to be added or modified.

This can be done efficiently if tuples are arranged in the order of key attribute values. The main purpose of the third and Boyce–Codd normal form is to allow such a simpler validation procedure for the functional dependencies, each represented by one relation schema. Note, however, that we should not forget assurance of into (and onto) constraints which are newly generated as the result of normal form decompositions.

There could exist some other cases for which a more efficient validation procedure than applying the universal search algorithm exists. These are left for future study.

Some assertions are always violated when a single-unit update, which adds, deletes, or replaces only one tuple, is performed. We have already discussed the cases where a relationship relation schema is defined on one or more (entity or relationship) relations (see Section 5.10). Assertions such as

$$(\forall x_1 / \mathcal{R}_{p_1})(\exists x_2 / \mathcal{R}_{p_2}) A_1(x_1) = A_2(x_2)$$

and

$$(\forall x_1 / \mathcal{R}_{p_1}) A_1(x_1) = \sum_{(x_2 \in \mathcal{R}_{p_2} \wedge A_2(x_1) = A_2(x_2))} A_1(x_2)$$

are also violated by some unit updates. For the former, deletion of a tuple t_2 in a relation R_2 in $\mathcal{R}_{p_2}$ violates the assertion if t_2 is the only tuple in R_2 for which the A_2 value is $A_2(t_2)$. For the latter, deletion of a tuple t_2 in a relation R_2 in $\mathcal{R}_{p_2}$ violates the assertion if $A_1(t_2) \neq 0$.

To keep the database consistent with regard to these assertions, all the related updates must be executed collectively. However, all these updates must be achieved by combining two or more unit updates—all add, delete, or replace only one tuple. A *temporary inconsistency* is generated during the term from the first unit update to the last unit update. For such cases, validation procedure must be undone, or be executed after all the related updates have been completed.

Some such updates can be implemented as collective updates. If an appropriate collective update is not implemented, the user must define a *transaction* by declaring *start-of-transaction* before the first unit update is executed and *end-of-transaction* after the last unit update is completed.

During the term in which a certain temporary inconsistency exists in the database, all tuples (including *phantoms*, which are currently not in the database but may be added to the database) related to the update that caused this inconsistency, must be prevented from other accesses. This matter will be discussed later in Section 6.3.

After the update has been validated with regard to all the static constraints registered as assertions, it must be determined if this update violates the registered dynamic constraints. The validation procedure varies according to the form of the dynamic constraint.

6.2. Security

The database may be used by a large number of users, although certain parts of the database must be protected against unauthorized disclosure to some users. In particular, provisions must be made to prevent a person with ulterior motives from surreptitious use or destruction of the database.

Many distinct levels of security or privacy protection must be made, and a variety of implementations have been proposed. However, database security design and implementation remain more an art than a science.

For the tuple-by-tuple operations of the read class, security can be considered as a set of pairs

$$\mathscr{S}_R \subset U \times \Gamma$$

where U is the set of users (which may be represented by the set of passwords given to the users) and Γ is the set of all possible alpha operations. If a pair (u, a) belongs to $\mathscr{S}_R$, the user u is authorized to make access to any element in the result of alpha operation a. Practically, security can be defined only in terms of the alpha operations that will be applied to a single relation, that is, $\mathscr{S}_R$ can be regarded as a set of quadruples

$$\mathscr{S}_R \subset U \times \Lambda \times B \times \mathscr{R}$$

where Λ is the set of search conditions on a relation (logical functions of points), B is the set of tuple-generating functions of points, and $\mathscr{R}$ is the set of relation schemas in the database. The set B can further be restricted to the tuple-generating functions that extract some attribute values from the given tuple. In this case, B can be replaced by $\mathscr{P}(\mathscr{A})$, the power set of the set $\mathscr{A}$ of all attributes of relation schemata in the database schema.

Given two quadruples $(u, \lambda_1, \beta_1, \mathscr{R}_{p_1})$ and $(u, \lambda_2, \beta_2, \mathscr{R}_{p_2})$ in $\mathscr{S}_R$, the user u is granted access to any tuples in $\mathsf{a}[\beta_1 : \lambda_1](R_1)$, $\mathsf{a}[\beta_2 : \lambda_2](R_2)$, $\mathsf{m}(\mathsf{a}[\beta_1 : \lambda_1](R_1), \mathsf{a}[\beta_2 : \lambda_2](R_2))$, and any relation obtained by applying a projection to one of these three, where R_1 and R_2 are the current relations in $\mathscr{R}_{p_1}$ and $\mathscr{R}_{p_2}$, respectively.

Let us assume here that user u is assigned m such quadruples $(u, \lambda_1, \beta_1, \mathscr{R}_{p_1}), (u, \lambda_2, \beta_2, \mathscr{R}_{p_2}), \ldots, (u, \lambda_m, \beta_m, \mathscr{R}_{p_m})$. When the user u

invokes a tuple-by-tuple search operation with a search condition

$$\lambda(x_1, x_2, \ldots, x'_m)$$

applied to $R'_1 \times R'_2 \times \cdots \times R'_{m'}$, the security assurance can be achieved by the following three steps:

1. Ascertain that

$$\{R''_1, R''_2, \ldots, R''_{m'}\} \subset \{R_1, R_2, \ldots, R_m\}$$

where R_k is the current relation in $\mathscr{R}_{p_k}$ for $k = 1, 2, \ldots, m$, and

$$R'_k \subset R''_k$$

for $k = 1, 2, \ldots, m'$. If λ contains bound variables, they must also be bound over some of $R_1, R_2, \ldots, R_m$. Let us assume that $R''_k = R_k$ for simplicity.

2. Execute the specified read class operation. Then, for each ordered set $(t_1, t_2, \ldots, t_m)$ of tuples (line) obtained, assure that $\lambda_k(t_k)$ becomes "true" for $k = 1, 2, \ldots, m'$. This assurance might be made without actual execution of the read class operation if

$$(\forall x_1 / R_1)(\forall x_2 / R_2) \cdots (\forall x_{m'} / R_{m'})\left(\lambda(x_1, x_2, \ldots, x_{m'}) \rightarrow \bigwedge_{k=1}^{m'} \lambda_k(x_k)\right)$$

could be proven in some other way. However, such a problem is in general recursively undecidable, and can be solved only in special cases.

3. Assure that the user u accesses only attribute values he is granted to access with reference to the third component of quadruples in $\mathscr{S}_R$.

When either the first or the second assurance fails, the subject read class operation must be rejected. For the third assurance, it is better to mask all the attribute values that are not disclosed to the user.

It is known that there are cases in which some attribute values not disclosed to a user can be guessed from other attribute values disclosed to him.[38] Security for such cases is being studied by several researchers.

For tuple-by-tuple operations in the write class, security can also be defined as a set of quadruples

$$\mathscr{S}_W \subset U \times \Lambda \times B \times \mathscr{R}$$

However, the security assurance procedure is different. If a user u is given a quadruple $(u, \lambda, \beta, \mathcal{R}_p)$ and he invokes a tuple-by-tuple update operation, the following condition must be examined:

If β covers all the attributes in $\mathcal{R}_p$, the user is allowed to add a tuple t to the current relation R in $\mathcal{R}_p$, delete a tuple from R, and replace a tuple t' in R by another tuple t, whenever $\lambda(t)$ and/or $\lambda(t')$ are "true." If this is not the case, he is not allowed to add a tuple to R, or delete a tuple t' from R. He is allowed only to replace a tuple t' by a tuple t, for which $A_k(t) = A_k(t')$ for all the attributes A_k he is not granted to update.

When this condition is violated, the subject write class operation must be rejected.

The sets $\mathcal{S}_R$ and $\mathcal{S}_W$ must be stored somewhere in the database. Each user is assigned a *password*, which is known only by him. The system identifies each user by means of the user's name, password, and some other messages submitted to the system by the user. After the user has been properly identified, the system has access to the tables for $\mathcal{S}_R$ and $\mathcal{S}_W$ upon the user's request for tuple-by-tuple operations in the read and write classes to preserve security.

6.3. Concurrency

When database updates are performed in a concurrent processing environment, we encounter many problems that do not occur when only one program is executed at a time. First, we should solve a classical update conflict problem, which has been dealt with by most advanced operating systems.

When a user wants to replace a tuple in a relation, he first reads it into the workspace provided for this relation. Then he applies the necessary modification to the tuple in the workspace, and, finally, he replaces the old tuple in the relation by the modified tuple. Reading an existing tuple in a relation is also necessary to locate this tuple when the user wants to delete it from this relation.

Let $r(u, t)$ and $w(u, t)$, respectively, be a read and write (replace or delete) operation applied to the tuple t by the user u. Since a $w(u, t)$ is always preceded by a $r(u, t)$, these two are invoked in one *transaction*, that is, the user must declare *start-of-transaction* before invoking $r(u, t)$ and *end-of-transaction* after invoking $w(u, t)$.

Assume two users u_1 and u_2 issue two transactions at the same time, both replacing or deleting the same tuple, t. The transaction issued by u_1 includes $r(u_1, t)$ and $w(u_1, t)$, while the transaction issued by u_2 includes

$r(u_2, t)$ and $w(u_2, t)$. These four operations are processed serially by the system. However, when they are executed in the sequence of

$$r(u_1, t) - r(u_2, t) - w(u_1, t) - w(u_2, t)$$

or

$$r(u_1, t) - r(u_2, t) - w(u_2, t) - w(u_1, t)$$

the third executed operation is not effective and an erroneous update results.

To avoid such erroneous updates, the tuple t must be locked immediately after the read operation. This prevents another read (with lock) operation for the tuple t, which might be requested by other users, until the tuple t is unlocked.

In the database management environment, we must define transactions to deal with temporary inconsistencies. This makes the situation much more complicated (see Section 6.1). During the term in which a temporary inconsistency exists, tuples involved in this inconsistency, which are called *dirty tuples*, must be locked against other updates. Other users may read the dirty tuples, but some may not.

We can see from the above that we need at least three modes for locking a tuple. The first allows other users to read this tuple whether or not it is in an inconsistent state. The second allows other users to read this tuple only when it is not in an inconsistent state; this is called the *shared lock* mode. The third disallows other users to read this tuple whether or not it is in an inconsistent state; this is called the *exclusive lock* mode. To avoid the update conflict, the exclusive lock mode is mandatory. Each lock option prohibits other users from making a lock that conflicts with this lock. Thus, a shared lock inhibits another exclusive lock, while the exclusive lock inhibits another shared lock as well as another exclusive lock.

In a transaction, one or more tuples are locked and then unlocked. It is known that the number of locked tuples must be constantly increased and then constantly decreased in a transaction, otherwise an inconsistency may occur in the database.[40]

The above locking mechanism can adequately protect the database against replace and delete operations that might cause an erroneous update. However, it cannot prohibit other users from adding a tuple that would cause an assertion to be violated. For example, for the assertion

$$(\forall x_1 / \mathcal{R}_{p_1})(A_1(x_1) = \sum_{(x_2 \in \mathcal{R}_{p_2} \wedge A_2(x_1) = A_2(x_2))} A_1(x_2)$$

an inconsistency occurs when a tuple t_2 in the current relation R_2 in $\mathcal{R}_{p_2}$ is modified or deleted. This inconsistency is removed when a tuple t_1 in the current relation R_1 in $\mathcal{R}_{p_1}$ for which $A_1(t_1) = A_1(t_2)$ is modified accordingly. The term between these two updates, t_1 and all tuples t_2' in R_2 for which $A_1(t_1) = A_1(t_2')$ are locked. However, it can happen to a tuple t_2'' for which $A_1(t_1) = A_1(t_2'')$ is newly added to R_2. This violates the assertion. The tuples such as t_2'', which do not exist in the current relation, but might be added to it, are called *phantoms*.

The phantom problem can be solved if we can lock tuples by specifying a sentence. In the above example, tuples x_2 in R_2 for which $A_1(x_2) = A_1(t_2)$ must be prevented from shared and exclusive lock requests by other users. Also, other users must be disallowed to add any tuple x_2 satisfying $A_1(x_2) = A_1(t_2)$ to R_2. Locking specified by such a sentence (a logical function of points) is called a *predicate lock*.[40]

If a user had made a predicate lock by a locking predicate $\lambda(x)$ defined on a relation schema $\mathcal{R}_p$, and if another user issues a predicate lock by $\lambda'(x)$ also defined on $\mathcal{R}_p$, then it is necessary to examine whether

$$(\forall x / \mathcal{R}_p)(\sim\lambda(x) \vee \sim\lambda'(x))$$

holds or not. In general, however, this is a recursively undecidable problem. Only for a limited form of predicates can we decide if its value is "true" or "false" without actually retrieving the tuples that are qualified for the condition λ'. Preventing irregular addition of tuples can be achieved easily by examining whether $\lambda(t)$ is "true" or "false" for the tuple t to be added.

Predicate lock can be expanded to allow a logical function of lines as a locking condition; however, examining whether two given predicates conflict with each other becomes much more difficult.

Essentially, only the tuples which are involved in the update must be locked in a transaction; however, it is too time- and space-consuming to achieve such a tuplewise lock. For this reason, a larger unit called a *locking granule* can be used. A locking granule may be a block composed of several tuples. Sometimes an entire relation or even several relations may become a locking granule. If a multilevel granularity is employed, several submodes must be devised for both the shared and exclusive lock modes. This problem is extensively studied by Gray *et al.*[43]

Use of the lock/unlock mechanism may cause *deadlocks*. For example, assume that two users issue two transactions: both lock two tuples t_1 and t_2. Let $l(u, t)$ be an exlusive lock request for a tuple t by a user u. Then both execution sequences

$$l(u_1, t_1) - l(u_2, t_2) - l(u_1, t_2) - l(u_2, t_1)$$

and

$$l(u_1, t_1) - l(u_2, t_2) - l(u_2, t_1) - l(u_1, t_2)$$

result in a deadlock. Deadlocks may occur in which three or more users are involved.

In the above example, the deadlock can be avoided if the tuples t_1 and t_2 are locked at the same time by each user. However, in most cases, one tuple is identified only after the other tuple is fetched and examined. There are several other methods to avoid deadlocks, but they all introduce inconsistencies into the database, which must be restored afterward. If it is impossible to avoid deadlocks, we are forced to deal with the deadlock detection and restoration problems.

Deadlocks have been extensively studied by many researchers with regard to resource sharing in operating systems. Coffman,[33] Collmeyer,[34] King,[52] and Chamberlin *et al.*[14] have discussed the concurrency problem in the database management environment.

6.4. Recoverability

Database relations are often destroyed due to some hardware, software, or operator errors. Also, a deadlock situation may occur. It is necessary to provide an appropriate mechanism to restore the database when such an error or a deadlock occurs. For this function, two major provisions must be made. They are logging functions to be integrated in the database update operations, and restoration functions to be provided as separate programs.

Three types of information can be logged. One is the *transaction logging.* Using (i) a *checkpoint dump* that records the database status at a certain time and (ii) the record of transactions that have occurred after the last checkpoint dump was created, we can reconstruct a correct database status. This is a complete and universally applicable recovery method, although unnecessarily time-consuming in many cases.

The second and third types of information are *before-image logging* and *after-image logging.* If it is known that some data are destroyed because of a specific improper transaction (update) applied to them. We can restore the correct data using the before images. In this case, all the transactions that used the destroyed data (which can be identified with reference to the transaction logging) must also be undone, and the data updated by these transactions must be restored. On the other hand, if it is known that some data are destroyed due to some other malfunction, and if the destroyed data are well located, then we can restore the correct data using the after images.

Recovery must be implemented as separate utility programs that can be activated automatically or by the database administrator. Checkpoint dumps may be taken repeatedly at certain time intervals, or they may be updated using the after-image logging.

Recovery procedures were also studied by many researchers in relation to operating systems. In the database management environment, Davies,[36] Bjork,[12] and Iizuka[46] have discussed the recovery problem.

6.5. Database Distribution

A database can be managed by one computer, or it can be managed by several computers that are installed in separate locations and connected by communication lines. Because of the rapid development of mini- and microcomputers, distributed processing is becoming more and more popular.

There are two types of distributed systems. Systems such as the ARPA network are constructed by connecting several freestanding systems with freestanding databases, while some systems are designed so that each computer and its database must play a part in the whole system function. The former can be called a *computer network*, while the latter can be called a *computer complex.*

For the computer network, data translation between different database schema definitions becomes necessary. This will be discussed later in relation to the view-support problem. No complicated data access protocols are necessary in this case because one database is essentially managed by a single computer. On the other hand, for the computer complex (in particular, if duplicate data elements are to be maintained by more than one computer) several types of locking and unlocking protocols are necessary in addition to those described in Section 6.3. This problem has been extensively studied by several researchers.[11,88]

6.6. Environmental Requirements

Before advancing to physical database design, we must clarify the needs regarding integrity, security, concurrency, recoverability, and, sometimes, database distribution. Since all these require very time- and space-consuming processing, general-purpose implementations seem very difficult or even impossible. It is more desirable to implement functions that are necessary and sufficient for the intended applications.

As for integrity, we should select semantic constraints to be registered as assertions, which cannot be violated by any user by applying improper updates. To examine whether an update violates a tuple constraint is easy. To examine whether an update violates the key dependency regarding the primary key of a relation is also easy. Relationship constraints and constraints determining relationship relation types can be preserved by providing appropriate collective update operations. However, it is difficult to devise a general integrity preservation mechanism to be integrated into the system. The user is requested, therefore, to be careful in updating the database (or in writing a database update programs) so that he does not violate any semantic constraint that is not already registered as assertions.

As for security, various levels of protection mechanisms are possible. Among them, to protect a whole relation against unauthorized read and/or write is easy. To protect values of specific attributes against unauthorized read is also easy. However, to protect values of specific attributes against unauthorized write is a little difficult. To protect tuples specified by a predicate is more difficult.

It is extremely difficult to preserve integrity and security when a relation is to be updated by a procedural combination of alpha operations (including relational algebra operations, information algebra operations, and setwise navigations). This is because an alpha operation always generates a relation, and an old relation when it is to be updated must be completely replaced by a newly generated relation. This disables the efficient update validating mechanism for universal constraints (see Section 6.1). Therefore, it is better to use alpha operations only for report generation (including outputs on display devices).

As for concurrency, we should determine what levels of locking granularity are appropriate. A small granularity may increase the system overhead to deal with lock/unlock, while a large granularity may decrease the number of transactions executed in parallel. We should also determine the locking modes to be implemented—the predicate lock is fine, but is not easy to implement—and decide how deadlocks are to be dealt with.

Some applications require a very quick recovery, but others do not. Some applications are running twenty-four hours a day, but others are not. The logging and recovery mechanisms must be determined with these factors taken into consideration. Some very critical parts of the database may be duplicated in the database. Two copies of these parts must be updated at the same time.

Although we will not go further into the problems regarding database distribution, designing the data translation between two different database systems and designing the locking protocols between different sites include many difficult problems.

7. PHYSICAL REPRESENTATION OF THE DATABASE

The next design step is the determination of physical representation of database relations that reflect the real world in which we are interested. Physical representation is basically the expression of individual values by bit strings stored in computer storage and the formation of various associations among these bit strings. The former is very common. We will first review the data associations.

7.1. Data Associations in Computer Storage

The organization of memory in the human brain is not well understood. We can suppose, however, that human memory uses many types of multilevel associations among data elements. There seem to be associations of various strengths. Some seem very strong, while other seem very weak.

In contrast, fewer methods of association are used in computer storage. The following four are basic. The first method is association by arranging individual values adjacently on the physical storage devices. One or more values can be associated in this way and are collectively called a (physical) *record*, in which each value is called a *field*.

The second method associates a set of records by allocating them to computer storage using a common address-assigning algorithm. Such a set of records is called a (physical) *file*.

The third method associates several records by giving them a common value in a specific field called a *linking field*. (A foreign key can be represented by a linking field.)

In the fourth method, a linking field is replaced by a *pointer field*, which is the physical (absolute or relative) address of another record associated

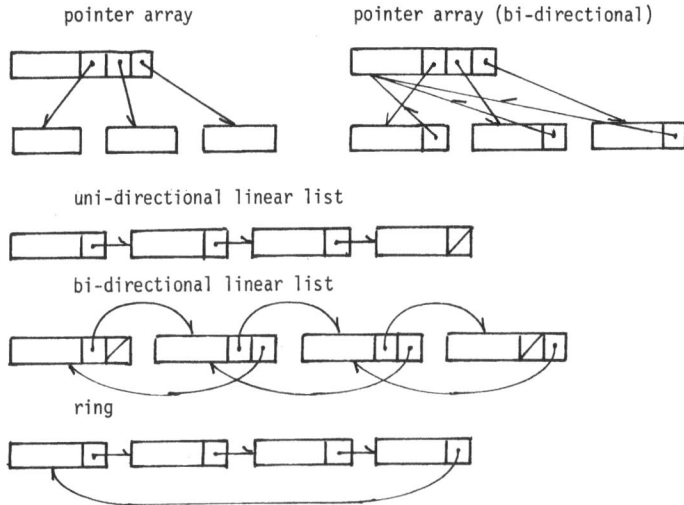

Fig. 24. Basic pointer organizations.

with the record containing the pointer field. Pointer organization can be bidirectional, that is, two records can have pointers pointing to each other. Several different pointer organizations are possible when this method is used to associate more than two records, some of which are illustrated in Fig. 24.

The logical data structure we have established in the logical database design phase must be mapped into a physical database that is structured using these associations.

7.2. Basic File Organizations

First we will discuss several different address assignment algorithms for organizing a file.

7.2.1. Heap File Organization

Records can be stored in a continuous storage area in the order of their arrival. If a record is to be deleted from this area, the location occupied by this record will be used to store new records arriving later. Such a file organization is called a *heap file*. To maintain a heap file area, an appropriate file area control program must be provided. This program monitors the area occupied by the existing records in addition to the area available for storing the newly added records.

The heap file organization can be used to store both fixed-length records and variable-length records. If it is used for the latter, a number of small slots that cannot be used to store newly added records may be generated after repeated updates of the file. A file reorganization, called *garbage collection*, should be performed at appropriate times. The garbage collection program rearranges records stored in the file area and eliminates such small slots.

7.2.2. Sequential File Organization

Records can be arranged in a contiguous storage area in the order of a certain field value. The field used to arrange records in this file is called the *key field* (usually the primary key attributes are represented by the key field). Such a file organization is called a *sequential file*.

The sequential file organization can be used to store both fixed-length and variable-length records. This organization is mandatory on sequential storage devices, but is not efficient for performing file updates on direct-storage devices.

7.2.3. Partitioned Sequential File Organization

In order to improve the update efficiency of a sequential file placed on direct-storage devices, it can be divided into partitions of an appropriate size. A partition contains a certain fixed number of records. This differs from a sequential file, in which addition or deletion of a record requires rewriting of all the records located after the added or deleted record. Update is propagated only within a partition in a partitioned sequential file. If an overflow occurs in a partition, it is divided into two partitions. Conversely if all records in a partition are deleted, the partition itself is removed from the file. Partitions are assigned addresses in a way similar to the heap file organization. Each partition in a file contains a pointer to the next partition. It is also desirable to have another pointer to the previous partition. In this sense, the partitioned sequential file organization uses both the second and fourth association methods described in Section 7.1.

7.2.4. Tree-Structured File Organization

We can embody an *n*-ary search mechanism as a file organization. A *tree-structured file* is composed of a number of partitions, each composed of $n - 1$ records and n pointers. Let $K(r)$ be the key field value of the record *r*. Records $r_1, r_2, \ldots, r_{n-1}$ in a partition are arranged in the order of the key field values, that is,

$$K(r_1) < K(r_2) < \cdots < K(r_{n-1})$$

The pointer p_1 points to a partition containing records whose key field values are smaller than $K(r_1)$. The pointer p_k $(2 \leq k \leq n - 1)$ points to a partition containing records all whose key field values are between $K(r_{k-1})$ and $K(r_k)$. The pointer p_n points to a partition whose key field values are greater than $K(r_k)$. Figure 25 shows a ternary tree-structured file.

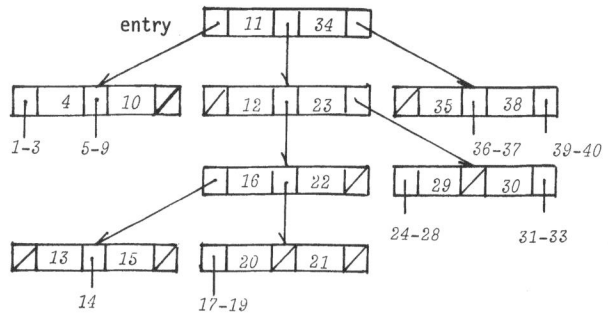

Fig. 25. A tree-structured file.

To achieve better search efficiency, all branches of each partition (node) must contain almost equal number of partitions. Such a tree is called a *balanced tree.* A B-tree is a tree-structured file organization in which a means to produce a balanced tree is integrated.

A tree-structured file can be maintained in a manner similar to maintaining a partitioned sequential file.

7.2.5. Direct-File Organization

The *direct-file organization* uses the key field for allocating records in a file but in a different way. This file organization is achieved for a file F by assigning the address calculated by

$$A(r) = l \times n(K(r)) + b$$

to each record r, where l is the record length that must be fixed for the file, n is an integer-valued function, and b is a constant that specifies the beginning address of the area assigned for the file.

The function n must be an injection (a one-to-one mapping from the set of key field values into a set of integers). In addition the cardinality of $I - I'$, where

$$I = \{i | \min_{r \in F} n(K(r)) \le i \le \max_{r \in F} n(K(r))\}$$

and

$$I' = \{n(K(r)) | r \in F\}$$

must be as small as possible. In general, it is very difficult to find such an integer-valued function.

One solution is to neglect the first restriction. We may provide a *bucket* that can accommodate several (or just one) records *colliding* with each other (i.e., assigned the same address). If a bucket overflow occurs, the record causing the overflow is assigned an open (not occupied by another record) address in the next bucket, or in an overflow bucket provided in some separate area (organized as a heap file) linked to the overflowed bucket by a pointer. To make the number of colliding records as small as possible, a certain *hashing function* is used for n.

7.2.6. Exclusiveness of the File Organization

The five basic file organizations we have mentioned are mutually exclusive except for the *binary* tree-structured file organization, that is, no more than one distinct organization can be applied to organizing a file. The binary tree-structured file is nonexclusive because every partition contains only one record. We can overlay a binary tree-structured file on whatever file organization we have constructed.

7.3. Representation of Entity Relations

A tuple in an entity relation may be represented by one record or by several records linked together by connecting fields or pointers. The latter type of representation is desirable when the tuple has several groups of attribute values accessed with considerably different freuqencies or when the typle has fixed-length attribute values and variable-length attribute values. In these cases, each group of attribute values may be represented by one record. One of the records that represent a tuple is called the *main record* (in most cases, composed of fixed-length attribute values), and others are called *subordinate records.*

An attribute value is represented in the record by a field. If the attribute value is compound, the corresponding field is composed of a fixed or variable number of *subfields.*

An entity relation is usually represented by a file that is a collection of main records representing tuples in the relation. Subordinate records, if generated, may comprise one or more additional files. One of the basic file organizations mentioned in Section 7.2 is used to organize these files.

The physical representation of entity relations is not uniquely determined. In fact, decomposition of a tuple into one or more parts, each represented by a separate record, selection of the linking method for associating the main and subordinate records, and selection of the storage allocation algorithm in organizing files, are not unique. We must select a specific representation from a variety of possible representations with various qualitative and quantitative factors taken into consideration. Next we will consider how each file organization behaves when basic database operations are applied to it.

7.3.1. Exhaustive Search

As a special case, the search condition can be T (which assigns the value "true" to each tuple in a relation). The search operation with T as the search condition is called *exhaustive search.* If an exhaustive search is performed in the order of primary key values, it is called a *sequential search.*

A heap file is efficient for an exhaustive search, but is inadequate for achieving an efficient sequential search. A sequential file as well as a partitioned sequential file is excellent for a sequential search. A tree-structured file is less efficient than these two for a sequential search, although a sequential search is still possible on it. A direct file is quite inadequate for an exhaustive search. It is almost impossible to achieve a sequential search on a direct file.

7.3.2. Equal Key Search

Equal key search is another special case of the search operation in which the search condition is of the form

$$\lambda(x) \equiv A_p(x) = \text{const}$$

where A_p is the primary key attribute (or the concatenation of primary key attributes).

To perform an equal key search (as well as other more complicated searches described later) on a heap file, a *seek* operation, which fetches all records in the file and then tests them against the given condition, must be performed.

This time-consuming procedure can be somewhat improved when searching a sequential file by using well-known binary or the n-ary search procedure. The search time required for a seek operation is $O(N)$ (order of N), where N is the number of records in the file, while that required for an n-ary search is $O(\log N)$. The n-ary search is difficult on a partitioned sequential field because partitions in it are linked to each other by a pointer. On the other hand, an n-ary tree-structured file is excellent for n-ary search because the n-ary search procedure is embedded into the associations among partitions that are made beforehand in an n-ary tree-structured file.

The equal key search can be implemented efficiently on a direct file if the key attributes are represented by the key field.

7.3.3. Key Search

Key search is a search operation with a search condition of the form

$$\lambda(x) \equiv A_p(x)\theta \text{ const}$$

where θ is an arbitrary relational operator. Equal key search is a special case of key search; however, the situation is a little different when the operator θ is not the equality operator. In this case the search efficiency cannot be improved for direct files. In contrast, the search efficiency can be improved if the n-ary search procedure on the sequential file is used. In consequence, a tree-structured file is excellent for key search.

7.3.4. Non-Key Search

Non-key search is a search operation with a search condition of the form

$$\lambda(x) \equiv A_k(x)\theta \text{ const}$$

where A_k is an arbitrary attribute. The attribute A_k can be replaced by an arbitrary function f whose value is calculated from several basic functions of points defined on the relation.

All the file organizations described in Section 7.2 are powerless to improve the search efficiency for this type of search condition, and hence a seek operation is indispensable.

One way to improve the seek process is to make the record size as small as possible. To cope with the non-key search, we may use the record that has only two fields, one representing the A_k value and the other representing the key field value (which can be replaced by a pointer field pointing to the main record having this key value). All these records are associated by some method to form the *index file* over the relation regarding the attribute A_k. The index file of the relation R regarding the attribute A_k can be considered as representing $p[\{A_k, A_p\}](R)$ which is a projection of R.

The non-key search can be performed by a seek operation applied to the index file, followed by an equal key search or by traversing along the pointer that replaces the primary key. If the main record contains a fairly large number of fields, this procedure is much more efficient than the seek operation on the main file.

The index file can be created so that each index record points to a partition in a partitioned sequential file. Only for the first record in each partition is an index record provided. Such an organization is called the *indexed sequential file organization*. It can be used only for indexing the primary key.

Index records with a common A_k value can be collected and represented by a single record that has this A_k value and an array of the primary key values of the tuples having this A_k value or a pointer array replacing it. The index field composed of such records is called an *inverted file*. The pointer array can be replaced by a chain of records linked by pointers. Such an index file is called a *multilist*. An inverted file and a multilist organization are shown in Fig. 26. Sometimes the last record in each chain is linked to the corresponding index record by a pointer to form a *multiring*.

If A_k has a power set-type domain, we can create an index file in which more than one index record points to the same main record. Two or more index files provided for a relation can be merged if the indexed attributes have a common domain.

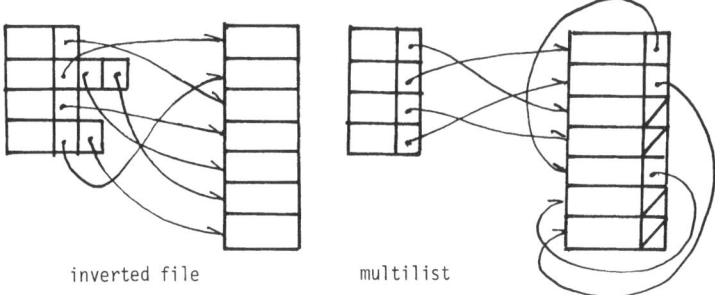

inverted file   multilist

Fig. 26. An inverted file and a multilist.

Like the binary tree-structured file organization, the index organization is nonexclusive. Therefore, index files can be created for any number of attributes (and functions which can be calculated from basic functions of points) of a relation regardless of what file organization is used to represent this relation. However, the presence of index files degrades the update performance because index files must be updated together with the main file (and subordinate files if they exist). An excessive number of index files is quite harmful for the total performance. We must be very careful in selecting the attributes (and functions) to be indexed. This problem has been extensively studied by several researchers.[53,61,64,73,83]

It is obvious that it is better to organize the index file as a sequential file, a partitioned sequential file, or an indexed sequential file. It can also be organized as an *n*-ary tree-structured file. The B-tree organization is excellent for the index file.

Index files, if they are sequentially organized, can be used to improve the search condition of the form

$$\lambda(x) \equiv f_1(A_i(x)) = f_2(A_j(x))$$

where f_1 and f_2 are constantly increasing functions. Two index files provided for A_i and A_j are sequentially collated and, for each match of two index records, it is determined whether the two have some common A_p values (or pointers). Such common values, if they exist, determine the tuples qualified for the search condition.

7.3.5. Compound Search on a Relation

So far we have discussed the file organizations that support some specific types of search operations. For other types of search operations we need an exhaustive search, which can be performed by a seek operation applied to the subject file.

In general, a search on a single file may be requested with a compound condition composed of several *unit conditions* combined by logical operators. We may consider only the "∨" and " ∧ " operators, since the "~" operator can be eliminated by changing the relational operator used in the unit condition appropriately.

A search with two unit conditions combined by a "∨" or "∧" operator can be performed by a seek operation. However, since we have

$$s[\lambda_1 \vee \lambda_2](R) = u(s[\lambda_1](R), s[\lambda_2](R))$$

and

$$s[\lambda_1 \wedge \lambda_2](R) = i(s[\lambda_1](R), s[\lambda_2](R))$$

we can use two searches with a unit condition followed by a union or an intersection procedure to obtain the same result. If some efficient search procedure supported by the file organization employed is applicable to both searches, the latter procedure may produce better performance than the former. Union and intersection can be efficiently achieved by sorting both search results and then sequentially collating them.

If two unit conditions are combined by an " ∧ " operator, we can improve the search efficiency even if one of them is not supported by the file organization employed. Since we have

$$s[\lambda_1 \wedge \lambda_2](R) = s[\lambda_2](s[\lambda_1](R)) = s[\lambda_1](s[\lambda_2](R))$$

we can first perform the search with the condition for which an efficient search is possible, and then perform a seek operation on its result.

Given a compound condition, we can make a syntactical transformation to maximize the use of efficient search procedures supported by the file organization. Astrahan and Chamberlin[4] gave an optimal execution sequence for the compound search on a single file (selection in the relational algebra). Kobayashi[57] presented a more general algorithm.

7.3.6. Compound Search on More Than One Relation

Generally, the search

$$s[\lambda](R_1, R_2, \ldots, R_m)$$

is performed with a logical function λ of lines of span m (an extended relational calculus). The function λ may have one or more bound variables.

The matrix part of its prenex normal form is composed of several unit conditions combined by logical operators. For some unit conditions defined on a single relation, we may have some means of improving the search efficiency.

If a unit condition is defined on $R_1 \times R_2 \times \cdots \times R_k$, then we should perform a seek operation on this Cartesian product of relations. However, if we find a unit or compound condition of the form

$$\lambda'(x_1, x_2, \ldots, x_k) \equiv \bigwedge_{j=2}^{k} (A_{i_1}(x_1) = A_{i_j}(x_j))$$

or one that is logically equivalent to one in this form, a sequential collation of k files, $R_1, R_2, \ldots, R_k$ can replace the seek operation on each compound unit condition. Sequential collation necessitates each file being arranged in the order of A_{i_j} ($j = 1, 2, \ldots, k$) values. Therefore, each file must be sorted before the sequential collation is executed. The time required for sorting a file with N records is $O(N \log N)$. As a consequence, the time required for sorting m files, each with N_j records followed by a sequential collation, is $O(\sum_{j=1}^{k} N_j \log N_j)$. It is expected to be less than $O(\prod_{j=1}^{k} N_j)$, which is the time required for a seek on the Cartesian product of m files.

Index files for A_{i_j}, if they exist, can be used in the sequential collation instead of the main files.

In general, there can be more than one (extended) relational calculus that are logically equivalent to each other. Given a compound search condition, we can make a syntactical transformation to obtain a condition that is equivalent to the given condition and maximizes the use of existing index organizations and also the use of sequential collation procedures. Unit or compound conditions for which an efficient search procedure is available must be processed before processing conditions for which a seek operation must be used.

An optimal search algorithm for search with a condition defined on two relations (join in relational algebra) was presented by Smith and Chang[85] and Yao.[100] Decomposition of a search with a condition defined on m ($m \geq 3$) relations into some relational algebra operations was first discussed by Codd.[30] However, no optimization was considered by him. Palermo[72] presented an improvement of Codd's algorithm for the search conditions without bound variables. Rothnie[76] studied search conditions of a more general form. In the INGRES project, several improvement were implemented which was reported by Wong and Youssefi[98] and Held et al.[45]

All these works were based on relational calculus. As suggested in Section 5.1, the search condition, which is a logical function of tuples of span m, can be of a more general form than the relational calculus.

Kobayashi[57] presented an optimal algorithm based on an extended relational calculus. He decomposed the search operation into certain more elementary operations, which resemble relational algebra operations but differ from them on several points. Sequential collation as well as index file organization was fully utilized in this algorithm.

7.3.7. Update

As for the update efficiency, the heap file is best, and the direct file is second best. The partitioned sequential file and the tree-structured file are not so bad, but the sequential file is very bad, as mentioned previously. Provision of index files considerably degrades the update efficiency.

In some applications, updates are not frequently required when compared with search operations, while in others updates are very frequent. In the latter cases, sequential file organization must be abandoned, and provision of index files must be minimized.

Quantitative discussions regarding selection of file organizations are not elaborated here. There are several excellent publications that elaborate quantitative discussions on various representations of entity relations.[62,65,94,98]

7.4. Representation of Relationship Relations

Unlike the representation of entity relations, tuples in a relationship relation are not always directly represented by physical records. In particular, when the relationship relation to be represented is binary and has no attributes other than its origin and destination attributes, we usually represent it quite differently from an entity relation. We will discuss these different representations and the efficiency of navigation and update operations applied to relationship relations.

7.4.1. Sequential Record Arrangement

A tuple in a binary relationship relation is a relationship between two tuples in one or two relations on which this relationship relation is defined. Such a relationship can be expressed by forming an association between the two records representing two tuples related to each other by this relationship. The first, third, and fourth methods of forming an association described in Section 7.1 can be used for this purpose.

The first method, which is to store the two records adjacently, can be used only when the relationship is a quasi sequence (see Section 4.6.4). A sequence is a connected quasi sequence. Conversely, a quasi sequence is a union of several sequences. If a sequence is represented in this way, we obtain a sequential file, although it is not the sequential file we defined in Section 7.2.2. If the relationship relation is a quasi sequence but not a sequence, an explicit indication to specify apices and/or terminals (by adding an additional field or by adding some special records) must be made.

This representation has two advantages. One is that it does not use any storage space to represent the relationship relation. The other is that navigations along the relationship relation can be efficiently performed by a physical sequential read (forward or backward). On the other hand, the update performance is very bad because it either updates the relationship relation or updates the relations on which it is defined necessitating rewriting a large part of the files representing the relation on which the relationship relation is defined.

7.4.2. Coding Representation

Association by providing a linking field can also be used to represent a relationship between two records. The linking field in this representation can be considered as representing an additional attribute in which the relationship relation is embedded.

Sometimes a recursive relationship can be embedded in a single attribute appended to the relation on which it is defined. For example, a sequence can be represented by an ordinal number, and a tree can be represented by a Dewey number, both appended as an attribute to the relation on which the relationship relation is defined. Such a method is called a *coding representation.*

In sequential storage devices such as magnetic tapes, such a coding representation must be made. In direct-access storage devices, however, such a representation is inadvisable because the generation and maintenance of such attribute values is not easy, and navigation is possible only after the file representing the relation on which the relationship relation is defined is sorted by this code.

7.4.3. Pointer Organization

Association by pointer fields is the most commonly used and the most efficient method for representing relationship relations. The types of pointers used vary according to the type of the relationship relation to be represented.

If the relationship relation is a quasisequence (which can be a sequence), it can be represented by a unidirectional or a bidirectional pointer contained in the records representing tuples in the relation on which this quasisequence is defined. This representation is called the *unidirectional* or *bidirectional linear list* according to the pointer organization. If the relationship relation is not a quasisequence, no single pointer can represent either or both directions of relationships relating two records. In fact, if the relationship relation is a tree, one origin (tuple) may have several destinations (tuples) and a pointer array is required for representing the forward direction of the relationship. If the relationship relation is a network, one origin may have several destinations and one destination may have several origins. Two pointer arrays are required if we would like to represent both directions of the relationship. All these must be variable-length arrays.

In most case, however, a fixed number of pointers can be used instead of a pointer array. The hierarchical normal form decomposition described in Section 4.6.5 and the three equivalence theorems presented in Section 4.6.6 are the basis of such substitutions.

Theorem 3 implies that a tree can be decomposed into two quasequences. This, in turn, implies that a tree can be represented by two uni- or bidirectional pointers. This representation of a tree is often called a *hierarchical list.*

Theorem 4 implies that an irrecursive tree (which can be a hierarchy) can be transformed into a quasisequence. This, in turn, implies that an irrecursive tree can be represented by a single uni- or bidirectional pointer.

Theorem 5 implies that a multilevel hierarchy can be transformed into a quasisequence. This, in turn, implies that a multilevel hierarchy can be represented by a single uni- or bidirectional pointer. In this case, however, the hierarchical skeleton must be kept somewhere in the database.

Finally, a network (as well as a recursive tree) can be decomposed into an entity relation (representing this relationship relation) and two hierarchies according to the hierarchical normal form decomposition. This implies that a network can be represented by a file representing an entity relation and two uni- or bidirectional pointers each representing a hierarchy.

Navigation along a path specified by the pointer organization is efficient. The choice between unidirectional and bidirectional pointer organization depends on the relative frequencies of forward and backward navigation. If navigation in these directions are almost equally likely, the bidirectional pointer is mandatory. If backward navigation is required but not as frequently as forward navigation, a *ring* pointer organization can be used.

Note that we need navigation in both directions to update the relationship relation and to update the relation on which the relationship relation is defined. In fact, if pointer organization is employed to represent a relationship relation, any addition and deletion of tuples in these relations causes the update of several other tuples. Unidirectional pointers are insufficient to perform such updates efficiently.

7.4.4. Relationship Records

The last method of representing a relationship relation is to represent it in the same manner as an entity relation. Tuples in the relationship relation are represented by records that are members of the file expressing the relationship relation.

This method can be used for representing an *n*-ary relationship relation. The relationship can also have any number of attributes in addition to its orgin and destination attributes.

Navigation must be performed by a search operation with a search condition defined on one or two relations (see Section 5.7) or a procedural execution of one or two searches on a single relation. Therefore, the navigation performance is rather poor. On the other hand, update of the relationship relation is very easy and efficient, since update of a relationship tuple does not cause any propagated update.

7.5. Localization

So far we have discussed a variety of representations of entity and relationship relations. A specific representation must be selected to efficiently execute various database operations.

If we employ a heap file, a sequential file, a partitioned sequential file or an *n*-ary ($n \geq 3$) tree-structured file, we can use *block buffering* techniques to reduce the number of data transfers between external and main storage. Block buffering can be regarded as a device that enables a quick access to the record r' which is next (in some sense) to the record r currently fetched (stored in the workspace). For a direct file, we cannot use block buffering techniques.

In general, if a record r' is frequently fetched immediately after a record r is fetched, the time $t(r, r')$ required for fetching r' under the condition that r is currently in the workspace provided in the program area must be as short as possible. Let $p(r, r')$ be the possibility of fetching r' immediately after fetching r. Here, records r and r' are not necessarily in the same file. For the whole database DB, we have

$$\sum_{r' \in DB} p(r, r') = 1$$

for all r, and also

$$\sum_{r \in DB} p(r, r') = 1$$

for all r'. It is desirable to minimize

$$\sum_{r \in DB} \sum_{r' \in DB} p(r, r') t(r, r')$$

Pointers certainly shorten $t(r, r')$ when $p(r, r')$ is expected to be considerably large. Block buffering also shortens $t(r, r')$ in the case that r and r' belong to the same file and r' is next to r with respect to a specified sequence.

Paging is a more general method. The whole database is divided into a number of pages of an appropriate size. We can use *page buffering* techniques to minimize the number of data transfers between external and main storage.

Paging can be regarded as a device by which two records logically near each other are placed in two locations physically near each other. For instance, we may define a logical distance between r and r' as

$$d(r, r') = \frac{2}{p(r, r') + p(r', r)} - 1$$

(It is not a distance in mathematical sense because the triangular inequality is not satisfied.) We can form the logical distance matrix D with the logical distance between ith and jth records in the database as its (i, j)-coefficient. Using this matrix, we can cluster the database records. One cluster may constitute one page.

For the program, which is a set of instructions, paging or virtual storage techniques are very popular. However, in comparison to the program, which has a strong *locality*, the database normally has only a very weak locality. This makes application of paging techniques to the database organization very difficult. In fact, improper application of page buffering may even worsen the total performance.

Sometimes, the extent of the page cluster is obvious because of some specific characteristics of the data to be stored in the database. For example, in a cartographic database for some regional information systems, page subdivision can be made according to the regional area subdivision on the map to be accommodated in the database. In such a case, we can apply a certain page buffering technique as the storage allocation algorithm for some part of the database.

8. DATABASE MANAGEMENT FUNCTIONS

After the physical representations of database relations have been determined, we must construct the physical database and also implement data manipulation programs to operate in it. This implementation could be done in a traditional programming manner; however, in order to build a soft system in the sense described in Section 3 with less programming effort, it is necessary to first implement several databse management functions. Such functions include the data description function, database routines, the binding function, and utility programs for the database administrators.

8.1. Data Description

In the past when advanced compiler languages were not available, programmers had to be aware of both logical data structure and its physical representation in storage media while writing programs. Modern compiler languages are capable of determining physical representation of logical data structure with the aid of advanced operating systems, if the programmer provides a relatively small amount of necessary information. This information is embedded in appropriate compiler directives as their arguments, is given to the compiler, and is analyzed and transcribed into information packets called *file descriptors*. File descriptors are given to the operating system when the compiled program is loaded. In some programming languages such as COBOL, these directives are collected to form the *data description* part of the program, which is written separately from the *procedure description* part. However, both parts are still closely related to each other and usually written by the same programmer.

In the database environment, we assume that many programs require access to a shared database. Therefore, the data description part should be written and maintained quite separately from any specific program. This is called *data independence* of the program (or *program independence* of data). In addition, the data in a database is usually much more complicated than data in traditional data files. Hence, representing the database relations is a much more difficult task than designing traditional data files.

In order to achieve data independence, all the file descriptors regarding database relations must be accommodated and maintained collectively somewhere in the database. Such information is concerned not with specific database relations (instances) but with relation schemata. The part of the database that contains schema information is called the *database directory* (or sometimes the *database schema*). The database directory must contain all the information necessary to define the relation schemata syntactically and semantically. It is used by the language translators at compilation time and by the database routines at execution time. Some additional information necessary to determine physical representation of the database relations can be included in the database directory.

8.1.1. Description of Entity Relation Schemata

To create the database directory easily, it is desirable to have a *data descrption language* (DDL) in which the user describes the relation schemata. Definition of the database schemata described in this language is given to the *data definition processor* (DDP), and is analyzed and registered in the database as the database directory.

To define an entity relation schema, the relation (schema) name and the names of the attributes constituting this schema are to be specified. Domain constraints and the key dependency regarding the selected primary key could be described in a more general way of describing semantic constraints; however, since a relation schema is always accompanied with these constraints, it seems better to describe them together with attribute names.

As the data description language must be used not only for defining a relation schema that is to be newly added to the database but also for modifying the definition of an already existing relation schema, some indication specifying addition, deletion, or modification of the schema definition is necessary.

For example, an entity relation schema can be defined by a statement such as

gtype relationname = σentity[primarykeyattributes] of tuples

$$\sigma_1 a_1 i_1 : t_1 ; \sigma_2 a_2 i_2 : t_2 \ldots ; \sigma_n a_n i_n : t_n \text{ end};$$

where a_k is an attribute name and t_k is the data type of the a_k value.

The gtype (grobal-type) statement is used to define this data type beyond the scope of any program. The data type of the a_k value can be one of those built into the programming language such as the scalar type in PASCAL or those defined by the user using devices in the programming language such as the subrange type and various structured types in PASCAL. A Cartesian product-type domain can be specified as record type; a power set-type domain as set type; and a repeating group type domain as set of record type. Sometimes we want to regard several relation schemata with some common attributes (including the primary key attributes) collectively as a relation schema (which is a join-union mentioned in Section 4.6.7). A device such as case of in PASCAL is convenient for defining such a relation schema.

Indicators σ and σ_k are either +, −, or blank. If σ is +, this gtype statement adds the definition of the specified entity relation schema to the database directory. If σ is −, it deletes the specified entity relation schema from the database directory. Only the relation name must be specified in the latter case. If σ is blank, the definition of the specified entity relation schema is to be modified. Attributes appearing in the statement are added if σ_k is +, deleted if σ_k is −, or modified if σ_k is blank.

Although it cannot be considered as a purely logical concept, an indicator i_k that specifies whether the attribute a_k is to be indexed is useful. The i_k is # if a_k is to be indexed, or blank if not.

8.1.2. Description of Binary Relationship Relation Schemata

Binary relationship relation schemata may be defined in a somewhat different manner from entity relations for the following two reasons: One is that the relationship relation schema is always accompanied by a relationship constraint; the other is that the binary relationship relation is very frequently represented differently from entity relations. The existence of a relationship constraint can be specified by declaring that this is a relationship relation schema definition. It is desirable to specify the relationship relation type because the type is important information to determine the representation of the relationship relation. Specifying the type implies registering the semantic constraints that classify relationship relation schemata (see Section 4.6.4). For example, a binary relationship relation schemata can be defined by a statement such as

gtype relationname = σrelationship[formula, relationshiptype] of tuples

$$\sigma_1 a_1 i_1 : t_1; \sigma_2 a_2 i_2 : t_2; \ldots ; \sigma_n a_n i_n : t_n \text{ end};$$

Indicators σ, σ_k, and i_k are the same as those for defining entity relation schemata. Only attributes other than those for origin and destination must be specified by arguments a_k. The type argument t_k is the same as that for defining entity relation schemata.

The formula argument is necessary to specify on what relation schemata the relationship relation schema is defined, and, if the relationship relation schema is for multilevel hierarchies, what its hierarchical skeleton is. For instance, the following BNF syntax can be used:

⟨formula⟩::=⟨relationname⟩|⟨relationame⟩ − ⟨aform⟩

⟨aform⟩::=⟨formula⟩|(⟨bform⟩)

⟨bform⟩::=⟨formula⟩, ⟨formula⟩|⟨bform⟩, ⟨formula⟩

Here $\mathscr{R}_{p_1} - \mathscr{R}_{p_2}$ means that the relationship relation schema is defined between $\mathscr{R}_{p_1}$ and $\mathscr{R}_{p_2}$, where $R_{p_1} - (\mathscr{R}_{p_2}, \mathscr{R}_{p_3})$ means that the relationship relation schema $\mathscr{R}_{p_1}$ is defined both between $\mathscr{R}_{p_1}$ and $\mathscr{R}_{p_2}$ and between $\mathscr{R}_{p_1}$ and $\mathscr{R}_{p_3}$. Several examples of multilevel hierarchies are shown in Fig. 27.

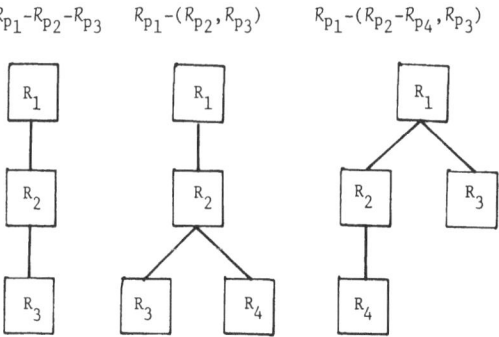

Fig. 27. Various multilevel hierarchies.

The origin and destination attributes can be supplied by the system. They may be the primary keys of the origin and destination tuples, or pointers replacing these primary keys.

The relationshiptype argument may be composed of two indicators c and d. The indicator c specifies the relationship relation type, which is one of S (sequence), Q (quasisequence), H (hierarchy or multilevel hierarchy), T (tree), or N (network). Various tuple-by-tuple navigations must be provided for traversing the relationship relation (see Section 5.9.1). The indicator d specifies what tuple-by-tuple navigations are to be provided. The indicator d is one of F, B, FB, $F(\lambda)$, $B(\lambda)$, and $FB(\lambda)$, where λ is an arbitrary function of points defined on each terminal set (see Section 4.6.7). If λ is specified, tuples in each terminal set are arranged in the order of the λ value. Otherwise they are arranged in the order of their arrival. If d is F or $F(\lambda)$, navigations G_{fa}, G_{na} (if c is not S), G_{fc}, G'_{fc}, G_{nc} (if c is H, T, or N), G'_{nc} (if c is H, T, or N), G'_{lc} (if c is H, T, or N), and G'_{pc} (if c is H, T, or N) are provided. If d is B or $B(\lambda)$, G_{fp}, G_{np} (if c is not S), G_{fp}, G'_{fp}, G_{np} (if c is N), G'_{np} (if c is N), G'_{lp} (if c is N), and G'_{pp} (if c is N) are provided. If d is FB or $FB(\lambda)$, all these tuple-by-tuple navigations are provided.

8.1.3. Registering Other Assertions

Domain constraints, key dependencies regarding primary keys, relationship constraints, and constraints classifying relationship relation schemata can be registered as assertions by means of defining entity and relationship relation schemata in the manner described in Sections 8.1.1 and 8.1.2. However, there can be many more semantic constraints, each of which brings a piece of data semantics and must be registered as assertions.

For registering assertions, we may have a statement such as

gtype assertionname = σassertions sentence end;

where σ is +, −, or blank, respectively, indicating adding, deleting, or replacing the assertion. For static constraints, the sentence part can be a schema calculus. Let R1 and R2 be the names of two relation schemata, and A1, A2, and A3 be the names of three attributes, all defined by means of gtype/entity statements mentioned in Section 8.1.1. Then we can write, for example, as

$$(\text{all } x/R1) \, A1(x) < 3^*A2(x)$$
$$(\text{all } x1/R1) \, A2(x1) = \text{sum}[x2/R2 \text{ and } A1(x1) = A2(x2)]A3(x2)$$

and

$$(\text{all } x1/R1)(\text{some } x2/R2) \, A1(x1) = A1(x2)$$

which correspond respectively to

$$(\forall x/\mathscr{R}_{p_1}) \, A_1(x) < 3 \times A_2(x)$$

$$(\forall x_1/\mathscr{R}_{p_1}) \, A_1(x_1) = \sum_{x_2 \in \mathscr{R}_{p_2} \wedge A_1(x_1) = A_1(x_2) A_3(x_2)}$$

and

$$(\forall x_1/\mathscr{R}_{p_1})(\exists x_2/\mathscr{R}_{p_2}) \, A_1(x_1) = A_1(x_2)$$

Dynamic constraints cannot be described by schema calculi. However, some of them can be described using some qualifiers such as old and new, which qualify attribute names. For example, we may write as

$$(\text{all } x/R1) \text{ new} \cdot A1(x) \geq \text{old} \cdot A1(x)$$

to express a dynamic constraint

$$(\forall \tau)(\forall \tau')(\tau > \tau' \to (\forall x/R_1^\tau)(\forall x'/R_1^{\tau'})(A_p(x) = A_p(x') \to A_1(x) \geq A_1(x')))$$

Assertions must be preserved at database update time. Update requests submitted by the user must be validated with regard to all the assertions as mentioned in Sec. 6.1.

Another way to register assertions is to integrate update validation procedures which the users supply. For integrity preservation, this method seems much more practical. However, these assertions may also be used as deductive rules. Since different uses of assertions require different procedures, this method is not suitable for implementing advanced capabilities such as deductive question answering.

8.1.4. View Support

A data description language requires the user to adopt a specific view of the real world. For instance, the data description mentioned in Sections 8.1.1 and 8.1.2 is based on an entity–relationship view of the real world. The relational view of the real world allows only the definition of entity relations in the sense described in Section 8.1.1. It disallows Cartesian-product-type and power-set-type domains. There are several other views such as the coset view which allows definition of entity relations and hierarchies and the hierarchical view which allows definition of entity relations and multilevel hierarchies. (At most one multilevel hierarchy can be defined on each entity relation in the hierarchical view.)

Often there may be a group of users who prefer a specific view of the real world which is different from the view supported by the given data description language. It is desirable to support the users' view by providing a proper data description language. For this purpose, an additional database directory (sometimes called a *subschema*) becomes necessary.

ANSI/X3/SPARC presented a report in which three levels of the database directory were proposed.[3] These were the *external schema*, the *conceptual schema*, and the *internal schema*. The system requires a basic data description language that is used to create the conceptual schema. It may have several other data description languages each of which is used to create an external schema. The internal schema is created by the system itself for describing the physical database organization. The report did not mention which view of the real world is the most appropriate for the conceptual schema.

Different schemata may be generated even within the same view of the real world. For example, in the relational view, a natural join of two relations can be regarded as a single relation by some users.[15]

If there are more than one database directory, all representing the same real world, a *data translation* mechanism, which transforms one directory to another directory, must be provided in the system. Data translation in both directions between various external schemata and the conceptual schema is basic. A similar situation occurs when we have several different database management functions (systems) in a distributed database environment.

Data translation is a transformation of logical data structure. However, we should transform data manipulation procedures and several environmental requirements as well. For example, in the entity–relationship view of the real world, we usually use navigation as a basic data manipulation (provided as database routines), while they are not provided in the relational view. Therefore, a program that invokes navigation operations must be transformable into a program that does not invoke navigation operations, particularly when we want to translate the database directory based on the entity–relationship view into others based on the relational view. This can be achieved by rewriting navigation operations as (conditional) searches (see Section 5.7). We will need different security, integrity, lock/unlock, and recovery procedures in different views. Many difficult problems still remain unsolved with regard to supporting more than one distinct view. They are left to future study.

8.1.5. Selection of Physical Representation

If we can establish a standard for representing entity and relationship relations, we can let the system select an appropriate representation for each database relation automatically. Although it does not always select an optimal representation, the following choice seems reasonable.

A tuple in an entity relation may or may not contain attribute values that are represented by a variable-length bit string. If such an attribute value is not present, a tuple can be represented by a fixed-length record. Otherwise, we can choose between a variable-length record and a fixed-length *main* record plus one or more fixed-length and/or variable-length *subordinate* records. This choice may depend on the users' applications and may be indicated in the definition of the entity relation schema. The number of subordinate records can be variable. In particular, when the entity relation schema has a repeating-group-type attribute, we may generate a subordinate record for each component of the repeating group.

It seems advisable to organize main records as an indexed sequential file. The indexed sequential file organization is applicable to both fixed- or variable-length records. Subordinate records are organized as one or more heap files. A main record and several subordinate records that together represent a tuple in an entity relation are associated by a pointer link, which may be a pointer array or a pointer chain.

If an attribute is specified to be indexed, an index file is created for this attribute. A *B*-tree is good for organizing an index file. An index record is associated with one or more main records corresponding to it by a pointer link. An inverted file is better than a multilist or multiring when we must deal with compound search conditions.

An *n*-ary relationship relation schema, if $n > 2$, must be decomposed into an entity relation and *n* binary relationship relations to obtain relations in relationship normal form. Otherwise we must register the relationship constraints in some other way. If the system has a certain statement for defining such relationship relations, the system must make this decomposition. If not, the user is responsible for making this decomposition. For a binary relationship relation defined by a statement such as gtype/relationship, we have a variety of representations. In order to allow efficient navigations along the binary relationship relation, representation by a pointer organization is usually the best choice if there are no attributes other than the origin and destination attributes.

If the indicator c in the gtype/relationship statement (see Section 8.1.2) is S (sequence), a linear list organization can be used to represent the relationship relation. To produce reasonable performance for updates as well as for navigation, a bidirectional linear list must be used.

If c is Q (quasisequence), a linear list organization can also be used, since a quasisequence is composed of several sequences. If a field indicating that this is a record representing an apex tuple is added, each linear list can be replaced by a ring. If the indicator d is F or B, the ring organization with a forward or backward pointer is advisable. If d is FB, the bidirectional linear list organization is advisable. In order to fetch all apex tuples efficiently, all the records representing apex tuples may be chained by a pointer link.

If c is H (hierarchy or multilevel hierarchy), the relationship relation can be transformed into a quasisequence and, in consequence, a linear list organization can be used. In this case, a unidirectional ring is advisable if d is F or B, and a bidirectional ring is advisable if d is FB. If d is B or FB, an additional pointer pointing to the record representing the parent tuple may be added. All the records representing apex tuples may be chained by a pointer link.

If c is T (tree), the relationship relation can be transformed into two quasisequences, the vertical and horizontal relations (see Section 4.6.6). Each of these two quasisequences can be represented by a linear list. A bidirectional linear list is advisable to each of them. All the records representing apex tuples may be chained by a pointer link. All the record-representing terminal tuples may also be chained by a pointer link.

If c is N (network), the relationship relation cannot be transformed into simpler relationship relations unless a new entity relation representing this relationship relation is added (see Section 4.6.5). Therefore, we can choose between representing the relationship relation by pointer arrays and representing it by creating an additional entity relation. For the latter case, we may represent two hierarchies obtained by decomposing the network. The former representation is better in the sense that we can produce better performance for navigation. However, as the pointer array size is variable, we need variable-length records. Two pointer arrays for forward and backward traversals should be provided. The former representation uses the representation of hierarchies mentioned above.

If the binary relationship relation schema has some attributes other than its origin and destination attributes, the relationship record representation is preferable. The created file can be regarded as representing a new entity relation, and two relationship relations each being a quasisequence of hierarchy can be defined between this entity relation and the relation on which the relationship relation to be represented is defined. These two relationship relations may also be represented by pointer organizations to allow efficient navigation.

8.1.6. Operational Statistics

When a specific logical data structure and a specific operational environment are determined, we can select an optimal representation of the database relations. We can determine physical file media, file organization for each entity relation, index organization for each attribute to be indexed, and physical representation of each binary relationship relation. However, it is usually very difficult to predict actual operational requirements. These may even change very rapidly as the society of which the enterprises are a part changes and the enterprises are reorganized.

It is desirable for the database management functions to be flexible enough to permit easy update of logical data structure and easy reorganization of physical representation. For the latter, it is best if the system has a feature for monitoring the system operation and collecting various operational statistics such as frequency of search operations with each type of the search conditions and frequency of update operations. Such information, if available, is given to the database administrators who are responsible for redefining the database structure or is used by the system in making an automatic database reorganization.

8.2. Data Manipulation

Data manipulation of the database relations can be described by several different levels of *data manipulation languages* (DML). We know that we can describe a very wide range of data processing operations by the language whose only statements specify alpha operations. We may have a data manipulation language composed of the statements corresponding to the relational algebra or to the information algebra. We may add statements corresponding to navigations if the language is based on the entity–relationship view of the real world.

We may even have some higher-level languages than those described above. For example, we may provide a language that activates several utility programs such as report writing and file maintenance. However, we can specify only a limited number of data processing patterns using such languages, and hence they can describe only a relatively narrow range of data processing operations.

Another direction along which to develop a higher-level language may be to adopt natural language statements. This approach will be discussed in Section 11.

As presented in Section 5.3, we need tuple-by-tuple operations if we want to achieve efficient database operations. In fact, the languages with executable statements corresponding to set operations never bring the best performance into data manipulation. Here we will discuss a data manipulation language based on tuple-by-tuple operations.

8.2.1. Host Languages

The tuple-by-tuple operations consist of the read class operations, the write class operations, and the calculate class operations. Of these, the calculate class operations can be specified in an existing basic programming language. Such a basic programming language is called a *host language*.[25] We must select a host language that is suitable for our applications. We may have more than one host language if we have several different types of applications.

Most existing basic programming languages have sufficient capability to describe the calculate class operations. They are, however, incapable of accurately describing the read class and write class operations to be performed on the database. Most of them are equipped with the read/write and get/put type statements and several compiler directives for specifying the file format, which are usually insufficient to control database operations. Hence, the host language must be enriched with additional *database routines* that can perform the read and write class operations.

8.2.2. Database Routines

As important standard procedures to be integrated in the system, we must implement database routines that can be invoked by the user's programs written in the host language. We have already discussed the basic tuple-by-tuple operations in Section 5.9. They are:

Read class:

$$G_f, G_n,$$
$$G_{fc}, G_{nc}, G_{fp}, G_{np},$$
$$G'_{fc}, G'_{nc}, G'_{lc}, G'_{pc}, G'_{fp}, G'_{np}, G'_{lp}, G'_{np},$$
$$G_{fa}, G_{na}, G_{ft}, G_{nt}$$

Write class:

$$U_a, U_d, U_r$$

Arguments appearing in each operation must be specified as formal parameters of the corresponding database routine. For example, G_f, G_{fc}, and U_a can be implemented as standard procedured headed respectively by

```
procedure getfirst(m: integer; r: array[1 .. m] of relation; t: type;
          function lambda: boolean; function lambda1: t;
          var c: array[1 .. m] of cursor);
procedure getfchild(r1, r2, r: relation; t: type; function lambda: t;
          car c1, c2: cursor);
procedure addtuple(r: relation);
```

Workspaces for the relations specified as actual parameters are reserved in the programming area with reference to the definition of these relations in the database directory. Workspaces for R can be referred to as R. The jth attribute value in the workspace in which a (current) record is stored may be referred to as $a_j(R\uparrow)$. After a read class operation has been executed, a record corresponding to a qualified tuple (or more than one record corresponding to a qualified ordered set of tuples) is fetched into the corresponding workspace(s). Before an update operation (except delete operations) is invoked, the corresponding workspace must be filled with the tuple to be added.

The cursor is a special data type which points to the tuple most recently fetched. The user need not be aware of its contents but must specify its name as an actual parameter.

The following is a complete program achieving a summary operation:

```
program summary(emp,dept)
        var cemp: cursor;
   begin getfirst(1,emp,integer,,deptno,cemp);
        while not eof(emp) do
     begin deptno(dept↑) := deptno(emp↑); stotal(dep↑)
               := salary(emp↑);
        getnext(1,emp,integer,,deptno,cemp);
        while deptno(dept↑) = deptno(emp↑) do
     begin stotal(dept↑) := stotal(dept↑) + salary(emp↑);
          getnext(l,emp,integer,,deptno,cemp)
        end;
        addtuple(dept)
     end
   end;
```

This program summarizes "salary" of employees in each department and generates a department relation. The default option of the lambda1 parameter specifies the T function, which assigns the value "true" to every tuple in the employee relation.

Standard procedures embodying these tuple-by-tuple operations need several features that are not integrated in the statements provided in the existing programming languages. The search procedure must be executed efficiently with the form of the search condition and the physical database organization taken into account. We know that a sort must be included to execute some types of search operations. The navigation procedures vary according to the physical representation employed for the relationship relation to be traversed. Update procedure also vary greatly according to the physical database organization. In particular, if the relationship relation is represented by pointers, its updates must be performed by updating one or more tuples in the relation on which the relationship relation is defined. Different pointer organizations require different update procedures.

All the additional requirements regarding integrity, security, concurrency, and recoverability must be dealt with by the database routines. Update procedures must be capable of validating the data that are used to update the database. To deal with temporary inconsistencies, we may provide a start-of-transaction procedure and an end-of-transaction procedure.

All the read and write procedures must be capable of protecting privacy with reference to the passwords that the user has submitted to the system and to the security table which the system maintains.

To allow concurrent accesses to the database, we must provide a lock option for the read procedures and an unlock option for the write procedures. We may also provide separate lock and unlock procedures, which specify a larger locking granule or a predicate lock.

Note that all the parts to be updated when the locked tuples are updated must be locked as well. For instance, the index records pointing to the locked records must be locked together. Update applied to the database must be logged in an appropriate *transaction journal*. Before and after images as well as the record of transactions must be logged.

If we have a distributed database some database routines that access a database maintained by another computer must be implemented. A proper protocol must be integrated in these routines to achieve data communication and data translation.

Implementation of the database routines is one of the most important and difficult tasks in constructing a database. In particular, dealing with various environmental requirements seems to remain more an art than a science.

8.2.3. Collective Updates

We know that some assertions with two or more bound variables are violated when a unit update is executed. In such cases, a temporary inconsistency occurs. The inconsistent state lasts until some other unit updates are executed. Declaration of start and end of transaction together with a predicate lock mechanism protects the inconsistent part of the database against access by other programs. However, for several special assertions we can provide collective update routines, which updates several tuples simultaneously.

For example, let R be a relationship relation defined between two relations R_1 and R_2. Deletion of any tuple either in R_1 or in R_2 violates the relationship constraint defined over the three relation schemata R_{p_1}, R_{p_2}, and R_p, to which R_1, R_2, and R, respectively, belong. The inconsistent state is removed when all the tuples in R whose origin or destination is the tuple deleted from R_1 or R_2. Therefore, we may provide a collective delete procedure that deletes a tuple in R_1 or R_2 and all the tuples in R whose origin or destination is the deleted tuple as well.

In the relationship relation schema several other constraints that determine the relationship relation type may hold. If the relationship relation is represented by a pointer organization, the forward and backward dependencies are embedded in this representation. If the pointer is bidirectional, the circuit constraint can be easily tested. It is relatively easy to provide collective update procedures that preserve the connectedness constraint (in particular, for a sequence) and the onto constraint (in particular, for a hierarchy).

If R is a sequence (a recursive connected quasisequence), the deletion of a tuple from the relation on which R is defined must be followed by the deletion of two tuples from R and the addition of one tuple to R. On the other hand, the addition of a tuple to the relation on which R is defined must be followed by the deletion of one tuple to R and the addition of two tuples to R. These are shown in Fig. 28.

If R is a multilevel hierarchy, the deletion of a tuple from one of the relations on which R is defined must be followed by the deletion of one or more tuples from R. This must be followed by the deletion of several

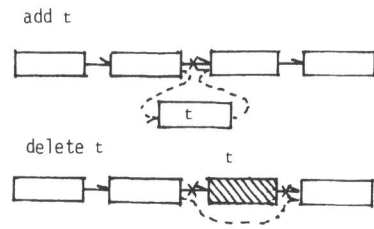

Fig. 28. Update of a sequence.

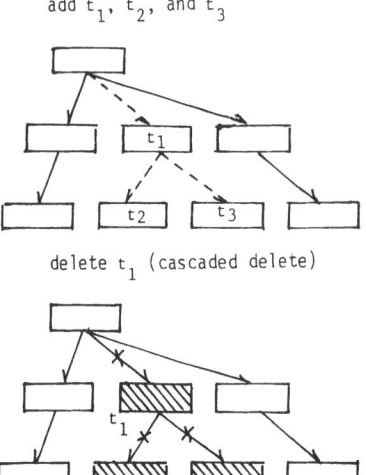

Fig. 29. Update of a multilevel hierarchy.

tuples from one of the relations on which R is defined to preserve the onto constraint, which must again be followed by the deletion of several tuples from R. This *cascaded deletion* must be continued until all the descendant tuples of the deleted ancestor tuple have been deleted. The addition of a tuple to one of the relations on which R is defined must be followed by the addition of a tuple to R. These are shown in Fig. 29. Database procedures for adding a new tuple must have some additional arguments specifying the position of the tuple to be added with respect to the relationship relation to be updated simultaneously.

If several such database routines are provided for such typical assertions, the user need not be aware of the most temporary inconsistencies and can write simpler programs that access the database.

8.2.4. Variable-Length Part of Tuples

The variable-length part of a tuple, if present, may be stored in the main record or in some subordinate record separate from the fixed-length part. Sometimes, repeating-group records are provided to store a repeating-group-type attribute value. Repeating-group records are usually dealt with differently from simple subordinate records.

Attribute values that are essentially of variable length may be stored in a subordinate record which is itself of variable length. Data types of such attributes must be indicated to be "variable." For example, a v indication may be prefixed to t_k in the **gtype** statement for the relation schema to be defined. When such an attribute is to be referred to, the user provides a workspace in his program that is large enough to hold the attribute value. Then he can invoke a database routine such as

getattribute(emp,address,ws)

where the first argument specifies the relation name, the second argument the attribute name, and the third argument the name of the workspace that the user provided in his program. He can update this attribute value by filling the workspace with the new value followed by invoking a database routine such as

replaceattribute(emp,address,ws)

The system accesses the specified attribute value using a workspace which the system provides for holding a subordinate record. This workspace is not necessarily large enough for an entire subordinate record. The system can read segments, each part of a subordinate record, one by one until the segment containing the specified attribute value has been reached. The attribute value can be replaced in this state.

A repeating group may be defined as

gtype groupname = set of record $a_1' : t_1'; a_2' : t_2'; \ldots ; a_m' : t_m'$ end;

If the data type t_k in the gtype/entity or gtype/relationship statement defining a relation schema is the groupname defined as above, a_k is a repeating-group-type attribute. Each component of a repeating group may be represented by a repeating-group record. The system provides a work-space large enough to hold one repeating-group record. When a main record is read into the workspace, the first repeating-group record linked to this main record is fetched into this workspace as well. If the next group becomes necessary, a database routine such as

getnextgroup(emp,family)

where the first argument specifies the relation name and the second argument the group name, can be invoked. For the update, we need database routines such as

addgroup(emp,family),
deletegroup(emp,family)

and

replacegroup(emp,family)

A repeating group can contain other repeating groups. The above access mechanism can be nested for nested repeating groups. At a specific moment, each of the workspaces for the main record and repeating-group records (forming a tree of workspaces) contains one record. The attribute values in a workspace for a repeating group can be referred to as if they were in the workspace for the main record.

Power-set-type attributes can be dealt with either as variable-length atrributes· or as repeating-group-type attributes. If the former is desirable (for example, a keyword list in the document records), the data type can be defined as

$$\text{gtype datatype} = \text{set of } t;$$

where t is a basic data type (for example, the data type of keywords). For the latter, the data type can be defined as

$$\text{gtype datatype} = \text{set of record } a:t \text{ end};$$

8.3. Binding

The information stored in the database directory is used by the compiler while it is reserving workspaces in the program area for database file control. The various symbolic specifications for database files that appear in the host language program are translated into an internal representation with reference to the database directory. Database routines may also use the directory information in selecting appropriate operation sequences to achieve necessary search or update operations. These are selected with the logical data structure and physical representation taken into consideration. These processes are called *binding.*

Some parts of the binding function can be easily integrated into a preprocessor for the host language translator. The preprocessor supplies the information necessary for compilation that is not given in the user's host language program. Since a relation may be represented by several physical files linked together, many compiler directives may be generated for a single relation.

Other parts of the binding function may be left to run-time binding. For example, we can make some run-time optimization of the search operation.[59] If run-time binding is required, a supervisory program must be provided which monitors all the processing programs that have access to the database. Some information, such as the number of tuples in each relation, is used by both types of binding functions. Such information must be contained in the database directory together with other data descriptions.

Implementation of binding functions largely depends on the operating system and the host language translators which will be used with the database management functions.

8.4. Functions for Database Administrators

The database must be searched and updated by many users. There may be various types of users, some well acquainted with computer programming and others not familiar with the computer. It is widely claimed that some experts must be responsible for administrating the database. They are called *database administrators.*[21]

Principal roles of the database administrators include monitoring system operations and restructuring the database when necessary. Several utility programs must be provided to assist them in performing their tasks.

8.4.1. Inspection

The database administrator needs to know the current status of some database parts. He might want to know what logical data structure is registered in the directory, what physical representation is used to express a specific relation, how many records are accommodated in a specific file, how many read and write class operations have been executed on a specific file, and so forth. To make such information available for the database administrator, a utility program that can extract and display the necessary information on request must be prepared. The system may also generate a warning message to the database administrator when some critical situation occur in the database.

8.4.2. Reorganization

When the database administrator encounters poor performance in the database, he would like to reorganize the database to remove the problem. Several kinds of database reorganization can occur. Relocation of database files, that is, moving some files between storage media, is a simple reorganization. For a heap file, particularly one with variable-length records, garbage collection is desirable. Garbage collection puts the database in order by cleaning up unnecessary data generated in a heap file. After many updates have been performed on a heap file, many areas too small to accommodate new records will have been generated in the heap file, which, therefore, must be reorganized to eliminate such unusable areas. Reorganization is also required when the data description (logical data structure) itself is updated.

8.4.3. Recovery

When the database is partially or completely destroyed by some hardware and/or software malfunctions or by operator errors, the database administrator must remove the cause and reconstruct the correct state of the database as soon as possible. He must examine the cause of the destruction, remove it, determine the error propagation, and restore the correct state. As described in Section 6.4, various recovery procedures can be used depending on the error types. We can use before images, after images, and/or checkpoint dumps, together with transaction logging depending on the error. The database administrator is also responsible for creating and maintaining the checkpoint dump. There must be several utility programs supporting these operations.

8.4.4. Table Maintenance

The database administrator has to maintain the security table in which $\mathscr{S}_R$ and $\mathscr{S}_W$ (see Section 6.2) and passwords assigned to users are stored.

Sometimes it is desirable to integrate an encoding/decoding mechanism into the system in order both to store some attribute values in an encoded form and to decode them when they are to be displayed. If such a function is integrated in the system, a code table must be created and maintained by the database administrator.

These roles of the database administrator must be supported by appropriate utility programs.

8.4.5. Database File Creation

When an entity or relationship relation schema is defined by means of the data description language, we may think that an empty relation is created in the database. However, we should note that an empty relation cannot satisfy any existential constraint (a constraint whose first quantification in prenex normal form is existential). Therefore, if such an existential constraint is registered as an assertion, the initial file creation procedure must be performed differently from other update operations. To handle this situation, a utility program that create a database file can be provided.

8.5. Database Management Languages

After all the database management functions we have discussed have been implemented, we can easily create, search, and update the database. These functions are activated by three different languages: the data description language, which is used to define logical data structure; the data manipulation language, which is used to describe data processing operations on the database; and the database administration language, which is used by the database administrator to activate various utility programs.

Design and implementation of database management functions and database management languages is a very time-consuming and expensive task. Fortunately, we have a number of the so-called generalized database management systems already developed and offered by computer manufacturers and software houses. In these systems, database management functions are implemented to a certain extent.

9. DATABASE MANAGEMENT SYSTEMS

Today, a number of generalized database management systems are available that can be used as a foundation for information systems construction. Several good surveys of the existing generalized database management systems have appeared.[24,25,42,93,96]

Two types of generalized database management systems, *host language systems* and *self-contained systems*, can be distinguished. A host language system is composed of one or more basic programming languages enriched with database management functions. A self-contained system is equipped with one or more end-user languages. The user can easily create, search, and update the database using these end-user languages.

Provision of the end-user languages might be the final goal of information systems construction; however, the self-contained systems have not been very successful until now. This is because the end-user language is not flexible enough for a wide range of applications.

Here we will discuss selection criteria for host language systems and will also review features of some typical generalized database management systems. Self-contained systems will be discussed later in relation to the end-user language design.

9.1. Selection Criteria for Database Management Systems

The database management functions we have discussed in Section 8 are those that must be embodied in the host language system. A host language system can therefore be used as a foundation for the information system to be constructed. There are a variety of host language systems, all having features somewhat different from one another. This makes comparison of these systems very difficult. The CODASYL Data Base Task Group (DBTG) proposed a standard functional specification for the host language system based on COBOL.[22] However, it is well known that the CODASYL DBTG proposal is not powerful enough to deal with all kinds of information systems.

If we want to be efficient in implementing database functions, we need to select one existing database management system that is most suitable for our application. There are many points to be considered in selecting one of the available systems. The following are important:

1. Can the system represent the logical data structure required in the users' application appropriately? Can the users define the data structure easily?
2. Is the system equipped with the database operations to be used frequently in the users' application? Can it process necessary search, navigation, and/or update operations efficiently?
3. Is the system suitable for the given operational environment? Does it provide enough capability for integrity preservation, privacy protection, concurrent processing, and recovery? If a distributed system is to be constructed, the system may have to have several functions such as data translation and locking protocols.
4. Is the physical representation employed by the system efficient enough for the users' application?
5. Is the host language of the system suitable for programming the users' application?
6. Does the system provide a database administrator language that well supports the database administrator's tasks?
7. Is the system flexible enough to cope with changes of environment? Can the users easily update the logical data structure as well as its physical representation?
8. Is it easy to develop end-user languages using the employed host language?
9. Is the total performance satisfactory for the users' application?

We will further discuss these criteria in the following, and we will see how each database function is implemented in several typical generalized database management systems.

9.2. Directory-Type Classification of Database Management Systems

The first criterion of classification of database management systems mainly concerns the data description language. According to the forms of their data description languages, database management systems are usually classified into three types: *network* (or coset), *hierarchical*, and *relational*.[42]

We will now add one more type called the *entity–relationship type*. The four types are characterized as follows:

1. *Entity–Relationship Type.* The systems that can represent any number of entity relations and any number of relationship relations of any type are said to be entity–relationship type.

2. *Coset Type.* The systems that can represent any number of entity relations and any number of (single-level) hierarchies are said to be coset type. Usually these are called network type systems. However, since they can represent neither recursive tree nor (recursive or irrecursive) network directly, network type is not an adequate name. Therefore, we will call them coset type systems after Nijssen.[70] In order to represent recursive trees and (recursive or irrecursive) networks, the user must decompose them into their hierarchical normal form expression as mentioned in Section 4.6.5.

3. *Hierarchical Type.* The systems that can represent any number of entity relations and any number of multilevel hierarchies are said to be hierarchical type. Unlike entity–relationship and coset type, only one multi-level hierarchy can be defined on each entity relation. Some systems that can represent repeating-group-type attributes may be classified in this type.

4. *Relational Type.* The systems that can represent any number of entity relation but can neither represent any relationship relation directly nor have repeating-group-type attributes are said to be relational type. Usually the first normal form of the relations is assumed.

FORIMS[60] is a typical entity–relationship type system. The relation schemata of entity relations (called FILEs) and relationship relations (called STRUCTUREs) are defined quite separately. Relationship relation schemata can have other attributes in addition to their origin and destination attributes. Data types for the attributes (PROPERTYs) can be any FORTRAN data type. In addition, variable-length attribute values can be specified.

TOTAL[20] is a coset type system. An entity relation, if it is specified as a hierarchically lower relation (VARIABLE-LENGTH DATA SET), can have as many linkage paths as the number of hierarchies defined on it. A linking field (LINK) must be provided in it in addition to the pointer field (CONTROL FIELD) which is provided for both the hierarchically upper relation (MSTER DATA SET) and hierarchically lower relation. This type of directory causes some difficulties in defining a multilevel hierarchy since the same relation can be both a hierarchically upper and lower relation in this sense. Only the number of bytes representing a unit datum is specified in the data-type specification of attribute values. All attribute values must be of fixed length.

All the systems based on the CODASYL DBTG proposal[22] are coset type. Entity relations (called RECORD aggregates) and hierarchies (called

SET aggregates) can be defined separately. One or more pointer fields are created by the system to represent a hierarchy. Unlike the pointer organization in TOTAL, no linking fields are necessary in generating pointer fields. The user can specify the order in which tuples in each terminal set (set of destinations with a common origin) are arranged. This introduces a quasisequence into the set of destination tuples and this quasisequence together with the hierarchy is represented at the same time (by a SET). Data types of the attributes (DATA ITEMs) are those in COBOL. This implies that repeating groups can also be represented. However, since the record size is fixed, the number of repetitions cannot exceed a predetermined limit.

IMS 1 was an example of the hierarchical system. There are two types of entity relations, which are the hierarchically highest class (ROOT SEGMENT files) and others (DEPENDENT SEGMENT files) of a multilevel hierarchy. All relations are defined with a part of hierarchical skeleton (using a PARENT SEGMENT indication). Data types are hexadecimal and alphanumeric.

IMS VS[47] is hybrid in the sense that the user can define both multilevel hierarchies (at most one on each entity relation) and (single-level) hierarchies (as many as required). (The former are represented by PHYSICAL POINTERs and the latter by LOGICAL POINTERs.) A pointer field (LCHILD) can be added to the relation that is to become the hierarchically upper class of the hierarchy. This system can be regarded as providing both the hierarchical type and coset type directory.

SYSTEM 2000[68] is a hierarchical system. The multilevel hierarchy is defined by means of a repeating-group-type attribute; but a separate record is generated for each component of the repeating group. If an appropriate linking field exists, a hierarchy (LINK) can be defined dynamically during program execution. In this sense, SYSTEM 2000 is also a hybrid system. A data-type specification defines only the length of attribute values. Variable-length attribute values are not allowed, but variable repetition of repeating-group components is permitted. SYSTEM 2000's data description seems to be the most easily used among the existing database management systems.

In most cases, ADABAS[85] is classified as the relational type. It allows, however, repeating-group-type attributes and hence does not impose the first normal-form restriction on defining database relation schemata. Essentially, the record size is of variable length and all the repeating-group components are fetched into the program area at the same time. Relationship relations are not explicitly defined by the data description language. In fact, the ADABAS file definition resembles that in COBOL. However, data compression is employed as a standard feature. In addition to the definition of entity relations (with repeating-group-type attributes, if necessary), ADABAS has a function (called COUPLING) which can be regarded as

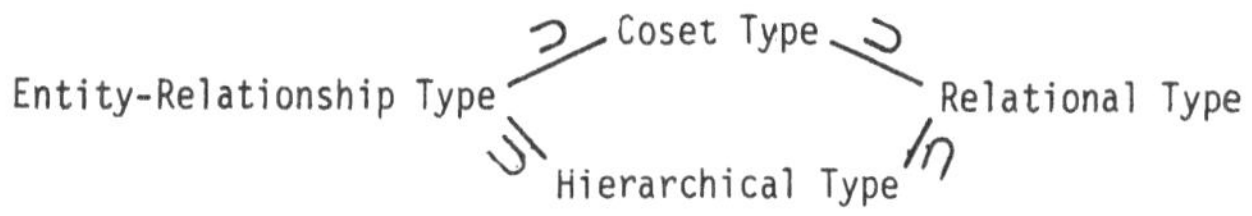

Entity-Relationship Type ⌒Coset Type⌒ Relational Type
Hierarchical Type

Fig. 30. Relationships among various directory types.

defining irrecursive relationship relations. If a common linking field is provided in the two relations between which an irrecursive relationship relation is to be defined, a bidirectional pointer array is generated by the system. Irrecursive networks as well as irrecursive trees can be defined by the (COUPLING) function. In this sense, ADABAS can be regarded as providing an entity–relationship type database directory, although definition of recursive relationship relations is not available.

INGRES[45] is a typical relational type system which is almost completely based on the relational model. SYSTEM R[3] seems to have aimed at implementing a relational type system to be used as a test bed of various database management functions. However, it now includes many compromises between relational and other types. For instance, it provides a linking function that is very similar to that provided in ADABAS. Links are based on a common linking field, and maintained automatically by the system. A link can represent a quasisequence (UNARY LINK) or an irrecursive tree (BINARY LINK).

Figure 30 shows the relationship among various database directory types. However, as seen above, not so many systems can be classified into a directory type in an exact sense. In fact, differences among the data description capabilities possessed by the existing database management systems tend to disappear, although different terminologies are still being used is their data description languages.

Some systems can serve users who want to have a view different from the view supported by the database directory. However, the view-support features in the existing database management systems are not powerful enough for supporting arbitrary views of the real world. For example, the subschema function provided in CODASYL DBTG-type systems only allows subsets of relation schema definitions registered in the directory (SCHEMA). SYSTEM R provides a somewhat more advanced view-support feature; however, the view must still be in a relational view.

9.3. Database Operations

To apply the second criterion, we must examine the database routines provided in each database management system. These include search operations, navigation operations, update operations, and some others that can be invoked in the user's host language program.

As described in Section 5.5, there are various levels of search conditions. Some system can only achieve the search with a condition of the form

$$A_p(x) = \text{const}$$

where A_p is a specified primary key or a system-supplied primary key called the *database key*. Only a few systems can answer queries with search conditions defined on more than one relation. In particular, it is very difficult to process conditions containing bound variables. Every database management system can process search conditions in a certain level.

Some systems provide index files to improve the efficiency of a search with a condition of the form

$$A_k(x)\theta \text{ const}$$

where A_k is an attribute and θ is an arbitrary relational operator. When an attribute A_k is specified to be indexed by means of a certain argument embedded in the data description language, an index file is created for this attribute. Some systems provide pointer links between tuples in two relations to improve the efficiency of a search with a condition of the form

$$A_i(x_1) = A_j(x_2).$$

This can be regarded as a provision for a special kind of navigation operations.

Systems dealing with relationship relations always provide navigation operations along the relationship relation which has been defined by means of the data description language. Navigation operations can be performed in several different directions. To achieve efficient navigation, pointer links connecting tuples are provided in most of the database management systems that have database routines for navigation operations.

Update routines that add, delete, and replace tuples in the database relation are provided in all the existing systems. However, their functions greatly vary.

FORIMS has three routines, each performing different search operations. The RTID retrieves a tuple using its primary key value, the RTD retrieves a tuple using its database key (RECORD NUMBER), and the RTC retrieves a tuple satisfying a given search condition one by one. The search condition can be an arbitrary FORTRAN logical function defined on one relation. This means FORIMS deals with extended relational calculi defined on one relation without quantified variables. To improve the search efficiency, any attribute can be indexed if so specified in the data description language. An inverted file is created for each attribute to be indexed. FORIMS database routines try to use these inverted files as much as possible in processing the given search condition.[17] If no inverted files are available for speeding up the search operation, a seek operation is performed. An optimization is integrated into the search process dealing with compound conditions (logical combinations of unit conditions).

For navigation, the RTS routine is provided, which can traverse any relationship relation in any direction. It is probably the most powerful navigation routine provided in the existing database management systems (in a logical sense). The navigation efficiency is worse than in other systems, because FORIMS represents relationship relations by relationship records (see Section 7.4.4).

For update, FORIMS provides ADD (addition), DLT (deletion), and MDF (replace) routines. They are used for updating both entity and relationship relations. To retrieve and update variable-length parts of tuples, the GETVP and PUTVP routines are provided.

In TOTAL, a number of database routines are provided; however, READM, which retrieves a tuple in a hierarchically upper class relation using its primary key (CONTROL FIELD) value, is the only available search routine.

TOTAL provides various database routines for navigation. The SEQRM and RESTM perform sequential access to a hierarchically upper-class relation. Hierarchies defined in the data description language can be traversed by one of SEQRV, READV, READR, and READD in various directions.

An update routine must be selected according to what retrieval routine has been used before the subject update. For adding a tuple, one of the routines ADD-M, LOADM, ADDVC, ADDVB, or ADDVR is used. The first two are used for hierarchically upper-class relations. LOADM performs the addition just as ADD-M does but it checks whether duplicate primary key values are generated (that is, checks if the key dependency regarding the primary key has been violated). The last three routines deal with updating the hierarchically lower-class relations and hierarchies themselves. For deleting a tuple, DEL-M or DELVD is used according to the case, while for replacing a tuple, either of SEQWV, WRITM, or WRITV is used. Thus, there are several collective update routines as mentioned in Section 8.2.3.

In a CODASYL DBTG proposal, only two special search routines are provided. One, the search using the database key, can be used only between the invocation of the KEEP routine and that of the RELEASE routine. Other users are prevented from modifying the subject tuple during this term. The other routine is the search with a condition of the form

$$A_p(x) = \text{const}$$

where A_p is the primary key.

In contrast, DBTG proposal provides a powerful command repertoire for navigation. The user can perform sequential access to tuples in a relation for which a sequence key is specified. Navigation along hierarchies (SETs) can be performed in any direction. It can pick up only the tuples that satisfy an additional condition. Such an operation can be regarded as a combination of search and navigation operations. All the search and navigation routines are invoked by the FIND and GET commands and a variety of FIND command formats are available.

There are various collective update routines. For example, addition is performed by STORE for entity relations, while it is performed by CON-NECT for hierarchies. These are unit update routines. If an AUTOMATIC option has been specified in a hierarchy definition, the STORE routine also add the tuples necessary for the hierarchy defined on the entity relation to which a tuple is added by this STORE. Deletion is performed by ERASE for entity relations, but by DISCONNECT for hierarchies. All the destination tuples of the deleted tuple with respect to the hierarchy for which an AUTOMATIC option is specified are deleted by ERASE. If the ERASE routine is invoked with an ALL option, a cascaded deletion results, that is, all descendant tuples in all the involved hierarchies are deleted. The DBTG proposal does not define multilevel hierarchies explicitly but deals with them in this sense. The replace operation is performed by the MODIFY routine.

IMS provides nine database routines, of which GU (GET UNIQUE) and GHU (GET HOLD UNIQUE) are for search operations. To perform a search, one of these must be invoked with a SSA (SEGMENT SEARCH ARGUMENT) which is declared elsewhere in the program. The search condition is a conjunction and/or disjunction of unit conditions of the form

$$A_k(x)\theta \text{ const}$$

where θ is one of $=$, $\neq$, $>$, $<$, $\geq$, and $\leq$. Any attribute can be indexed, if so specified in the data description language.

Navigation is achieved in two different ways. The GN (GET NEXT) and GHN (GET HOLD NEXT) routines traverse a multilevel hierarchy along the sequence that is obtained by connecting all component sequences in the quasisequence, which is the result of transformation mentioned in Theorem 5 (see Section 4.6.7). The GNP (GET NEXT WITHIN PARENT) and GHNP (GET HOLD NEXT WITHIN PARENT) routines fetch the destination tuples with a common origin tuple one by one. They both can be combined with some search operation is specified in the SSA. In order to lock the retrieved tuple, the hold option must be specified for all the read routines that precede an update routine.

The ISRT, DLET, and REPL routines are used respectively for adding, deleting, and replacing a tuple. These routines make the necessary updates of the multilevel hierarchy at the same time.

SYSTEM 2000's host language interface has a number of verbs. Of these, LOCATE and GET1 are used with a WHERE clause specifying a search condition, which is a logical combination of unit conditions of the form

$$A_k(x)\,\theta\text{ const}$$

and of some other forms. Any attribute is indexed if so specified in the data description language. When a search has been invoked by the LOCATE verb, the qualified tuples can be arranged using the ORDER BY verb. The results can be fetched one by one using the GET verb.

Navigation can be performed by GETA and GETD. The GETA verb fetches the parent tuple, while the GETD verb the fetches the child tuple, both with respect to a multilevel hierarchy. SYSTEM 2000 has the LINK verb which is used to reorganize a multilevel hierarchy at run time.

Adding and replacing a tuple can be performed by INSERT and MODIFY, respectively. For deleting tuples, two verbs, REMOVE and REMOVE TREE, are provided. The latter is a collective update which performs a cascaded deletion with respect to the multilevel hierarchy.

In ADABAS, nine commands are provided, of which two are search commands. The S1 command returns a list of ISNs (INTERNAL SEQUENCE NUMBERs) of the tuples satisfying the search condition which is a logical combination of unit conditions of the forms

$$A_k(x_i)\,\theta\text{ const}$$

and/or

$$A_k(x_i) = A_k(x_j)$$

This implies that the search condition is some special logical function of lines (of span less than five). The search condition must be specified using the SEARCH BUFFER and VALUE BUFFER upon calling the command. An inverted file can be created for any attribute to improve the search with a condition of the former form, while the COUPLING can be made to improve the search with a condition of the latter form. The S2 command returns a sorted list of ISNs. The tuple pointed to by an ISN can be fetched one by one by the L1 command.

As a special operator, ADABAS permits phonetic comparison. Phonetic equivalents are found by dropping vowels and one letter of each double consonant. ADABAS provides three types of sequential read operations. The D2 command is for physical sequential read while the L3 command is for sequential read in the order of values of a specified indexed attribute. Finally, the L9 command is used to retrieve (1) all values of a specified indexed attribute and (2) the number of occurrences of each value. Updates are achieved by N1 for adding a tuple, E1 for deleting a tuple, and A1 for replacing a tuple.

The host language interface of SYSTEM R is called the *relational data interface* (RDI). It includes an operator called SEQUEL that allows the use of the SEQUEL sublanguage. The search condition is specified by a part of the large SEQUEL syntax. The search condition is a logical combination of unit conditions of the form

$$A_x(x_i)\, \theta \text{ const}$$

and/or

$$A_k(x_i)\, \theta A_l(x_j)$$

This is a logical function of lines of a limited form. Some intrinsic function on an attribute can replace an attribute in the above form. The search result is a list of TIDs (TUPLE IDENTIFIERs). The qualified tuples can be fetched one by one by the FETCH command. The FETCH-HOLD command is used for preventing other users from updating the qualified tuples. If the user knows the tuple format, he may issue a BIND command before the SEQUEL command to specify the workspace into which a qualified tuple is to be fetched. If the format is unknown, the user may issue a DESCRIBE command to examine the tuple format. To enable an efficient search with a unit condition of the former form, any attribute can be indexed by IMAGE. Unit conditions of the latter form can be processed efficiently if the user lets the SYSTEM R provide pointers between tuples in two relations by BINARY LINK. This is possible only when θ is the equality operator.

Navigation can be invoked in a lower-level language called the *relational storage interface* (RSI), which is oriented toward the use of formatted control blocks. In this level, sequential read can be performed in the order of values of an indexed attribute (IMAGE) or of an attribute for which a sequential scan is declared by UNARY LINK. Also, traversals along a hierarchy defined by means of the BINARY LINK pointers can be performed in various directions.

Updates are also specified by SEQUEL operators. The SEQUEL syntax allows both setwise and tuplewise updates. It provides INSERT for adding, DELETE for deleting, and UPDATE for replacing.

The SEQUEL syntax includes a huge statement repertoire and can specify many other finer functions than those mentioned above. Furthermore, due to its nature as an experimental system, it is still expanding.

As seen above, database routines in the existing database management systems are very diverse. Some systems have powerful navigation routines but only the search routine corresponding to direct access. Some others have powerful search routines but no navigation routines. We must be very careful in examining what operations are required for our application, and what database management systems are suitable in the sense that they provide database routines powerful enough to meet such requirements both qualitatively and quantitatively.

9.4. Environmental Requirements

The third criterion is related to operational requirements including integrity, security, concurrency, and recoverability. Most existing database management systems provide these functions to some extent. We will review only some of the extraordinary functions supplied in several systems.

We encounter two major problems with distributed databases. One is data translation among different database directories, and the other is locking protocols between different sites. The distributed database technology is still under development, and is not fully supported by the existing database management systems.

9.4.1. Integrity

Many database management systems automatically execute data-type checks for attribute domains. Some of them have an additional range check function. For example, DBTG has a check option in its attribute definition.

Some of them validate the key dependencey regarding the primary key of each relation. For instance, we already saw that TOTAL has the LOADM command that checks if duplicate primary key values are generated when a tuple is added to the relation. IMS guarantees no two tuples contain the same sequence field value if M (MULTIVALUED) is not specified. DBTG assures uniqueness in the primary key value when a DUPLICATES NOT ALLOWED clause is given in the data description language.

Relationship constraints are preserved in many systems by means of providing collective update routines. We have seen that many systems have a cascaded deletion routine to maintain hierarchies.

An advanced provision is seen in SYSTEM R, which allows an explicit declaration for registering static constraints by an ASSERT statement. Since quantifications cannot be specified explicitly; only some aggregate constraints and tuple constraints can be specified. The ASSERT statement can also be used to register dynamic constraints of certain forms. For example

ASSERT assertionname ON UPDATE OF relationname (attributename):
NEW attributename θ OLD attributename

assures the specified condition at update time.

Many systems allow integration of user-coded validation procedures. For example, DBTG is capable of integrating the PROCEDURE that is to be invoked at an appropriate time to perform desired validation.

9.4.2. Security

As described in Section 6.2, database security can be specified by a table expressing $\mathscr{S}_R$ and $\mathscr{S}_W$. Each entry of this table determines the parts of the database to which a user is granted access.

FORIMS provides privacy protection both for an entire relation and for each attribute in a relation. The specified relations and/or attributes are protected against unauthorized read and/or write. However, FORIMS cannot specify privacy protection for tuples satisfying a given condition.

IMS provides privacy protection for a relation specified by means of PCB (PROGRAM COMMUNICATION BLOCK). DBTG enables the user to specify privacy protection for a SUBSCHEMA. However, both the PCB and SUBSCHEMA are exact copies of some parts of the database directory, and they can not specify tuples satisfying a given condition. Therefore, security mechanisms in these two systems are not very flexible.

Again, SYSTEM R has an interesting feature which assigns the user a virtual database relation he can access by defining a VIEW. The VIEW corresponds to an alpha operation, which is defined by both a relational calculus of a certain limited form (a search condition that can be described in the SEQUEL syntax) and a tuple-generating function. The calculus part of the VIEW definition extracts the tuples satisfying it, while the tuple-generating function extracts the attribute values or some values calculated from the attribute values, that are disclosed to the user. The GRANT command in SEQUEL assigns such VIEWs to the user with rights of READ, INSERT, DELETE, and/or UPDATE.

9.4.3. Concurrency

Most existing database management systems have two levels of locking protocols: the shared lock and the exclusive lock. Some of them provide a multilevel locking granularity.

FORIMS provides the OPN routine to specify a lock mode for a transaction. The lock mode is one of mode 0 read, mode 0 write, mode 1 read, and mode 1 write. Mode 0 corresponds to the shared lock, while mode 1 refers to the exclusive lock. This lock is made for an entire relation. Each mode inhibits other OPN routines that might inhibit the operations this transaction can execute. The lock is released by RLS during the transaction or by CLS at the end of transaction. If the mode 0 write is specified, any read routine locks the read tuple until the next read is invoked for the relation to which this tuple belongs. Also, the add routine locks the added tuple until the next read is invoked. The replace and delete routine assure that any other updates are not made by other transactions during the execution of these routines.

DBTG has the READY command to specify one of five access modes at the beginning of a transaction. These access modes are: retrieval, update, protected retrieval, protected update, and exclusive update (exclusive retrieval has the same effect). The lock is made for an AREA that is part of the database which the user specified in the data description language. The READY command inhibits other READY commands that might inhibit the operations which are allowed by this READY command. The lock is released by the FINISH command. If one of the first four modes is specified, the user can perform tuplewise locking by means of invoking KEEP. This lock is released by the FREE command.

IMS provides the HOLD option to be specified with various read operations for tuplewise locking.

SYSTEM R enables the user to assign three consistency levels for a transaction by means of the BEGIN-TRANS command. Level 1 allows reading a tuple even if it is in an inconsistent state, while Level 2 allows reading a tuple only if it is not in an inconsistent state. Finally, Level 3 corresponds to the exclusive lock. If one of the first two is specified, the transaction can issue FETCH command with the HOLD option to lock the fetched tuple exclusively. The BEGIN-TRANS is released by END-TRANS and FETCH-HOLD by RELEASE. SYSTEM R provides various locking granularities based on the locking mechanism proposed by Gray *et al.*[43]

9.4.4. Recoverability

Most existing database management systems create a transaction journal that logs transactions thrown into the system: before images and after images. Checkpoint dump, recovery (using the newest checkpoint dump and after images), backout (using before images), and some other utilities are also provided.

FORIMS employs a general error-recovery model proposed by Iizuka and Chiba[46] that determines the causes of errors, examines error propagation, and backs out the database into the consistent state.

DBTG provides the COMMIT and ROLLBACK commands which can be included in the user's program. The COMMIT command is used for establishing a quiet point where all active locks are released. All the updates applied after the newest quiet point are undone when the ROLLBACK command is invoked. Therefore, the destruction of a part of the database, to which the transaction has exclusive access, can be restored automatically if it has been detected by the transaction itself.

ADABAS and SYSTEM R have a function similar to that in DBTG. However, SYSTEM R incidentally employs a *differential file* technique,[82] in which updates are not applied directly to the database. Instead they are recorded in a physically distinct file and are merged with the database at the END-TRANS time. This makes the backout process very simple. The SAVE-TRANS command directs a quiet point, and the RESTORE-TRANS command activates a backout.

9.5. Physical Representation

The preceding three criteria are mainly concerned with external (logical) features of database management systems. Such external features are implemented internally in various ways. As seen in Section 7, a variety of physical representations are applicable to the very same logical data structure. The physical representation selected determines the storage space necessary for the database, the search efficiency, the navigation efficiency, the update efficiency, and so forth. In general, there are various trade-offs among these factors. Which factors are the most important varies according to the users' applications. Every existing database management system has been implemented with an assumption of some specific application requirements or with a compromise of requirements in various applications.

FORIMS generates a heap file for the main records provided for each relation. Each tuple is assigned a unique identification called RN (RECORD NUMBER) by applying a hashing function to the special primary key. An inverted file that gives a correspondence between RN and the main record address is created. Variable-length parts, if exist in tuples, are represented by subordinate records which are accommodated in a separately provided heap file. An inverted file can be created for any attribute, each making a correspondence between an attribute value to one or more RNs. Both entity and relationship relations are represented in this way. Thus, navigation is internally translated into a special search operation applied to more than one file.

The DBTG proposal mentions nothing explicit about physical database representation. However, it includes several commands and clauses that are somehow related to the physical characteristics of the database. An attempt to separate the specification of physical database organization from the data description language to form a sublanguage called DSDL. Most of the DBTG implementations employ the direct or indexed sequential file organization for the entity relations. The CALC access mode may be embodied by a certain hashing function. Hierarchies (SETs) are in most cases represented by ringed lists. A number of additional features have been appended to the original proposal. For example, the secondary key specification may be achieved by providing a certain kind of index organization (SEQUENCE KEY). The DSDL sublanguage will have the CLUSTERED clause that specifies a certain paging mechanism.

In TOTAL, hierarchies are represented by linear lists rather than ringed lists. The LINK FIELD, which are explicitly declared in the data description language, are used to store pointers.

IMS uses two different file organizations, the hierarchical sequential and hierarchical direct, to represent entity relations together with multilevel hierarchies defined on them. The former is a sequential file organizations that uses the sequence obtained by connecting all component sequences in the quasisequence, which is the result of the transformation mentioned in Theorem 5 (see Section 4.6.6). The latter is a direct-file organization for the hierarchically highest-class (ROOT) relation with a hashing function. Hierarchically lower-class relations are linked to it by pointers, for which two different pointer organizations are possible. One is the linear list expressing the sequence obtained by transforming the multilevel hierarchy, and the other is the linear list provided for each hierarchy. Only for the hierarchically highest-class relations can index files be provided. Two access methods, HSAM and HISAM, are available if the former file organization is used, while two other access methods, HDAM and HIDAM, are available if the latter file organization is used.

ADABAS and SYSTEM R employ a representation somewhat similar to that in FORIMS. The unique tuple identification is called ISN (INTERNAL SEQUENCE NUMBER) in ADABAS and TID (TUPLE IDENTIFIER) in SYSTEM R. In ADABAS the record length is essentially variable. The data compression feature greatly reduces the storage space necessary for storing tuples. In SYSTEM R, a paging mechanism is employed, which is controlled by the lower level language RSI.

9.6. Host Language Interfaces

Host language systems have one or more host language interfaces. Usually, we must select one primary basic programming language that is the most suitable for programming our applications. It is desirable for the selected database management system to have an appropriate interface to this language. Other basic programming languages, if necessary, can be used to implement some parts of the program.

FORIMS has only one host language interface to FORTRAN. Many arguments in FORIMS statements are written in FORTRAN format. For instance, the search condition to be given as an argument to the search routine RTC is a FORTRAN logical expression. A FORTRAN logical function can also be used as a logical expression just as in FORTRAN programs. Thus, FORTRAN programmers can very easily learn and use the FORIMS statements. Other basic programming languages can be used via standard linkage processors provided in the operating system.

TOTAL can interface with COBOL, FORTRAN, PL/1, and various assembly languages. All the database routines are invoked by the CALL DATBAS statement.

DBTG employs COBOL as the primary host language. A FORTRAN interface has been added recently. Its data description language and data manipulation language are so designed as to be embedded in the COBOL syntax. This enables COBOL programmers to learn the language syntax easily.

SYSTEM 2000 was originally designed as a self-contained system; hence, its interfaces to COBOL, FORTRAN, PL/1, and an assembler language are optional features. The host language program is first passed through a SYSTEM 2000 compiler where SYSTEM 2000 commands are translated into appropriate calls of the host language interface.

ADABAS can be interfaced with COBOL, FORTRAN, PL/1, and an assembly language for batch operations. The database routines can be invoked by the CALL ADABAS statement with several arguments specifying a proper operation.

SYSTEM R can be used with various basic programming languages. Thirteen distinct routines, SEQUEL, FETCH, FETCH-HOLD, OPEN, CLOSE, KEEP, DESCRIBE, BIND, BEGIN-TRANS, END-TRANS, SAVE, RESTORE, and RELEASE, all provided in the RDI interface, can be invoked by CALL statements.

9.7. Other Criteria

There are several other criteria for selecting a generalized database management system. However, we will only review some functions implemented in several systems.

Generally, several utility programs are provided for the database administrators. FORIMS has seven such utility functions: DISPLAY for looking into the database directory; DBDUMP and DBLOAD to dump and reload database relations; DBRLBK and DBRSTR to back out and restore the database; DBGBCL for garbage collection; and PRVCY for maintaining the privacy protection table. All existing database management systems have similar utility programs.

This is not the case for the function of updating the data definition in the database directory. The DEFINE command in FORIMS that activates the data definition processor can be used both for registering a new relation schema description into the directory and for modifying an existing relation schema description in the directory. The physical representation of the corresponding relation is modified accordingly by the system. ADABAS can add new attributes to an existing relation schema description using the A2 command. These two are very rare systems which allow modifications of directory information.

In most cases, devices for defining procedures provided in the host language are used in developing end-user languages. Some systems have their own procedure (or macro) definition functions in addition.

Finally, evaluating the total system performance is a very difficult task. Usually, several kinds of bench mark tests are unavoidable.

A sample checklist for evaluating database management systems is shown in Table I. It is by no means a complete checklist. Several additional criteria that are important for the users' specific application must be included in it.

10. END-USER LANGUAGES

The final step of information systems construction is the design and implementation of the end-user languages. The end-user language is a language that invokes various application programs. There are various types of information system users. The following three types are typical.

The first type is the real-time user, who uses the database in his routine work. Usually, the real-time user accesses only a specific part of the database for some specific applications. His requests can be classified into a relatively small number of patterns of data processing, each able to be embodied in a separate application program. These programs can be activated by an appropriately designed control command language.

The second type is the casual user, who consults the database mainly in achieving a certain kind of planning tasks. It is hard to predict what parts of the database he will access. A wide range of data processing

TABLE I
Checklist for Evaluating Database Management Systems

1. Identification
   1.1. Name of the system
   1.2. Year developed
   1.3. Developer
   1.4. Computers and minimum configuration
   1.5. Price schedule
2. Data description
   2.1. Entity relations
      2.1.1. Attribute domains
         2.1.1.1. Scalar-type domains (integer, real, boolean, char)
         2.1.1.2. Subrange-type domains
         2.1.1.3. Structured-type domains (array, list, (power) set, repeating group, nest of repeating group, etc.)
      2.1.2. Index specification
      2.1.3. Primary key specification
      2.1.4. Other specifications if available
   2.2. Relationship relations
      2.2.1. Attributes other than origin and destination
      2.2.2. Relationship relation types (sequence, quasisequence, hierarchy, tree, network)
      2.2.3. Multilevel hierarchy specification
      2.2.4. Sequence in the terminal set
      2.2.5. Traversal direction
      2.2.6. Other specifications if available
   2.3. View definition
   2.4. Update of database directory and views
   2.5. Description of other assertions
3. Database routines
   3.1. Search routines
      3.1.1. Unit condition format
      3.1.2. Logical combinations
      3.1.3. Bound variables
      3.1.4. Sequencing among qualified elements
      3.1.5. Cursor
   3.2. Navigation routines
      3.2.1. Relationship relation to be traversed
      3.2.2. Direction of traversals
      3.2.3. Fetching apices and terminals
      3.2.4. Cursor
   3.3. Update routines
      3.3.1. Basic update (add, delete, replace)
      3.3.2. Collective updates if available
   3.4. Dealing with variable-length parts
      3.4.1. Variable-length attribute values
      3.4.2. Repeating groups

TABLE I (*Cont.*)

4. Operational requirements
    4.1. Integrity
        4.1.1. Domain constraints
        4.1.2. Key dependencies regarding primary keys
        4.1.3. Relationship constraints
        4.1.4. Constraints regarding relationship relation type
        4.1.5. Other static constraints
        4.1.6. Dynamic constraints
    4.2. Security
        4.2.1. Protection for an entire relation
        4.2.2. Protection for attributes
        4.2.3. Protection for tuples
        4.2.4. Password mechanism
    4.3. Concurrency
        4.3.1. Read lock and write release
        4.3.2. Start and end of transaction
        4.3.3. Locking levels for the transaction
        4.3.4. Locking granules
        4.3.5. Predicate lock if available
        4.3.6. Deadlock avoidance, detection, and restoration
    4.4. Recoverability
        4.4.1. Examining error causes and propagation
        4.4.2. Restoration
        4.4.2. Backout
    4.5. Provisions for distributed database if any
5. Other logical features
6. Physical representation
    6.1. Entity relations
        6.1.1. File organization
        6.1.2. Indexing mechanism
    6.2. Relationship relation
7. Other physical features
8. Host language interfaces
9. Database administrator utilities
    9.1. Inspection
    9.2. Reorganization
    9.3. Recovery
    9.4. Table maintenance
    9.5. Others if available
10. High-level languages
    10.1. Names
    10.2. User classes
    10.3. Types
    10.4. Extensibility

capabilities may be requested. Usually the search operations are very frequently requested but the update operations are not. We may allow the user to perform only some very special types of update operations, or sometimes we may even forbid him to make any update.

The last type is the parameter user, who performs database file maintenance and prepares reports mostly in batch mode. He specifies a relatively small number of parameters upon calling utility programs for these tasks. The parameter user requests only a limited number of patterns of data processing. Some files not in the database may be used together with the database relations.

10.1. Application Routines

First we must integrate application-oriented subroutines into the system. Generalized database management systems certainly provide powerful database routines; however, they do not provide any application-oriented function.

If we want to construct a management information system, various mathematical, statistical, and management science routines must be integrated into the system. For an engineering information system, we need various scientific and engineering routines. For a regional information system, several routines for geographical data processing are required.

Application routines written in the host language can be easily integrated into the system. Application routines in the host language library can be linked to the user's program at compilation time or loading time. If the application routine includes some read/write statements, these statements must be replaced by appropriate database routines.

10.2. Language for Real-Time Users

Real-time users may request some specific information to be extracted from the database and may transmit some specific information to be used for updating the database through remote terminals and communication lines.

Since the real-time users have access to a restricted part of the database and use a limited number of patterns of data processing, it is a relatively easy task to implement all the programs they may use as transaction-processing programs. These programs can be implemented very efficiently. The database routines invoked by these programs are not necessarily general-purpose. In fact, the search conditions used in search operations, the relationship relations along which navigation operations are performed, traversal directions in navigation, integrity, security, concurrent processing, and recovery procedure can all be designed just for the users' specific requirements. Database routines tailored for specific application environments are desirable for real-time users.

Data communication functions are important for supporting real-time users. Fortunately, most operating systems are capable of providing such functions.

We can design and implement a real-time user language that is very suitable for the user who is invoking necessary application programs. Because real-time users are usually not computer experts, it is desirable to integrate various tutorial aids into this language.

10.3. Languages for Casual Users

Casual users request a wide range of data from a database and also relatively complicated data manipulation to be performed on the database. However, in most cases, these manipulations do not include database updates.

One way to cope with such a situation is to provide a statement language in which each statement activates a set-oriented operation. As collections of elementary set operations, we have the set composed of only one alpha operation, the set of relational algebra operations, the set of information algebra operations, and so on. Each of these is a good candidate for the set of operations that are evoked by a statement language.

Since such a statement language must be implemented for a general purpose, the operational efficiency will be worse than for other types of end-user languages. However, quick responses are not an absolute requirement for casual users.

Sometimes a more application-oriented language is desirable for some users. If this is the case, a special-purpose language can be designed and implemented, which resembles the languages for real-time users but which is a little more flexible. In fact, casual users may request a variety of patterns of data processing that cannot be predicted beforehand. Such application-oriented languages are usually implemented for systems such as management information systems, engineering information systems, medical information systems, and regional information systems.

Several attempts are being made to employ a natural language as the language for casual users. However, since there exist many difficult problems in manipulating natural languages, these attempts remain in an experimental stage.

According to the type of the users' application, some advanced terminal devices can be used. In fact, various devices for image display are now becoming available in the computer market.

10.4. Languages for Parameter Users

Parameter users extract information from the database and update the database, mainly in batch mode. Some patterns of data processing commonly required can be provided as standard utility programs. File maintenance and report writing are typical examples. Again, some users may require more application-oriented utility programs. These may be separately designed and implemented. Some special devices such as dot printers and plotters can be used to prepare special reports. These utility programs can be activated by a language for parameter users, in which the user specifies the parameters necessary for calling utility programs. Usually, a tabular language is designed.

10.5. Self-Contained Systems

Languages designed for casual users and those designed for parameter users, which are not application dependent, can be provided in general-purpose database management systems. There are a number of database management systems that are equipped with such languages. If a database management system does not expose the host language capability to the users but provides only some end-user languages, it is called a *self-contained system*. Self-contained systems have been developed using some basic programming language but they do not expose these languages to the users.

As for the directory-type classification, most existing self-contained systems fall into the hierarchical type. This seems reasonable since the hierarchical (or repeating-group) view of the real world is probably the most intuitive view of the data structure. In practice, recursive trees and (recursive or irrecursive) networks are not frequently dealt with in business applications.

Two distinct types of end-user languages exist: tabular languages and command languages. MARK IV[74] and QWICK-QWERY[36] provide typical tabular languages. MARK IV uses two tables for specifying file maintenance and report preparation. Hence the language is for parameter users. It is very easy for parameter users to use this language, but the language is not flexible enough for casual users. In fact, since we cannot classify data processing operations into a finite number of patterns, a finite number of tabular forms can hardly cover all patterns of data processing the user may request.

TDMS[90] and GIS[48] provide command languages which are much more flexible than systems using tabular languages to specify data manipulation. However, these command languages are suitable only for casual users who are well trained in computer programming.

Since the existing self-contained systems have been developed with a specific class of end-users in mind, they are hardly general-purpose. This seems to be the major reason why these systems are not so widely used as the host language systems. They do not seem to be successful enough in the software market.

10.6. High-Level Languages on the Host Language Systems

Recently, several database management systems have appeared with one or more host languages and also one or more high-level end-user languages. For example, FORIMS, in its initial implementation, provides two high-level languages: a language for casual users based on Information Algebra and enriched with several navigation operations, and a language for parameter users including statements that activate database creation, database update, and report preparation. As mentioned previously, SYSTEM 2000 is basically a self-contained system with a command language. This command language includes statements activating database creation, database update, report preparation, and control transfer operation. ADABAS provides an interactive query language called ADASCRIPT, which includes statements for retrieving tuples using various retrieval conditions. As optional statements, coupling, sorting, and database updates are provided.

Some host language systems can be interfaced with many other languages. TOTAL can be interfaced with ENVIRON I, CICS, and TASKMASTER. ADABAS can be interfaced with TSO, ENVIRON I, CICS, TASKMASTER, and INTERCOM. All these languages are for on-line operations.

CODASYL DBTG did not propose any specification for high-level languages. However, many high-level languages have been implemented on the specific implementation of the DBTG proposal.

SYSTEM R's high-level language interface is called the *user friendly interface* (UFI). Currently, stand-alone SEQUEL and QUERY-BY-EXAMPLE (QBE) are interfaced. The latter provides an excellent tutorial aids for casual users.

10.7. Language Extensibility

End-user languages must be analyzed by a supervisory program provided in the system, which extracts the parameters from the end-user language for invoking appropriate programs.

There may be various classes of application-oriented users who want to add new application programs as they expand their tasks. Hence, the end-user languages must be expandable. The supervisory program must be capable of integrating new control statements into its statement repertoire when new application programs have been developed.

11. FUTURE RESEARCH DIRECTIONS

There remain many problems left to future research. We have already seen that implementation of security, integrity, concurrent processing, and distribute databases involves many unsolved difficulties. In particular, the view support and data translation problems in relation to these functions have not been thoroughly studied as yet. Optimal query evaluation is being attacked by many researchers, but its implementation is still in a very primitive stage.

In the past few years, many attempts have been made to construct so-called database machines. All these attempts are still in an experimental stage; however, we can probably expect that some of these machines will be put to practical use in the relatively near future.

One interesting direction for research is the introduction of deductive processing into database systems and natural language query processing. These have been studied for a long time in relation to the development of question-answering systems, a major topic in artificial intelligence. However, database researchers are now penetrating more and more into this field and, conversely, artificial intelligence researchers are becoming more and more involved in the database management problems.

11.1. Database Machines

We can find a primitive database machine concept in existence as far back as the associative storage devices. Various attempts had been made to generate considerably large content-addressable storage devices.[37] Thanks to the development of large-scale IC memories we now have some gigabyte content-addressable storage devices. However, they are not yet sufficient to store a total database. Nevertheless, they will be very efficiently used, for example, to accommodate inverted files.

For the database operations applied to a relational database, several database machines have been proposed and some have actually been implemented. RAP[71] developed at the University of Toronto and RARES[63] developed at the University of Utah are among these. They both are devices that execute some relational algebra operations using rotating storage devices with a logic-per-track provision. However, they do not seem fully successful because they can execute only a part of the database management functions, and there are many other functions to be implemented as well. It is somewhat doubtful that the implementation of relational algebra operations is really effective in processing queries in general. Some researchers have presented sets of elementary operations that are more suitable to be embodied as database machines than relational algebra operations.[59] It is pointed out that a sort engine, if it is implemented, is powerful for performing many database operations.

Some other researchers proposed back-end database computers[8] which are not yet fully implemented but seem more promising than the logic-per-track approach.

Several levels of hardware (or firmware) logic may be integrated into the database computer. For example, we may have the following three levels. The lowest level consists of basic devices such as high-speed sort engines that can reorder tuples in a database relation very quickly. It would be very effective if we had a device which could deal with variable-length tuples as easily as with fixed-length tuples. The intermediate level is composed of devices that perform algebraic operations such as relational algebra or its extention using the lowest-level devices. The highest level is the device that decomposes a given alpha operation into a series of algebraic operations that can be processed by the intermediate level devices, that is, the highest level is a predicate-calculus processing machine.

Providing several parallel devices at each level, database operations can be processed very efficiently without causing a great deal of trouble for the host computer. The database directory itself may also be a part of the database which can be maintained and referred to by the database computer along with the database relations.

11.2. Deductive Processes

We have already discussed the intension database that stores predicates to be used as assertions. If we have an intension database, we can also introduce a deductive question-answering function. Some facts, even though they are not explicitly represented by tuples in the (extension) database, can be inferred from other facts explicitly represented in it by using some predicates in the intension database as deductive rules.

In particular, deduction for binary propositions can be made by relatively simple matrix calculation.[57,66] Generally, we can use a universal search algorith[59] in inferring n-ary propositions.

The major problem is in finding a proper combination of the predicates in the intension database to infer the given propostion. The basic deductive pathfinder was presented by Robinson[77] as the resolution principle. Several improvements have been proposed for deductions on the database.[50,54,64]

Once an appropriate deductive path has been found, the problem becomes a simple database search procedure.

From the predicate logic viewpoint, the extension and intension databases can be regarded collectively as a database composed of (first-order) predicate calculi.[75] This view of the database may lead us to a new unified approach to the database problem and predicate logic. Propositions in the extension database and predicates in the intension database together constitute an axiom system, and we may deduce various theorems from this axiom system.

Nonclassic logics such as modal logic and fuzzy logic may also be incorporated into the database issues and deductive procedures. These are other interesting research areas.[6]

11.3. Natural-Language Query Processing

Many commercial and experimental database management systems provide a natural-language-like query description. They can be regarded as providing a subset of natural-language statements that can be transformed into predicate calculi which can be processed by the system. Although all the existing systems provide very small subclasses, it may be possible to expand them into a fairly large subclass which can be transformed into predicate calculi which can in turn be processed by a universal search algorithm.

Such a system must have a data dictionary that stores possible attribute values and also various metadata describing the logical database organization. The system must perform syntax persing and semantic analysis of given natural-language queries with reference to the data dictionary and transform these queries into a proper predicate-calculus expression.

An advanced natural-language query processing can be seen in TORUS[69] and RENDEZVOUS.[31] The former attempts to convert natural language queries into somewhat extended relational algebra operations with an aid of the semantic network. The latter transforms the given query step by step through a man–machine interaction.

Natural-language query processing has long been studied in relation to the question-answering systems development[84] but is still a very difficult problem. It will remain as an extremely important but difficult problem in both artificial intelligence and database management research.

ACKNOWLEDGEMENT

I am greatly indebted to Yasuhiro Chiba and several other colleagues at Nippon Univac Research Institute, who implemented an experimental system, FORIMS, that is based on the Information Space Model, and gave me a lot of fruitful suggestions for the enhancement of the data model.

I am grateful to Professor Fernão Stella de Rodrigues Germano and several graduate students of Universidade de São Paulo, who made many fruitful discussions on logical database design during my stay in Brazil.

I also thank members of the Database Modelling Committee of the Japan Information Processing Society, with whom I studied many research materials for ten years.

Finally, I would like to deeply thank Professor J. T. Tou of the University of Florida, who recommended me to write this chapter and corrected many errors in the English in the first manuscript.

REFERENCES

1. J. R. Abrial, Data semantics, in *Data Base Management* (J. W. Klimbie and K. L. Koffman, eds.), pp. 1–59, North-Holland, Amsterdam (1974).
2. A. V. Aho, C. Beeri, and J. D. Ullman, The theory of joins in relational databases, *ACM Trans. Database Syst.* **4**(3), 297–314 (1979).
3. ANSI/X3/SPARC, *Interim Report ANSI/X3/SPARC Study Group on Data Base Management Systems*, ANSI 75-02-08 (1975).
4. M. M. Astrahan, and D. D. Chamberlin, Implementation of structured English query language, *Commun. ACM* **18**(10), 580–588 (1975).
5. M. M. Astrahan, M. W. Blasgen, D. D. Chamberlin, K. P. Eswaran, J. N. Gray, P. P. Griffiths, W. F. King, R. A. Lorie, P. R. McJones, J. W. Mehl, G. R. Putzolu, I. L. Traigaer, E. W. Wade, and V. Watson, System R: Relational approach to database management, *ACM Trans. Database Syst.* **1**(2), 97–137 (1976).
6. Auerbach Associates, Inc., *Design Concept for an Augmented Relational Intelligence Analysis System*, RADC-TR-73-342, Rome Air Development Center, Air Force Systems Command, New York (1973).
7. C. W. Bachman, The data structure set model, in *Proc. ACM SIGMOD, Data Models: Data Structure Set versus Relational* (R. Rustin, ed.), pp. 1–10 (1974).
8. J. Benerjee, R. I. Baum, and D. K. Hsiao, Concept and capabilities of a database computer, *ACM Trans. Database Syst.* **3**(4), 347–384 (1976).
9. R. Bayer, and E. M. McCreight, Organization and maintenance of large shared indexes, *Acta Inf.* **1**(3), 37–52 (1972).
10. P. A. Bernstein, Synthesizing third-normal-form relations from functional dependencies, *ACM Trans. Database Syst.* **1**(4), 277–298 (1976).
11. P. A. Bernstein, D. W. Shipman, and W. S. Wong, Formal aspect of serializability in database concurrency control, *IEEE Trans. Software Eng.* **5**(3), 203–215 (1979).
12. L. A. Bjork, Recovery scenario for a DB/DC system, in *Proc. ACM Nat. Conf.*, pp. 142–145 (1973).
13. G. Bracchi, P. Paolini, and G. Pelagatti, Binary logical associations in data modelling, in *Modelling in Data Base Systems* (G. M. Nijssen, ed.), pp. 125–148, North-Holland, Amsterdam (1976).
14. D. D. Chamberlin, R. F. Boyce, and T. L. Traiger, A dead-lock-free scheme for resource locking in a database environment, in *Proc. IFIP Congr.*, pp. 340–343, North-Holland, Amsterdam (1974).

15. D. D. Chamberlin, J. N. Gray, and T. L. Traiger, Views, authorization, and locking in a relational database system, in *Proc. Nat. Comp. Conf.*, pp. 425–430 (1974).

16. P. P. Chen, The entity–relationship model: Toward a unified view of data, *ACM Trans. Database Syst.* 1(1), 9–36 (1976).

17. Y. Chiba, A database search algorithm based on complicated retrieval conditions, *The Soken Kiyo* 5(1), 159–176, Nippon Univac Sogo Kenkyusho, Inc. (1975).

18. D. L. Childs, Description of a set-theoretic data structure, in *Proc. Fall Joint Comp. Conf.*, pp. 557–564 (1968).

19. D. L. Childs, Extended set theory: A general model for very large, distributed, backend information systems, in *Proc. 3rd Int. Conf. Very Large Data Bases*, pp. 28–46 (1977).

20. Cincom Systems, Inc., *TOTAL/7 Reference Manual, Application Programming*, P02-1321-2; and *TOTAL/7 Reference Manual, Data Base Administration*, P02-1322-2.

21. R. J. Clark, The database administrator, *EDP In-Depth Rep.* 3(12); 4(1) (1974).

22. CODASYL DBTG, CODASYL Data Base Task Group Report, ACM, New York (1971).

23. CODASYL Development Committee, An information algebra: Phase I report, *Commun. ACM* 5(4), 190–204 (1962).

24. CODASYL Systems Committee, *A Survey of Generalized Data Base Management Systems*, ACM, New York (1969).

25. CODASYL Systems Committee, *Feature Analysis of Generalized Data Base Management Systems*, ACM, New York (1971).

26. E. F. Codd, A relational model of data for large shared data banks, *Commun. ACM* 13(6), 377–387 (1970).

27. E. F. Codd, Normalized database structure: A brief tutorial, in *Proc. ACM SIGFIDET Workshop on Data Description, Access, and Control*, pp. 1–17 (1971).

28. E. F. Codd, A database sublanguage founded on the relational calculus, in *Proc. ACM SIGFIDET Workshop on Data Description, Access, and Control*, pp. 35–68 (1971).

29. E. F. Codd, Further normalization on the database retrieval model, in *Data Base Management*, Courant Comput. Sci. Symp. 6 (R. Rustin, ed.), pp. 33–64, Prentice-Hall, Englewood Cliffs, NJ (1972).

30. E. F. Codd, Relational completeness of database sublanguage, in *Data Base Management*, Courant Comput. Sci. Symp. 6 (R. Rustin, ed.), pp. 65–98, Prentice-Hall, Englewood Cliffs, NJ (1972).

31. E. F. Codd, Seven steps to RENDEZVOUS with the casual user, in *Data Base Management* (J. W. Klimbie, and K. L. Coffman, eds.), pp. 179–199, North-Holland, Amsterdam (1974).

32. E. F. Codd, Recent investigation in relational database systems, in *Proc. IFIP Congr.*, pp. 1017–1021, North-Holland, Amsterdam (1974).

33. A. J. Coffman, Jr., N. J. Elphnick, and A. Shoshani, System deadlocks, *Comput. Surv.* 3(2), 67–78 (1971).

34. A. J. Collmeyer, Data management in a multiaccess environment, *Computer* 4(6), 36–46 (1973).

35. Consolidated Analysis Center Corp., *Qwick Qwery User's Manual.*

36. C. T. Davis, Jr., Recovery semantics for DB/DC system, in *Proc. ACM Annual Conf.*, pp. 136–141 (1973).

37. C. Delobel and R. Casey, Decomposition of a database and the theory of switching functions, *IBM J. Res. Dev.* 17(3), 374–386 (1973).

38. D. E. Denning, A review of research on statistical database security, in *Foundation of Secure Computation* (R. A. Demilo, D. P. Dobkin, A. K. Jones, and R. J. Lipton, eds.), pp. 15–26, Academic Press, New York (1978).

39. J. A. Dugan, R. S. Green, J. Minker, and W. E. Shindle, A study of the utility of associative memory processors, in *Proc. ACM Annual Conf.*, pp. 347–360 (1966).

40. K. P. Eswaran, J. N. Gray, R. A. Lorie, and I. L. Traiger, On the notions of consistency and predicate locks in a database system, RJ 1487, IBM Research (1974).

41. R. Fagin, Multivalued dependencies and a new normal form for relational data bases, *ACM Trans. Database Syst.* **2**(3), 262-278 (1977).

42. J. P. Frey, and E. H. Sibley, Evolution of database management systems, *Comput. Surv.* **8**(1), 8-42 (1976).

43. J. N. Gray, R. A. Lorie, and G. R. Putzolu, Granularity of locks in a shared database, in *Proc. 1st Int. Conf. Very Large Data Bases*, pp. 428-451 (1975).

44. J. L. Hainaut, and B. Lacharlier, An extensible semantic model of a database systems and its data language, in *Proc. IFIP Congr.*, pp. 1026-1030, North-Holland, Amsterdam (1975).

45. G. D. Held, M. R. Stonebraker, and E. Wong, INGRES: A relational database system, in *Proc. Nat. Comput. Conf.*, pp. 409-416 (1975).

46. S. Iizuka, and Y. Chiba, GERM: General error-recovery model of shared databases, *The Soken Kiyo* **5**(1), 211-226, Nippon Univac Sogo Kenkyusho, Inc. (1975).

47. International Business Machines Corp., *Information Management System IMS/360*; *Application Description Manual*, GH20-0765-1; *Information Management System/Virtual Storage*; *General Information Manual*, GH-20-1260-3; *Information Management System/Application Design Guide*, SH-20-9025-2; *Information Management System/Application Programming Reference Manual*, SH-9026-2, *Information Management System/System Programming Reference Manual*, SH-9027-2; *Information Management System/Operator's Reference Manual*, SH-20-9028-2; *Information Management System/Utilities Reference Manual*, SH-9029-2; and *Information Management System/Messages and Codes Reference Manual*, SH-9030-2.

48. International Business Machines Corp., *Generalized Information System GIS/360*; *Application Description Manual*, H-0574-1.

49. K. Jensen, and N. Wirth, *PASCAL User Manual and Report*, Lecture Notes in Computer Science, Vol. 18, Springer-Verlag, Berlin (1976).

50. C. Kellog, P. Klahr, and L. Travis, A deductive capability for data management, in *Systems for Large Data Bases* (P. C. Lockemann, and E. J. Neuhald, eds.), pp. 181-196, North-Holland, Amsterdam (1977).

51. L. Kerschberg, A. Klug, and D. C. Tsichritzis, A taxonomy of data models, in *Systems for Large Data Bases* (P. C. Lockemann, and E. J. Neuhold, eds.), pp. 43-64, North-Holland, Amsterdam (1977).

52. D. F. King, and A. J. Collmeyer, Data sharing: An efficient mechanism for supporting concurrent processes, in *Proc. Nat. Comput. Conf.*, pp. 271-275 (1974).

53. W. F. King, On the selection of indices for a file, RJ 1341, IBM Research (1974).

54. P. Klahr, *The Deductive Pathfinder: Creating Derivation Plans for Inferential Question-Answering*, SP-3842, System Development Corp. (1975).

55. I. Kobayashi, Information and information processing structure, *Inf. Syst.* **1**(2), 39-50 (1975).

56. I. Kobayashi, An optimal database search strategy for retrievals on one file, *The Soken Kiyo* **6**(2), 79-95 (1976).

57. I. Kobayashi, File-oriented approach: A new design method for constructing information systems, in *Short-Course Lecture Notes of International Computer Symposium*, pp. 143-247, Taipei (1978).

58. I. Kobayashi, Cartographic databses, in *Pictorial Information Systems* (S. K. Chang, and K. S. Fu, eds.), Lecture Notes in Computer Science, Vol. 80, pp. 322-350, Springer-Verlag (1980).

59. I. Kobayashi, Evaluation of queries based on the extended relational calculi, *Int. J. Comput. Inf. Syst.* **10**(2), 63-102 (1981).

60. K. Kohri, and Y. Chiba, FORIMS phase-2 design specification: A FORTRAN-oriented information management system, *The Soken Kiyo* **5**(1), 177–210, Nippon Univac Sogo Kenkyusho, Inc. (1975).

61. J. G. Kollias, A heuristic approach for determining the optimal degree of file inversion, *Inf. Syst.* **4**(4), 307–318 (1979).

62. D. E. Knuth, *Sorting and Searching: The Art of Computer Programming*, Vol. 3, Addison-Wesley, Reading MA (1968).

63. C. S. Lin, D. C. P. Smith, and J. M. Smith, The design of rotating associative memory for relational database management applications, *ACM Trans. Database Syst.* **1**(1), 53–65 (1976).

64. V. Y. Lum, and H. Ling, An optimization problem on the selection of secondary keys, in *Proc. ACM Annual Conf.*, pp. 349–356 (1971).

65. J. Martin, *Principles of Database Management*, Prentice-Hall, Englewood Cliffs, NJ (1976).

66. J. Minker, Binary relations, matrices, and inference developments, *Inf. Syst.* **3**(1), 37–47 (1978).

67. J. Minker, Search strategy and selection function for an inferential relational system, *ACM Trans. Database Syst.* **3**(1), 1–31 (1978).

68. MRI Systems Corp., *SYSTEM 2000 General Information Manual*; *Basic Reference Manual*, and *Immediate Access Feature*.

69. J. Mylopoulos, A. Borgida, P. Cohen, N. Roussopoulos, J. Tsotsos, and H. Wong, TORUS: A step toward bridging the gap between databases and the casual user, *Inf. Syst.* **2**(2), 49–64 (1976).

70. G. M. Nijssen, Set and CODASYL set or coset, in *Data Base Description* (B. C. Douque, and G. M. Nijssen, eds.), pp. 1–70, North-Holland, Amsterdam (1975).

71. E. A. Ozkrahan, S. A. Schuster, and K. C. Smith, RAP: An associative processor for database management, in *Proc. Nat. Comput. Conf.*, pp. 379–387 (1975).

72. F. P. Palermo, A database search problem, in *Proc. 4th Int. Symp. Comput. Inf. Sci.*, pp. 67–101, Plenum, New York (1972).

73. F. P. Palermo, A quantitative approach to the selection of secondary indexes, RJ 730, IBM Research (1970).

74. J. A. Postley, The MARK IV system, *Datamation* **14**(1), 28–30 (1968).

75. R. Reiter, Equality and domain closure in first-order databases, *J. Assoc. Comput. Mach.* **27**(2), 235–249 (1980).

76. J. Rissanen, Independent component of relations, *ACM Trans. Database Syst.* **2**(4), 317–325 (1977).

77. J. A. Robinson, A machine-oriented logic based on the resolution principles, *J. Assoc. Comput. Mach.* **12**(1), 23–41 (1965).

78. J. B. Rothnie, Evaluating interentry retrieval expressions in a relational database management system, in *Proc. Nat. Comput. Conf.*, pp. 417–423 (1975).

79. F. Sadri and J. D. Ullman, The interaction between functional dependencies and template dependencies, in *Proc. ACM SIGMOD Int. Conf.*, pp. 45–51 (1980).

80. G. Salton, and A. Wong, Generation and search of clustered files, *ACM Trans. Database Syst.* **3**(4), 321–346 (1978).

81. M. B. Senko, E. B. Altman, M. M. Astrahan, and P. L. Fehder, Data structures and accessing in database systems, *IBM Syst. J.* **12**(1), 30–93 (1973).

82. D. G. Severance, and G. M. Lohman, Differential files: Their application to maintenance of large databases, *ACM Trans. Database Syst.* **1**(3), 256–267 (1976).

83. M. Schkolnick, The optimal selection of secondary indices for files, *Inf. Syst.* **1**(4), 141–146 (1975).

84. R. Schwarcz, J. F. Burger, and R. F. Simmons, A deductive question–answer for a natural-language interface, *Commun. ACM* **18**(10), 568–588 (1975).

85. J. M. Smith, and P. Y. T. Chang, Optimization and performance of relational algebra database interface, *Commun. ACM* **18**(10), 568–588 (1975).

86. Softward AG, *ADABAS General Information Manual*; *Reference Manual*; and *Utilities Manual*.

87. M. R. Stonebraker, Implementation of integrity constraints and views by query modification, in *Proc. ACM SIGMOD*, pp. 65–78 (1975).

88. M. R. Stonebraker, Concurrency control and consistency of multiple copies of data in distributed INGRES, *IEEE Trans. Software Eng.* **5**(3), 188–194 (1979).

89. B. Sundgren, Conceptual foundation of the Infological approach to databases, in *Database Management* (J. W. Klimbie, and L. L. Koffeman, eds.), pp. 61–96, North-Holland, Amsterdam (1974).

90. System Development Corp., *TS/DMS User's Guide*, TM-4132.

91. J. T. Tou, Design of medical knowledge system for diagnostic consultation and clinical decision-making, in *Proc. Int. Comput. Symp.*, pp. 80–99, Taipei (1978).

92. D. C. Tsichritzis, and F. H. Lochovsky, Hierarchical database management: A survey, *Comput. Surv.* **8**(2), 105–123 (1976).

93. D. C. Tsichritzis, and F. H. Lochovsky, *Database Management Systems*, Academic, New York (1977).

94. J. D. Ullman, *Principles of Database Systems*, Computer Science, Potomac, MD (1980).

95. H. Weber, A semantic model of integrity constraints on a relational database, in *Modelling in Data Base Management Systems* (G. M. Nijssen, ed.), pp. 269–292 (1976).

96. G. Wiederhold, *Database Design*, McGraw-Hill, New York (1977).

97. H. K. T. Wong, and J. Mylopoulos, Two views of data semantics: A survey of data models in artificial intelligence and database management, *Inf.* **15**(3), 344–383 (1971).

98. E. Wong, and K. Youssefi, Decomposition: A strategy for query processing, *ACM Trans. Database Syst.* **1**(3), 233–241 (1976).

99. S. B. Yao, Modeling and performance evaluation of physical database structure, in *Proc. ACM Annual Conf.*, pp. 303–309 (1976).

100. S. B. Yao, Optimization of query evaluation algorithms, *ACM Trans. Database Syst.* **4**(2), 133–155 (1979).

Chapter 3

PROCESSING OF PATTERN-BASED INFORMATION: PART I

INDUCTIVE INFERENCE METHODS SUITABLE FOR USE IN PATTERN RECOGNITION AND ARTIFICIAL INTELLIGENCE

Yoh-Han Pao and Chi-Heng Hu*

Department of Electrical Engineering and Applied Physics
Case Western Reserve University
Cleveland, Ohio 44106

1. INTRODUCTION

1.1. Preamble

This paper is the first of a series in which we attempt to formulate a conceptual framework for the combined use of some aspects of the pattern recognition (PR) and artificial intelligence (AI) approaches to the processing of information represented in the form of patterns. This is not to say that there is no such interaction at the present time, but it is of limited extent, and it would be helpful if a more comprehensive and systematic understanding of the relationships between the two information processing areas was available.

This paper deals with inductive inference. In Sections 1.2–1.4 we provide brief discussions of the roles played by induction in the PR and AI milieus. These discussions are in the nature of selective reviews, which is to say that we mention selectively those instances of work which are related to and have influenced our approaches directly. We also describe the basic tenets on which our approach is founded.

Subsequent sections deal with pattern description, systematic generation of hypotheses, control of the hypotheses formulation and test sequences, and illustration of inductive inference of decision rules for some examples of sets of patterns.

* Dr. Hu's permanent address is: Institute of Automation, Beijing, China.

1.2. The Decision Rule Inference Problem in Pattern Recognition

Typically, in the pattern recognition environment, the raw data, i.e., the patterns themselves, are usually represented in a rich variety of forms. Thus, a very large number of patterns may in fact all be representing the same object (i.e., they may belong to the same class), not only because that object has many manifestations but also because the raw data include the obscuring effects of noise and distortion due to other unrelated phenomena.

In the absence of revelation, determining the regularities and rules that truly specify class membership is a very difficult task. However, this formulation of decision rules is perhaps also the primary task of pattern recognition.

The nature of the task is not independent of the manner in which patterns are described. If recognition is to be achieved only on the basis of an exact match, then clearly there is almost no further difficulty with deciding what constitutes a good decision rule. In the realm of decision-theoretic pattern recognition (actually geometric pattern recognition), if the patterns are represented in the form of vectors in an N-dimensional metric space, then discriminants can always be obtained which will allow classification on the basis of a sequence of binary decisions. There are no conceptual difficulties. There exist systematic procedures for deriving those discriminants even though the procedures might differ in details depending upon the circumstances.

It is often said that geometric representations of patterns, e.g., in the form of an array of unrelated and equally important features, are deficient in that neither structural relationships nor semantics can be represented. The former is true, the latter is not. Actually, the features can be given meaning, but the true deficiency lies in the fact that the semantics so incorporated do not take part in the recognition or classification process.

In that branch of structural pattern recognition known as syntactic, patterns correspond to sentences in a language (L). Classification corresponds to parsing a sentence (a concatenation of terminal symbols in the form of a string) to see if it obeys the generation rules of a grammer (G). Induction of decision rules would be termed inference of grammar. Given the positive and sometimes also the negative training sets S^a and S^b, the inferred grammar G should have the following properties, namely,

$$S^a \subseteq L(G) \tag{1}$$

$$S^b \not\subseteq L(G) \tag{2}$$

$$n(c)/n(a) \geq \alpha \tag{3}$$

$$n(r)/n(a) \leq \beta \tag{4}$$

$$n(e)/n(b) \le \gamma \tag{5}$$

where $L(G)$ is the language generated by the inferred grammar G, or equivalently the pattern set which can be generated by the inferred rules; $n(a)$ and $n(b)$ are the numbers of samples in the positive and negative test sets, respectively; $n(c)$ and $n(r)$ are the numbers of test samples in S^a which have been classified correctly and rejected, respectively; $n(c)$ is the number of test samples in S^b which have been incorrectly classified as being members of $n(a)$ by the inferred rules; α, β, and γ are prescribed requirements for recognition, rejection, and error rates, respectively.

In syntactic pattern recognition, the inference problem has been solved in general only for the very restricted circumstance of regular grammar. But even for this restricted case there is no general method for ensuring that the inferred grammar will satisfy condition (2).[1]

For other instances of structural pattern recognition, the inference problem can be viewed as an automaton synthesis problem. For example, in the structural recognition of handwritten characters,[2,3] the decision making device is a bank of sequential logic networks, each of which describes the structural properties that are common to all samples of the same class but are not shared with those not in that class. In such structural pattern recognition, the automata are usually synthesized "by hand." Automatic inference of decision rules under those circumstances is thus revealed to be the task of duplicating the very powerful human capability of being able to distinguish subtle differences between characters which resemble each other in shapes but actually belong to different classes. Moreover, the duplicated capability has to be in a form suitable for mechanical implementation.

The rule inference or rule learning approaches advocated by Banerji[4] and by Michalski[5] are off the two main streams of pattern recognition and are more in the spirit of the present work, bridging the gap between artificial intelligence and pattern recognition.

Both Banerji and Michalski advocate the use of pattern description languages that would allow us to escape the restrictive limitations imposed by the geometric and syntactic modes of pattern description.

In works by Michalski,[5-7] a pattern is described by a conjunctive formula of descriptors in a manner conceptually comprehensible to humans, capable of expressing numerical measurements as well as structural relationships, and convenient for representing semantic information. Each training set pattern is viewed as an input rule, i.e.,

Description $::>$ Class (known)

The task of decision rule inference is to reconstruct and transform the input rule (training samples) to yield a compact set of consistent and complete output rules:

General description (complete for positive training set; consistent for negative training set) ::> Class (predictive)

1.3. Inference in Artificial Intelligence

In AI information processing, inference may be of deductive and/or inductive nature, and there are some instances where it would be extremely difficult to differentiate between the two. Attainment of new production rules by some exercise similar to following arcs in a semantic net, or through a resolution procedure, would certainly be considered a deductive procedure in nearly all cases. Learning from examples either in the manner of Quinlan and Hunt,[8] or following the practice of Winston,[9] would be considered inductive inference exercises. To be more specific, given the statement that

For all persons, if that person has pneumonia,
then that person has a fever

and the fact that

John has pneumonia

then it may be deduced that

John has a fever

(or at least, logically, he should be in a feverish condition). This would be deductive inference. However, in this case the original rule was probably arrived at by induction, namely, that over many decades and for many different communities, pneumonia patients were all observed to have the symptom of having above-normal temperatures, whereas no patient with a normal temperature ever turned out to be ill from pneumonia. Deductive inference may take place in a variety of forms such as through the chaining of rules, or *modus ponens*, or by "resolution."[10] In contrast, induction always seems to involve the generalization of conditions formed to be true for a number of positive examples and a number of negative examples. In so doing, new concepts are synthesized and predictive powers are acquired. But it would seem that in AI information processing, if there is the capability for autonomous inductive inference, then there also should be a facility for directing and acknowledging errors if those occur. Quite often, induced rules can be invalidated by the addition of a single new sample. However, matters are not always clear-cut and, for example, the automatic acquisition of new rules for an expert system by sifting through new data and also drawing upon the existing knowledge base might represent an exercise in combined inductive and deductive inference.[11]

There are many AI studies of "learning" and/or inductive inference that serve as examples of successful endeavors and might perhaps also serve as prototypes for future studies. References (12) and (13) contain brief reviews of many of the interesting studies that are known. In view of this, no comparable review will be attempted in this discussion and only work impacting directly on this present study will be cited. Previous work indicates that certain principles are important and certain practices are helpful in inductive reasoning, but there is a need for further exploration and study, especially with the aim of identifying general systematics which might be useful for a variety of circumstances.

The problem of rule inference is especially interesting in the area of AI activity known as expert systems. At first thought, one might have thought that in expert systems we are able finally to circumvent the task of rule induction. After all, why is there need for rule inference when in fact the rules can be supplied by human experts? It turns out, however, quite disappointingly, that this is not so. It is true that in the solving of practical complex problems, the knowledge of domain experts is indispensible and it is also well-known that the capability of an intelligent program depends to a large extent on the amount of knowledge it possesses. Unfortunately, human knowledge is usually comprehensive and implicit; in many cases it is not in the form suitable for representation by well-formed rules of the "If ... , then ... " variety, as is necessary for use in a "mechanical" intelligent system. The task of organizing human expert knowledge into forms compatible for use in expert system programs turns out to be akin to the task of rule inference.

Presently it is mostly done "by hand" and is a tiresome and tedious task often comprising several man-years of effort. Referring to the nature of experts' knowledge and to the task of knowledge acquisition, Feigenbaum says, for example, that

> No textbook of medicine currently records these rules. They constitute the partly public, partly private knowledge of an expert ... and were extracted and polished by project engineers working intensively with the experts over a period of time.[14]

It is worth noting that even if we were satisfied with expert systems fashioned in such a manner, no such expert system could remain viable if it were not capable of acquiring new internal decision rules on its own. Therefore, both in the original construction and in the growth of the system we are again confronted with the task of devising means for systematic and automatic inference of new knowledge, e.g., new decision rules from new data and expert opinions. The "meta-" systems such as META-DENDRAL and TEIRESIAS are systems designed to help in inference of new rules and/or to provide assistance in the interactive transfer of knowledge from a human expert to the knowledge base of a high-performance system.[15,16]

Winston's study of the "learning of concepts from examples" is an early and important example of inductive reasoning or learning from the observation of positive and negative examples.[9] Given a positive example, say, of an arch, the system derives from it a fairly general idea of what an arch is. A series of carefully designed negative examples, each of which is slightly but suitably different from the positive example, are then shown to the machine, telling it at the same time that these are no longer arches. In such manner, the previously formed general idea about an arch is modified, corrected, and restricted by the near-misses until the machine has a good and useful idea of what constitutes an arch.

1.4. Basic Tenets of the Present Approach to Inductive Inference of Decision Rules

We consider here those basic tenets which may be of use in both pattern recognition and artificial intelligence. Our present work is motivated by and owes a great deal to the examples provided by the works of Michalski and Winston. More specifically, we base our approach on the following three tenets.

1. We believe that using a suitable representation for the patterns under consideration is critical to the success of the inference process. The geometric and syntactic pattern descriptions are often not suited to the problem of interest. And we believe that a picture description language identical or similar to that used by Michalski[6] would provide a suitable basis for describing various complex situations (patterns) for a variety of purposes including the inductive inference of decision rules.

2. Following the example of Winston's work,[9] we make use of negative samples. We believe that the negative sample set is as important as the positive sample set in so far as inference or learning is concerned.

It seems that in the human concept formation process a significant factor is the contrast condition, or, in other words, the identity of the entities which are to be distinguished from the concept under consideration. Usually it is necessary to say much more to describe a concept in general fully than it is, say, to describe the same concept just in contrast with some other specified concepts. The most compact and accurate description for a class of objects would be quite different depending on what are the other classes against which it is to be contrasted. The contrast classes provide the boundary conditions for identifying the extent to which a certain concept is distinct from others. Without the boundary restrictions a pattern class might be defined so generally that patterns of other classes might be inadvertently included in that general definition. Therefore, the use of negative-sample sets is extremely important in the decision rule inference process. The resulting decision rules should be economical in the sense that they comprise just those descriptors which distinguish the described class from all other given contrast classes.

In the present work, we refer to S^a and S^b as the positive and negative patterns, when we actually mean S^a and $\sim S^a$, but we will continue to use the S^a and S^b notation because it is more convenient. Furthermore, even in the general multiclass case, both the inference of rules and the actual classification procedure would be carried out on the basis of a sequence of binary decisions. That is, we decide S^1 or $\sim S^1$, and subsequently if not S^1, then S^2 or not S^2, and so on. The task is therefore always the inference of decision rules for a single sample set S^a and all other patterns at that juncture would be considered to be members of $\sim S^a$, the negative sample set.

3. Newell and Simon have proposed that "generation and test" is a law of AI science.[14] We find that in a sense we rely on that operational principle as we strive to provide a systematic procedure for the decision rule inference process. It is interesting to note that the order and manner in which hypotheses are generated and presented for test can still be influenced by *a priori* knowledge, and this aspect turns out to be important in making systems capable of acquisition of knowledge and improvement of decision rules.

2. REPRESENTATION OF PATTERNS

As mentioned previously, we believe that the manner in which patterns are described, i.e., the representation, is crucial to the extent to which inference and other information processing procedure can be carried out.

It would seem that representations should be

- capable of describing objects or situations in terms of patterns which convey the information in the original situation to a degree of precision sufficient for processing purposes (that is, for example, it should be capable of accommodating and representing complex objects and complex structural relationships and subtle changes in those of both quantitative and qualitative nature);

- easily expressible in high-level programming languages, and readily manipulated and processed in symbolic logic manner; and
- comprehensible both to humans and computers, with both semantics and quantitative values available for use in the inference process.

Toward this end, we adopt a pattern description format very close to that of Michalski, namely, each pattern $P(l)$ is represented by a conjunctive expression of descriptors:

$$P(l) = \text{Descriptor } 1 \wedge \text{Descriptor } 2 \wedge \cdots \wedge \text{Descriptor } N$$

where $l = 1, \ldots, M$ (M is the number of samples in the given sample set). Each descriptor is a triplet:

$$\text{Descriptor } i = [F(i), A(i), V(i)], \qquad i = 1, \ldots, N$$

where $F(i)$ is the ith feature symbol or label (i.e., it is the "name" of the feature). By retaining this slightly redundant feature label, the order in which the descriptors in the pattern are written becomes immaterial. $A(i)$ is an attribute associated with feature $F(i)$ and gives the physical meaning of the ith feature, e.g., in simple cases it might be size, color, texture, and so on. $V(i)$ is the value of the attribute $A(i)$.

When the value is referred to conceptually, i.e., when we refer to the third entity in the descriptor $[F(i), A(i), V(i)]$, we use the symbol $V(i)$. However, in any instantiation of pattern description, that quantity will take on a specific value $V(i, j)$—one of the values of $V(i)$ in its domain. We find it useful to consistently regard $V(i)$ as a set defined by

$$V(i) \equiv \{V(i,j)\}, \qquad j = 1, \ldots, ki \qquad (6)$$

In equation (6), the second index may refer to any arbitrary indexing of all the elements in the domain of that value, and the indexing scheme may be the same one as that used for providing a label to the patterns in the sample sets S^a and S^b.

Correspondingly, the generic description of the ith descriptor, $[F(i), A(i), V(i)]$, may be abbreviated to $D(i)$, and it is always understood to represent a set of descriptors which differ only in the actual values of $V(i)$, i.e.,

$$D(i) \equiv \{D(i,j)\}$$

where $D(i, j)$ is the abbreviation for $[F(i), A(i), V(i,j)]$.

Attributes which describe relationships between descriptors such as

$$[F(i), A(i), V(i, k)] \wedge [F(i + 1), A(i + 1), V(i + 1, l)]$$

and attributes which are statements about relationships between the values of feature attributes such as

$$V(i + 2) = \alpha V(i + 1) - \beta V(i)$$

are also allowed. In those cases, the attribute corresponds to a two-valued predicate with possible values of (true, false). Such descriptors represent details of the internal structure of objects. In the above expression, $V(i, k)$ is a specific value which the ith attribute takes on from the set $V(i)$.

In practice, the existence of those structural relationships may be discovered by evaluating the second- and/or higher-order correlations between descriptor attribute values, and new descriptors are added onto the patterns to reflect those relationships explicitly. Inference of rules may then be carried out in the manner described in this chapter.

Also, it may be noted that although it is common practice to represent knowledge in the form of associations of the form (attribute, object, value), which in turn might correspond readily to the form predicate (object, value), the descriptors in the present pattern representation are written in the order (object, attribute, value). This was done so that the resulting format might correspond more directly to some practices of pattern recognition.

It is easy to see that this formalism is compatible with the geometrical representation of patterns. If the total number of selected features is N, then each pattern can be represented as a vector defined in the N-dimensional feature space

$$P = (V(1), \ldots, V(j), \ldots, V(N))$$

where each component $V(j)$ is associated with a certain physical meaning but neither the feature label nor the meaning of the attribute is used in processing, and all $V(j)$ have numeric values.

In other words, in the N-dimensional feature space each pattern can be represented as a dot which is the intersection of N $(N - 1)$-dimensional subspaces or hyperplanes, each of which is "defined" by fixing the value of one descriptor with all hyperplanes generated by taking each descriptor in turn.

Structural pattern representation by strings of (terminal) symbols can also be viewed to be a special case of the general formalism where the precise order in the sequence of descriptors in the conjunctive formula expresses the syntactic structure of the object, and the value domains of all the features (i.e., of all the attributes) are the same—a domain consisting of all terminal symbols.

For the representations afforded by this general formalism, the inferred decision rule will be a disjunction of conjunctive expressions of descriptors, which specify properties common to all positive training set members and possessed by none of the negative training set members. The systematic procedure for obtaining such rules is formulated in the form of an algorithm described in Section 3.

3. ALGORITHM FOR DECISION RULE INFERENCE

3.1. The Nature of the Task

The input data for an inference system are the positive and negative training sample sets S^a and S^b for classes A and B, respectively, where each sample is described by a conjunction of descriptors, each descriptor representing a statement regarding certain physical properties of the sample. The task is to find a rule in the form of a disjunctive–conjunctive combination of descriptors that defines a subspace R in the N-dimensional sample space such that the following conditions are satisfied

$$S^a \subseteq R \tag{7}$$

$$S^b \nsubseteq R \tag{8}$$

The accuracy of the predictive capability of the inferred decision rule depends to a large extent upon how well the training sets are representative of the classes under consideration.

It is obvious that condition (7) can be satisfied if we define R as the disjunction of all the S^a pattern descriptions, but the satisfaction of condition (8) would be quite fortuitous. In order to be able to satisfy condition (8) it is important to use S^b for eliminating from the description of R those descriptors which are formed not only in S^a but also in S^b, or, in other words, those which are not significant in distinguishing S^a from S^b.

The basic idea which underlies the algorithm presented in this chapter is that we use the negative sample set as a boundary condition in the inference process. The decision rule is constructed as a disjunction of conjunctions of descriptors such that the rule covers S^a completely and is consistent for S^b (i.e., includes none of S^b).

3.2. *Some Concepts and Definitions Used in the Algorithm*

(i) *Common descriptor and common values.* Some descriptors, e.g., $D(i, j)$, will be found in both the pattern samples in S^a and in S^b. Those descriptors will be referred to as *common descriptors*, i.e., descriptors common to S^a and S^b, denoted $CD(i, j)$.

Accordingly, $CD(i) \equiv \{CD(i, j)\}$ is the set of all descriptors $CD(i, j)$.

The corresponding *common values* are $CV(i, j)$ and $CV(i)$, with the relationship

$$CV(i) \equiv \{CV(i, j)\} \tag{9}$$

We note that

$$CV(i) = V^a(i) \cap V^b(i)$$

and

$$CV \equiv \{CV(i)\} = \{V^a(i) \cap V^b(i)\} \equiv V^a \cap V^b \tag{10}$$

where

$$V^a(i) \equiv \{V^a(i, j)\} \tag{11}$$

is a subset of $V(i)$, being in fact all those values in the value domain of the ith attribute which occur in S^a samples. Similar remarks apply to $V^b(i)$ and S^b;

$$V^b(i) \equiv \{V^b(i, j)\} \tag{12}$$

and

$$V^a \equiv \{V^a(i)\} \equiv \{\{V^a(i, j)\}\} \tag{13}$$

$$V^b \equiv \{V^b(i)\} \equiv \{\{V^b(i, j)\}\} \tag{14}$$

(ii) *Distinct descriptor and distinct value subsets.* Some attribute values are only to be found in samples of set S^a and not in those of S_b. We refer a specific instance of that as $DV^a(i, j)$. For the ith descriptor, the set of such instances would be $DV^a(i)$, defined by

$$DV^a(i) \equiv \{DV^a(i, j)\} \tag{15}$$

The set of all such distinct descriptors would be

$$DV^a \equiv \{DV^a(i)\} \equiv \{\{DV^a(i,j)\}\} \tag{16}$$

and

$$DV^a = V^a - CV \tag{17}$$

where V^a and CV are sets defined by expressions (13) and (10), respectively. Correspondingly, the *distinct descriptors* are $DD^a(i,j)$ and the set

$$DD^a(i) \equiv \{DD^a(i,j)\} \tag{18}$$

and

$$DD^a \equiv \{DD^a(i)\}$$

Correspondingly, expressions exist for $DV^b(i,j)$, $DV^b(i)$, DV^b, $DD^b(i,j)$, $DD^b(i)$, and DD^b.

(iii) *Common and distinct pattern subsets.* All the members of a common pattern subset of S^a have at least one common descriptor in their description.

For example, $CP^a(i,j)$ are those patterns in S^a which have $CD(i,j)$ in common.

The set $CP^a(i,j \wedge l, m \wedge \cdots \wedge x, y)$ are those patterns in S^a which have descriptors $CD(i,j)$, $CD(l,m)$, and $CD(x,y)$ in each and every pattern. In general, the set $CP^a(i,j \wedge l, m \wedge \cdots \wedge x, y)$ would not be the union of the individual subsets $CP^a(i,j)$, $CP^a(l,m), \ldots, CP^a(x,y)$.

On the other hand, if $CP^a(i,j \vee l, m \vee \cdots \vee x, y)$ is defined to be the set of patterns in S^a that contained one or more of the descriptors $CD^a(i,j)$ and so on, it is clear that $CP^a(i,j \vee l, m \vee \cdots \vee x, y) = CP^a(i,j) \cup CP^a(l,m) \cup \cdots \cup CP^a(x,y)$, and therefore it needs no additional definition.

The S^a set of common pattern subsets is defined to be CP^a as follows

$$CP^a \equiv \{CP^a(i,j)\} \tag{19}$$

and similarly

$$CP^b \equiv \{CP^b(i,j)\} \tag{20}$$

It is also useful to define a subset of S^a patterns as a S^a *distinct pattern subset* if each and all of the members of such a subset contain one or more descriptors unique to S^a. Thus, $DP^a(i, j)$ is the subset of all patterns in S^a that contain the distinct descriptor $DD^a(i, j)$.

The subset of S^a patterns which contain more than one distinct descriptor in common is simply the intersection of the single distinct descriptor subsets, i.e., we have

$$DP^a(i, j \land l, m \land \cdots \land x, y) \equiv DP^a(i, j) \cap DP^a(l, m) \cap \cdots \cap DP^a(x, y)$$

The set of all S^a patterns that contain one or more distinct discriptors is

$$DP^a \equiv \{DP^a(i, j)\} \tag{21}$$

Corresponding definitions exist for $DP^b(i, j)$ and DP^b,

$$DP^b \equiv \{DP^b(i, j)\} \tag{22}$$

(iv) *The negation set of a descriptor.* The negation of the descriptor $D(i, j) \equiv [F(i), A(i), V(i, j)]$ is defined to be the set $\{[F(i), A(i), \overline{V(i, j)}]\}$, *where* $\overline{V(i, j)}$ may range over all the values in the domain of $V(i)$ except $V(i, j)$, and may be represented in an abbreviated manner as $\overline{D(i, j)}$.

(v) *Cover ratio of a common descriptor.* The cover ratio $CR(i, j)$ of the common descriptor $[F(i), A(i), V(i, j)]$ is the cardinality of $CP^a(i, j)$ divided by the cardinality of $CP^b(i, j)$, i.e.,

$$CR(i, j) = \frac{C(CP^a(i, j))}{C(CP^b(i, j))}$$

3.3. Hypotheses Generation and Test

The process of decision rule inference is essentially a process of hypotheses generation and test. A hypothesis might be a single conjunctive formula or a disjunction of conjunctive formulas of descriptors which is complete for S^a and consistent for S^b.

In the generation of hypotheses the first priority is given to the descriptors that are the components of the original descriptions of the given samples. However, the algorithm is not restricted to generating only hypotheses expressed explicitly in terms of the original descriptors. When this strategy fails to yield an appropriate decision rule, it is possible to create hypotheses consisting of descriptors with attributes representing certain structural relationships between the properties of the sample objects that are described by the original descriptors.

The generation of hypotheses from the original descriptors is performed in the order of the simplicity of the resulting decision rule. A test for success is performed for each hypothesis. If the test succeeds, then the hypothesis is confirmed to be a subrule, otherwise the hypothesis with lower priority is generated and tested.

A few of the hypotheses that might be used in the inference procedure are enumerated below:

(1) *Disjunction of the S^a distinct descriptors* (DDD). The concept of distinct sample subsets developed in Eqs. (21) and (22) may now be used in the development of a particularly simple way of forming the decision rule. Namely, if the union of all the S^a distinct sample subsets equals S^a, then the disjunction of the corresponding descriptors is a decision rule for distinguishing sample set S^a from S^b.

The hypothesis: A pattern belongs to class A iff any descriptor in the pattern $\subseteq DDD$, where

$$DDD = \bigcup_{\{(i,j)\}} DD^a(i,j) \tag{23}$$

and $\{(i,j)\}$ indicates that the set operation is taken over all those pairs of (i,j) which together combine to make expression (24) true.

The test condition:

$$\bigcup_{\{(i,j)\}} \{DP^a(i,j)\} = S^a \tag{24}$$

In Eq. (24) the expression $DD^a(i,j)$ represents the distinct descriptor distinguishing S^a from S^b in which the attribute value is $V(i,j)$ and $\{DP^a(i,j)\}$ is the set of patterns all of which contain the distinct descriptor $DP^a(i,j)$ as defined in Eq. (21).

(2) *Conjunction of the negations of the S^b distinct descriptors* ($CNDD$). If the union of certain S^b distinct pattern subsets equals S^b, then the conjunction of the negations of the corresponding discriptors is a decision rule setting S^a apart from S^b.

Let $\{(i,j)\}$ be the set of index pairs that label these S^b distinct pattern subsets. Then the hypothesis is: A pattern belongs to class A iff all of the descriptors $D^a(i,j)$ in the pattern $\subseteq CNDD$ where

$$CNDD = \bigcap_{\{(i,j)\}} \overline{DD^b(i,j)} \equiv \bigcap_{\{(i,j)\}} \{[F(i), A(i), \overline{V(i,j)}]\} \tag{25}$$

The test condition:

$$\bigcup_{\{(i,j)\}} \{DP^b(i,j)\} = S^b \tag{26}$$

We remind ourselves that the set $\{(i, j)\}$ in Eq. (25) and in the hypothesis are those pairs of (i, j) for which expression (26) is true.

(3) *Single distinct descriptor (SDD).* If the cardinality of a S^a distinct pattern subset $DP^a(t, q)$ is greater than that of any of the other S^a distinct pattern subsets, and if the cardinality $C(DP^a(t, q))$ is larger than a threshold value which is calculated in accordance with the cardinality of the positive pattern set $C(S^a)$, then the corresponding distinct descriptor is a disjunctive component of a decision rule setting S^a apart from S^b.

The hypothesis: A pattern belongs to class A if any descriptor in the pattern equals *SDD*, where

$$SDD = DD^a(t, q) \tag{27}$$

The test conditions:

1. $\quad C(DP^a(t, q)) = \max_{\substack{\text{for all } DP^a(i, j) \\ \text{in } DP^a}} C(DP^a(i, j)) \tag{28}$

2. $\quad C(DP^a(t, q)) > (1 + \tfrac{1}{6}C(S^a)) \tag{29}$

(4) *Negation of single S^b distinct descriptor (NSDD).* If there exists an S^b distinct sample subset $DP^b(t, q)$ with cardinality greater than that of any of the other elements of the entire set of DP^b, and if the cardinality $C(DP^b(t, q))$ is larger than or equal to a threshold value which is calculated in accordance with the cardinalities of S^a and S^b and the maximum cover ratio CR_{max} for all the common pattern subsets, then the negation (set) of the corresponding S^b distinct descriptor $DD^b(t, q)$ is a conjunctive component of a decision rule setting S^a apart from S^b.

The hypothesis: The necessary condition for a pattern to be a member of class A is that the descriptor with attribute $A(t)$ in the pattern be in the set *NSDD*, where

$$NSDD = \overline{DD^b(t, q)} = [F(t), A(t), \overline{V(t, q)}] \tag{30}$$

The test conditions:

1. $\quad C(DP^b(t, q)) = \max_{\substack{\text{for all } DP^b(i, j) \\ \text{in } DP^b}} C(DP^b(i, j)) \tag{31}$

2. $\quad C(DP^b(t, q)) \geq C(S^b) - \dfrac{C(S^a)}{CR_{max}} \tag{32}$

where

$$CR_{\max} = \max_{\substack{\text{for all} \\ CP(i,j)}} \frac{C(CP^a(i,j))}{C(CP^b(i,j))} \tag{33}$$

(5) *Conjunction of the common descriptors complete for S^a (CCD).* If there exist common-pattern subsets each of which equals S^a (i.e., is complete for S^a) and the intersection contains no pattern of S^b, then the conjunction of the corresponding common descriptors is a decision rule setting sample set S^a apart from S^b.

The hypothesis: A pattern belongs to class A iff expression CCD is included in the description of the pattern, where

$$CCD = \bigcap_{\{(t,\,q)\}} CD(t,q) \tag{34}$$

The test conditions:

1. $CP^a(t, q) = S^a$ $\hspace{4cm}$ (35)

2. $\bigcap_{\{(t,\,q)\}} \{CP^b(t, q)\} = \phi$ $\hspace{2.6cm}$ (36)

In Eqs. (34) and (36) the set operation is carried out over the same set of (t, q) value for which Eq. (35) is true.

(6) *Common descriptor with the maximum cover ratio (CD).* If the maximum cover ratio of the common descriptors is larger than a threshold value calculated in accordance with the maximum cardinality of the S^b distinct sample subsets and the cardinalities of the sample sets S^a and S^b, then the common descriptor with the maximum cover ratio is a conjunctive component of a decision rule setting S^a apart from S^b.

The hypothesis: The necessary condition for a pattern to be a member of class A is that any descriptor in the pattern is equal to CD, where

$$CD = CD(t, q) \tag{37}$$

The test conditions:

1. $\dfrac{C(CP^a(t, q))}{C(CP^b(t, q))} = CR_{\max} = \max_{\substack{\text{for all} \\ CP(i,j) \\ \text{in } CP}} \dfrac{C(CP^a(i,j))}{C(CP^b(i,j))}$ $\hspace{1cm}$ (38)

2. $CR_{\max} > \dfrac{C(S^a)}{C(S^b) - C(DP^b(u, v))}$ $\hspace{2.2cm}$ (39)

In Eq. (39) $C(DP^b(u, v))$ is the maximum cardinality of elements of the entire set DP^b, as defined in Eq. (31).

As has been mentioned above, the samples described by N descriptors can be represented as dots in the N-dimensional sample space, and a geometrical interpretation can be given to the hypotheses described above.

The DDD [Eq. (23)] is the union of subspaces each of which contains a number of sample dots in S^a and none in S^b and their union covers S^a completely. The $CNDD$ [Eq. (25)] is actually the negation of a DDD obtained for the negative sample set S^b. The SDD [Eq. (27)] is only one subspace (or hyperplane) which contains none of samples of S^b and the largest possible number of samples of S^a. The SDD rule by itself distinguishes only that part of S^a contained in the subspace SDD apart from the contrast set S^b; thus, it is only a disjunctive component of a decision rule. The test condition [Eq. (29)] is used to restrict the total amount of disjunctive components in the resulting decision rule which distinguishes the whole set S^a from S^b.

The $NSDD$ [Eq. (30)] is actually the negation of a SDD obtained for the negative set S^b. The hypothesis CCD [Eq. (34)] defines in the N-dimensional sample space a subspace which is the interaction of a number of subspaces each of which contains all of the sample dots of S^a and a few sample dots of S^b, and, in addition, the intersection subspace contains none of sample dots in S^b. The hypothesis CD [Eq. (37)] defines a subspace containing sample dots from both S^a and S^b. The test condition of Eq. (38) is used to select the subspace containing the largest number of samples in S^a and the least in S^b. The test conditions of Eqs. (32) and (39) are used to indicate whether it is more worthwhile to implement a $NSDD$ or a CD hypothesis, the criterion of choice being based on maximizing the difference between the numbers of samples in S^a and S^b described by the chosen subrule.

The decision rule obtained from each of the hypotheses DDD, $CNDD$, and CCD sets the sample set S^a apart from S^b completely. The rule SDD is a disjunctive component of the decision rule, and both $NSDD$ and CD are only conjunctive components of the decision rule. In the case of CD the problem reduction approach can be used to provide a hierarchical process for inferring the entire decision rule.

3.4. Problem Reduction in the "CD" Hypothesis Generation

In a sense the sixth hypothesis, the CD hypothesis, serves as a catch-all hypothesis, likely to be of use even when all else fails.

As described previously, the cover ratio of a common descriptor is used as a test criterion for selecting the "best" dimension-reducing descriptor. Among all common descriptors the one which has the maximum cover ratio is the one which provides the greatest amount of information in distinguishing S^a from S^b.* The selected CD (common descriptor) is then excluded from further consideration in the process of decision rule inference for the reduced subsets S_1^a and S_1^b, and the selected CD is attached conjunctively to the decision rules attained for S_1^a and S_1^b.

This dimension reduction process can be and in many cases needs to be repeated recursively, and each time the hypothesis descriptor is attached conjunctively to the subrule obtained for the further reduced subsets S_i^a and S_i^b.

We note that use of a particular $CD(t, q)$ as a conjunctive component of the decision rule means in effect that we have decided to deal at first with only those members of S^a that contain $CD(t, q)$. We use $CD(t, q)$ as one conjunctive component of the decision rule and restrict further processing of that subset of S^a patterns to the circumstance of $V(t) = V(t, q)$, i.e., to the $(N - 1)$-dimensional hyperplane defined by that specified value of $V(t)$. Processing of the sets S_1^a and S_1^b might yield another conjunctive component to the decision rule and the further reduced sets S_2^a and S_2^b, and the entire process is repeated until a complete decision rule is inferred.

However, we note that even at the very first step of the procedure, only a part of S^a was covered by the choice of the descriptor $CD(t, q)$. Therefore we must remember to put aside at that stage all those other S^a patterns that need to be recognized as such. Consideration of this aspect of the procedure reveals the fact that the procedure could be a recursive one. At each stage part of the input set of S_i^a patterns is accommodated by the selected CD, the remaining part is set aside for further processing (i.e., to be distinguished from S^b), and S_i^a and S_i^b is reduced to S_{i+1}^a and S_{i+1}^b by excluding the selected descriptor from further consideration. For example, at processing stage j with input pattern sets S_j^a and S_j^b, it might develop that some hypothesis other than CD could terminate the inference process more rapidly. An overall structure for control of the entire procedure is described briefly in Section 4 and in detail in a companion paper.

3.5. Sentential Form of the Decision Rules

The decision rules that result from the proposed inference procedure are of the form

$$\text{Rule} = \{\text{clause } 1\} \vee \{\text{clause } 2\} \vee \cdots \vee \{\text{clause } k\}$$

where each clause is a conjunction of pattern descriptors, which may be

---

* Other information measures may also be used without invalidating this approach.

either original descriptors or synthesized descriptors or a mixture of both types. The various hypotheses contribute to the formulation of such rules in different ways.

The hypothesis DDD, for example, contributes a disjunction of distinct descriptors. If such an expression constituted the decision rule all by itself, then the rule would be of the form

$$\text{Rule} = DD^a(i, \alpha) \vee DD^a(j, \beta) \vee \cdots \vee DD^a(l, \gamma)$$

However, if the DDD contribution were only part of a clause, then it would be convenient and conventional when presenting the rule in the final and operational form to rewrite that single clause into a disjunction of several clauses as dictated by the DDD contribution, that is, an expression such as

$$\text{Rule} = \text{subclause} \wedge DDD$$

which would be rewritten as

$$\text{Rule} = [\text{subclause} \wedge DD^a(i, \alpha)] \vee [\text{subclause} \wedge DD^a(j, \beta)]$$

$$\vee \cdots \vee [\text{subclause} \wedge DD^a(l, \gamma)]$$

The hypothesis $CNDD$ could be retained as a conjunctive statement of negations of descriptors or it could be unraveled.

The hypothesis SDD contributes a single descriptor which is always connected disjunctively to the main body of the rule. The $NSDD$ is appropriate when a SDD has been found for S^b and we wish to formulate the rule to apply to S^a. Again, the contribution from $NSDD$ might be retained in the form of a conjunction of negations of descriptors or it might be unraveled.

The hypothesis CCD contributes a conjunctive statement in a straightforward manner.

The hypothesis CD contributes a single descriptor, but use of that hypothesis often implies the need for repeated recursive use of that hypothesis, at least until the sample sets have been simplified sufficiently so that some other hypothesis can take over.

While on the subject of forms, it is appropriate to make some remarks regarding some related representational matters. Typically, in the interest of economy of effort, a rule might be stated in the following manner:

The DDD Rule: A pattern is in class A iff any descriptor in the pattern is included in DDD where

$$DDD = \bigcup_{\{(i, j)\}} DD^a(i, j)$$

and the $\{(i, j)\}$ is that set for which the test condition is true. The test condition is

$$\bigcup_{\{(i,j)\}} \{DP^a(i, j)\} = S^a$$

In these expressions, and in many other similar expressions in this discussion, an entity such as *DDD* is taken to represent both a logical statement as well as all the elements of a corresponding set. The logical statement is in the form of descriptors joined by logical "and" or "or" connectives. In the case of ambiguity, the elements of the set are always determined by carrying out the intersection operations first and the union operations subsequently. Although there are occasional hints of awkwardness, this practice does not seem to give rise to actual ambiguities. Those slight improprieties could be resolved if we followed, for example, more closely the practice of Ashby[17] and Bourbaki[18] defined sets and properties of elements of the sets, but there does not seem to be a need for that additional formalism at the present time.

3.6. An Illustration of Suggested Algorithm

To illustrate tha basic ideas that underly the proposed algorithm, we consider a very simple example from Michalski's work[6] (Fig. 1).

Following Michalski, the attributes for the samples shown in Fig. 1 are:

$A(1)$ = number of "O" $A(2)$ = number of "$\bigcirc$"

$A(3)$ = number of "$\triangle$" $A(4)$ = number of "$\square$"

and are represented in a simplified form in Fig. 1.

According to the suggested algorithm, the first step is to look for the distinct descriptors. For this purpose we identify for each feature the subsets of attribute values associated respectively with S^a and S^b

$$V^a = (V^a(1) = (1, 2), V^a(2) = (2), V^a(3) = (1, 2, 3), V^a(4) = (0, 1, 2))$$

$$V^b = (V^b(1) = (2), V^b(2) = (2), V^b(3) = (0, 1, 3), V^b(4) = (0, 1, 2))$$

According to equations (10), (17), and (19)-(22), we can write

$$CV = \{V^a(i) \cap V^b(i)\} = (CV(1) = (2), CV(2) = (2), CV(3) = (1, 3),$$

$$CV(4) = (0, 1, 2))$$

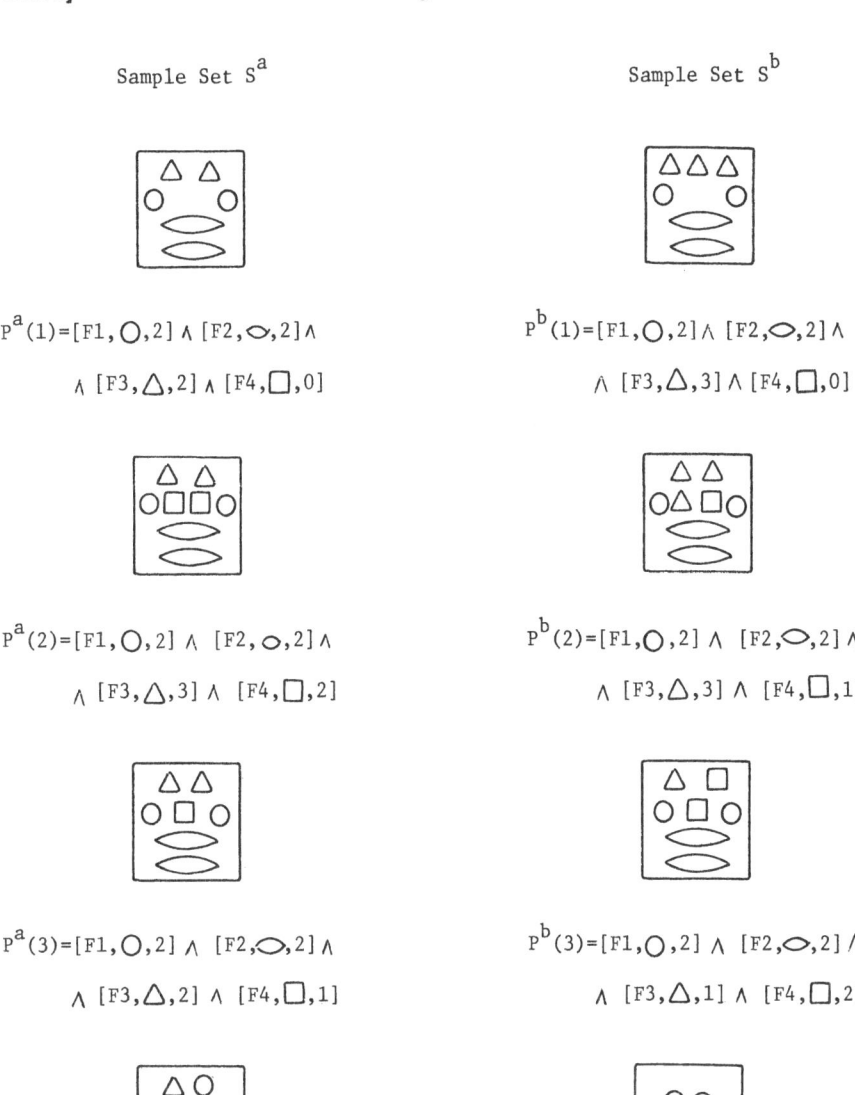

Fig. 1. Illustration of two sample sets. (From Ref. 6.)

$$DV^a = V^1 - CV = (DV^a(1) = (1), DV^a(3) = (2))$$

$$DV^b = V^b - CV = (DV^b(3) = (0))$$

$$CP^a = \{CP^a(1, 2) = (P^a(1), P^a(3)),$$

$$CP^a(2, 2) = (P^a(1), P^a(2), P^a(3), P^a(4)),$$

$$CP^a(3, 1) = (P^a(4)), CP^a(3, 3) = (P^a(2)), CP^a(4, 0) = (P^a(1)),$$

$$CP^a(4, 1) = (P^a(3), P^a(4)), CP^a(4, 2) = (P^a(2))\}^*$$

$$CP^b = \{CP^b(1, 2) = (P^b(1), P^b(2), P^b(3), P^b(4)),$$

$$CP^b(2, 2) = (P^b(1), P^b(2), P^b(3), P^b(4)),$$

$$CP^b(3, 1) = (P^b(3)), CP^b(3, 3) = (P^b(1), P^b(2)),$$

$$CP^n(4, 0) = (P^b(1)),$$

$$CP^b(4, 1) = (P^b(2), P^b(4)), CP^b(4, 2) = (P^b(3))\}$$

$$DP^a = \{DP^a(1, 1) = (P^a(2), P^a(4)), DP^a(3, 2) = (P^a(1), P^a(3))\}$$

$$DP^b = \{DP^b(3, 0) = (P^b(4))\}$$

The next step is to generate and test various hypotheses. In this very simple case it is easy to see that the hypothesis *DDD* constitutes a successful rule describing S^a apart from S^b since the test condition for *DDD*, equation (24), is satisfied

$$DP^a(1, 1) \cup DP^a(3, 2) = (P^a(1), P^a(2), P^a(3), P^a(4)) = S^a$$

Thus the decision rule is obtained from the hypothesis *DDD*; namely, a pattern belongs to class *A* iff it satisfies the following rule

$$[F1, \text{number of } \bigcirc, V(1) = 1] \wedge [F3, \text{number of } \triangle, V(3) = 2]$$

---

* NOTE: $CP^a(1, 2)$ represents all those patterns for which the value of the attribute is 2. Other indexing schemes could also have been used, as described in this text.

Obviously, in more complicated cases, the generation of hypotheses with lower priority and the dimension reduction procedure can be performed recursively in a hierarchical way.

4. STRUCTURE OF THE CONTROLS FOR SYSTEMATIC IMPLEMENTATION OF THE INFERENCE PROCEDURE

In order that the inference procedure might be achieved in a systematic manner, it is necessary to impose a control structure on it. The control structure also provides means for incorporating additional problem domain knowledge and for interactive acquisition of such knowledge as needed. Laying aside those additional considerations for the time being, we find that a useful control structure is obtained if we model the procedure in terms of a special kind of recursive transition network. It is similar to the augmented transition network (ATN) of Woods,[19] but there are significant differences. To differentiate it from the ATNs we refer to the present structure as an *inductive inference transition network* (ITN).

The details of the modeling are contained in a separate companion paper,[20] but the main ideas underlying the modeling can be described briefly as follows.

As we know, ATNs are used primarily for natural language analysis. In that approach a finite-state transition graph is made recursive (and hence into a network) by allowing labels on the arcs to be state names as well as terminal symbols. When such an arc is traversed, the state at the end of the arc will be saved on a pushdown store and the control will jump (without additional new input) to the state that is the arc label. In addition, in an ATN, an arbitrary condition is added to each arc. The condition must be satisfied in order for the arc to be followed, and a set of structure building actions are to be executed if the arc is followed.

In the present case, the ITN consists of a network of recursively called subnetworks, all identical in structure. The input for each subnetwork is always in the form of two sets, the positive and negative sample sets. In that ith subnetwork, properties such as CV, CD, DV, DD, CP, and DP are extracted, tests are conducted, a hypothesis is validated, certain sets are pushed onto pushdown stores A and B, a component of the decision rule is stored in either the "disjunctive" register or the "conjunctive" register and finally reduced sets of patterns are passed on to the $(i + 1)$th subnetwork. Those subnetworks also provide for the wrapping-up procedures by which the sample sets which had been pushed down onto the stores are popped up for processing, and the subrules are collected to form the final inferred decision rule.

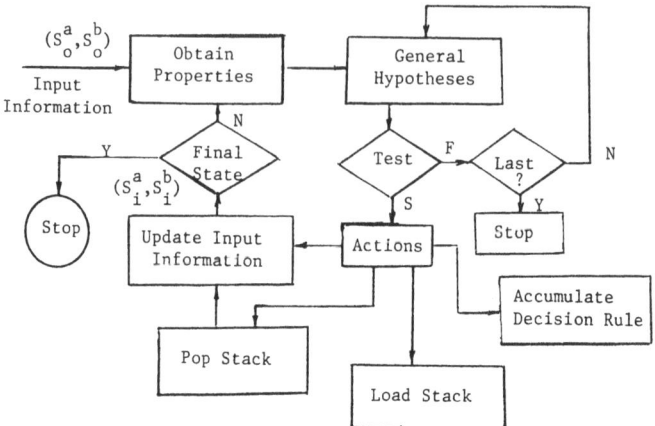

Fig. 2. Schematic representation of the functions of INFER.

5. A BRIEF DESCRIPTION OF THE IMPLEMENTATION

The algorithm presented in this report has been programmed in PASCAL on the PDP-11/45 RSX-11M system. The implemented system contains the interface facilities PATTIN and PATMOD which serve to enter the input information and to provide means for modifying the training set interactively as needed.

The inference system INFER has been built in a modular manner according to the ITN structure. The modular structure provides for extension and modification of the system without major changes to the entire structure. A schematic representation of the functions of INFER is shown in Fig. 2.

The implemented system has been used for several illustrative examples, the results of which are shown in Section 6.

6. EXAMPLES

Examples

Example 1. To illustrate the suggested algorithm (Fig. 3) we take from Michalski's work[6] a well-known example consisting of two groups of texture patterns.

Each of the two classes of textures *A* and *B* contains 20 samples, each of which is described by 9 features all of which have the same attribute—grey level—and take on values from the same value domain $\{1, 2, 3, 4\}$.

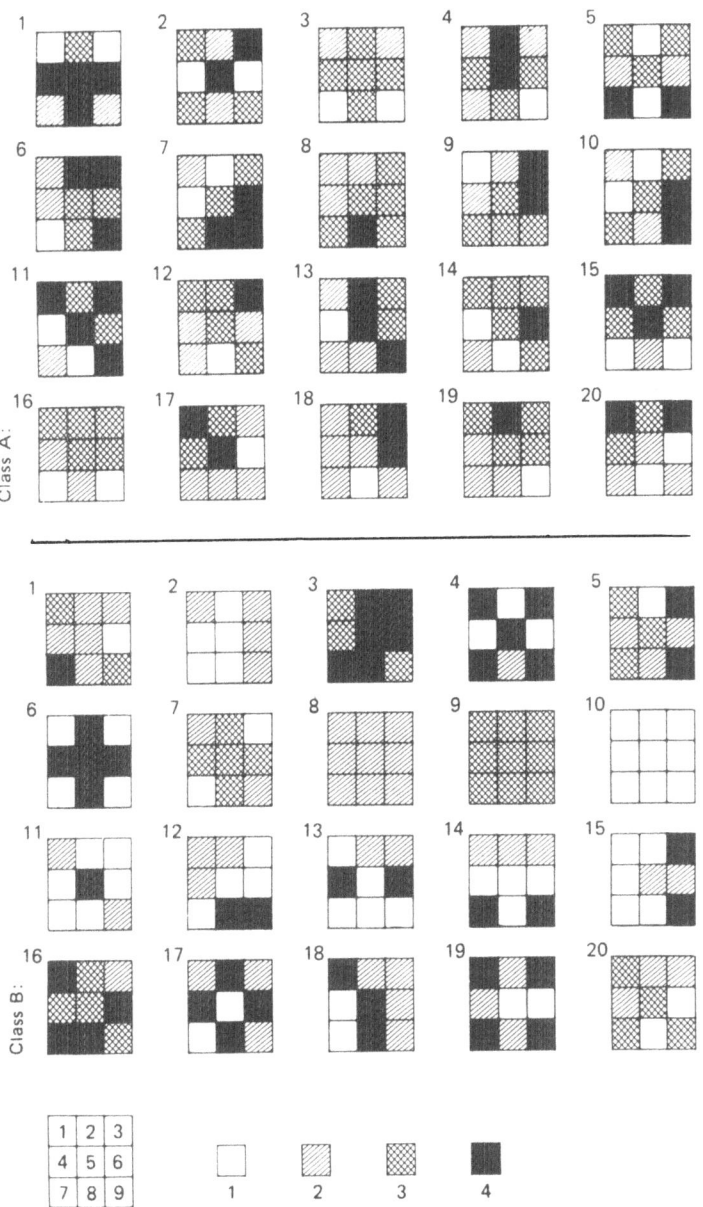

Fig. 3. Illustration of two groups of texture patterns. (From Ref. 6.)

Run of a modified version of INFER, the program TXRINF, where only hypotheses *DDD* and *CD* are considered, resulted in a number of alternative decision rules describing class *A* apart from class *B*. One of them is shown below

$$[F7, V(7) = 2] \land ([F2, V(2) = 4] \lor [F2, V(2) = 3])$$

$$[F3, V(3) = 3] \land [F4, V(4) = 2] \lor [F1, V(1) = 2])$$

$$[F6, V(6) = 3] \land ([F9, V(9) = 1] \lor [F2, V(2) = 4])$$

$$[F7, V(7) = 3] \land ([F4, V(4) = 1] \lor [F1, V(1) = 1])$$

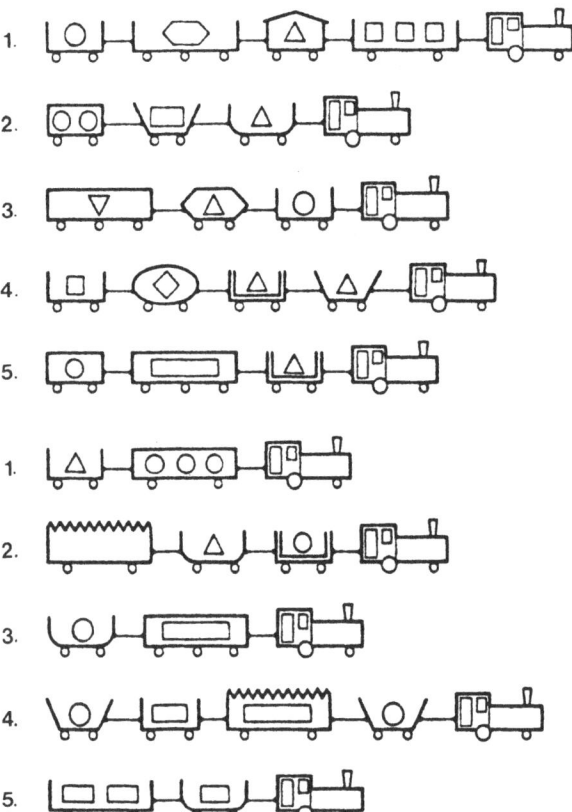

Fig. 4. Illustration of trains going east and trains going west. (From Ref. 5.)

In the above description the attribute is ignored since it is the same (grey level) in all of the descriptors. There are four clauses in the rule and seven features out of the total of nine are involved.

Example 2. In another example taken from Michalski's work,[5] the task is to infer decision rules for telling apart the trains going east from those going west (Fig. 4).

We defined the attributes as follows

$A(1)$: number of cars in a train

$A(2)$: car shape of 1st car

$A(3)$: load shape of 1st car

$A(4)$: number of wheels of 1st car

$A(5)$: number of load-parts in 1st car

$A(6)$: length of 1st car

$A(7)$: car shape of 2nd car

$A(8)$: load shape of 2nd car

$A(9)$: number of wheels of 2nd car

$$\vdots \qquad \vdots$$

$A(21)$: length of 5th car

Run of the program TXRINF resulted in a number of alternative decision rules, one of which is shown below.

For trains going east:
$[F(13)$, load shape of 3rd car, $V(13) =$ triangle$]$
   $\vee [F(2)$, car shape of 1st car, $V(2) =$ close-top rectangle$]$

For trains going west:
$[F(1)$, number of cars in a train, $V(1) = 2]$
   $\vee [F(2)$, car shape of 1st car, $V(2) =$ zigzag $\vee$ open-top trapezoid$]$

Example 3. The data used in Example 3 were taken from the work of Pao *et al.*[21] It is a set of patient assessment profiles, each of which is described by 12 components. Each component represents a symptom and is coded numerically according to the degree of severity.

A tentative diagnosis of disease type was made by a group of physicians for each patient profile. In addition, a SEVILL value was assigned to each profile according to the assessed overall severity.

The original data including patient assessment profiles, the assigned SEVILL values and the tentative diagnosis represented in a numerically coded form are shown in Table I (Appendix). The coding for 12 components in the patient assessment profiles is listed in Table II. The coding for the tentative diagnosis of disease types is listed in Table III.

TABLE I
Patient Assessment Profile

No.														SEVILL
1	4	0	0	0	0	0	0	0	0	0	0	0	0	5*
2	3	0	0	0	0	0	0	0	0	0	0	0	0	5
3	3	0	0	0	1	0	0	0	0	0	0	0	0	10
4	30	1	0	0	0	0	0	0	0	0	0	0	0	7*
5	5	1	0	0	0	0	0	0	0	0	0	0	0	7*
6	7	1	0	0	0	0	0	0	0	0	0	0	0	7
7	8	1	0	0	0	0	0	0	0	0	0	0	0	7*
8	10	1	0	0	0	0	0	0	0	0	0	0	0	7
9	8	0	0	0	0	0	0	1	0	0	0	0	0	20*
10	4	0	0	0	0	0	0	1	0	0	0	0	0	15
11	3	0	0	0	0	0	0	1	0	0	0	0	0	15*
12	3	0	0	0	0	0	0	0	1	0	0	0	0	10
13	5	1	0	0	1	0	0	0	0	0	0	0	0	10*
14	8	1	0	0	1	0	0	0	0	0	0	0	0	10
15	6	0	0	0	1	0	0	1	0	0	0	0	0	15*
16	17	0	0	0	1	0	0	1	0	0	0	0	0	32
17	3	0	0	0	1	0	0	1	0	0	0	0	0	20*
18	6	0	0	0	1	0	0	0	1	0	0	0	0	15
19	8	1	0	0	0	0	0	0	1	0	0	0	0	38*
20	8	0	0	0	0	0	0	0	0	1	0	0	0	20
21	8	0	0	0	0	0	0	0	0	1	0	0	0	30*
22	6	0	0	0	0	0	0	0	0	1	0	0	0	30
23	17	0	0	0	0	0	0	0	0	1	0	0	0	54*
24	5	1	0	0	1	0	0	1	0	0	0	0	0	40
25	6	1	0	0	1	0	0	1	0	0	0	0	0	40*
26	7	1	0	0	1	0	0	1	0	0	0	0	0	40
27	8	1	0	0	1	0	0	0	1	0	0	0	0	40*
28	8	0	0	0	1	0	0	0	1	0	0	0	1	60
29	17	0	0	0	1	0	0	0	0	1	0	0	0	75*
30	7	0	0	0	1	0	0	1	1	0	0	0	0	40
31	6	1	0	0	1	0	0	0	0	0	0	1	0	40*
32	6	1	0	0	0	0	0	0	0	1	0	0	0	25
33	6	1	0	0	0	0	0	1	1	0	0	0	0	30*
34	8	1	0	0	0	0	0	0	2	0	0	0	0	40
35	8	1	0	0	1	0	0	1	0	0	0	0	1	60*
36	8	1	0	0	1	0	0	0	0	1	0	0	0	40
37	6	1	0	0	1	0	0	0	0	1	0	0	0	50*
38	17	0	0	0	1	0	0	1	0	1	0	0	0	95
39	31	1	0	0	1	0	0	1	0	0	0	1	0	75*
40	5	1	0	0	0	0	0	0	0	1	0	1	0	60
41	8	1	0	0	1	0	0	1	0	1	0	0	0	90*
42	8	1	0	0	1	0	0	2	1	0	0	0	0	110
43	17	0	0	0	1	0	0	0	0	2	0	0	0	140*
44	6	1	0	0	1	0	0	0	0	1	0	1	0	75
45	8	1	0	0	1	0	0	0	0	1	0	1	0	90*
46	6	1	0	0	1	0	0	1	1	0	0	1	0	5
47	8	1	0	0	0	0	0	1	1	1	0	0	0	115*
48	17	0	0	0	0	0	0	0	1	2	0	0	0	153
49	6	1	0	0	0	0	0	1	0	1	0	1	0	110
50	7	1	0	0	1	0	0	2	2	0	0	0	0	150*
51	5	1	0	0	1	0	2	0	0	0	0	0	0	150*
52	6	0	0	0	1	0	0	1	1	1	0	1	0	125
53	17	0	0	0	1	0	0	0	2	1	0	1	0	177*
54	6	1	0	0	1	1	0	0	0	1	0	1	0	115
55	1	0	0	0	0	0	3	0	0	0	0	0	0	160*
56	17	0	0	0	1	0	0	1	1	1	0	1	1	140
57	17	0	0	0	1	0	0	1	0	2	0	1	0	185*
58	17	1	0	0	0	0	0	1	1	1	0	1	1	140
59	17	0	0	0	1	2	0	0	0	2	0	0	0	177*
60	17	0	0	0	0	0	0	2	0	2	0	1	0	185
61	17	1	0	0	1	0	2	0	0	1	0	0	0	235*
62	1	0	0	0	0	0	3	1	0	0	0	0	0	175
63	17	0	0	0	1	0	0	2	0	1	1	0	0	245*
64	1	0	0	0	0	0	3	0	0	0	0	1	0	175
65	1	0	0	0	1	0	3	1	0	0	0	0	0	190*
66	1	0	0	0	1	0	3	0	1	0	0	0	0	190
67	2	0	0	0	1	0	3	0	0	0	0	1	0	190
68	6	1	0	0	1	0	0	1	1	0	0	3	1	250*
69	1	0	0	0	1	1	3	0	0	0	0	0	0	225*

(*continued*)

TABLE I (cont.)

70	8 1 0 0 1 0 0 2 2 1 0 1 0	200	98	17 1 0 0 1 2 0 2 2 5 0 3 0	575*
71	2 0 0 0 1 0 3 1 1 0 0 0 0	225*	99	21 1 2 0 0 0 0 0 0 0 0 0 0	150*
72	17 0 0 0 1 2 0 2 2 0 0 1 0	185	100	21 1 2 0 1 0 0 1 0 0 0 0 0	180
73	30 1 0 0 1 0 3 0 0 0 0 1 0	225*	101	21 0 2 0 0 0 0 1 0 1 0 0 0	190*
74	17 0 0 0 0 2 0 1 1 2 0 0 0	245	102	21 1 2 0 0 0 0 1 0 0 0 0 1	180
75	17 0 0 0 0 2 2 0 0 1 0 0 0	235*	103	21 1 2 0 1 0 0 1 1 0 0 0 1	220*
76	1 0 0 0 1 1 3 1 0 0 0 0 0	230	104	21 1 2 0 0 0 0 1 0 1 0 0 0	220
77.	2 1 0 0 0 0 3 1 0 0 0 1 0	235*	105	21 2 2 0 0 0 0 1 0 1 0 1 1	290*
78	2 0 0 0 1 0 3 1 0 1 0 0 0	205	106	21 2 2 0 0 0 0 0 1 1 0 1 0	290
79	2 0 0 0 1 0 3 2 1 0 0 0 0	225	107	21 2 2 0 1 2 0 2 0 0 0 0 1	290*
80	5 2 0 0 1 0 0 2 2 0 0 3 0	300*	108	21 0 2 0 1 0 0 2 1 1 0 0 0	290
81	1 1 0 0 0 0 3 0 0 1 0 1 0	235*	109	21 2 2 0 0 2 0 1 0 1 0 0 0	290*
82	17 0 0 0 0 0 0 1 0 5 0 0 0	312	110	21 2 2 0 1 0 0 0 2 1 0 0 0	290
83	2 0 0 0 1 1 3 0 1 1 0 0 0	250*	111	21 1 2 2 0 1 0 0 1 0 0 0 0	290*
84	17 0 0 0 1 0 0 2 0 2 0 3 1	285	112	21 2 2 2 1 0 0 1 0 0 0 0 1	315
85	17 0 0 0 1 2 2 0 0 2 0 0 0	312*	113	21 2 2 0 1 2 0 2 1 0 0 1 0	335*
86	30 1 0 0 1 0 3 1 1 0 0 1 1	310	114	21 4 0 2 1 0 0 2 0 1 0 0 1	400
87	1 0 0 0 1 2 3 0 1 0 0 1 0	300*	115	21 2 2 0 0 2 0 1 0 5 0 1 0	400*
88	17 0 0 0 1 0 0 0 1 5 0 1 0	342	116	21 4 2 2 1 0 0 2 0 0 0 3 0	440
89	17 0 0 0 1 2 0 0 0 5 0 0 0	342*	117	21 4 2 0 1 2 0 2 1 2 0 1 0	450*
90	17 1 0 0 1 2 2 0 2 2 0 0 0	400	118	21 4 4 0 1 2 0 1 1 1 0 1 0	450
91	17 0 0 0 1 2 0 0 0 5 0 1 0	355*	119	21 4 2 0 0 2 4 1 0 1 0 1 0	475*
92	30 0 0 0 1 1 3 1 2 1 0 1 0	375	120	21 4 2 2 1 0 0 2 0 1 0 0 0	425
93	8 2 0 0 1 0 2 2 1 2 0 1 0	400*	121	21 4 0 3 0 0 0 1 1 1 0 3 0	500*
94	30 1 0 0 1 1 3 0 2 1 0 1 1	400	122	21 4 2 0 1 2 2 2 1 1 0 3 1	475
95	17 2 0 0 1 2 2 2 1 1 0 1 0	400*	123	21 4 0 3 1 2 0 2 2 1 0 1 0	550*
96	17 0 0 0 1 2 2 1 0 5 0 0 0	500*			
97	30 1 0 0 1 2 3 0 2 1 1 1 1	500*			

Experiment 1. The patient assessment profiles are divided into four groups according to their tentative diagnosis.

Group A consists of profiles with the diagnosis coding 01, 02, 03, and 04. It is a chest disease group. Group B consists of profiles of the abdominal diseases and the corresponding codings are 05, 06, 07, 08, and 31. Group C is the cardiac disease group and the coding is 17. Group D is the neurologic disease group and the coding is 21.

In this experiment the decision rule for each group is inferred. Execution of INFER for the four training sets in a pairwise manner resulted in three decision rules for each group. The training set for each group consisted of eight samples.

Patient profiles for the four disease type groups are shown in Table IV where the samples with asterisks are members of the training set. The

TABLE II
Coding of Patient Assessment Profile

	Dimension

Central nervous system

1. Levels of consciousness.   1
   0 Fully alert.
   1 Will raise hand, stick out tongue, wiggle toes, etc., on command. Patient
     may be mentally confused but not comatose.
   2 Withdraws leg or arm, or grimmaces with painful stimulus, e.g., pressure
     on nail beds, hard squeezing of shoulder muscles, etc.
   4 Unresponsive.

2. Reflexes.   2
   0 Deep tendon reflexes intact (knee jerk, ankle jerk, biceps jerk).
   4 Deep tendon reflexes absent.

3. Pupil size and response.   3
   0 Normal size and reaction to light.
   2 Unequal size (if previously equal).
   3 Dilated, fixed, no light reaction.

Respiratory System

1. Rate.   4
   0 10–20/min.
   1 Less than 10 or greater than 20.

2. Type.   5
   0 Normal *chest* movement.
   1 Chest does not move, but abdomen raises and falls with breathing.
   2 Gasping or irregular breathing.

3. Chest signs.   6
   0 Clear, coarse rhonchi, scattered rales.
   2 Widespread rales (at least one-half of one lung).
   3 Severe chest trauma, first-day thoracotomy, first-day thoracostomy tube.
   4 Pulmonary edema, untreated tension pneumothorax.

Cardiovascular System

1. Blood pressure.   7
   0 ±20% of usual level (systolic).
   1 ±20–50% of usual level (systomic).
   2 +More than 50% of usual level (systolic or diastolic).
   5 Absent.

N.B. If usual pressure is not available, use 120/80 under 50 years of age and
     140/90 if 50 years of age or over. If on boundary, give the higher score.

2. Pulse.   8
   0 ±20/min from usual rate.
   1 ±20–40/min from usual rate.
   2 ±More than 40/min from usual rate.
   5 Absent.

N.B. If usual pulse is not available, use 80/min. If on boundary give the higher
     score.

(*continued*)

TABLE II (*cont.*)

	Dimension

3. Electrocardiogram.   9

   0 No significant abnormalities.

   1 All atrial arrythmias, first- and second-degree heart block, occasional PVCs, bundle branch block, *any abnormal* EKG not covered elsewhere.

   2 Unifocal PVCs (more than 6/min), ischemia.

   5 Multifocal PVCs, third-degree heart block without operating pacemaker, recent M.I.

4. Venous pressure.   10

   A. If central venous pressure is available:

      0 0–12 cm water.

      1 13–25 cm water.

      2 More than 25 cm water.

   B. If central venous pressure is not available, the following approximation is made:

   With the patient lying flat, raise arm slowly until the veins of the back of the hand collapse; then, measure with a yardstick the distance from the hand to the level of the heart (approximately the anterior iliac spine).

   0 0–18 cm

   1 19–35 cm

   2 More than 35 cm

Skin Color[a], Skin Moisture, Body Temperature (*Rectal*).   11

   0 Pink, 37 ± 1 °C.

   1 Pale, or jaundiced, or wet, or body temperature less than 36 °C or greater than 38 °C, or all four present.

   3 Blue or temperature less than 33 °C greater than 41 °C, or both.

Renal System.   12

   0 Normal kidney function and urine output.

   1 Urine output decreased but greater than 30 cc/hr, or albumin or blood (except females during menstruation), or all three present.

   3 Anuria or less than 30 cc/hr urine output.

---

[a] For black patients, use mucous membrane inside mouth or eyelids to detect color changes.

decision rules of the four groups inferred in pairwise manner are listed in Table V.

The final decision rule describing each group apart from the other three is obtained as the conjunction of three pairwise discriminators. A recognition test was carried out and the results are tabulated in Table VI.

It is interesting to note that the profiles which were diagnosed to be combined chest and abdominal diseases are classified into either group A or group B, indicating perhaps that one or the other was the more prominent aspect.

TABLE III
Coding of Patient's Tentative Diagnosis

Code	Tentative diagnosis
01	Surgical chest intrapleural trauma
02	Surgical chest intrapleural disease
03	Surgical chest extrapleural trauma
04	Surgical chest extrapleural disease
05	Upper abdominal intraperitoneal trauma
06	Upper abdominal intraperitoneal disease
07	Lower abdominal intraperitoneal trauma
08	Lower abdominal intraperitoneal disease
10	Abdominal extraperitoneal disease
30	01 and 05 combined
31	06 and 08 combined
17	Cardiac disease
21	Neurologic disease

TABLE IV
Samples of Four Disease Type Groups

	F1	F2	F3	F4	F5	F6	F7	F8	F9	F10	F11	F12
Group A												
P1*	0	0	0	1	0	0	1	0	0	0	0	0
P2*	0	0	0	0	0	3	1	0	0	0	0	0
P3	0	0	0	0	0	3	0	0	0	0	1	0
P4	0	0	0	1	0	3	1	0	0	0	0	0
P5	0	0	0	1	0	3	0	1	0	0	0	0
P6*	0	0	0	1	1	3	0	0	0	0	0	0
P7	0	0	0	1	1	3	1	0	0	0	0	0
P8*	1	0	0	0	0	3	0	0	1	0	1	0
P9	0	0	0	1	2	3	0	1	0	0	1	0
P10	0	0	0	1	0	3	0	0	0	0	1	0
P11*	0	0	0	1	0	3	1	1	0	0	0	0
P12	1	0	0	0	0	3	1	0	0	0	1	0
P13	0	0	0	1	0	3	1	0	1	0	0	0
P14*	0	0	0	1	0	3	2	1	0	0	0	0
P15*	0	0	0	1	1	3	0	1	1	0	0	0
Group B												
P1	1	0	0	1	0	0	0	0	0	0	0	0
P2	1	0	0	1	0	0	1	0	0	0	0	0
P3*	1	0	0	0	0	0	0	0	1	0	1	0
P4	1	0	0	1	0	2	0	0	0	0	0	0
P6	0	0	0	1	0	0	1	0	0	0	0	0
P7*	0	0	0	1	0	0	0	1	0	0	0	0

(continued)

TABLE IV (*cont.*)

	F1	F2	F3	F4	F5	F6	F7	F8	F9	F10	F11	F12
P8*	2	0	0	1	0	2	2	1	2	0	1	0
P9	1	0	0	1	0	0	0	0	0	0	1	0
P10*	1	0	0	0	0	0	0	0	1	0	0	0
P11	1	0	0	0	0	0	1	1	0	0	0	0
P12	1	0	0	1	0	0	0	0	1	0	0	0
P13	1	0	0	1	0	0	0	0	1	0	1	0
P14	1	0	0	1	0	0	1	1	0	0	1	0
P15	1	0	0	0	0	0	1	0	1	0	1	0
P16	0	0	0	1	0	0	1	1	1	0	1	1
P17	1	0	0	1	1	0	0	0	1	0	1	0
P18	1	0	0	1	0	0	1	0	0	0	0	0
P19*	0	0	0	1	0	0	1	1	0	0	0	0
P20*	1	0	0	1	0	0	2	2	0	0	0	0
P21	1	0	0	1	0	0	0	0	0	0	0	0
P22	1	0	0	0	0	0	0	1	0	0	0	0
P23	1	0	0	1	0	0	0	1	0	0	0	0
P24	0	0	0	1	0	0	0	1	0	0	0	1
P25	1	0	0	0	0	0	0	2	0	0	0	0
P26	1	0	0	1	0	0	1	0	0	0	0	1
P27	1	0	0	1	0	0	0	0	1	0	0	0
P28	1	0	0	1	0	0	1	0	1	0	0	0
P29	1	0	0	1	0	0	2	1	0	0	0	0
P30	1	0	0	1	0	0	0	0	1	0	1	0
P31	1	0	0	0	0	0	1	1	1	0	0	0
P32	2	0	0	1	0	0	2	2	0	0	3	0
P33*	1	0	0	1	0	0	1	1	0	0	3	1
P34*	1	0	0	1	0	0	2	2	1	0	1	0
Group C												
P1*	0	0	0	1	0	0	0	2	1	0	1	0
P2	0	0	0	1	0	0	1	0	2	0	1	0
P3*	0	0	0	1	2	0	0	0	2	0	0	0
P4*	0	0	0	0	0	0	2	0	2	0	1	0
P5*	1	0	0	1	0	2	0	0	1	0	0	0
P6	0	0	0	1	0	0	2	0	1	1	0	0
P7*	0	0	0	1	2	0	2	2	0	0	1	0
P8*	0	0	0	0	2	0	1	1	2	0	0	0
P9	0	0	0	0	2	2	0	0	1	0	0	0
P10	0	0	0	0	0	0	1	0	5	0	0	0
P11	0	0	0	1	0	0	2	0	2	0	3	1
P12	0	0	0	1	2	2	0	0	2	0	0	0
P13*	0	0	0	1	0	0	0	1	5	0	1	0
P14	0	0	0	1	2	0	0	0	5	0	0	0
P15	1	0	0	1	2	2	0	2	2	0	0	0
P16	0	0	0	1	2	0	0	0	5	0	1	0

(*continued overleaf*)

TABLE IV (*cont.*)

	F1	F2	F3	F4	F5	F6	F7	F8	F9	F10	F11	F12
P17*	2	0	0	1	2	2	2	1	1	0	1	0
P18	0	0	0	1	2	2	1	0	5	0	0	0
P19	1	0	0	1	2	0	2	2	5	0	3	0
P20	0	0	0	1	0	0	1	0	0	0	0	0
P21	0	0	0	1	0	0	0	0	1	0	0	0
P22	0	0	0	1	0	0	1	0	1	0	0	0
P23	0	0	0	1	0	0	0	0	2	0	0	0
P24	0	0	0	0	0	0	0	1	2	0	0	0
P25	0	0	0	1	0	0	1	1	1	0	1	1
P26*	1	0	0	0	0	0	1	1	1	0	1	1

Group D

	F1	F2	F3	F4	F5	F6	F7	F8	F9	F10	F11	F12
P1	1	2	0	0	0	0	0	0	0	0	0	0
P2	1	2	0	1	0	0	1	0	0	0	0	0
P3*	0	2	0	0	0	0	1	0	1	0	0	0
P4	1	2	0	0	0	0	1	0	0	0	0	1
P5*	1	2	0	1	0	0	1	1	0	0	0	1
P6	1	2	0	0	0	0	1	0	1	0	0	0
P7*	2	2	0	0	0	0	1	0	1	0	1	1
P8	2	2	0	0	0	0	0	1	1	0	1	0
P9	2	2	0	1	2	0	2	0	0	0	0	1
P10	0	2	0	1	0	0	2	1	1	0	0	0
P11	2	2	0	0	2	0	1	0	1	0	0	0
P12*	2	2	0	1	0	0	0	2	1	0	0	0
P13	1	2	2	0	1	0	0	1	0	0	0	0
P14*	2	2	2	1	0	0	1	0	0	0	0	1
P15	2	2	0	1	2	0	2	1	0	0	1	0
P16	4	0	2	1	0	0	2	0	1	0	0	1
P17	2	2	0	0	2	0	1	0	5	0	1	0
P18*	4	2	2	1	0	0	2	0	0	0	3	0
P19*	4	2	0	1	2	0	2	1	2	0	1	0
P20	4	4	0	1	2	0	1	1	1	0	1	0
P21	4	2	0	0	2	4	1	0	1	0	1	0
P22	4	2	2	1	0	0	2	0	1	0	0	0
P23	4	0	3	0	0	0	1	1	1	0	3	0
P24	4	2	0	1	2	2	2	1	1	0	3	1
P25*	4	0	3	1	2	0	2	2	1	0	1	1

Experiment 2. In this experiment the patient assessment profiles were divided into two groups according to their assigned SEVILL value. Clinical judgement would place a patient under intensive care if his SEVILL value exceeded 160. In this experiment, group A profiles have assigned SEVILL values greater than 160, and those in group B have assigned SEVILL values

TABLE V
Decision Rules of Four Groups in a Pairwise Manner

Group A

A/B: $[F(6),$ chest signs, $V(6) = 3]$ ∨
       $([F(8),$ pulses, $V(8) < > 1] \wedge [F(1),$ levels of consciousness, $V(1) = 1])$

A/C: $[F(6),$ chest signs, $V(6) = 3]$ ∨
       $([F(9),$ electrocardiogram, $(9) = 0] \wedge [F(5),$ respiratory type, $V(5) = 0])$

A/D: $[F(2),$ central nervous reflexes, $V(2) = 0]$ ∧
       $[F(3),$ Pupil size and response, $V(3) = 0]$

Group B

B/A: $[F(6),$ chest signs, $V(6) < > 3]$ ∨
       $([F(8),$ pulses, $V(8) = 1] \wedge [F(1),$ consciousness, $V(1) = 1])$

B/C: $([F(9),$ electrocardiogram, $V(9) = 0] \wedge [F(5),$ respiratory type, $V(5) = 0])$ ∨
       $([F(1),$ consciousness, $V(1) = 1] \wedge [F(7),$ blood pressure, $V(7) < > 1] \wedge$
       $[F(6),$ chest signs, $V(6) < > 2])$ ∨
       $([F(9),$ electrocardiogram, $V(9) < > 1] \wedge [F(1),$ consciousness, $V(1) < > 0])$

B/D: $[F(2),$ central nervous reflexes, $V(2) < > 2]$ ∧
       $[F(1),$ consciousness, $V(1) < > 4]$

Group C

C/A: $[F(6),$ chest signs, $V(6) < > 3] \wedge [F(9),$ electrocardiogram, $V(9) < > 0]$

C/B: $[F(5),$ respiratory type, $V(5) = 2]$ ∨
       $([F(9),$ electrocardiogram, $V(9) < > 0] \wedge [F(1),$ consciousness, $V(1) = 0])$ ∨
       $([F(9),$ electrocardiogram, $V(9) < > 0] \wedge [F(7),$ blood pressure, $V(7) = 1])$ ∨
       $([F(9),$ electrocardiogram, $V(9) < > 0] \wedge [F(7),$ blood pressure, $V(7) < > 2] \wedge$
       $[F(4),$ respiratory rate, $V(4) = 1])$

C/D: $[F(2),$ central nervous reflexes, $V(2) < > 2]$ ∧
       $[F(1),$ consciousness, $V(1) < > 4]$

Group D

D/A, D/B, D/C:
       $[F(2),$ central nervous reflexes, $V(2) = 2]$ ∨
       $[F(1),$ consciousness, $V(1) = 4]$

TABLE VI

Class	Diagnosis of disease type	Test set size	Recognition rate	Rejection rate	Error rate
A	Chest	15	100%	0	3.6%
B	Abdominal	34	82.4%	17.6%	1.5%
C	Cardiac	25	92%	8%	12%
D	Neurologic	24	100%	0	0

TABLE VII
Two Groups of Patient Profiles Divided According to the SEVILL Value

	F1	F2	F3	F4	F5	F6	F7	F8	F9	F10	F11	F12
Group A (SEVILL value > 160)												
P1	0	0	0	0	0	3	1	0	0	0	0	0
P2	0	0	0	0	0	3	0	0	0	0	1	0
P3	0	0	0	1	0	3	1	0	0	0	0	0
P4	0	0	0	1	0	3	0	1	0	0	0	0
P5	0	0	0	1	1	3	0	0	0	0	0	0
P6	0	0	0	1	1	3	1	0	0	0	0	0
P7	1	0	0	0	0	3	0	0	1	0	1	0
P8	0	0	0	1	2	3	0	1	0	0	1	0
P9	0	0	0	1	0	3	0	0	0	0	1	0
P10	0	0	0	1	0	3	1	1	0	0	0	0
P11	1	0	0	0	0	3	1	0	0	0	1	0
P12*	0	0	0	1	0	3	1	0	1	0	0	0
P13	0	0	0	1	0	3	2	1	0	0	0	0
P14*	0	0	0	1	1	3	0	1	1	0	0	0
P15	2	0	0	1	0	0	2	2	0	0	3	0
P16*	1	0	0	1	0	0	1	1	0	0	3	1
P17*	1	0	0	1	0	0	2	2	1	0	1	0
P18	2	0	0	1	0	2	2	1	2	0	1	0
P19*	0	0	0	1	0	0	0	2	1	0	1	0
P20*	0	0	0	1	0	0	1	0	2	0	1	0
P21	0	0	0	1	2	0	0	0	2	0	0	0
P22	0	0	0	0	0	0	2	0	2	0	1	0
P23*	1	0	0	1	0	2	0	0	1	0	0	0
P24	0	0	0	1	0	0	2	0	1	1	0	0
P25	0	0	0	1	2	0	2	2	0	0	1	0
P26	0	0	0	0	2	0	1	1	2	0	0	0
P27*	0	0	0	0	2	2	0	0	1	0	0	0
P28*	0	0	0	0	0	0	1	0	5	0	0	0
P29*	0	0	0	1	0	0	2	0	2	0	3	1
P30	0	0	0	1	2	2	0	0	2	0	0	0
P31	0	0	0	1	0	0	0	1	5	0	1	0
P32	0	0	0	1	2	0	0	0	5	0	0	0
P33	1	0	0	1	2	2	0	2	2	0	0	0
P34	0	0	0	1	2	0	0	0	5	0	1	0
P35	2	0	0	1	2	2	2	1	1	0	1	0
P36	0	0	0	1	2	2	1	0	5	0	0	0
P37	1	0	0	1	2	0	2	2	5	0	3	0
P38*	1	0	0	1	0	3	0	0	0	0	1	0
P39	1	0	0	1	0	3	1	1	0	0	1	1
P40*	0	0	0	1	1	3	1	2	1	0	1	0
P41	1	0	0	1	1	3	0	2	1	0	1	1
P42	1	0	0	1	2	3	0	2	1	1	1	1
P43	1	2	0	1	0	0	1	0	0	0	0	0

(continued)

TABLE VII (*cont.*)

	F1	F2	F3	F4	F5	F6	F7	F8	F9	F10	F11	F12
P44	0	2	0	0	0	0	1	0	1	0	0	0
P45	1	2	0	0	0	0	1	0	0	0	0	1
P46	1	2	0	1	0	0	1	1	0	0	0	1
P47	1	2	0	0	0	0	1	0	1	0	0	0
P48	2	2	0	0	0	0	1	0	1	0	1	1
P49	2	2	0	0	0	0	0	1	1	0	1	0
P50	2	2	0	1	2	0	2	0	0	0	0	1
P51*	0	2	0	1	0	0	2	1	1	0	0	0
P52	2	2	0	0	2	0	1	0	1	0	0	0
P53	2	2	0	1	0	0	0	2	1	0	0	0
P54	1	2	2	0	1	0	0	1	0	0	0	0
P55	2	2	2	1	0	0	1	0	0	0	0	1
P56	2	2	0	1	2	0	2	1	0	0	1	0
P57	4	0	2	1	0	0	2	0	1	0	0	1
P58*	2	2	0	0	2	0	1	0	5	0	1	0
P59*	4	2	2	1	0	0	2	0	0	0	3	0
P60	4	2	0	1	2	0	2	1	2	0	1	0
P61*	4	4	0	1	2	0	1	1	1	0	1	0
P62*	4	2	0	0	2	4	1	0	1	0	1	0
P63	4	2	2	1	0	0	2	0	1	0	0	0
P64*	4	0	3	0	0	0	1	1	1	0	3	0
P65	4	2	0	1	2	2	2	1	1	0	3	1
P66	4	0	3	1	2	0	2	2	1	0	1	0

Group B (SEVILL value ≤ 160)

	F1	F2	F3	F4	F5	F6	F7	F8	F9	F10	F11	F12
P1	0	0	0	0	0	0	0	0	0	0	0	0
P2	0	0	0	1	0	0	0	0	0	0	0	0
P3	0	0	0	0	0	0	1	0	0	0	0	0
P4	0	0	0	0	0	0	0	1	0	0	0	0
P5	0	0	0	1	0	0	1	0	0	0	0	0
P6	0	0	0	0	0	0	1	0	0	0	0	0
P7	0	0	0	1	0	0	0	0	0	0	0	0
P8	0	0	0	0	0	0	0	1	0	0	0	0
P9	1	0	0	0	0	0	0	0	0	0	0	0
P10*	1	0	0	1	0	0	0	0	0	0	0	0
P11*	1	0	0	1	0	0	1	0	0	0	0	0
P12	1	0	0	0	0	0	0	0	1	0	1	0
P13	1	0	0	1	0	2	0	0	0	0	0	0
P14	0	0	0	1	0	0	1	0	0	0	0	0
P15	0	0	0	1	0	0	0	1	0	0	0	0
P16	0	0	0	0	0	0	0	0	1	0	0	0
P17	1	0	0	1	0	0	1	0	0	0	0	0
P18	1	0	0	1	0	0	0	0	0	0	1	0
P19*	1	0	0	0	0	0	0	0	1	0	0	0

(*continued overleaf*)

TABLE VII (*cont.*)

	F1	F2	F3	F4	F5	F6	F7	F8	F9	F10	F11	F12
P20	1	0	0	0	0	0	1	1	0	0	0	0
P21*	1	0	0	1	0	0	0	0	1	0	0	0
P22	1	0	0	1	0	0	0	0	1	0	1	0
P23	1	0	0	1	0	0	1	1	0	0	1	0
P24	1	0	0	0	0	0	1	0	1	0	1	0
P25*	0	0	0	1	0	0	1	1	1	0	1	0
P26	1	0	0	1	1	0	0	0	1	0	1	0
P27	1	0	0	0	0	0	0	0	0	0	0	0
P28	1	0	0	1	0	0	1	0	0	0	0	0
P29*	0	0	0	1	0	0	1	1	0	0	0	0
P30*	1	0	0	1	0	0	2	2	0	0	0	0
P31	1	0	0	1	0	0	0	0	0	0	0	0
P32	0	0	0	0	0	0	1	0	0	0	0	0
P33	1	0	0	0	0	0	0	1	0	0	0	0
P34	0	0	0	0	0	0	0	0	1	0	0	0
P35*	1	0	0	1	0	0	0	1	0	0	0	0
P36*	0	0	0	1	0	0	0	1	0	0	0	1
P37*	1	0	0	0	0	0	0	2	0	0	0	0
P39*	1	0	0	1	0	0	1	0	0	0	0	1
P40	1	0	0	1	0	0	0	0	1	0	0	0
P41*	1	0	0	1	0	0	1	0	1	0	0	0
P42*	1	0	0	1	0	0	2	1	0	0	0	0
P43*	1	0	0	1	0	0	0	0	1	0	1	0
P44*	1	0	0	0	0	0	1	1	1	0	0	0
P45*	0	0	0	1	0	0	1	0	0	0	0	0
P46	1	2	0	0	0	0	0	0	0	0	0	0
P47	0	0	0	1	0	0	0	0	1	0	0	0
P48	0	0	0	1	0	0	1	0	1	0	0	0
P49	0	0	0	1	0	0	0	0	2	0	0	0
P50*	0	0	0	0	0	0	0	1	2	0	0	0
P51	0	0	0	1	0	0	1	1	1	0	1	1
P52	1	0	0	0	0	0	1	1	1	0	1	1
P53	1	0	0	0	0	0	0	0	0	0	0	0
P54	1	0	0	1	0	0	1	0	0	0	1	0
P55	1	2	0	0	0	0	0	0	0	0	0	0

less than or equal to 160. Sixty-six profiles were available for group A and fifty-five for group B. A training set consisting of 18 samples from each was selected for this experiment. These are marked with an asterisk in Table VII.

Execution of INFER for the training sets resulted in the following decision rule for distinguishing group A profiles from those of group B:

$[F(1)$, level of consciousness, $V(1) = 4]$

$\quad \vee [F(2)$, central nervous system reflexes, $V(2) = 2]$

$\quad \vee [F(5)$, respiratory system type, $V(5) = 2]$

$\quad \vee [F(6)$, chest signs, $V(6) = 2 \vee 3]$

$\quad \vee [F(9)$, electrocardiogram, $V(9) = 5]$

$\quad \vee [F(11)$, body temperature, $V(11) = 3]$

$\quad\quad \wedge [F(9)$, electrocardiogram, $V(9) = 2]$

$\quad \vee [F(11)$, body temperature, $V(11) = 3] \wedge [F(8)$, pulse, $V(8) = 2]$

There are seven clauses in the decision rule and seven attributes out of the total of twelve were involved.

The result of a classification test for the two groups is listed below:

Recognition rate:	98.5%
Rejection rate:	1.5%
Error rate:	3.6%

It should be noted that the predictive capability of the inferred decision rule depends to a large extent upon how well the training sets are representative of the classes under consideration, or, in other words, the error rate might be due to human judgement in the original assignment of SEVILL value rather than to any inadequacy of INFER. In addition, the training sets should be selected carefully to span the variety of objects in the considered classes.

REFERENCES

1. K. S. Fu, and T. L. Booth, Grammatical inference: Introduction and survey—1, *IEEE Trans. Syst. Man Cybern.* **5** (1975).
2. C. H. Hu, P. Lin, H. Y. Ning, and F. F. Wu, A handwritten numeral recognition machine for automatic mail-sorting, *Signal Processing: Theories and Applications*, EURASIP (1980).
3. J. W. Tai, C. H. Hu, P. Lin, H. Y. Ning, and F. F. Wu, The investigation of handwritten character recognition methods, *Acta Automatica Sinica* **5**(1) (1979).
4. R. B. Banerji, A language for pattern recognition, *Pattern Recognition*, 63–74 (1968).
5. R. S. Michalski, Pattern recognition as rule-guided inductive inference, *IEEE Trans. PAMI* **2**(4), 349–361 (1980).
6. R. S. Michalski, A variable-valued logic system as applied to picture description and recognition, *Graphic Languages* (F. Nake and N. Rosenfeld, eds.), North Holland, Amsterdam (1972).
7. R. S. Michalski, AQVAL/1 computer implementation of a variable-valued logic system: VL 1 and examples of its applications to pattern recognition, *Proc. 1st IJCPR* (1972).

8. J. Quinlan and E. Hunt, A formal deductive problem-solving system, *J. ACM*, **15**(4), 625–646 (1968).

9. P. H. Winston, *Artificial Intelligence*, Addison-Wesley, New York (1977).

10. N. J. Nilsson, *Principles of Artificial Intelligence*, Tioga (1980).

11. F. Hayes-Roth, and J. McDermott, Knowledge acquisition from structural descriptions, *Proc. of 5th IJCAI* (1977)

12. D. A. Waterman, and F. Hayes-Roth, Introduction, in *Pattern-Directed Inference Systems* (D. A. Waterman and F. Hayes-Roth, eds.) (1978).

13. B. G. Buchanan, and T. M. Mitchell, Model-directed learning of production rules, in *Pattern-Directed Inference Systems* (D. A. Waterman and F. Hayes-Roth, eds.) (1978).

14. E. A. Feigenbaum, The art of AI: 1. Themes and case studies of knowledge engineering, *Proc. 5th IJCAI* (1977).

15. B. G. Buchanan, G. Sutherland, and E. A. Feigenbaum, Heuristic dendral: A program for generating explanatory hypotheses in organic chemistry, *Machine Intelligence*, Vol. 4 (1969), (B. Meltzer and D. Michie, eds.), pp. 209–254.

16. R. Davis, Interactive transfer of expertise: acquisition of new inference rules, *Proc. 5th IJCAI* (1977).

17. W. R. Ashby, The set theory of mechanism and homeostasis, in *Automaton Theory and Learning Systems* (D. J. Stewart, ed.), Thompson, Washington, D.C. (1967).

18. N. Bourbaki, Elements de mathematique theorie des ensembles; fascicule de resultates, ASEI 1141, Hermann and Cie, Paris, Third Edition (1958).

19. W. A. Woods, Transition network grammars for natural language analysis, *C. ACM*, pp. 591–606 (1970).

20. Y. H. Pao, and C. H. Hu, Some characteristics of attributed ATN's, Case Western Reserve University, Technical Report MI 102-82 (1982).

21. Y. H. Pao, W. L. Schultz, M. Kiley, J. L. Altman, and A. J. L. Schneider, Implementation of human "Judgement" and "Experience" in computer-aided interpretation of medical images, *Proc. 3rd IJCPR* (1976).

Chapter 4

PROCESSING OF PATTERN-BASED INFORMATION: PART II
DESCRIPTION OF INDUCTIVE INFERENCE IN TERMS OF TRANSITION NETWORKS

Chi-Heng Hu[†] and Yoh-Han Pao

Department of Electrical Engineering and Applied Physics
Case Western Reserve University
Cleveland, Ohio 44106

1. INTRODUCTION

In a previous publication[1] we discussed the nature of inductive inference and its role in pattern information processing. More specifically, for patterns described in a manner such as that advocated by Michalski[2]—as conjunctions of triplets of the form (name, attribute, value)—we described how inductive inference might be employed systematically to yield decision rules for the classification of such patterns.

Whereas, for example, predicate calculus and artificial intelligence (AI) processing are primarily concerned with deductive inference and are well suited to that task, inductive inference (that is, learning a formation of new concepts) remains a difficult task seemingly not easily handled in any direct manner by existing methodology. The type of inductive inference described in Ref. 1 may be used in image understanding, acquisition of rules for expert systems, and in the formation of new concepts in the control of systems.

This present discussion is concerned with the description of the inductive inference procedure of Ref. 1 in terms of a sequence of *inductive inference transition networks* (ITNs). That is, we say that a systematic decision-rule inference process can be viewed as a generalized recursive information processing system and can be modeled by a series of interconnected automata, each of which is an ITN. By "interconnection" of automata

[†] Permanent address: Institute of Automation, Beijing, China.

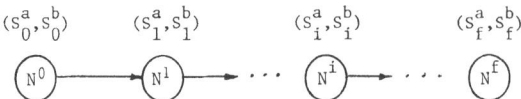

Fig. 1. Description of the inductive inference procedure in terms of a sequence of inductive inference transition networks (ITNs).

we mean the identifying of the output information of the foregoing automaton with the input information of the successive one, as shown in Fig. 1.

In this system each automaton N^i is a transition network (the ITN) that is unlike other networks such as the conventional ATNs of natural language processing and the semantic nets for associative retrieval.[3,4]

For example:

1. In the present case the input is not a sequence of symbols but a list of "training set" patterns, comprising two sets of patterns, one being the positive set S_i^a and the other the negative set S_i^b.
2. In part, the function of the automaton is to extract a property list from the two sets, and this property list together with the input list determines the path traversed in the network.

The following considerations provided strong motivation for representing the decision-rule inference process by a sequence of INTs:

1. The process of inferring decision rules from the training samples is quite complicated in most of the tasks that are of practical interest. In many cases the inference task is problem-oriented and the inference algorithm cannot be immutable. When represented by ITNs, the inference system can easily be decomposed into a set of elementary components each of which is described in a simple and formal way. This representation allows for easier rearrangement and modification of the algorithm and results in more flexible and powerful systems.

2. The formal nature of the description and the decomposable nature of the ITNs lead to a deeper understanding of the inference process and an easier task in programming.

3. A formal and simple description may contribute to the building of better interactive inference systems for use as interfaces between the human expert and the expert system in knowledge acquisition tasks.

Finally, we need to make a very important point regarding the form of the end result, namely, the inferred decision rules. Although they can be stated simply enough in the form of disjunctions of conjunctive statements, it is quite difficult to keep track of different parts of subrules as they are inferred. We find it helpful to think of the function of the ITN as being the synthesis of yet another automaton, the acceptor-automaton, which accepts all patterns of the positive pattern set S^a and rejects all patterns of the contrast pattern set S^b. This account of the ITN representation of the inductive inference of decision rules is entirely couched in terms of acceptor-automaton synthesis.

Therefore, the entire inductive inference process can be viewed as two sets of patterns being inserted as input to a sequence of ITNs. These ITNs work successively on the input information, extracting subrules and synthesizing a completely separate acceptor-automaton as the patterns pass through. The end result is another transition network which can serve as an acceptor-automaton for patterns of the type used as input to the ITNs.

Although the present account is very specific in the description of every arc and every action in the ITN, actually this discussion is only meant to be an illustrative example. The idea is that each problem may require variations in the hypothesis and that corresponding changes in the ITNs would be made accordingly.

2. DESCRIPTION OF THE INDUCTIVE INFERENCE TRANSITION NETWORK

An inductive inference transition network (ITN) is a directed graph with labeled states and arcs, a set of pushdown stacks, and a set of registers. Among the states there is a distinguished initial state and a distinguished final state.

An ITN is characterized by an input list which is to be processed in the network and is associated formally with the initial state of this network. Information contained in the input list is extracted in some initial steps and is used subsequently in the control of the path actually traversed in the network.

The function of the ITN is to determine a sequence of internal states on the basis of the input list associated with the ITN. A new list is obtained in accordance with the sequence of states. The new list and the sequence of states are the output of an ITN.

In the ITN each internal state is associated with a finite number of property lists that are extracted from the original input list. The properties associated with a certain state can be used as arguments in executing functions on those arcs that start from that state.

The arcs in an ITN are labeled numerically. Arcs starting from the same state are examined in the order of their labels. If any arc is followed, then the remaining arcs originating from that same state are not examined. If no arc can be followed, then the ITN fails to reach its final state for the given input information.

We can describe an ITN in Backus–Naur form:

⟨ITN⟩ ::= (⟨initial state⟩⟨arc⟩⟨arc⟩∗)(⟨state-arc set⟩)|

        (⟨initial state⟩⟨arc⟩⟨arc⟩∗)(⟨state-arc set⟩)⟨ITN⟩

⟨state-arc set⟩ ::= (⟨state⟩⟨arc⟩∗)

                (⟨state⟩⟨arc⟩∗)⟨state-arc set⟩

⟨initial state⟩ ::= (⟨input list⟩⟨input list⟩∗)

⟨input list⟩ ::= (⟨list⟩)

⟨state⟩ ::= (⟨property list⟩⟨property list⟩∗)

⟨arc⟩ ::= (⟨ACT⟩⟨function list⟩)|

        (⟨JUMP⟩⟨test⟩⟨function list⟩)|

        (⟨TST⟩⟨register⟩⟨form⟩⟨function list⟩)|

        (⟨PUSH⟩⟨stack⟩⟨stack⟩∗⟨form⟩⟨form⟩∗⟨function list⟩)|

        (⟨POP⟩⟨stack⟩⟨stack⟩∗⟨list⟩⟨list⟩∗⟨function list⟩)

⟨function list⟩ ::= (⟨action⟩∗⟨destination⟩)

⟨action⟩ ::= (⟨MAP⟩⟨form⟨list⟩⟨list⟩)|

        (⟨SYNTH⟩⟨list⟩⟨tail⟩⟨head⟩)|

        (⟨SET⟩⟨form⟩⟨record⟩⟨record⟩∗|

        ⟨form⟩⟨destination⟩⟨destination⟩∗)

⟨form⟩ ::= ⟨record⟩˙|⟨record⟩|(⟨functional expression⟩)

⟨tail⟩ ::= ⟨form⟩

⟨head⟩ ::= ⟨form⟩

⟨record⟩ ::= ⟨list⟩|⟨register⟩

⟨destination⟩ ::= ⟨state⟩

⟨test⟩ ::= (⟨Boolean expression⟩)⟨form⟩∗

In this formal description the asterisk is used to indicate arbitrarily repeatable (including zero times) constituents and the vertical bar separates alternative ways of forming a rewriting rule. The expressions enclosed in parentheses are elements of a list, e.g., ⟨state-arc set⟩ is a list where the first element is the state label and the subsequent elements are arcs emanating from that state.

The item ⟨stack⟩ is a pushdown store for information in the form of a list. Similarly, ⟨list⟩ is a memory device for the storage of information in the form of a list, but ⟨register⟩ is for storage of numerical information. The dot in ⟨record⟩˙ indicates that the elements of the list ⟨record⟩ have to satisfy conditions specified by TST. The entities ⟨tail⟩ and ⟨head⟩ are not to be found in an ITN but are numerical designation of nodes in the acceptor-automaton synthesized by ITNs.

Entities such as ⟨ACT⟩, ⟨JUMP⟩, ⟨TST⟩, ⟨PUSH⟩, and ⟨POP⟩ are the names of arc categories. The function of each category is given below.

1. *ACT arc.* The ACT arc can be followed without making any test; a series of actions is executed in accordance with the specification given in the ⟨function list⟩.

2. *JUMP arc.* The JUMP arc is followed if the ⟨test⟩ conditions are satisfied. The actions specified in the function list are executed if a JUMP arc is followed.

3. *TST arc.* The TST arc entails a test for the number stored in the register; if the number is not zero, then the TST arc is followed, the number in the register is replaced by that in ⟨form⟩, and the actions specified in the ⟨function list⟩ are executed.

4. *PUSH arc.* The PUSH arc causes a pushdown of certain ⟨forms⟩ into the corresponding pushdown stacks. In addition, a series of actions are executed.

5. *POP arc.* The POP arc is the opposite of the PUSH arc, or, in other words, the POP arc causes an unwrapping action, i.e., in following a POP arc, the pushdown stacks are "popped" by one element and the lists at the top of those stacks are delivered to assigned devices. In addition, the actions specified by the ⟨function list⟩ are executed.

The ⟨function list⟩ specifies two things, one being the action to be executed and the other the destination state.

1. *The actions that are to be executed:* The set of actions necessary for implementing the basic function of the system can be defined in a problem-oriented manner. In the description presented above a set of three basic

actions is defined for implementing the decision-rule inference algorithm: (i) MAP, (ii) SYNTH, and (iii) SET.

(i) MAP is a list construction action. It is also a table look-up action in the following sense. In following an arc with a MAP action, at the start of the arc there are a ⟨form⟩ and an accompanying ⟨list⟩. The arc action consists of going to the ⟨form⟩ and for each element of the ⟨form⟩ constructing a subset from the set of elements in the ⟨list⟩ following the ⟨form⟩. The constructed is *not* the ITN but the automaton that will actually be used in one or more memory devices, named ⟨list⟩.

(ii) SYNTH is an automaton-constructing action. The automaton so constructed is not the ITN but the automaton that will actually be used for classification of the patterns. The automaton is an embodiment or representation of the decision rule inferred through use of the ITN. Since the decision rule is usually a disjunction of subrules, each of which may be either a single descriptor or a conjunction of descriptors, the automaton is accordingly also a transition network with many arcs in parallel corresponding to each of the disjunctive clauses. Some of these arcs may consist of a number of nodes connected sequentially, corresponding to the conjunction of descriptors. Therefore, there are two different types of SYNTH actions depending on the subrule type.

If the list (subrule) that follows the action name is of disjunctive type, then the action is to assign the content of the list to parallel arcs, one element to each arc, all of which start from the ⟨tail⟩ node and point to the ⟨head⟩ node—which is actually the final node of the acceptor-automaton. If the list is of conjunctive type, then the elements in the list are assigned sequentially to a series of arcs, one element to each arc. The first one starts from the ⟨tail⟩ node and ends at the ⟨head⟩ node. If in the list there is more than one component, then the ⟨head⟩ label of the foregoing arc is the ⟨tail⟩ label of the successive one and the ⟨head⟩ label of that is obtained by adding one to the ⟨head⟩ label of the foregoing arc. The last component in the list is assigned to an arc pointing to the final state, i.e., R_f.

(iii) SET includes two alternative actions. One is to store a certain ⟨form⟩ (at least one, but more than one is allowed) into the ⟨record⟩* following that ⟨form⟩. The other is to equate the ⟨property list⟩ of the ⟨destination⟩ state (at least one, but more than one is allowed) with ⟨form⟩.

The "action" in ⟨function list⟩ might be an empty list, i.e., no actions are expected.

2. *The destination state of the arc*: This is the destination state to which control is transferred if the arc is followed.

In ⟨action⟩, ⟨form⟩ can be represented by any of three alternatives:

(i) ⟨record⟩˙ is a list or the content of a register; in both cases ⟨record⟩˙ has to satisfy the test conditions specified by the TST arc;

(ii) ⟨record⟩ (without superscript dot) is simply a list or the content of a register;

(iii) ⟨functional expression⟩ describes operations on members of the input list or property lists, or on the content of registers.

The test conditions ⟨test⟩ are Boolean expressions followed by forms that define the items in that expression.

3. AN INFERENCE ALGORITHM REPRESENTED BY AN INDUCTIVE INFERENCE TRANSITION NETWORK

To show the representation of an inference algorithm by an ITN, we take a systematic procedure for inductive inference of decision rules[1,5], for example, and give the description of the ITN as an abstract model for this procedure. To make this chapter complete, a brief review of this procedure is given below.

3.1. A Brief Description of the Inference Algorithm

3.1.1. Input Information—Training-Pattern Sample Sets

The input information for the inference system is the group of training pattern sets for Class A and the contrast Class B, (S_0^a, S_0^b), which comprise M_a and M_b members, respectively.

$$S_0^a = \{P^a(1), P^a(2), \ldots, P^a(i), \ldots, P^a(M_a)\} \tag{1}$$

$$S_0^b = \{P^b(1), P^b(2), \ldots, P^b(i), \ldots, P^b(M_b)\} \tag{2}$$

Each member in equations (1) and (2) is described by a conjunctive expression of N descriptors:

$$P^a(i) = [F(1), A(1), V(1)] \cdots [F(j), A(j), V(j)] \cdots [F(N), A(N), V(N)] \tag{3}$$

In equation (3) N is the number of features used in the pattern description. In the jth descriptor $D(j)$, $F(j)$ is the feature label, $A(j)$ is the attribute of the jth feature, and $V(j)$ is the value that the attribute $A(j)$ takes on, which represents the value domain for the jth attribute, i.e.,

$$V(j) \equiv \{V(j, k)\} \qquad k = 1, \ldots, k_j \tag{4}$$

The jth descriptor with an attribute value $V(j) = V(j, k)$ is written as $D(j, k)$. In this connection $D(j)$ can be written as a set

$$D(j) \equiv \{D(j, k)\} \qquad k = 1, \ldots, k_j \tag{5}$$

3.1.2. Properties of the Pattern Sets and the Operations for Obtaining the Properties

As the first step of the inference process a series of properties is to be extracted from the original input data—the positive and negative training pattern sets. Information useful for differentiation between the two sets is condensed in the properties and the most significant factors are extracted from those properties in the hypotheses generation and test process to form the final decision rules.

Common Descriptor and Pattern Subsets. A descriptor $D(i, k)$ is said to be a common descriptor if it can be found in both the patterns of S^a and S^b. Common descriptor is denoted as $CD(i, k)$.

Similar to (4) and (5) we can write

$$CD(i) \equiv \{CD(i, k)\} \quad \text{for} \quad V(i, k) \in CV(i) \tag{6}$$

where

$$CV(i) \subseteq V(i)$$

and

$$CV(i) = V^a(i) \cap V^b(i) \tag{7}$$

where $V^a(i) \subseteq V(i)$ is the collection of those values $V(i, q)$ that can be found in the ith descriptors of samples in S^a. The same remark applies to $V^b(i)$ with regard to S^b.

The entire set of common descriptors is

$$CD \equiv \{CD(i)\}, \qquad i \in (1, \ldots, N) \tag{8}$$

The corresponding common value set is

$$CV \equiv \{CV(i)\}, \qquad i \in (1, \ldots, N) \tag{9}$$

The subsets of S^a and S^b, each member of which contains at least one common descriptor, are the common pattern subsets CP^a and CP^b, respectively, and can be written as

$$CP^a \equiv \{CP^a(i, k)\} \tag{10}$$

$$CP^b \equiv \{CP^b(i, k)\} \tag{11}$$

for the corresponding $V(i, k) \in CV(i)$, where the component $CP^a(i, k)$ is the pattern subset in S^a, each member of which contains the common descriptor $CD(i, k)$.

Distinct Descriptor and Pattern Subsets. A descriptor $D(i, k)$ is said to be a S^a distinct descriptor and is denoted as $DD^a(i, k)$ if the attribute value $V(i, k)$ in this descriptor is unique to samples of S^a. The subset of the ith attribute values unique to samples of S^a is

$$DV^a(i) \equiv \{DV^a(i, k)\} \tag{12}$$

Correspondingly, the set of ith S^a distinct descriptors

$$DD^a(i) \equiv \{DD^a(i, k)\} \tag{13}$$

and the entire S^a distinct descriptor set:

$$DD^a \equiv \{DD^a(i)\} \tag{14}$$

Those samples in S^a that have at least one S^a distinct descriptor constitute the S^a distinct pattern subsets

$$DP^a \equiv \{DP^a(i, k)\} \tag{15}$$

corresponding to the DD^a set.

Similar definitions exist for the S^b distinct descriptors and the corresponding S^b distinct pattern subsets DV^b, DD^b, $DD^b(i)$, $DD^b(i, k)$, and DP^b.

3.1.3. Hypothesis Generation and Test

In the described inference procedure a number of hypotheses are generated and tested. If the test condition for a hypothesis is satisfied, then this hypothesis is confirmed to be a subrule, otherwise the hypothesis with lower priority is generated and tested. The hypotheses that might be used and the associated test conditions are enumerated below.

Hypothesis DDD. The test condition:

$$\bigcup_{\{(i,q)\}} \{DP^a(i, q)\} = S^a \tag{16}$$

Iff any descriptor in a pattern $\subseteq DDD$, where

$$DDD = \bigcup_{\{(i,q)\}} DD^a(i, q) \tag{17}$$

then this pattern belongs to Class A. The set operation in equation (17) is taken over all those pairs of (i, q) that together combine to make equation (16) true.

Hypothesis CNDD. The test condition is

$$\bigcup_{\{(i,q)\}} \{DP^b(i, q)\} = S^b \tag{18}$$

Iff all of the descriptors $D(i, q)$ in a pattern $\subseteq CNDD$, where

$$CNDD = \bigcup_{\{(i,q)\}} \overline{DD^b(i, q)} \tag{19}$$

then this pattern belongs to Class A. The set operation in equation (19) is taken over all those pairs of (i, q) that together combine to make equation (18) true. $DD^b(i, q)$ is a set of descriptors in each member of which the attribute value might equal any element in the value domain $V(i)$ except $V(i, q)$.

Hypothesis SDD. The test condition is

$$C(DP^a(t, q)) = \max_{\substack{\text{for all} \\ DP^a(i,j) \\ \text{in } DP^a}} C(DP^a(i, j)) \tag{20}$$

$$C(DP^a(t, q)) > (1 + \tfrac{1}{6}C(S^a)) \tag{21}$$

In the above expressions C(certain set) is the cardinality of this set. If any descriptor in a pattern is SDD, where

$$SDD = DD^a(t, q) \tag{22}$$

then this pattern belongs to Class A. In equation (22) the pair of indexes (t, q) makes equations (20) and (21) true.

Hypothesis NSDD. The test condition is

$$C(DP^b(t, q)) = \max_{\substack{\text{for all} \\ DP^b(i,j) \\ \text{in } DP^b}} C(DP^b(i, j)) \tag{23}$$

$$C(DP^b(t, q)) \geq C(S^b) - \frac{C(S^a)}{CR_{max}} \tag{24}$$

where

$$CR_{max} = \max_{\substack{\text{for all} \\ CP(i,k) \\ \text{in } CP}} \frac{C(CP^a(i, k))}{C(CP^b(i, k))} \tag{25}$$

If a pattern belongs to Class A, then the descriptor with attribute $A(t)$ in this pattern should be included in the set NSDD, where

$$NSDD = \overline{DD^b(t, q)} \tag{26}$$

Hypothesis CCD. The test condition is

$$\{CP^a(i, q)\} = S^a \tag{27}$$

$$\bigcap_{\{(i,q)\}} \{CP^b(i, q)\} = \phi \tag{28}$$

Equation (27) should be true for each and all pairs of (i, q) that together combined to make equation (28) true.

Iff expression CCD is included in the description of a pattern then this pattern belongs to Class A, where

$$CCD = \bigcap_{\{(i,q)\}} CD(i, q) \tag{29}$$

Hypothesis CD. The test condition is

$$\frac{C(CP^a(t, q))}{C(CP^b(t, q))} = CR_{max} \tag{30}$$

$$CR_{max} > \frac{C(S^a)}{C(S^b) - C(DP^b(u, v))} \tag{31}$$

CR_{max} in equation (30) is the same as defined in equation (25). $DP^b(u, v)$ in equation (31) is the same as $DP^b(t, q)$ defined in equation (23).

If a pattern belongs to Class A, then there is at least one descriptor in this pattern that is a CD, where

$$CD = CD(t, q) \tag{32}$$

3.1.4. Processing Actions That Are Executed after the Confirmation of a Hypothesis

When a certain hypothesis has been confirmed to be a subrule, then a set of actions is executed according to prescribed associated rules. In order to organize the inference process and to synthesize the acceptor-automaton based on the inferred decision rule, the following registers and memory stacks are used:

1. *Registers*:

    (i) Register L: The label of a node at which branching occurs is held in L and is used as the first index in the labeling of all the other acceptor-automaton nodes that form that branch.

    (ii) Register NLR: A number is held in NLR and is used as the second index in the labeling of nodes on a branch. As the inference process proceeds, and as node after node is generated, this number is updated by increasing it by one each time. The node label is obtained by juxtaposition of the two indices.

    (iii) Register NT(L): NT(L) is a set of registers that can be accessed using L as a key. In each NT(L) stored the NLR index of the most recent node in the branch *L*.

In the following, [L] and [NLR] mean the content of the register L and NLR, respectively.

For example, for branch A of an acceptor–automaton shown in Fig. 2, for [L] = 0, [NLR] = takes on the value of 0, 1, 2, 3, consecutively, and [NT(L)] at the end of the synthesis of branch A is 3. This guides the labeling of the node 04, i.e., [L] = 0 and [NLR] = [NT(L)] + 1 = 4. For branch B, [L] = 01, [NLR] = 1, 2, for the corresponding nodes.

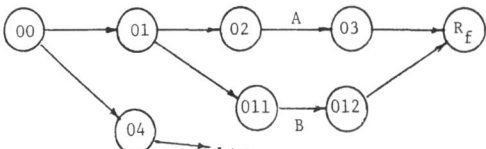

Fig. 2. Structure of an acceptor-automaton.

(iv) PUSH-COUNTER register PC: PC is an indicator for keeping track of the branching actions in the synthesized acceptor-automaton. [PC] is advanced by 1 each time a CD hypothesis is confirmed.

2. *Memory stacks for list-structured information for the synthesis of subrules.* There are two such stacks, namely,

(i) DISJ
(ii) CONJ

A sequence of expressions of the form

$$[V(i) = V(i, j)]$$

can be held in DISJ and in CONJ.

3. *Pushdown stacks*:

(i) PUSHA
(ii) PUSHB

Both PUSHA and PUSHB can accommodate arrays of the form

$$(a_1, a_2, \ldots, a_i, \ldots, a_n)$$

where each component a_i is also an array with a formal name P_i:

$$a_i = P_i(V(1, j_1^i), \ldots, V(l, j_l^i), \ldots, V(N, j_N^i))$$

It should be noted that, formally, the entire array $(a_1, a_2, \ldots, a_n)$ is pushed onto stack in one single action.

(iii) PUSHL: The PUSHL is actually a first-in last-out register for numerical information.

The actions that are executed after a hypothesis has been confirmed as a subrule can be categorized into four groups:

1. *Decision Rule or Subrule Formation*

Confirmed hypothesis	Rule formation actions
DDD|SDD:	The expression DDD|SDD is stored into the DISJ stack.
CNDD|CCD|NSDD|CD:	The expression CNDD|CCD|NSDD|CD is stored into the CONJ stack.

2. Input Information Updating Rules

Confirmed Hypothesis	Information Updating Actions
DDD|CNDD|CCD:	Replace the input sets of patterns S_i^a and S_i^b by the pattern sets shown on the top of the PUSHA and PUSHB stacks, respectively.

SDD:
$$S_{i+1}^a = S_i^a - DP^a(t, q)$$
$$S_{i+1}^b = S_i^b \qquad\qquad (33)$$

NSDD:
$$S_{i+1}^a = S_i^a$$
$$S_{i+1}^b = S_i^b - DP^b(t, q) \qquad\qquad (34)$$

CD:
$$S_{i+1}^a = CP^a(t, q)$$
$$S_{i+1}^b = CP^b(t, q) \qquad\qquad (35)$$

where the expressions $DP^a(t, q)$, $DP^b(t, q)$ and $CP^a(t, q)$, $CP^b(t, q)$ are defined in equations (20), (23), (24) (30), and (31), respectively.

3. Automaton Construction Rules. Since the inference process is carried out hierarchically and recursively, the extracted subrules should be organized in accordance with the inference hierarchy. The role of the automaton construction rules is actually to assign each subrule that is formed on a different level of the inference hierarchy to the associated arc in the corresponding acceptor-automaton, which is to be synthesized on the basis of an inferred decision rule.

Confirmed hypothesis	Actions
DDD:	(1)

Each component of the content of a DISJ stack is assigned to one of the arcs connecting nodes R_s and R_d as a test condition in order that this arc can be followed, where the label of R_s is $[L] \cdot [NLR]$ and the label of R_d is R_f; and where R_f is a distinguished label for the final state for the entire inference process.

(2) Set $[L] = PUSHL$

(3) Set $[NLR] = 0$

(4) If $[PC] > 0$ then set $[PC]$ to $[PC] - 1$.

Confirmed hypothesis	Actions

CNDD|CCD: (1)

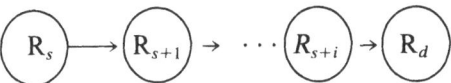

Each component of the content of a CONJ stack is assigned to an arc successively, where the label of R_s is $[L] \cdot [NLR]$. The labeling of successive nodes R_{s+1}, $R_{s+2}, \ldots, R_{s+n}$ is determined by the content of NLR as follows. If $[NLR] \neq 0$, then $[NLR]$ is advanced by 1; if $[NLR] = 0$, then $[NLR] = [NT(L)] + 1$ and the label of R_{s+1} is $[L] \cdot [NLR]$. The successive nodes are labeled by increasing $[NLR]$ by 1 for each additional node. The last component of $[CONJ]$ is assigned to the arc pointing to the final node of the synthesized automaton, i.e., $R_d = R_f$, where R_f is the final state as defined previously.

(2) Set $[L] = $ PUSHL.

(3) Set $[NLR] = 0$.

(4) If $[PC] > 0$, then set $[PC]$ to $[PC] - 1$.

SDD:

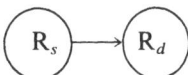

The content of DISJ is associated with the arc connecting R_s and R_d, where the label of R_s is $[L] \cdot [NLR]$ and the label of R_d is R_f.

NSDD:

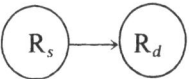

The content of CONJ is assigned to the arc connecting R_s and R_d, where the label of R_s is $[L] \cdot [NLR]$, and if $[NLR] \neq 0$, then $[NLR]$ is advanced by 1. If $[NLR] = 0$, then $[NLR] = [NT(L)] + 1$ and the label of R_d is $[L] \cdot [NLR]$.

Confirmed hypothesis	Actions

CD: (1) Push [L] · [NLR] into PUSHL.

(2)

The content of CONJ is assigned to the arc connecting R_s and $\bar{R}_d$ where the label of R_s is [L] · [NLR]. If [NLR] $\neq$ 0, then [NLR] is advanced by 1; if [NLR] = 0, then [NLR] = [NT(L)] + 1, and the label of R_d is [L] · [NLR].

4. The Pushdown Rules. Pushdown action will take place only if the hypothesis CD is accepted.

$$PUSHA = S_i^a - CP^a(t, q) = S_i^a - S_{i+1}^a \qquad (36)$$

$$PUSHB = S_i^b$$

As an indicator for branching, the PUSH-COUNTER (PC) is set to [PC] + 1.

3.2. The ITN Representing the Inference Algorithm

The inference algorithm described above can be represented using the ITN as a model. The directed graph with labeled arcs shown in Fig. 3 is a pictorial representation of the internal structure of the *i*th network in the ITN shown in Fig. 1.

The memory stacks for list-structured information used in the formal description of Fig. 3 and their correspondence with the associated information needed in the inference procedure are given below.

1. Input Lists AL1 and AL2. The input information for the inference system (S_i^a, S_i^b) is stored in AL1 and AL2, respectively. AL1 and AL2 are actually variables of the array type, for example:

$$AL1 \sim S_i^a = a_1, a_2, \ldots, a_l, \ldots$$

Each element a_l in AL1 represents an array with a formal name P_l^a:

$$a_l = P_l^a(V^a(1, j_1^l), \ldots, V^a(i, j_i^l), \ldots, V^a(N, j_N^l))$$

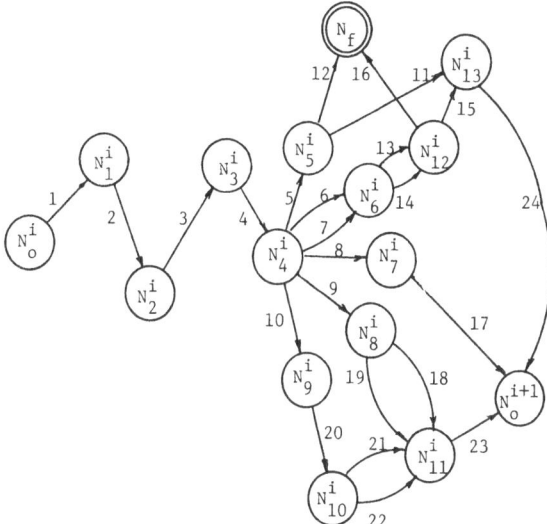

Fig. 3. An ITN representation of the inference algorithm.

where the element $V(i, j_i^l)$ is the value of the ith attribute in the lth sample of set S_i^a.

2. Property Lists. According to the inference procedure described in Section 3.1, a number of properties needs to be extracted from the input lists S_i^a and S_i^b. To simplify the description we identify the formal names of memory stacks with the names of the associated property lists. Those property lists can be categorized into two groups according to their structure.

(1) *Value Property Lists*: V^a, V^b, CV, DV^a, DV^b. These are variables of the array type similar to the input lists, for example,

$$V^a = a_1, \ldots, a_t, \ldots$$

where each element a_t represents an array of values:

$$a_t = V(t) = V(t, j_t^1), \ldots, V(t, j_t^i), \ldots$$

where the element $V(t, j_t^i)$ is the ith value of the tth attribute that belongs to the subset V^a.

(2) *Sample Property Lists:* DP^a, DP^b, CP^a, CP^b. These are variables of the array type, too, for example,

$$DP^a = b_1, \ldots, b_m, \ldots$$

where each element represents an array of samples, namely,

$$b_m = DP^a(i,j) = a_1, \ldots, a_s, \ldots$$

where each a_s is an array with the same structure as elements in AL1 and AL2:

$$a_s = P_s^a(V(1, j_1^s), \ldots, V(i, j_i^s), \ldots, V(N, j_N^s))$$

Before giving the formal description of the network, we describe briefly the operations represented in Fig. 3 by each arc and the lists associated with each state.

The initial state N_0^i is associated with the input lists AL1 and AL2 (e.g., S_i^a, S_i^b).

The arcs 1, 2, 3, and 4 are all ACT arcs, i.e., the associated function lists are executed without making any tests. The operations represented by these arcs are specified by their corresponding function lists, namely,

- *Arc 1:* Extract from S_i^a and S_i^b the value subsets V^a and V^b, respectively, and send both of them to states N_1^i and N_2^i.
- *Arc 2:* Extract from V^a and V^b the common value subsets CV and send CV to states N_2^i, N_3^i, N_4^i.
- *Arc 3:* Extract from V^a, V^b, and CV the distinct value subsets DV^a and DV^b, and send them to states N_3^i, N_4^i.
- *Arc 4:* In this arc, we find the pattern sets DP^a corresponding to DV^a, DP^b to DV^b, and CP^a and CP^b to CV. These property lists are sent to state N_4^i.

Thus, all property lists needed for decision-rule inference are accessible at state N_4^i. There is a set of JUMP arcs starting from N_4^i, namely, arcs 5-10. The test condition for each of these represents the test condition for a certain hypothesis. Arcs 5-10 are examined sequentially in the order of their labels and when the test condition on a certain arc is satisfied, that arc is followed and the rest of the arcs are not examined.

The actions executed by arcs 5-10 are basically the decision-rule/subrule formation operations, i.e., to send the subrule expression corresponding to the confirmed hypothesis into either DISJ or CONJ—buffers for storage of decision rules. In addition, the actions for arcs 8-10 include the updating operations for the input lists.

If hypothesis DDD has been accepted, then the corresponding decision-rule/subrule stored in DISJ is transferred to the state N_5^i. If either hypothesis CNDD or CCD has been accepted, then the corresponding rules stored in CONJ are transferred to the state N_6^i.

The arc 11 starting from N_5^i and the arc 15 starting from N_{12}^i are the TST arcs that are used to check if the PUSH-COUNTER [PC] $\neq$ 0, in which case the pushdown stacks would have to be accessed. Thus, if [PC] $\neq$ 0, either arc 11 or 15 is followed and control is transferred to the state N_{13}^i from which POP arc 24 is used to access the PUSHDOWN stacks for obtaining the updated input lists (S_{i+1}^a, S_{i+1}^b) and the content of NT(L) for further processing at the initial state of the successive network N_0^{i+1}. In this manner, the next cycle in acceptor-automaton synthesis is initiated, or, equivalently, the next ITN is called.

If at states N_5^i and N_{12}^i the PUSH counter [PC] = 0, then either arc 12 or arc 16 is followed, leading in both cases to the final state N_f of the inference machine. This is because [PC] = 0 means that there is no remaining branching that needs to be processed, and the inference process terminates.

If the accepted hypothesis was SDD, then arc 8 implements the input lists updating action and leads to state N_7^i. Arc 17 starting from N_7^i carries out the automaton construction and leads to the initial state of the successive network N_0^{i+1}.

If the hypothesis NSDD was accepted, then the input lists updating action are carried out by arc 9 and control is transferred to N_8^i. At N_8^i it is necessary to check the status of NLR. Depending on that status, the automaton construction task is implemented differently, following either arc 18 or arc 19, and control goes to N_0^{i+1}.

If the accepted hypothesis was CD then arc 10 is followed, the input lists (S_i^a, S_i^b) are held in buffers SA and SB, respectively, which can accommodate information of the same structure as of AL1 and AL2. This temporary storage is necessary for the pushdown action since the input list updating action implemented by arc 10 will remove information needed subsequently for the pushdown action to be implemented in arc 23.

At state N_{10}^i the status of NLR is checked by a TST arc 21. The automaton construction task is carried out differently by either arc 21 or arc 22 depending on the status of NLR and control is transferred to N_{11}^i.

At this point, we point out that there are actually two pushdown actions to be implemented in any one ITN. One of these occurs at arc 20 and the other at arc 23. The function of PUSH arc 23 starting from N_{11}^i is to push the appropriate input information into PUSHA and PUSHB according to the PUSHDOWN rules (36) and the purpose of PUSH arc 20 starting from N_9^i is to push the current contents of registers L and NLR into PUSHL, to be used for route marking in the automaton construction task together with the associated information in PUSHA and PUSHB.

A formal description of the graphic representation for the inference process is given below.

$$N^i \rightarrow (N_0^i\ 1)(N_1^i\ 2)(N_2^i\ 3)(N_3^i\ 4)(N_4^i\ 5\ 6\ 7\ 8\ 9\ 10)$$

$$(N_5^i\ 11\ 12)(N_6^i\ 13\ 14)(N_7^i\ 17)(N_8^i\ 18\ 19)(N_9^i\ 20)$$

$$(N_{10}^i\ 21\ 22)(N_{11}^i\ 23)(N_{12}^i\ 15\ 16)(N_{13}^i\ 24)$$

$$N_0^i \rightarrow (\text{AL1}\ \text{AL2})$$

$$\text{Arc } 1 \rightarrow \left(\text{ACT}\left(\text{SET}\left(\left\{ V^a(i) = \bigcup_j V^a(i,j) \right\} \right) V^a \right) \right.$$

$$\left(\text{SET}\left(\left\{ V^b(i) = \bigcup_j V^b(i,j) \right\} \right) V^b \right)$$

$$\left. (\text{SET } V^a\ N_1^i\ N_2^i)(\text{SET } V^b\ N_1^i\ N_2^i)\ N_1^i) \right)$$

$$N_1^i \rightarrow (V^a\ V^b)$$

$$\text{Arc } 2 \rightarrow (\text{ACT}(\text{SET}(V^a \cap V^b)\ \text{CV})(\text{SET } \text{CV}\ N_2^i\ N_3^i\ N_4^i)\ N_2^i)$$

$$N_2^i \rightarrow (V^a\ V^b\ \text{CV})$$

$$\text{Arc } 3 \rightarrow (\text{ACT}(\text{SET}(V^a - \text{CV})\ \text{DV}^a)(\text{SET}(V^b - \text{CV})\ \text{DV}^b)$$

$$(\text{SET } \text{DV}^a\ N_3^i\ N_4^i)(\text{SET } \text{DV}^b\ N_3^i\ N_4^i)\ N_3^i)$$

$$N_3^i \rightarrow (\text{DV}^a\ \text{DV}^b\ \text{CV})$$

$$\text{Arc } 4 \rightarrow (\text{ACT}(\text{MAP } \text{CV}\ \text{AL1}\ \text{CP}^a)(\text{SET } \text{CP}^a\ N_4^i)$$

$$(\text{MAP } \text{CV}\ \text{AL2}\ \text{CP}^b)(\text{SET } \text{CP}^b\ N_4^i)$$

$$(\text{MAP } \text{DV}^a\ \text{AL1}\ \text{DP}^a)(\text{SET } \text{DP}^a\ N_4^i)$$

$$(\text{MAP } \text{DV}^b\ \text{AL2}\ \text{DP}^b)(\text{SET } \text{DP}^b\ N_4^i)\ N_4^i)$$

$$N_4^i \to (DV^a \ DV^b \ CV \ DP^a \ DP^b \ CP^a \ CP^b)$$

$$\text{Arc } 5 \to \left(\text{JUMP}\left(\bigcup_{i,j} DP^a(i,j) = AL1 \right)(C\{(i,j)^\cdot\} < T) \right.$$

$$(\text{SET}(\{V(i) = V(i,j)^\cdot\}) \ \text{DISJ})$$

$$\left. (\text{SET DISJ } N_5^i) \ N_5^i \right)$$

$$\text{Arc } 6 \to \left(\text{JUMP}\left(\bigcup_{i,j} DP^b(i,j) = AL2 \right)(C\{(i,j)^\cdot\} < T) \right.$$

$$(\text{SET}(\{V(i) \neq V(i,j)^\cdot\}) \ \text{CONJ})$$

$$\left. (\text{SET CONJ } N_6^i) \ N_6^i \right)$$

$$\text{Arc } 7 \to \left(\text{JUMP}\left(\bigcap_{i,j} CP^b(i,j) = \varnothing \right)(CP^a(i,j)^\cdot = AL1) \right.$$

$$(C\{(i,j)^\cdot\} < T)(\text{SET}(\{V(i) = V(i,j)^\cdot\}) \ \text{CONJ})$$

$$\left. (\text{SET CONJ } N_6^i) \ N_6^i \right)$$

$$\text{Arc } 8 \to (\text{JUMP}(C(DP^a(t,q)) > (1 + \tfrac{1}{6}C(AL1)))$$

$$(C(DP^a(t,q)) = \max_{i,j} C(DP^a(i,j)))$$

$$(\text{SET}(V(t) = V(t,q)^\cdot)\text{DISJ})(\text{SET DISJ } N_7^i)$$

$$(\text{SET}(AL1\text{-}DP^a)(t,q)^\cdot) \ AL1) \ N_7^i)$$

$$\text{Arc } 9 \to \left(\text{JUMP}(C(DP^b(t,q)) \geq C(AL2) \right.$$

$$\left. - \frac{C(AL1)}{\max_{i,j}[C(CP^a(i,j))/C(CP^b(i,j))]} \right)$$

$$(C(DP^b(t,q)) = \max_{i,j} C(DP^b(i,j)))$$

$$(SET(V(t) \neq V(t, q)^{\cdot})\ CONJ)(SET\ CONJ\ N_8^i)$$

$$(SET(AL2 - DP^b(t, q)^{\cdot})\ AL2)\ N_8^i)$$

$$Arc\ 10 \rightarrow \left(JUMP \left(\frac{C(CP^a(t, q))}{C(CP^b(t, q))} = \max_{i,j} \frac{C(CP^a(i, j))}{C(CP^b(i, j))} \right) \right.$$

$$(SET(V(t) = V(t, q)^{\cdot})\ CONJ)(SET\ CONJ\ N_{10}^i)$$

$$(SET\ AL1\ SA)(SET\ AL2\ SB)$$

$$(SET\ CP^a(t, q)^{\cdot}\ AL1)(SET\ CP^b(t, q)^{\cdot}\ AL2)$$

$$\left. (SET\ SA\ N_{11}^i)(SET\ SB\ N_{11}^i)\ N_9^i \right)$$

$N_5^i \rightarrow (DISJ)$

$\quad Arc\ 11 \rightarrow (TST\ PC\ (PC - 1)(SYNTH\ DISJ\ (L \cdot NLR)\ R_f)$

$$\qquad\qquad\qquad\qquad (SET\ NLR\ NT(L))(SET\ 0\ NLR)\ N_{13}^i)$$

$\quad Arc\ 12 \rightarrow (ACT\ (SYNTH\ DISJ\ (L \cdot NLR)\ R_f)\ N_f)$

$N_6^i \rightarrow (CONJ)$

$\quad Arc\ 13 \rightarrow (TST\ NLR\ (NLR + 1)$

$$\qquad\qquad\qquad\qquad (SYNTH\ CONJ\ (L \cdot NLR - 1)(L \cdot NLR))$$

$$\qquad\qquad\qquad\qquad (SET\ (R_f - 1)(L \cdot NT(L)))$$

$$\qquad\qquad\qquad\qquad (SET\ 0\ NLR)\ N_{12}^i)$$

$\quad Arc\ 14 \rightarrow (ACT\ (SYNTH\ CONJ\ (L \cdot NLR)(L \cdot NT(L) + 1))$

$$\qquad\qquad\qquad (SET\ (R_f - 1)(L \cdot NT(L)))(SET\ 0\ NLR)\ N_{12}^i)$$

$N_7^i \rightarrow (DISJ)$

$\quad Arc\ 17 \rightarrow (ACT\ (SYNTH\ DISJ\ (L \cdot NLR)\ R_f)\ N_0^{i+1})$

$N_8^i \rightarrow$ (CONJ)

    Arc 18 → (TST NLR (NLR + 1)

                    (SYNTH CONJ $(L \cdot NLR - 1)(L \cdot NLR)$) N_0^{i+1})

    Arc 19 → (ACT (SYNTH CONJ $(L \cdot NLR)(L \cdot NT(L) + 1)$)

                    (SET $(NT(L) + 1)$ NLR) N_0^{i+1})

$N_9^i \rightarrow$ ( )

    Arc 20 → (PUSH PUSHL $(L \cdot NLR)$(SET $(PC + 1)$ PC) N_{10}^i)

$N_{10}^i \rightarrow$ (CONJ)

    Arc 21 → (TST NLR (NLR + 1)

                    (SYNTH CONJ $(L \cdot NLR - 1)(L \cdot NLR)$ N_{11}^i)

    Arc 22 → (ACT (SYNTH CONJ $(L \cdot NLR)(L \cdot NT(L) + 1)$)

                    (SET $(NT(L) + 1)$ NLR) N_{11}^i)

$N_{11}^i \rightarrow$ (SA SB)

    Arc 23 → (PUSH PUSHA PUSHB $(SA - AL1)$ SB N_0^{i+1})

$N_{12}^i \rightarrow$ ( )

    Arc 15 → (TST PC $(PC - 1)$ N_{13}^i)

    Arc 16 → (ACT ( ) N_f)

$N_{13}^i \rightarrow$ ( )

    Arc 24 → (POP PUSHA PUSHB PUSHL AL1 AL2 L N_0^{i+1})

In the above description the expression $C\{X\}$ denotes the cardinality of a set and X, T is a predetermined numerical threshold value. The expression $L \cdot NLR$ indicates an index string consisting of the content of register L followed by the content of register NLR. R_f is a fixed index indicating the final node of the automaton. The expression $(R_f - 1)$ indicates the tail node label of the last arc which points to the final state R_f.

It is interesting to note that the described ITN network model has the attractive feature of being capable of generating an acceptor-automaton that implements the decision rule inferred by following the paths through ITN from the initial state N_0^0 to the final state N_f. The synthesized automaton is able to accept all samples of the positive training set and to reject any sample of the negative training set. The predictive capability depends to a large extent on how representative the training sets of the classes to be differentiated are.

4. IMPLEMENTATION AND ILLUSTRATIVE EXAMPLES

A program in PASCAL on the PDP 11/45 RSX-11M based on the ITN model described in this report and implementing the algorithm suggested in Refs 1 and 2 has been used for inferring decision rules that are valid for binary classification tasks. Multiclass classification is carried out in the form of a tree of binary decisions.

As illustrations, two medical diagnosis (classification) tasks were considered and the results are described in the following.

Data in the examples are taken from the work of Pao et al.[6] In all cases, each sample represents a patient assessment profile described by twelve features that are coded numerically to indicate the degree of severity of corresponding symptoms. A tentative diagnosis was made by a group of physicians for each patient profile. The original data with the tentative diagnosis and the test and training sample sets for different classes can be found in Ref. 1.

Example 1:
A training set consisting of eight samples was taken for each of classes A and B where class A consists of profiles for chest disease patients and class B for cardiac cases. A decision rule for differentiating class A from B was obtained. The acceptor-automaton for class A constructed on the basis is inferred decision rules following the paths in the ITN model is shown in Fig. 4.

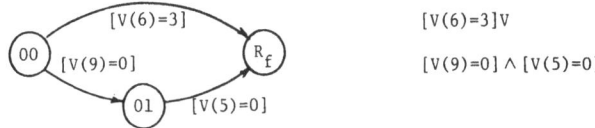

[V(6)=3]V

[V(9)=0] ∧ [V(5)=0]

Fig. 4. Acceptor-automaton for distinguishing between the two medical diagnosis classes of Example 1.

Fig. 5. Acceptor-automaton for distinguishing between the two medical diagnosis classes of Example 2.

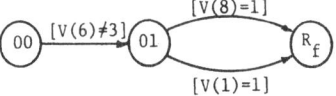

Example 2:

In this example, class A and class B correspond to the profiles of abdominal and chest diseases, respectively. A training set of eight samples was selected for each class and the synthesized decision rule is shown below:

$$([V(6) \neq 3] \wedge [V(8) = 1])V$$

$$([V(6) \neq 3] \wedge [V(1) = 1])$$

The corresponding acceptor-automaton was synthesized in the inference process (Fig. 5). A recognition test was carried out for the test sets consisting of 15 samples for chest diseases, 25 samples for cardiac diseases, and 34 samples for abdominal diseases, respectively. The results are shown below:

	Recognition rate (%)	Rejection (%)	Error (%)
Example 1:			
Chest/Cardiac	100	0	0
Example 2:			
Abdominal/Chest	94	6	0

NOTE ADDED IN PROOF

Since preparation of this manuscript there has been a resurgence of activity in "machine learning" or inductive inference in AI research. See, for example, *Machine Learning*, R. S. Michalski, J. G. Carbonell, and T. M. Mitchell (Eds.), Tioga Publishing Co., Palo Alto, CA. (1983).

REFERENCES

1. Y.-H. Pao and C. H. Hu, Methods for manipulating pattern information: suitable for use in machine intelligence, CWRU Technical Report MI 101-82 (1982).
2. R. S. Michalski, Pattern recognition as rule-guided inductive inference, *IEEE Trans. PAMI* **2** (4), 349–361 (1980).

3. W. A. Woods, Transition network grammars for natural language analysis, *Commun. ACM* **13** (10), 591–606 (1970).

4. S. M. Chou and K. S. Fu, Inference for transition network grammars, *Proc. 3rd IJCPR*, pp. 79–84 (1976).

5. Y.-H. Pao and C. H. Hu, A systematic procedure for inductive inference of decision rules applicable to certain instances of pattern recognition, *Proc. of 6th IJCPR* (1982).

6. Y.-H. Pao, W. L. Schultz, M. Kiley, J. L. Altman, and A. J. L. Schneider, Implementation of human "judgement" and "experience" in computer-aided interpretation of medical images, *Proc. 3rd IJCPR* (1976).

7. J. E. Hopecroft and J. D. Ullman, *Formal Languages and Their Relation to Automata*, Addison-Wesley, Reading, MA (1969).

8. M. A. Aiserman, L. A. Gusen, L. I. Rozonoer, I. M. Smirnova, and A. A. Tal', *Logic, Automata, and Algorithms* (Translated by Scripta Technica, Inc.; translation editor: G. M. Krane), Academic, New York (1971).

9. J. R. Sampson, *Adaptive Information Processing; An Introductory Survey*, Springer-Verlag, New York, (1976).

Chapter 5

AUTOMATED LOGIC DESIGN OF MOS NETWORKS

Hung Chi Lai

and

Saburo Muroga

Department of Computer Science
University of Illinois
222 Digital Computer Laboratory
1304 West Springfield Ave.
Urbana, Illinois 61801

1. INTRODUCTION

With the technological progress of integrated circuits of very large scale integration (VLSI), MOS logic families such as nMOS and C/MOS are becoming increasingly important because large integration size can be attained with MOSFETs (metal–oxide–semiconductor field-effect transistors) due to low power consumption and simple integrated circuit structure.[1] Compared with other logic families, MOS logic families have a unique feature: each MOS logic gate in any logic network can express a negative function.[2] A *negative function* is a switching function that can be expressed as the complement of a disjunctive (or conjunctive) form of only noncomplemented literals. Examples are $\overline{x_1 \vee x_2 x_3}$, $\overline{x_1 x_2 \vee x_2 x_3 \vee x_1 x_3}$, and $\overline{(x_1 \vee x_2)(x_3 \vee x_4 \vee x_5)}$. A negative function is more general than the NOR, NAND, AND, or OR operations that a conventional simple logic gate expresses. Logic gates that express negative functions are called *negative gates*. Thus, for any switching functions, networks of negative gates require no more gates than those of conventional simple logic gates. As a matter of fact, they generally require much less.

When we compare the logic designs of networks with different types of gates, networks with AND and OR gates are the easiest because these gates are directly related to the AND and OR operations, and consequently networks can be designed based on switching expressions. Multilevel networks with NOR or NAND gates are much harder to design because these gates are not directly related to simple logic operations. At least for manual design, the map-factoring method is convenient and powerful,[2] but it is not as easy to use as the Karnaugh maps which are useful for two-level AND/OR gate network design. Networks with negative gates look even more difficult because negative gates express more complex functions than NAND or NOR gates. But as discussed in Sections 3–5, negative-gate networks are easy to design—if we are not concerned with the complexity of each gate—because of the flexibility that any negative function can be expressed as a gate. Furthermore, networks with a minimum number of negative gates are easy to derive, unlike the multilevel networks of AND/OR gates or NOR gates where the minimization of the number of gates is not easy, though network design without minimization is easy.[2] But it is not so easy if we are concerned with the complexity of each gate (see Section 6).

The first procedure to design a logic network with a minimum number of negative gates was developed by Ibaraki and Muroga.[3] Though this was restricted to two-level networks, the procedure, unlike those developed later, can be extended to the minimization of the number of interconnections, as was done by Ibaraki.[4] An efficient procedure was developed by Nakamura *et al.*[5] for designing negative-gate networks, whether the networks were to be in two- or multi-levels. A similar approach was independently developed by Liu.[6] Although the two approaches differ in certain aspects, they are essentially based on the same type of grouping of input vectors. Two-level networks have been discussed in detail by Nakamura.[7]

All these procedures minimize the number of negative gates in designed networks, but they have no control over the complexity of each gate or the number of interconnections. For layout on VLSI chips the number of interconnections as well as the number of gates are important for the reduction of layout area. Design procedures for multilevel networks with a minimum number of negative gates and with irredundant MOSFETs in each negative gate were developed.[8] Irredundant MOSFETs in each negative gate means that the network outputs will change if any MOSFET is deleted from any gate. This also results in irredundant interconnections among negative gates. In this case the number of interconnections among negative gates is not necessarily the minimum, but if any interconnection is deleted the network outputs will change. In the following, we present these procedures along with discussions of their significance and relationship with recent research works.

2. BASIC PROPERTIES

In this section, we present the basic properties related to negative functions that are discussed in Ibaraki and Muroga,[3] Nakamura *et al.*,[5] Muroga,[9] and Gilbert.[10] Consider the switching functions of n variables $x_1, \ldots, x_n$. Let V_n be the set of all n-dimensional binary vectors, where each component is 1 or 0. Suppose two vectors, $A = (a_1, \ldots, a_n)$ and $B = (b_1, \ldots, b_n)$, in V_n are given. $a_i = b_i$ for every $i = 1, \ldots, n$ is denoted by $A = B$, and $a_i \leq b_i$ for every $i = 1, \ldots, n$, but $a_i < b_i$ for at least one i is denoted by $A < B$. $A \leq B$ means $A < B$ or $A = B$. If none of the relations $A > B$, $A < B$, or $A = B$ holds between A and B, then A and B are said to be *incomparable*. For convenience, let O denote $(0, \ldots, 0)$ and I denote $(1, \ldots, 1)$.

For a graphical representation, an n-dimensional lattice C_n is defined as follows:

Each vector in V_n is represented as a distinct node in C_n. Henceforth, a node in C_n may be referred to by the vector that it represents. Then (i) there is an edge between two nodes A and B if and only if A differs from B at exactly one component, and (ii) the edge between A and B is directed from A to B if $A > B$ and is denoted by $\overrightarrow{AB}$.

The *weight* of a node A is defined as the number of "1" components in the vector which represents node A.

Let $f_1, \ldots, f_m$ be the completely specified switching functions on n variables. An n-dimensional lattice C_n is referred to as a *labeled n-lattice* with respect to the functions $f_1, \ldots, f_m$ when a binary integer

$$L(A) \equiv l(A; f_1, \ldots, f_m) = \sum_{i=1}^{m} f_i(A) 2^{m-i}$$

is attached to each node A of C_n as a label. A labeled n-lattice with respect to $f_1, \ldots, f_m$ is denoted by $C_n(f_1, \ldots, f_m)$. Figure 1 shows a labeled 3-lattice with respect to functions $f_1 = \bar{x}_1 \vee \bar{x}_3$ and $f_2 = x_1 x_3 \vee \bar{x}_1 x_2 \bar{x}_3$.

Definition 1. A directed edge $\overrightarrow{AB}$ is said to be an *inverse edge* of a labeled n-lattice $C_n(f_1, \ldots, f_m)$ if $l(A; f_1, \ldots, f_m) > l(B; f_1, \ldots, f_m)$.

In the labeled 3-lattice shown in Fig. 1, the directed edge $\overrightarrow{(010)(000)}$ in the bold line is the only inverse edge. Based on the definition of inverse edges, a negative function can be defined as follows.

Definition 2. A completely specified switching function f of n variables is a *negative function* if there is no inverse edge in $C_n(f)$, the labeled n-lattice with respect to f.

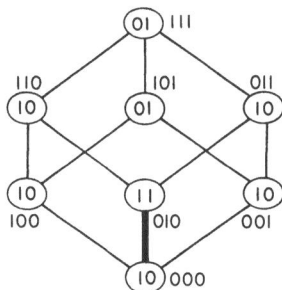

Fig. 1. Labeled 3-lattice with respect to $f_1 = \bar{x}_1 \vee \bar{x}_3$ and $f_2 = x_1 x_3 \vee \bar{x}_1 x_2 \bar{x}_3$, where the binary number inside each circle is the label attached to the corresponding node.

This definition is consistent with the conventional definition of negative function (stated in Section 1) as can be seen from the following lemmas and theorems, as stated in Ibaraki and Muroga.[3]

Lemma 1. If a switching function f is a negative function, then $f(A) > f(B)$ does not hold for any pair of input vectors A, B such that $A > B$.

Corollary 1. If a switching function f is a negative function and $f(A) = 1$ for some $A \in C_n$, then $f(B) = 1$ for every $B \in C_n$ such that $B < A$. Also, if $f(A) = 0$ for some $A \in C_n$, then $f(B) = 0$ for every $B \in C_n$ such that $B > A$.

From Lemma 1, the following theorem can be easily proved.

Theorem 1. A function f of n variables is a negative function if and only if for every pair of input vectors such that $f(A) = 1$ and $f(B) = 0$ there exists a subscript $i(1 \leq i \leq n)$ such that $a_i = 0$ and $b_i = 1$ hold.

Because of this characterization, it is sometimes convenient to determine whether or not a function is a negative function by checking whether or not every 0-1 combination in the values of the function has a corresponding 1-0 combination in the values of the variables. For convenience, let us use the term *0-1 pair* to refer to any combination of "0" and "1" in the values of the function, and use the term *1-0 cover* to refer to the corresponding combination of "1" and "0" in the values of a particular variable of this function. Theorem 1 asserts that function f is a negative function if and only if all 0-1 pairs in f are covered by 1-0 covers in its variables.

Another characterization of negative functions is given by the following theorem, which can be easily proved based on a theorem of positive functions in Gilbert.[10]

Theorem 2. A function is a negative function if and only if it has a disjunctive form consisting of complemented variables only.

Figure 2 shows a labeled 3-lattice for a negative function $f = \bar{x}_1\bar{x}_3 \vee \bar{x}_1\bar{x}_2 = \overline{x_1 \vee x_2x_3}$. Obviously, this labeled 3-lattice has no inverse edge, and for every 0-1 pair in f, there is a 1-0 cover. For example, the 0-1 pair, $f(110) \equiv f(A) = 0$ and $f(000) \equiv f(B) = 1$, is covered by the 1-0 cover $a_1 = 1$ and $b_1 = 0$ or $a_2 = 1$ and $b_2 = 0$.

The above definitions and discussions are concerned with completely specified functions, i.e., functions whose values are specified for every input vector. For incompletely specified functions, i.e., functions whose values for some input vectors are not specified ("don't cares"), we need the following definitions and theorems. We use "∗" to denote those unspecified values of a function.

Definition 3. A *completion* of an incompletely specified function f is a completely specified function obtained from f by specifying each unspecified value of f to either "1" or "0". If the resulting completion is a negative function, it is called a *negative completion*.

Definition 4. An incompletely specified function f of n variables is *negative with respect to* these n-variables if and only if it has a negative completion.

The following theorem in Ibaraki and Muroga[3] gives a criterion to judge whether an incompletely specified function is negative with respect to its input variables. For convenience, we sometimes refer to a function that is negative with respect to its input variables simply as an *incompletely specified negative function.*

Theorem 3. An incompletely specified function f of n variables is negative with respect to these n variables if and only if for each pair of specified input vectors A, $B \in V_n$ such that $f(A) = 0$ and $f(B) = 1$, there exists a subscript i such that $a_i = 1$ and $b_i = 0$ where $1 \leq i \leq n$.

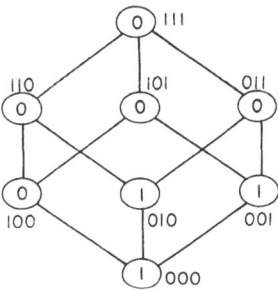

Fig. 2. Labeled 3-lattice for $f = \bar{x}_1\bar{x}_3 \vee \bar{x}_1\bar{x}_2$ which has no inverse edge.

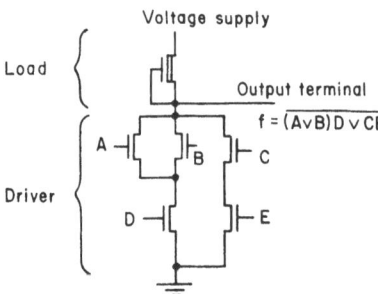

Fig. 3. Typical MOS cell.

There are generally many negative completions for a given function f. The following corollaries are sometimes more convenient in judging whether an incompletely specified function is negative.

Corollary 2. A function f of n variables is negative with respect to these n variables if and only if for every vector $A \in C_n$ such that $f(A) = 0$, we have $f(B) = 0$ or $*$ for every $B \in C_n$ such that $B > A$.

Corollary 3. A function f of n variables is negative with respect to these n variables if and only if for every vector $A \in C_n$ such that $f(A) = 1$, we have $f(B) = 1$ or $*$ for every vector $B \in C_n$ such that $B < A$.

Next let us consider MOS cells as a means to realize negative gates, though negative gates can be realized by other electronic circuits. Figure 3 shows a typical *MOS cell* which consists of a *load FET* and many *driver FETs*. (MOSFETs are often abbreviated as FETs.) The load FET is always conductive. Each driver FET operates like a make-contact relay: it is conductive when its input is a logic "1" (represented by a voltage close to the supply voltage), and it is nonconductive when its input is a logic "0" (represented by a voltage close to the ground voltage). As discussed in Muroga,[2] the MOS cell shown in Fig. 3 realizes the function $\overline{(A \vee B)D \vee CE}$. The output is always the complement (negation) of the transmission function realized by the driver alone. Thus, theoretically, any negative function can be realized by a single MOS cell, though it may become impractical if the cell is excessively complex.

In Sections 3–5, we derive procedures to design irredundant networks with a minimum number of negative gates.[8] In these sections, we will use the term *a network with negative gates* or *a negative-gate network* to mean a network consisting of only negative gates. Each of such gates realizes a function that is negative with respect to its inputs, but we are not concerned with the structure of each gate. This will be distinguished from *a network with MOS cells* or *a MOS network* which is a negative-gate network with each negative gate realized by an MOS cell.

3. ALGORITHMS FOR DESIGNING NETWORKS WITH A MINIMUM NUMBER OF NEGATIVE GATES

In this section we discuss two algorithms for the synthesis of networks with a minimum number of negative gates which are basic algorithms for the design procedure of irredundant MOS networks to be introduced in Section 5. Only feed-forward networks, i.e., loop-free networks, will be considered.

Definition 5. A *minimum negative-gate network* for a switching function f is a feed-forward network for f that consists of R_f negative gates, where R_f is the minimum number of negative gates required for the realization of f with only negative gates.

Our problem is to design a network for a given function using a minimum number of negative gates alone. This problem was solved by Nakamura *et al.*[5] by considering the relationship between a general feed-forward negative-gate network and the labeled n-lattice with respect to the functions realized by the gates in this network. Figure 4 shows a generalized form of a feed-forward network with R negative gates, where $x_1, \ldots, x_n$ denote the n input variables, g_i denotes the ith gate from the left for $i = 1, \ldots, R$ with g_R being the output gate. Let $u_i(x_1, \ldots, x_n)$ denote the function realized by the gate g_i with respect to the input variables $x_1, \ldots, x_n$. Since every gate is a negative gate, u_i is negative with respect to the inputs $x_1, \ldots, x_n, u_1, \ldots, u_{i-1}$ of g_i. In other words, $u_i(x_1, \ldots, x_n, u_1, \ldots, u_{i-1})$ is an incompletely specified negative function of $n + (i - 1)$ variables. This network is a generalized form of a feed-forward network with R negative gates, since every feed-forward network of R negative gates can be expressed in this form with some (or none of the) connections deleted.

Since this generalized form of Fig. 4 represents all the possible configurations of networks consisting of R negative gates, the problem of the synthesis of networks with a minimum number of gates for a given function

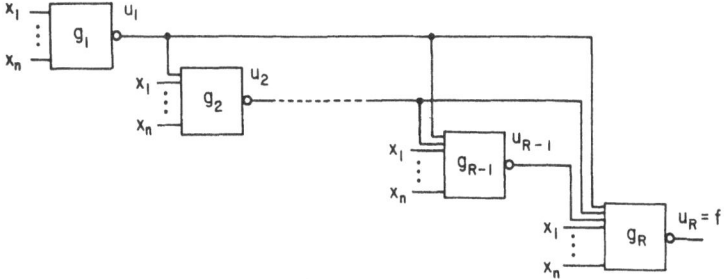

Fig. 4. Generalized form of a feed-forward network consisting of R negative gates.

f becomes the problem of finding a sequence of functions, $u_1, u_2, \ldots, u_R$, defined in the following, while R is minimized.

Definition 6. A *negative-function sequence of length R for function f*, denoted by NFS(R, f), is an ordered set of R functions in C_n, $u_1, u_2, \ldots, u_R$, such that (1) u_1 is a negative function in C_n; (2) u_i is negative with respect to $x_1, \ldots, x_n, u_1, \ldots, u_{i-1}$ for $i = 2, \ldots, R$; and (3) $u_R = f$.

The following lemma[5] characterizes an NFS(R, f) in terms of a labeled n-lattice.

Theorem 4. A sequence of functions $u_1, u_2, \ldots, u_R$ in C_n is an NFS(R, u_R) if and only if the labeled n-lattice with respect to $u_1, \ldots, u_R$, i.e., $C_n(u_1, \ldots, u_R)$, has no inverse edge.

Based on Theorem 4, an algorithm for the synthesis of a network realizing a given function f with a minimum number of negative gates has been derived.[5] The basic concept of this algorithm is to find a labeled n-lattice $C_n(u_1, \ldots, u_R)$ such that (1) $u_R = f$; (2) $C_n(u_1, \ldots, u_R)$ has no inverse edge; and (3) the label for node A, $l(A; u_1, \ldots, u_R)$, is minimized under the above two conditions for each A, and therefore R, the bit length of binary numbers $l(A; u_1, \ldots, u_R)$, is minimized. This algorithm stated in the following will be referred to as the *algorithm MNL*.

Algorithm 1. Algorithm based on minimum labeling *(MNL)*.
The symbol $L^f_{mn}(X)$ denotes the label assigned to node X in the following:
Step 1. Assign as $L^f_{mn}(I)$ the value of $f(I)$.
Step 2. When $L^f_{mn}(A)$ is assigned to every node A of weight w in C_n, assign as $L^f_{mn}(B)$ to each node B of weight $w - 1$ the smallest binary integer satisfying the following two conditions: (a) The least significant bit of $L^f_{mn}(B)$ is $f(B)$; (b) $L^f_{mn}(B) \geq L^f_{mn}(A)$ for every directed edge $\overrightarrow{AB}$ terminating at B.
Step 3. Repeat Step 2 until $L^f_{mn}(O)$ is assigned.
Step 4. The number of bits in $L^f_{mn}(O)$ is R_f, the minimum number of negative gates required to realize f, and the ith significant bit of $L^f_{mn}(A)$ is $u_i(A)$ for each A and for $i = 1, \ldots, R_f$.

The validity of this algorithm is obvious from Theorem 4. The algorithm obtains an NFS$(R_f, f) = (u_1, \ldots, u_{R_f} \equiv f)$, where R_f is the number of bits in $L^f_{mn}(O)$. From the definition of NFS(R_f, f), u_i for $i = 1, \ldots, R_f$ can be realized by a negative-gate network of the form of Fig. 4. Since the minimum possible $L^f_{mn}(A)$ to guarantee no inverse edge in the labeled n-lattice is chosen at each node $A \in C_n$, R_f is the minimum number of negative gates required to realize f by a feed-forward configuration of negative gates.

Example 1. Let us design a minimum negative-gate network for $f = x_1x_2 \lor x_2\bar{x}_3$ in C_3. The true nodes of $C_3(f)$ are (111), (110), and (010) as shown in Fig. 5(a). According to Algorithm 1 (MNL), the labeled 3-lattice $C_3(u_1, u_2, f)$ is obtained as shown in Fig. 5(b). (u_1, u_2, f) as an NFS$(3, f)$ can then be realized by a network with three negative gates in the generalized form as shown in Fig. 5(c).

Corollary 4. Let NFS$(R_f, f) = (u_1, \ldots, u_{R_f})$ be a minimum negative-function sequence for f, and $C_n(u_1, \ldots, u_{R_f})$ be the corresponding labeled n-lattice. Then the labels in this lattice must satisfy $l(A; u_1, \ldots, u_{R_f}) \geq L_{mn}^f(A)$ for every node $A \in C_n$.

Next, let us investigate the label attached to each node by MNL.

Definition 7. A *directed path* from a node A_1 to another node A_p satisfying $A_1 > A_p$ in an n-lattice C_n is a sequence of directed edges connecting the two nodes, $\overrightarrow{A_1A_2}, \overrightarrow{A_2A_3}, \ldots, \overrightarrow{A_{p-1}A_p}$.

Obviously there may be more than one directed path between two nodes in C_n.

Definition 8. In a labeled n-lattice $C_n(f)$ for a function f, the *number of inversions* in a directed path between two nodes is the number of inverse

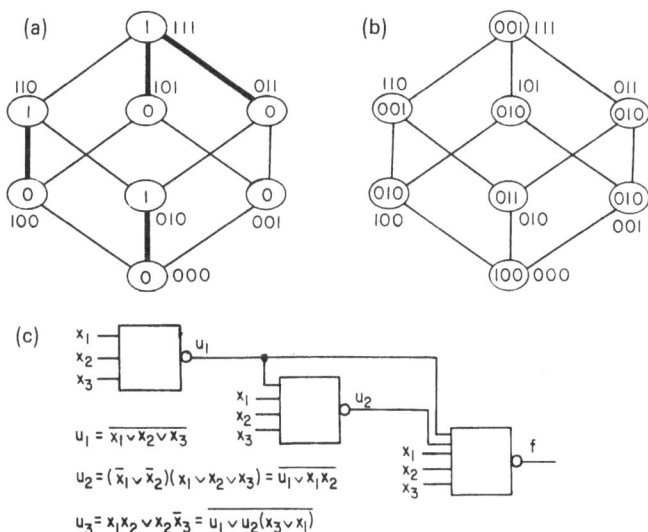

Fig. 5. Example 1. (a) $C_3(f)$ for $f = x_1x_2 \lor x_2\bar{x}_3$, where bold lines denote inverse edges. (b) $C_3(u_1, u_2, f)$ based on minimal labeling. (c) Minimum negative-gate network for f based on minimal labeling.

edges included in this path. The *inversion degree* of a node A *with respect to node* I in $C_n(f)$ is the maximum number of inversions over all directed paths from node I to node A, and is denoted by $D_I^f(A)$.

Definition 9. The *number of inversions* of a function f is the maximum number of inversions over all directed paths from node I to node O in $C_n(f)$, i.e., $D_I^f(O)$.

Example 2. In Fig. 5(a) for Example 1, $D_I^f(111) = D_I^f(110) = 0$, $D_I^f(100) = D_I^f(101) = D_I^f(011) = D_I^f(010) = D_I^f(001) = 1$, and $D_I^f(000) = 2$.

The number of inversions of a function determines the number of negative gates required to realize this function. This relation is stated in Corollary 5 which is an immediate consequence of Theorem 5.

Theorem 5. $L_{mn}^f(X)$, the label attached to node $X \in C_n$ by Algorithm 1 (MNL) for a function f, has the value

$$L_{mn}^f(X) = 2D_I^f(X) + f(X).$$

Proof. According to Theorem 4 and also $D_I^f(I) = 0$ by definition, $L_{mn}^f(I) = f(I) = 2D_I^f(I) + f(I)$. Therefore, the theorem holds for the node of weight n. Next assume $L(X) = 2D_I^f(X) + f(X)$ holds for every node of weight w or greater, and we will prove that it holds for every node of weight $w - 1$. Let us consider a node B of weight $w - 1$ and select a node A of weight w such that

$$L_{mn}^f(A) = \max\{L_{mn}^f(X) | \overrightarrow{XB} \in C_n\} \tag{1}$$

Because $L_{mn}^f(X) = 2D_I^f(X) + f(X)$ holds for every X of weight w or greater,

$$L_{mn}^f(A) = 2D_I^f(A) + f(A) \tag{2}$$

holds. Since $L_{mn}^f(A)$ is chosen as the maximum of $L_{mn}^f(X)$ by Eq. (1) and $f(A)$ is constant 1 or 0 in Eq. (2),

$$D_I^f(A) = \max\{D_I^f(X) | \overrightarrow{XB} \in C_n\} \tag{3}$$

must hold. The following cases may occur:

(1) $f(A) = 0$, i.e., $L_{mn}^f(A) = 2D_I^f(A)$. According to Step 2 of algorithm MNL, $L_{mn}^f(B)$ will then be assigned the value satisfying $L_{mn}^f(B) = L_{mn}^f(A) + f(B) = 2D_I^f(A) + f(B)$. Since $\overrightarrow{AB}$ does not constitute an inverse edge in $C_n(f)$ and Eq. (3) holds (the case where $D_I^f(C) = D_I^f(A) =$

$\max\{D_I^f(X)|\overrightarrow{XB} \in C_n\}$ holds for another node C as well as for A and also $f(C) = 1$ holds can not occur because otherwise $L_{mn}^f(C) = 2D_I^f(C) + f(C) \geq 2D_I^f(A) + f(A) = L_{mn}^f(A)$ hold, contradicting Eq. (1)), we have $D_I^f(B) = D_I^f(A)$. Therefore, $L_{mn}^f(B) = 2D_I^f(B) + f(B)$ holds.

(2) $f(A) = 1$, $f(B) = 1$. None of $\overrightarrow{XB}$ is an inverse edge in C_n, so we have $D_I^f(B) = D_I^f(A)$. According to algorithm MNL, $L_{mn}^f(B) = L_{mn}^f(A) = 2D_I^f(B) + f(B)$ must hold.

(3) $f(A) = 1$, $f(B) = 0$. $\overrightarrow{AB}$ is an inverse edge in C_n, so $D_I^f(B) = D_I^f(A) + 1$. According to algorithm MNL, $L_{mn}^f(B) = L_{mn}^f(A) + 1 = 2D_I^f(A) + f(A) + 1 = 2D_I^f(B)$ must hold.

Consequently, $L_{mn}^f(B) = 2D_I^f(B) + f(B)$ holds for every node B of weight $w - 1$. By induction, $L_{mn}^f(X) = 2D_I^f(X) + f(X)$ holds for every $X \in C_n$. $\qquad\square$

Corollary 5. R_f, the minimum number of negative gates required to realize function f, is given by

$$R_f = \lceil \log_2(D_I^f(O) + 1) \rceil + 1$$

where $\lceil r \rceil$ denotes the smallest integer not smaller than r.

Proof. By Theorem 5, $L_{mn}^f(O) = 2D_I^f(O) + f(O)$, which requires R_f bits in binary number representation. This means that R_f is the smallest integer satisfying

$$2^{R_f} - 1 \geq 2D_I^f(O) + f(O) \tag{4}$$

Therefore,

$$R = \lceil \log_2(2D_I^f(O) + f(O) + 1) \rceil = \lceil \log_2(D_I^f(O) + 1) \rceil + 1 \qquad\square$$

From Eq. (4), it is obvious that

$$D_I^f(O) \leq 2^{R_f-1} - 1 \tag{5}$$

is always satisfied. This relation will be used later.

The above relations are consistent with the results that are obtained by Markov[11] and independently by Muller.[12]

Next let us consider the labeled n-lattice $C_n(u_1, \ldots, u_{R_f-1}, f)$ obtained by algorithm MNL for function f. We can partition the entire set of nodes in C_n into disjoint subsets such that two nodes A and B belong to the same subset if and only if $L_{mn}^f(A) = L_{mn}^f(B)$. It is obvious that if A and B are in the same subset, $f(A) = f(B)$ must hold, i.e., A and B must be both true or false vectors. Each of the above subsets is called a *cluster based on MNL.*

In general, given any labeled n-lattice $C_n(u_1, \ldots, u_{R_f-1}, f)$ that has no inverse edges, we can partition the entire set of nodes into disjoint subsets in the same manner as above. Each of these subsets is simply called a *cluster*, in contrast to a cluster based on MNL above. A *true cluster* consists of true vectors, whereas a *false cluster* consists of false vectors. An n-lattice where all nodes are partitioned into clusters is called a *clustered n-lattice.* The concept of clustered n-lattice is a generalization of the concept of the stratified structure of a switching function defined in Liu.[6] We will show later that the stratified structure of a switching function is essentially the clustered n-lattice based on Algorithm 2 (MXL) to be introduced later.

In general, the clustered n-lattice based on algorithm MNL is different from the clustered n-lattice based on algorithm MXL, and accordingly different from the stratified structure of Liu.[6] Nevertheless, most of the properties possessed by the stratified structure of a switching function are also possessed by the clustered n-lattice based on MNL. This will be discussed in more detail later.

The negative-gate network for a function f produced by algorithm MNL is usually not the only minimum negative-gate network for f. If $D_I^f(O) \neq 2^{R_f-1} - 1$, we can relabel the nodes in C_n according to the following.

Relabeling of a Clustered n-Lattice Based on MNL. (1) Arrange the clusters based on MNL in such an order that a cluster with a smaller label precedes a cluster with a greater label (assigned by algorithm MNL). (2) Assign to every node in each cluster the same label of R_f bits such that: (a) the last bit of the label is "1" or "0", depending on whether this cluster is a true or false cluster, respectively; and (b) the label assigned to each cluster must be greater than those assigned to clusters preceding it.

Through relabeling, we can obtain a different minimum negative-gate network. This way of relabeling is similar to the procedure given in Liu[6] where a realizable stratified truth table (corresponding to a labeled n-lattice without an inverse edge) can be obtained by assigning each cluster (based on MXL, to be introduced) a unique label such that the resulting labeled n-lattice has no inverse edge. Example 3 shows how one can obtain different minimum negative-gate networks from the clustered n-lattice based on MNL by relabeling.

Example 3. For the function shown in Fig. 5(b) for Example 1, there are four clusters based on MNL.

(i) True cluster: (111), (110). (ii) False cluster: (101), (011), (100), (001). (iii) True cluster: (010). (iv) False cluster: (000).

Since $D_I^f(O) = 2$, at least three negative gates are required to realize f according to Corollary 5. Table I shows five different labelings obtained by relabeling the clustered n-lattice based on MNL. All five labelings result in a different NFS$(3, f)$'s (though NFS$(3, f)_2$ and NFS$(3, f)_4$ become identical by permuting gates). It should be noted that NFS$(3, f)_1$ in Table I is the one obtained by algorithm MNL.

As we can see from this simple example, we may have different ways for attaching labels to a given clustered n-lattice, and yet the resulting labeled n-lattices have no inverse edges. If $D_I^f(O) = 2^{R_f - 1} - 1$, we have only one way to label these clusters with R_f bits for each label. Even if $D_I^f(O) = 2^{R_f - 1} - 1$, however, the way of clustering is usually not unique, and therefore the labeled n-lattice [the NFS(R_f, f)] is usually not unique. One way to generate a different clustering is to use Algorithm 2.

Algorithm 2 is based on the idea of attaching to each node in an n-lattice a maximum possible label consisting of a minimum number of bits such that the resulting n-lattice has no inverse edge. From this labeled n-lattice, an NFS(R_f, f) is obtained where $R_f = \lceil \log_2(D_I^f(O) + 1 \rceil + 1$. The algorithm stated in the following will be referred to as *algorithm MXL*.

Algorithm 2. Algorithm based on maximum labeling with a minimum number of bits (MXL).

Let $L_{mn}^f(A)$ be the label attached to each node $A \in C_n$ by this algorithm for a given function f. Let $R_f = \lceil \log_2(D_I^f(O) + 1 \rceil + 1$.

Step 1. Assign as $L_{mx}^f(O)$ the value of $2^{R_f} - 2 + f(O)$.

Step 2. When $L_{mx}^f(A)$ is assigned to every node A of weight w in C_n, assign as $L_{mx}^f(B)$ to each node B of weight $w + 1$ the largest binary integer satisfying the following two conditions: (a) The least significant bit of $L_{mn}^f(B)$ is $f(B)$; (b) $L_{mx}^f(B) \le L_{mx}^f(A)$ for every directed edge $\overrightarrow{BA}$ originating from B.

TABLE I

Possible NFS$(3, f)$'s Obtained from Clusters Based on MNL for Function
$$f = x_1 x_2 \vee x_2 \bar{x}_3$$

Clusters based on MNL	Nodes	NFS$(3, f)_1$ u_1 u_2 f	NFS$(3, f)_2$ u_1 u_2 f	NFS$(3, f)_3$ u_1 u_2 f	NFS$(3, f)_4$ u_1 u_2 f	NFS$(3, f)_5$ u_1 u_2 f
1	(111), (110)	0 0 1	0 0 1	0 0 1	0 0 1	0 1 1
2	(101), (011), (100), (001)	0 1 0	0 1 0	0 1 0	1 0 0	1 0 0
3	(010)	0 1 1	0 1 1	1 0 1	1 0 1	1 0 1
4	(000)	1 0 0	1 1 0	1 1 0	1 1 0	1 1 0

Step 3. Repeat Step 2 until $L^f_{mx}(I)$ is assigned.

Step 4. Let the ith significant bit of $L^f_{mx}(A)$ be $u_i(A)$ for every $A \in C_n$. Then the resulting $(u_i, \ldots, u_{R_f})$, where $R_f = \lceil \log_2(D^f_I(O) \rceil + 1$, is an NFS($R_f, f$) for function f.

Example 4. Consider the function discussed in Example 1, $f = x_1 x_2 \vee x_2 \bar{x}_3$. As seen in Fig. 5(a) for Example 1, $D^f_I(O) = 2$, and three negative gates are required. According to MXL, $2^3 - 2 + f(O) = 110$ is assigned to node O as $L^f_{mx}(O)$, and the labeled 3-lattice is completed according to algorithm MXL as shown in Fig. 6(a). Figure 6(b) shows the negative-gate network obtained in the general form. The actual network can be obtained by deleting certain connections from this network, as will be discussed in Section 4.

The validity of this algorithm is obvious from Theorem 4 and the fact that the number of inversions of function f satisfy $D^f_I(O) \leq 2^{R_f-1} - 1$ by Eq. (5). The following discussion gives a formal proof.

Definition 10. The *inversion degree* of a node A *with respect to node* O in $C_n(f)$ is the maximum number of inversions over all directed paths from node A to node O, and is denoted by $D^f_O(A)$.

From this definition and the definition of the number of inversions of a function obviously $D^f_O(I) = D^f_I(O)$ holds.

Theorem 6. $L^f_{mx}(X)$, the label attached to a node $X \in C_n$ by algorithm MXL for function f, has the value

$$L^f_{mx}(X) = 2^{R_f} - 2(D^f_O(X) + 1) + f(X)$$

Proof. By definition, $D^f_O(O) = 0$ holds. According to Algorithm 2, $L^f_{mx}(O) = 2^{R_f} - 2 + f(O) = 2^{R_f} - 2(D^f_O(O) + 1) + f(O)$ holds, i.e., the

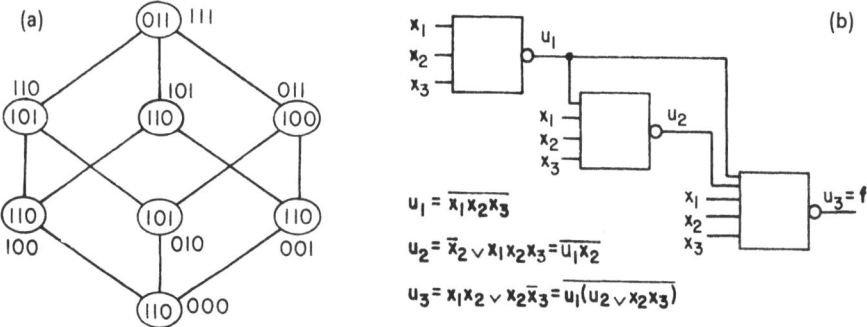

Fig. 6. Example 4 with function f in Fig. 5(a). (a) $C_3(u_1, u_2, f)$ based on MXL. (b) A minimum negative-gate network for f based on MXL.

theorem holds for the node of weight 0. Assume $L^f_{mx}(X) = 2^{R_f} - 2(D^f_O(X) + 1) + f(X)$ holds for each node X of weight w or less. Consider an arbitrary node A of weight $w + 1$. Select a node B of weight w such that

$$L^f_{mx}(B) = \min\{L^f_{mx}(X)|\overrightarrow{AX} \in C_n\} \tag{6}$$

Because $L^f_{mx}(X) = 2^{R_f} - 2(D^f_O(X) + 1) + f(X)$ holds for every X of weight w or less, we have

$$L^f_{mx}(B) = 2^{R_f} - 2(D^f_O(B) + 1) + f(B) \tag{7}$$

Since $L^f_{mx}(B)$ is chosen as the minimum by Eq. (6) and $f(B)$ is constant 1 or 0 in Eq. (7),

$$D^f_O(B) = \max\{D^f_O(X)|\overrightarrow{AX} \in C_n\} \tag{8}$$

must hold. The following cases may occur:

(1) $f(B) = 1$. According to Step 2 of algorithm MXL, $L^f_{mx}(A)$ is assigned a maximum possible value less than or equal to $L^f_{mx}(B) = 2^{R_f} - 2(D^f_O(B) + 1) + f(B)$. Because $\overrightarrow{AB}$ does not constitute an inverse edge in $C_n(f)$ and Eq. (8) holds [the case where $D^f_O(C) = D^f_O(B) = \max\{D^f_O(X)|\overrightarrow{AX} \in C_n\}$ holds for another node C and we have $f(C) = 0$ cannot occur because otherwise $L^f_{mn}(C) = 2^{R_f} - 2(D^f_O(C) + 1) + f(C) < 2^{R_f} - 2(D^f_O(B) + 1) + f(B) = L^f_{mn}(B)$ holds, contradicting Eq. (6)], we have $D^f_O(A) = D^f_O(B)$. Therefore, $L^f_{mx}(A) = 2^{R_f} - 2(D^f_O(B) + 1) + f(A) = 2^{R_f} - 2(D^f_O(A) + 1) + f(A)$ holds.

(2) $f(B) = 0$, $f(A) = 0$. None of $\overrightarrow{AX}$ is an inverse edge in $C_n(f)$, so $D^f_O(A) = D^f_O(B)$ holds. According to algorithm MXL, $L^f_{mn}(A) = L^f_{mx}(B) = 2^{R_f} - 2(D^f_O(B) + 1) + f(B) = 2^{R_f} - 2(D^f_O(A) + 1) + f(A)$ holds.

(3) $f(B) = 0$, $f(A) = 1$. $\overrightarrow{AB}$ is an inverse edge in $C_n(f)$, so $D^f_O(A) = D^f_O(B) + 1$. According to algorithm MXL,

$$L^f_{mx}(A) = L^f_{mx}(B) - 1 = 2^{R_f} - 2(D^f_O(B) + 1) - 1$$
$$= 2^{R_f} - 2(D^f_O(B) + 2) + 1$$
$$= 2^{R_f} - 2(D^f_O(A) + 1) + f(A)$$

must hold.

Therefore, $L^f_{mx}(A) = 2^{R_f} - 2(D^f_O(A) + 1) + f(A)$ holds for every A of weight $w + 1$. By induction, $L^f_{mx}(X) = 2^{R_f} - 2(D^f_O(X) + 1) + f(X)$ holds for every $X \in C_n$. $\square$

From Theorem 6 it is clear that $L^f_{mx}(I) = 2^{R_f} - 2(D^f_O(I) + 1) + f(I) \geq 0$ since $D^f_O(I) = D^f_I(O) \leq 2^{R_f-1} - 1$ holds by Eq. (5). This means that when we use algorithm MXL, we can continue labeling up through the node I. This proves the validity of algorithm MXL because the resulting labeled n-lattice is indeed a labeled n-lattice, with a minimum number of bits in each label, which has no inverse edges.

Having proved the validity of algorithm MXL, we can now present Corollary 6 which directly follows from algorithm MXL.

Corollary 6. Let $\text{NFS}(R_f, f) = (u_1, \ldots, u_{R_f} = f)$ be a minimum negative-function sequence for f, and $C_n(u_1, \ldots, u_{R_f})$ be the corresponding labeled n-lattice. Then the labels of this lattice must satisfy $l(A; u_1, \ldots, u_{R_f}) \leq L^f_{mx}(A)$ for every $A \in C_n$.

Similar to the discussion following algorithm MNL, we can partition the entire set of nodes into clusters such that all nodes in each cluster have the same label based on MXL. These clusters based on MXL constitute the stratified structure of a switching function defined by Liu.[6]

Definition 11. The *stratified structure* of a function f of n variables is a sequence of subsets of input vectors—$(M^f_0, M^f_1, \ldots, M^f_{2r})$, where $r = D^f_0(I)$—defined as:

(i) $M^f_{2(i+f(O))-1}$ for $i = (1 - f(O)), \ldots, r - 1$, contains every vector A such that $f(A) = 1$ and $D^f_0(A) = i$.

(ii) $M^f_{2(i+f(O))}$ for $i = 0, \ldots, r$, contains every vector A such that $f(A) = 0$ and $D^f_0(A) = i$.

The wording of this definition is different from that in Liu,[6] but it defines the same concept—the stratified structure of a function. Liu discussed various properties of the stratified structure of a function which we will not repeat here. However, it should be emphasized that the algorithm based on the maximal labeling attaches to all nodes in each cluster the same label unique to that cluster because of Theorem 6.

Liu also gave several algorithms to design minimum negative-gate networks for a given function. All the networks designed by his algorithms are *based on the stratified structure of that function*. In other words, in the labeled n-lattice corresponding to a minimum negative-gate network given by algorithms in Liu,[6] all nodes in each M^f_i are assigned the same label unique to that M^f_i. It implies that, in general, the algorithms given in Liu consider only a subset of all possible $\text{NFS}(R_f, f)$'s for the given function f. Sometimes these algorithms design minimum negative-gate networks whose corresponding MOS networks, regardless of how well each cell is designed, may contain redundant FETs and interconnections. This problem will be discussed in detail in Sections 4 and 5 along with examples.

Example 5. Consider the function discussed in Examples 1-4, $f = x_1 x_2 \lor x_2 \bar{x}_3$. The stratified structure for f is: $M^f_0 = \{(000), (001), (100), 101)\}$,

TABLE II

NSF$(3, f)$'s Based on the Stratified Structure for $f = x_1 x_2 \vee x_2 \bar{x}_3$

	NFS$(3,f)_1$			NFS$(3,f)_2$			NFS$(3,f)_3$			NFS$(3,f)_4$			NFS$(3,f)_5$		
Cluster	u_1	u_2	f	u_1	u_2	f	u_1	u_2	f	u_1	u_2	f	u_1	u_2	f
M_3^f	0	0	1	0	0	1	0	0	1	0	0	1	0	1	1
M_2^f	0	1	0	0	1	0	0	1	0	1	0	0	1	0	0
M_1^f	0	1	1	0	1	1	1	0	1	1	0	1	1	0	1
M_0^f	1	0	0	1	1	0	1	1	0	1	1	0	1	1	0

$M_1^f = \{(010), (110)\}$, $M_2^f = \{(011)\}$, and $M_3^f = \{(111)\}$. All possible NFS$(3, f)$'s based on this stratified structure for f are listed in Table II.

We can prove that a function f has a unique NFS(R_f, f) and hence a unique minimum negative-gate network, if and only if $L_{mn}^f(A) = L_{mx}^f(A)$ holds for every $A \in C_n$. Here "unique" means that two NFS(R_f, f)'s are considered to be identical if they become identical by permuting gates. A proof for this and other properties on the uniqueness will be published elsewhere.

4. SYNTHESIS OF MOS CELLS

Given a switching function f of n variables, the design procedures discussed in the previous sections can generate networks of a minimum number of negative gates realizing the given function, by specifying the function u_i realized by each negative gate g_i in the network. These functions u_i's are specified in the form of a labeled n-lattice $C_n(u_1, \ldots, u_R = f)$ which is equivalent to a truth table where the function u_i realized by each negative gate g_i is specified for 2^n input vectors. Although Theorem 4 asserts that each function u_i can be realized by a negative gate with $x_1, \ldots, x_n$, $u_1, \ldots, u_{i-1}$ as inputs, the explicit expression of u_i as a negative function with respect to $x_1, \ldots, x_n, u_1, \ldots, u_{i-1}$ is not yet given. When a logic network of MOSFETs is constructed to realize a given function, each MOS cell (i.e., negative gate), which theoretically can be made to realize an arbitrary negative function, must be properly designed. This requires each u_i to be explicitly expressed as a negative function of $x_1, \ldots, x_n, u_1, \ldots, u_{i-1}$ for $1 \le i \le R_f$.

As explained in Section 2 (for details, see Ref. 2), the driver part of an MOS cell operates exactly like a relay contact network where each FET corresponds to a "make-contact" (i.e., normally open) relay contact. Therefore, the problem of designing an MOS cell for a given negative function can be treated as the problem of designing a relay contact network with only make-contact relays for the complement of the given function. The problem of designing a relay contact network with a minimum number of contacts has been studied by many authors. If a series–parallel-type network is to be designed, a procedure proposed by Lawler[13] can be applied. If a network of a general type (i.e., not necessarily series–parallel type) is to be designed, a procedure proposed by Moriwaki[14] can produce an absolutely minimum network. Although these procedures are very useful in some cases, they are complicated and time-consuming even with the assistance of a high-speed computer when the size of the network is relatively large. Although these procedures, which are developed based on the assumption that both make-contacts and break-contacts are available, can be simplified to fit our special situation where only make-contacts are available, they would still be very complicated and time-consuming if minimality is to be guaranteed.

The procedure to be presented in the next section designs for a given function an "irredundant MOS network" with a minimum number of negative gates (MOS cells). In other words, the number of gates in the designed network is minimum, and if any MOSFET (and accordingly any interconnection) is removed from the network, the network will not realize the given function. (The rigorous definition of "irredundant MOS network" will be given later.) We are not concerned with whether or not each MOS cell is of series–parallel type, although an MOS cell of such type is easier to design. In order to guarantee that the designed network is irredundant, each MOS cell should be irredundant as defined by the following definitions.

Definition 12. The *s-extraction* of an FET from an MOS network is the replacement of this FET by a short circuit between its source and drain. The *o-extraction* of an FET from an MOS network is the replacement of this FET by an open circuit between its source and drain. A *single extraction* of an FET is either a single *s-* or *o-*extraction of the FET, and a *multiple*

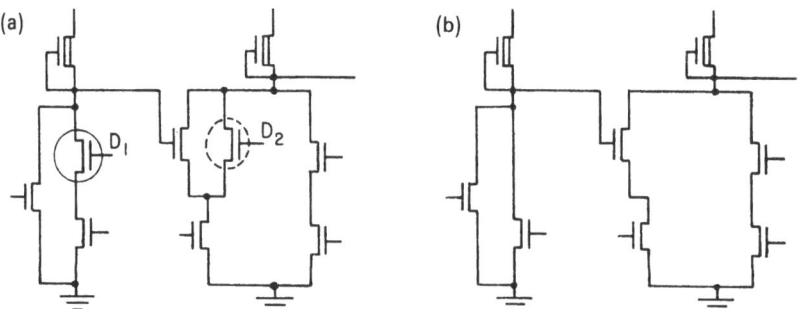

Fig. 7. Example of extraction of FETs. (a) Original MOS network. (b) Network after *s*-extraction of D_1 and *o*-extraction of D_2 from (a).

extraction of more than one FET is more than one simultaneous s- and/or o-extraction of these FETs.

Figure 7(a) shows an MOS network. Figure 7(b) shows the network obtained from the network in (a) by the s-extraction of the FET D_1 (within the solid-line circle) and the o-extraction of the FET D_2 (within the dashed-line circle).

Definition 13. An FET in an MOS network is *redundant* if a single extraction of this FET does not change the output values of the network. A group of FETs in an MOS network are *redundant* if there exists a multiple extraction of these FETs such that this multiple extraction of these FETs does not change the output values of the network.

Definition 14. An *irredundant MOS cell configuration* with respect to a negative (possibly incompletely specified) function f is an MOS cell realizing f (or a completion of f) that has no redundant FETs.

It should be noted that there are usually more than one irredundant MOS cell configuration for a given function.

Definition 15. An *irredundant MOS network* for a function f (possibly incompletely specified) is an MOS network realizing f (or any completion of f) that has no redundant FETs and consequently no redundant intercon-nection.

According to the above definitions, it is obvious that each MOS cell in an irredundant MOS network must have an irredundant MOS cell configuration with respect to the function realized by the cell.

It should be noted that even if each MOS cell in an MOS network is irredundant, the network may not be irredundant, as examples will show in Section 5.

Definition 16. A *complemented irredundant disjunctive form* for a nega-tive function f (possibly incompletely specified) is the complement of an irredundant disjunctive form for the complement of f, $\bar{f}$. A *complemented irredundant conjunctive form* for a negative function f (possibly incompletely specified) is the complement of an irredundant conjunctive form for the complement of f, $\bar{f}$. (See Ref. 2 for discussion of the irredundant disjunctive and conjunctive forms.)

Definition 17. A *complemented minimum sum-of-products form* for a negative function f (possibly incompletely specified) is a complemented irredundant disjunctive form for f that has the minimum number of terms and the minimum number of literals among all complemented irredundant disjunctive forms for f. A *complemented minimum product-of-sums form* for a negative function f (possibly incompletely specified) is a complemented irredundant conjunctive form for f that has the minimum number of alterms and the minimum number of literals among all complemented irredundant conjunctive forms of f.

___**Example 6.**___ Suppose a completely specified negative function $f = \overline{x_1 x_2 \vee x_2 x_3 \vee x_1 x_3 x_4}$ is given. The MOS cells shown in Fig. 8(a)–8(d) are irredundant MOS cell configurations for f. The MOS cell shown in Fig. 8(a) is obtained from the complemented minimum sum-of-products form of f, i.e., $f = \overline{x_1 x_2 \vee x_2 x_3 \vee x_1 x_3 x_4}$. Figure 8(b) shows a cell obtained from the complemented minimum product-of-sums form of f, i.e., $f = \overline{(x_1 \vee x_2)(x_2 \vee x_3)(x_2 \vee x_4)(x_1 \vee x_3)}$. These two cells are not the simplest irredundant ones for f. Figures 8(c) and 8(d) show two other simpler irredundant MOS cells for f which are obtained by factoring out common terms from Figures 8(a) and 8(b), respectively.

___**Example 7.**___ An incompletely specified f for four variables is given in the truth table form [i.e., $C_4(f)$ with don't-cares denoted by an asterisk] as shown in Fig. 9(a). Two complemented minimum sum-of-products forms of f, $f_1 = \overline{x_1 x_2 \vee x_1 x_3 \vee x_2 x_3 \vee x_2 x_4}$ and $f_2 = \overline{x_1 x_2 \vee x_1 x_4 \vee x_2 x_3 \vee x_2 x_4}$, are obtained by assigning $f(1010) = 0$ and $f(1001) = 1$, and also by assigning $f(1010) = 1$ and $f(1001) = 0$, respectively. MOS cells based on these expressions or their derivatives obtained by factorization of common terms are irredundant MOS cell configurations for f (not shown). However, the direct implementation of the complemented minimum sum-of-products form for another completion of f (notice that this is the complemented minimum sum-of-products form for a completion of f but not for the

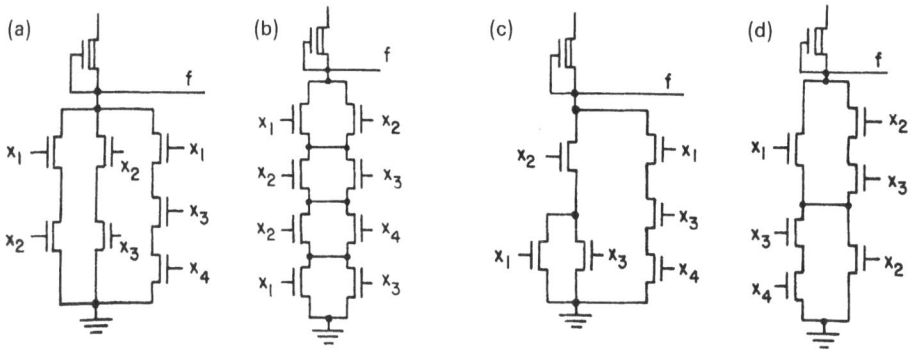

Fig. 8. Example 6. Irredundant MOS cell configurations for $f = \overline{x_1 x_2 \vee x_2 x_3 \vee x_1 x_3 x_4}$. (a) Irredundant MOS cell configuration for f based on complemented minimum sum-of-products form of f. (b) Irredundant MOS cell configuration for f based on the complemented minimum product-of-sums of f. (c) Irredundant MOS cell configuration for f derived from (a). (d) Irredundant MOS cell configuration for f derived from (b).

incompletely specified function f), $f_3 = \overline{x_1x_2 \vee x_2x_3 \vee x_2x_4 \vee x_1x_3x_4}$, obtained by assigning $f(1010) = f(1001) = 1$, yields a redundant MOS cell with respect to the incompletely specified function f. Figure 9(b) shows this cell where the s-extraction of either FET D_1 or D_2 does not change the output values corresponding to the specified input vectors of f. The MOS cell obtained by the s-extraction of D_1 or D_2 realizes function f_2 or f_1, respectively, each of which is a negative completion of f. However, if an MOS cell is designed as shown in Fig. 9(c) which realizes the same function as Fig. 9(b), it is an irredundant MOS cell configuration of f since any single or multiple extraction of FETs in Fig. 9(c) will make the MOS cell no longer realize a completion of f.

In general, the exhaustion of all irredundant MOS cell configurations for a given negative function requires an enormous effort. As a matter of fact, if all irredundant MOS cell configurations are obtained, the ones with a minimum number of FETs among them will be the minimum MOS cell configurations for the given function. For our irredundant MOS network

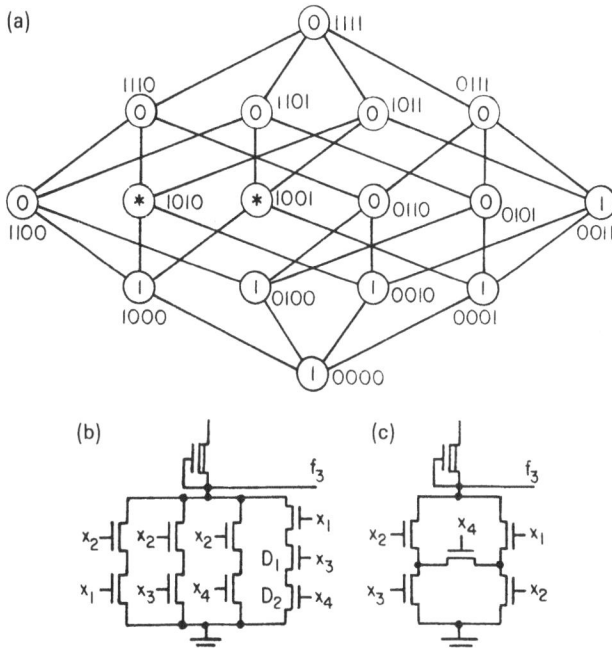

Fig. 9. Example 7. (a) Incompletely specified function f. (b) Redundant MOS cell configuration for f. The single s-extraction of either D_1 or D_2 from the network results in a cell realizing f_2 or f_1, which is a completion of f. (c) Irredundant MOS cell configuration for f. Although it realizes the same function f_3 as (b) does, it is an irredundant MOS cell configuration for the incompletely specified function f.

design procedure to be presented in the next section, however, an arbitrary irredundant MOS cell configuration is sufficient.

The following algorithm is based on the algorithm given by Ibaraki[4] which obtains a complemented irredundant disjunctive form for a negative function (Definition 16).

Algorithm 3. Derivation of a complemented irredundant disjunctive form for a given incompletely specified negative function f of n variables. (This algorithm is illustrated in Example 8.)

Step 1. Obtain a subset S_{0*}^f of the set V_n of all n-dimensional binary vectors such that $X \in S_{0*}^f$ if and only if $f(X) = 0$ or $*$ holds and no $Y > X$ satisfying $f(Y) = 1$ exists.

Step 2. Obtain Min$[S_{0*}^f]$, the set of minimum vectors of S_{0*}^f, such that $X \in$ Min$[S_{0*}^f]$ if and only if there exists no $Y \in S_{0*}^f$ satisfying $Y < X$.

Step 3. Obtain Irr$[S_{0*}^f]$, an irredundant subset of Min$[S_{0*}^f]$, such that, for every X satisfying $f(X) = 0$, there exists a $Y \in$ Irr$[S_{0*}^f]$ satisfying $Y \leq X$, and that the deletion of any vector from Irr$[S_{0*}^f]$ will cause the above condition not to be satisfied. (Because of this, the subset is called "irredundant".) Irr$[S_{0*}^f]$ will be referred to as an *irredundant cover* of Min$[S_{0*}^f]$. (The problem of obtaining an irredundant cover is a covering problem.)

Step 4. For each $A = (a_1, \ldots, a_n) \in$ Irr$[S_{0*}^f]$, make the corresponding product term of input variables $P_A = x_1^{a_1} x_2^{a_2} \cdots x_n^{a_n}$ such that if $a_i = 0$, $x_i^{a_i} = 1$ (i.e., x_i is not included in P_A) and if $a_i = 1$, $x_i^{a_i} = x_i$. The complement of the sum of these product terms

$$f_I = \overline{\bigvee_{A \in \text{Irr}[S_{0*}^f]} P_A}$$

is a complemented irredundant disjunctive form for f.

From a complemented irredundant disjunctive form, it is easy to construct an irredundant MOS cell configuration for f. For each term P_A in f_I, make a serial connection of FETs such that corresponding to each literal in P_A there is an FET with the input represented by the literal. Then, parallelly connect all these serially connected FETs. The resulting MOS configuration constitutes the driver part of the irredundant MOS cell configuration designed for f.

Steps 1 and 2 of Algorithm 3 involve only simple calculations. Step 3 requires the solution of a covering problem which is relatively simple since any irredundant cover will be sufficient for our purpose. Step 3 is necessary since f is generally an incompletely specified function (see Example 8). If f is a completely specified negative function, there exists only one complemented irredundant disjunctive form. In such a case Step 3 is unnecessary because $\mathrm{Irr}[S_{0*}^f] = \mathrm{Min}[S_{0*}^f]$. In Step 3, if a minimum cover is obtained the resulting configuration will contain a smaller number of FETs. (This may not be true, if factorization is considered.) Step 4 of this algorithm is trivial.

We can easily prove that an irredundant MOS cell configuration for f can be constructed from a complemented irredundant disjunctive form derived by this algorithm. First, to prove that the constructed MOS cell realizes a completion of f, we need to prove that for every specified false vector, there is a path between the two terminals of the driver part of the cell. This is obvious because Step 3 guarantees that for each vector A such that $f(A) = 0$, there is a vector B in $\mathrm{Irr}[S_{0*}^f]$ such that $B \leq A$. Therefore, when input A is applied to the cell, the serially connected FETs corresponding to B forms a conductive path. Similarly for each vector A such that $f(A) = 1$, no vector $B \in \mathrm{Irr}[S_{0*}^f]$ satisfies $B \leq A$ according to Steps 1 and 2. Therefore, when A is applied, there will be no path in the driver part of the constructed cell. This proves that the constructed MOS cell realizes a completion of f. Next, we need to prove that the MOS cell obtained is an irredundant MOS cell configuration for f. If it is not, there must exist one or more FETs such that the extractions of them do not affect the realization of f. Let us consider the case where an FET is redundant. According to the manner in which the cell is constructed, the s-extraction of an FET which corresponds to literal x_i in a term P_A means the replacement of $A \in \mathrm{Irr}[S_{0*}^f]$ by a vector $B \notin \mathrm{Irr}[S_{0*}^f]$ such that $b_i = 0$ ($a_i = 1$) and $b_j = a_j$ for $j \neq i$. Because $B \notin \mathrm{Min}[S_{0*}^f]$ (otherwise $A \in \mathrm{Irr}[S_{0*}^f]$ can not hold), there must exist a vector B' such that $B' \geq B$ and $f(B') = 1$. However, when B' is applied to the cell obtained by the s-extraction of the FET, a conductive path from the output terminal to the ground will appear which results in the output value 0 since $B' \geq B$, and the s-extraction of the FET causes the replacement of term P_A by term P_B in the corresponding expression. Therefore, no s-extraction of any FET can be performed without changing the output values of f corresponding to some specified inputs. On the other hand, the o-extraction of an FET corresponding to any literal in term P_A from the cell means the removal of the vector A from $\mathrm{Irr}[S_{0*}^f]$. Since $\mathrm{Irr}[S_{0*}^f]$ is, according to Step 3, an irredundant cover of $\mathrm{Min}[S_{0*}^f]$ satisfying that for every X satisfying $f(X) = 0$, there exists a $Y \in \mathrm{Irr}[S_{0*}^f]$ satisfying $Y \leq X$, the removal of term A from $\mathrm{Irr}[S_{0*}^f]$ means that for some vector B satisfying $B > A$ and $f(B) = 0$, there exists no $Y \in \mathrm{Irr}[S_{0*}^f]$ satisfying $Y < B$. This, in turn, means that the resulting MOS cell after the o-extraction will produce an output "1" for input B. Consequently, the MOS cell designed by Algorithm 3 is an irredundant MOS cell configuration for f.

The number of FETs in an MOS cell designed by Algorithm 3 can be sometimes reduced by factoring out common literals in the expression obtained in Step 4. Obviously, this factorization does not change the irredundancy of the MOS cell.

Example 8. Suppose a switching function f specified as shown in Fig. 10(a) is given. By Step 1 of Algorithm 3, $S_{0*}^f = \{(11111), (11110), (11101), (11011), (10111), (01111), (11100), (11010), (11001), (10110), (10101), (10011), (01110), (01101), (11000), (10001), (01100)\}$. Then Step 2 calculates $\text{Min}[S_{0*}^f] = \{(11000), (10001), (01100), (10110)\}$. Since (10110) and (10001) must be included in every irredundant subset $\text{Irr}[S_{0*}^f]$ defined in Step 3 of Algorithm 3, the only $\text{Irr}[S_{0*}^f]$'s are $\text{Irr}[S_{0*}^f]_1 = \{(11000), (10001), (10110)\}$ and $\text{Irr}[S_{0*}^f]_2 = \{(10001), (01100), (10110)\}$. The complemented irredundant disjunctive forms for f are $f_1 = \overline{x_1 x_2 \vee x_1 x_5 \vee x_1 x_3 x_4}$ and $f_2 = \overline{x_1 x_5 \vee x_2 x_3 \vee x_1 x_3 x_4}$, respectively. The corresponding irredundant MOS cell configurations for f are shown in Fig. 10(b) and Fig. 10(c), respectively. Although these two expressions are the only complemented minimum sum-of-products forms for f, other irredundant MOS cells with fewer FETs

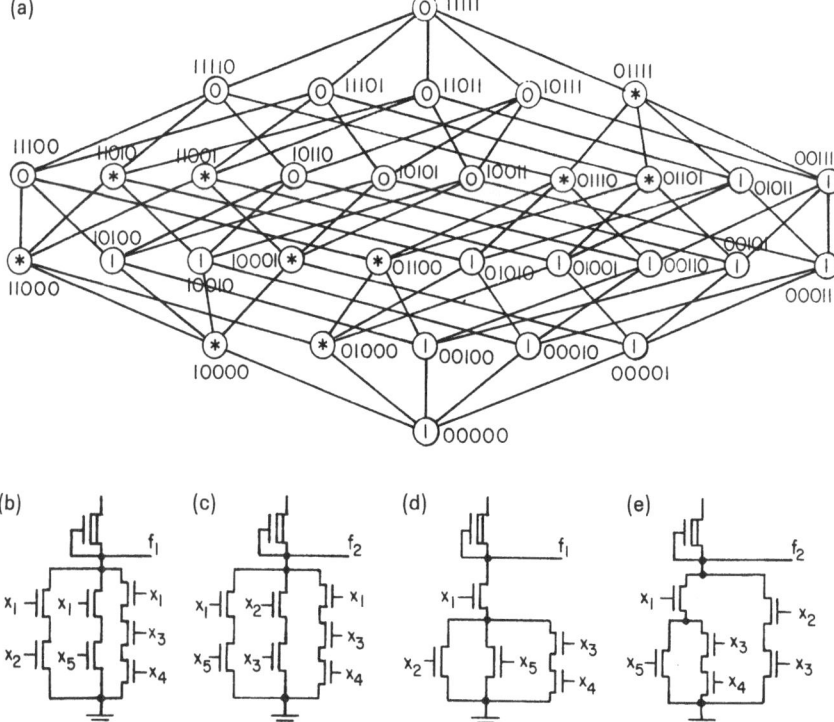

Fig. 10. Example 8. (a) Incompletely specified function f. (b) Irredundant MOS cell for f based on f_1. (c) Irredundant MOS cell for f based on f_2. (d) Irredundant MOS cell for f based on factorization of f_1. (e) Irredundant MOS cell for f based on factorization of f_2.

can be derived from them by factorization. The MOS cell shown in Fig. 10(d) corresponds to

$$f_1 = \overline{x_1(x_2 \vee x_5 \vee x_3 x_4)}$$

which uses only five driver FETs. The MOS cell shown in Fig. 10(e) corresponds to

$$f_2 = \overline{x_1(x_5 \vee x_3 x_4) \vee x_2 x_3}$$

which requires one more FET than in Fig. 10(d).

By the dual property, it is easy to obtain a complemented irredundant conjunctive form for a given function.

5. DESIGN OF IRREDUNDANT MOS NETWORKS

This section presents an algorithm for the synthesis of irredundant MOS networks defined in Definition 15. As shown in Section 5.1, the conventional approaches for MOS network design sometimes produce redundant MOS networks. Then the algorithm introduced in Section 5.4 is outlined in Section 5.2, introducing some concepts necessary for the algorithm in Section 5.3. Examples in Section 5.5 display the effectiveness of the algorithm.

5.1. Conventional Design Procedures of MOS Networks

The algorithms given in Nakamura *et al.*[5] and Liu[6] design MOS networks for a given function in two separate phases:

Phase I. Design an NFS(R_f, f) (a negative-gate network) in which the function to be realized by each negative gate (MOS cell) is specified with respect to the external inputs.

Phase II. Design an MOS cell to realize each of the functions specified by Phase I (i.e., the design of the internal configuration of each cell).

As discussed in the previous sections, algorithms MNL and MXL design networks with a minimum number of negative gates. These algorithms and the algorithm based on the relabeling of the clustered n-lattices obtained by algorithm MNL or MXL (as demonstrated in Examples 3 and 5) correspond to Phase I in the above two-phase design procedures since the internal structure of each negative gate (MOS cell in an MOS network) is not designed by them. In order to design an MOS network, each negative gate should be realized by an MOS cell; this corresponds to Phase II of

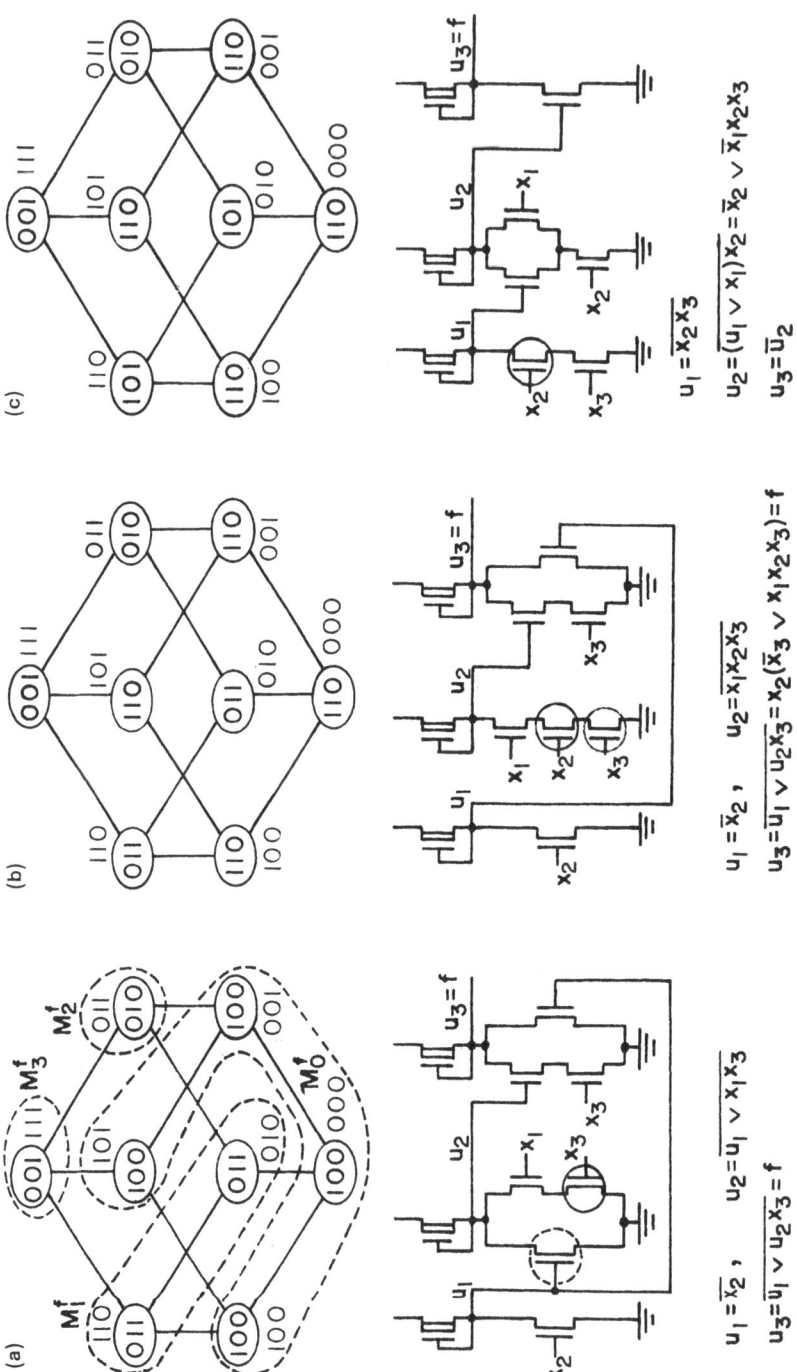

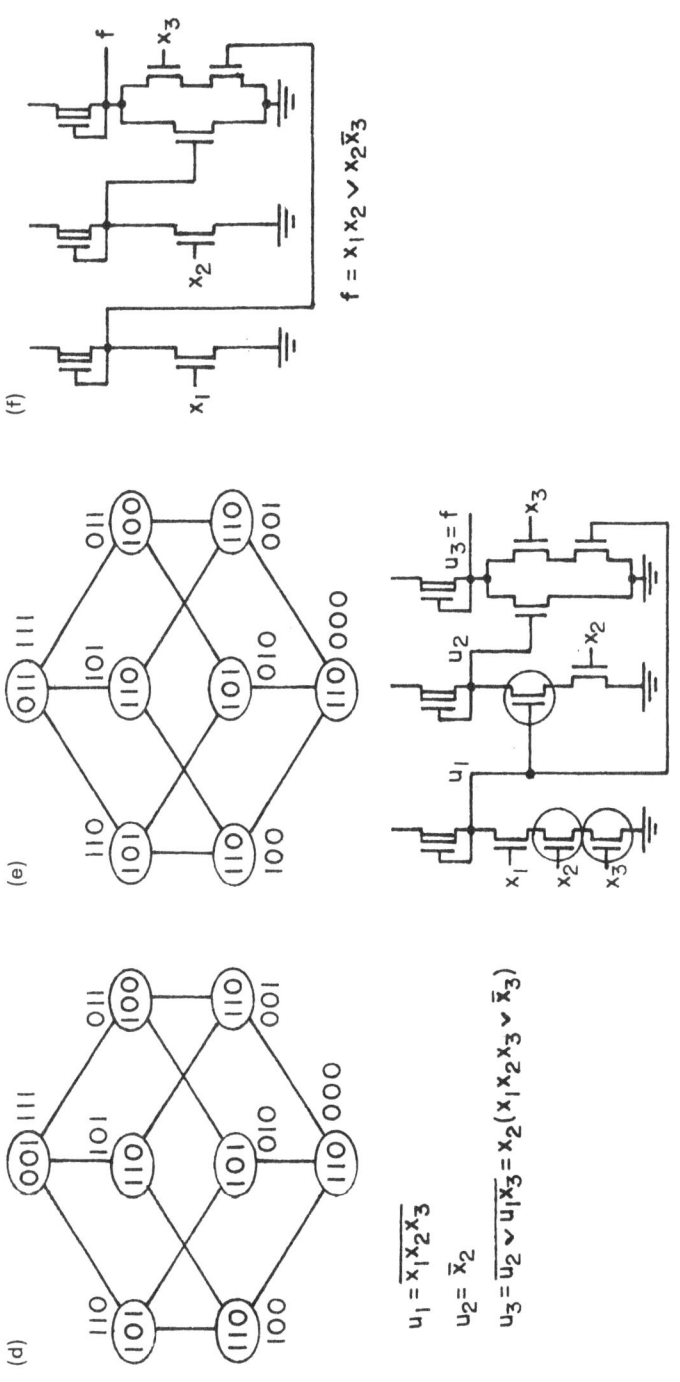

$$u_1 = \overline{x_1 x_2 x_3}$$
$$u_2 = \overline{x}_2$$
$$u_3 = \overline{u_2 \vee u_1 x_3} = x_2(x_1 x_2 x_3 \vee \overline{x}_3)$$

$$u_1 = \overline{x_1 x_2 x_3}, \quad u_2 = \overline{u_1 x_2}, \quad u_3 = \overline{u_2 \vee u_1 x_3}$$

$$f = x_1 x_2 \vee x_2 \overline{x}_3$$

Fig. 11. Example 9. MOS networks based on stratified structure of Liu[6] for $f = x_1 x_2 \vee x_2 \overline{x}_3$ (see Example 5). (a) Labeled 3-lattice and MOS network for NFS$(3, f)_1$. (b) Labeled 3-lattice and MOS network for NFS$(3, f)_2$. (c) Labeled 3-lattice and MOS network for NFS$(3, f)_3$. (d) Labeled 3-lattice for NFS$(3, f)_4$. [An MOS network for NFS$(3, f)_4$ can be obtained from the network shown in (b) by interchanging u_1 and u_2.] (e) Labeled 3-lattice and MOS network for NFS$(3, f)_5$. (f) Irredundant MOS network for f.

the design procedures. The design algorithms of irredundant MOS cell configurations in Section 4 can be applied for this purpose although they are different from the algorithms given by Nakamura *et al.* and Liu which may not yield an irredundant MOS cell configuration for each negative function specified by Phase I.

Even if each MOS cell configuration is irredundant, the conventional design approaches with two separate phases have a disadvantage in that the designed MOS network may contain redundant FETs. In other words, even if we use an irredundant MOS cell design procedure for Phase II, we may not obtain an irredundant MOS network as a whole. This is demonstrated by the following example.

Example 9. Consider five minimum $NFS(3, f)$'s in Table II for $f = x_1 x_2 \vee x_2 \bar{x}_3$ discussed in Example 5. If we design an irredundant MOS cell for each negative function in each $NFS(3, f)$, we obtain five MOS networks for f as shown in Fig. 11(a)–11(e). Each figure shows the labeled 3-lattice corresponding to each $NFS(3, f)$ in Table II and an MOS network obtained by designing an irredundant MOS cell for each function in this $NFS(3, f)$. For example, Fig. 11(a) shows the labeled 3-lattice corresponding to the $NFS(3, f)_1$ in Table II that is obtained based on the stratified structure of f given by Liu.[6] The clusters of the stratified structure of f are enclosed in broken lines in the labeled 3-lattice. Figure 11(a) also shows an MOS network corresponding to $NFS(3, f)_1$: the ith MOS cell realizes the ith function in $NFS(3, f)_1$, for $i = 1, 2,$ and 3. Although each MOS cell is irredundant with respect to the corresponding function of $NFS(3, f)_1$, which it realizes, the MOS network as a whole has some redundant FETs. The two encircled FETs are redundant: the s-extraction of the FET encircled in the solid line and the o-extraction of the FET encircled in the broken line yield the MOS network shown in Fig. 11(f) which also realizes f. All other MOS networks based on the stratified structure of f in Fig. 11 are also redundant as shown by the encircled FETs in the networks.

Example 10. An MOS network derived from the $NFS(3, f)$ by algorithm MNL for the same function $f = x_1 x_2 \vee x_2 \bar{x}_3$ (Example 1) as that in Example 9 is shown in Fig. 12. The MOS network is redundant as indicated by the encircled FETs.

The above two examples demonstrate that the design procedures of networks with a minimum number of MOS cells given by Nakamura *et al.* and Liu do not yield irredundant MOS networks for some functions.

5.2. Outline of the Design Algorithm of Irredundant MOS Networks

This section outlines a procedure for the synthesis of irredundant MOS networks with a minimum number of MOS cells for a single function. This

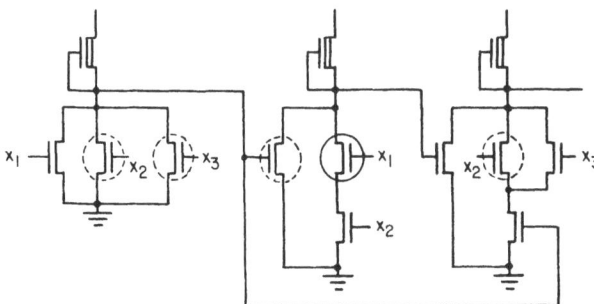

Fig. 12. Example 10. MOS network derived from the NFS$(3, f)$ by algorithm MNL for function $f = x_1 x_2 \vee x_2 \bar{x}_3$.

procedure also consists of two phases of design, i.e., the design of functions realized by negative gates (MOS cells) and the design of an irredundant MOS cell for each of these functions. However, in order to guarantee the irredundancy of the designed network, the two phases are not performed separately but interactively, unlike the case of Nakamura *et al.* and Liu. In other words, the network will not be designed by single-pass application of Phase I followed by Phase II, but iterations of application of Phase I followed by Phase II. The motivation is to allow the function realized by the gate in the remotest level from the network output be specified by Phase I as flexible as possible (containing as many unspecified values as possible). Phase II can then design the internal structure of an irredundant MOS cell for this function which is usually incompletely specified with respect to the set of external variables, $x_1, \ldots, x_n$. Only when Phase II for this gate has been completed, does this function become completely specified with respect to the set of external variables, $x_1, \ldots, x_n$. This process will be repeatedly applied to the gate in the next remotest level until the network output is reached. This design procedure will guarantee that the designed MOS network is irredundant because each function will be specified to contain as many don't-cares as possible. This means that each specified value (i.e., not a don't-care) of the function for each gate is absolutely required for the realization of the network output, and, therefore, any change in these specified values caused by extraction of FETs from this cell will change the network output.

In order to explain the irredundancy of the designed network, let us consider an MOS network designed by this approach. Since each MOS cell g_i in this network is irredundant with respect to the function that has been specified so as to contain as many don't-cares as possible, any extraction of FETs from this cell g_i will cause some change in specified values, say $u_i(A)$, of its corresponding function u_i, which in turn will definitely lead to changes in the output function of the entire network. Otherwise, those changed values of the corresponding function, $u_i(A)$, would have been specified as don't-cares during the design process. This means that the designed MOS network is irredundant. A formal proof will be given after the algorithm is introduced.

The above is the motivation for the procedure to be introduced in Section 5.4. The outline of the procedure is given below. Let us consider the problem of designing an irredundant MOS network with a minimum number of MOS cells for a completely specified function of n variables, $f(x_1, \ldots, x_n)$. Let $\text{NFS}(R_f, f) = (u_1, \ldots, u_{R_f-1}, u_{R_f} = f)$ be the minimum negative-function sequence corresponding to an irredundant MOS network to be designed.

Outline of a Design Algorithm of Irredundant MOS Networks. Given a function f, R_f is the minimum number of negative gates (MOS cells) required for the realization of f. At the start of this procedure, the entire NFS except u_{R_f} is unspecified, i.e., $\text{NFS}^0(R_f, f) = \{u_1^*, \ldots, u_{R_f-1}^*, f\}$ where superscript 0 means that no function except $u_{R_f} = f$ is specified and u_i^* means the unspecified function for u_i, i.e., all components in the value vector of u_i^* are don't-cares.

Step 0. Set $i = 1$.

Step 1. Specify $\tilde{u}_i$, in such a manner that $\tilde{u}_i$ contains as many don't-care components as possible, which is negative with respect to $x_1, \ldots, x_n$, $u_1, \ldots, u_{i-1}$. [This step is entered with a partially specified negative-function sequence $\text{NFS}^{i-1}(R_f, f) = (u_1, \ldots, u_{i-1}, u_i^*, \ldots, u_{R_f-1}^*, f)$, and will yield $\widehat{\text{NFS}}^{i-1}(R_f, f) = (u_1, \ldots, u_{i-1}, \tilde{u}_i, u_{i+1}^*, \ldots, u_{R_f-1}^*, f)$.]

Step 2. Obtain an irredundant MOS cell configuration for the incompletely specified function $\tilde{u}_i$ with inputs chosen from $x_1, \ldots, x_n, u_1, \ldots, u_{i-1}$. (Algorithm 3 may be used.) Let u_i be the function realized by this MOS cell which is now completely specified with respect to $x_1, \ldots, x_n$. [By this step $\text{NFS}^i(R_f, f) = (u_1, \ldots, u_i, u_{i+1}^*, \ldots, u_{R_f-1}^*, f)$ is obtained.]

Step 3. If $i = R_f - 1$, design an irredundant MOS cell configuration for f with possible inputs from $x_1, \ldots, x_n, \ldots, u_1, \ldots, u_{R_f-1}$, and terminate this procedure; otherwise set i to $i + 1$, and go to Step 1.

The nucleus of this algorithm is Steps 1 and 2. Step 2 designs an irredundant MOS cell configuration for a given incompletely specified function which has been discussed in Section 4, so we will, in Section 5.3, concentrate on Step 1, i.e., specifying $\tilde{u}_i$ based on a partially specified negative-function sequence, $\text{NFS}^{i-1}(R_f, f) = (u_1, \ldots, u_{i-1}, u_i^*, \ldots, u_{R_f-1}^*, f)$ so as to contain as many don't-cares as possible.

5.3. Maximum Permissible Function

The following definitions formally define partially specified negative-function sequences and $\tilde{u}_i$ mentioned in Section 5.2.

Definition 18. A *partially†* *specified negative-function sequence* of length R_f and degree i for a function f is a sequence of R_f functions denoted by $\text{NFS}^i(R_f, f) = (u_1, \ldots, u_i, u^*_{i+1}, \ldots, u^*_{R_f-1}, u_{R_f})$ such that

(i) $u_1, \ldots, u_i$ are completely specified functions of $x_1, \ldots, x_n$;

(ii) $(u_1, \ldots, u_i)$ is an NFS of length i;

(iii) $u^*_{i+1}, \ldots, u^*_{R_f-1}$ are unspecified functions (i.e., all components are don't-cares); and

(iv) $u_{R_f} = f$.

A partially specified $\text{NFS}^i(R_f, f)$ is *feasible* if there exists at least one complete specification (with respect to $x_1, \ldots, x_n$) $u_{i+1}, \ldots, u_{R_f-1}$ of $u^*_{i+1}, \ldots, u^*_{R_f-1}$, such that $(u_1, \ldots, u_{R_f-1}, f)$ which will be referred to as a feasible completion of $\text{NFS}^i(R_f, f)$ is an $\text{NFS}(R_f, f)$; otherwise $\text{NFS}^i(R_f, f)$ is an *infeasible* partially specified NFS.

Example 11. Let us consider a function f of four variables as shown in Fig. 13(a). Figure 13(b) shows a feasible partially specified NFS of length 3 and degree 1 for f, $\text{NFS}^1(3, f)$, where u_1 is specified as $u_1 = \bar{x}_1$. This is feasible because a completion of this partial specification shown in Fig. 13(c) results in an $\text{NFS}(3, f)$. On the other hand, another partially specified NFS of length 3 and degree 1 for f, $(u_1 = \bar{x}_2, u^*_2, f)$ shown in Fig. 13(d) is an infeasible $\text{NFS}^1(3, f)$, because no matter how u_2 is specified, one of the two inverse edges will remain along the critical path $(1111) \to (0111) \to (0011) \to (0010)$ (there are two inverse edges along the path but only one bit can be used to cover them).

Definition 19. The *maximum permissible function* $\tilde{u}_i$ for a feasible partially specified NFS of length R_f and degree $i - 1$ for function f, $\text{NFS}^{i-1}(R_f, f) = (u_1, \ldots, u_{i-1}, u^*_i, \ldots, u^*_{R_f-1}, f)$, is an incompletely specified function for u^*_i such that:

(i) $\tilde{u}_i$ is negative with respect to $x_1, \ldots, x_n, u_1, \ldots, u_{i-1}$;

(ii) every negative completion u_i of $\tilde{u}_i$ yields a feasible $\text{NFS}^i(R_f, f) = (u_1, \ldots, u_i, u^*_{i+1}, \ldots, u^*_{R_f-1}, f)$; and

(iii) any function $\tilde{u}'_i$ that has different values from those specified in $\tilde{u}_i$ will make the corresponding $\text{NFS}'^i(R_f, f) = (u_1, \ldots, u_{i-1}, \tilde{u}'_i, u^*_{i+1}, \ldots, u^*_{R_f-1}, f)$ infeasible.

It should be noted that the condition (iii) is necessary because we want to have a *maximum* permissible function that contains as many don't-cares as possible. In other words, each specified value of u_i is absolutely required.

---

† Although the term "partially specified" has a meaning similar to "incompletely specified," the latter is used only in conjunction with a single function in order to avoid confusion.

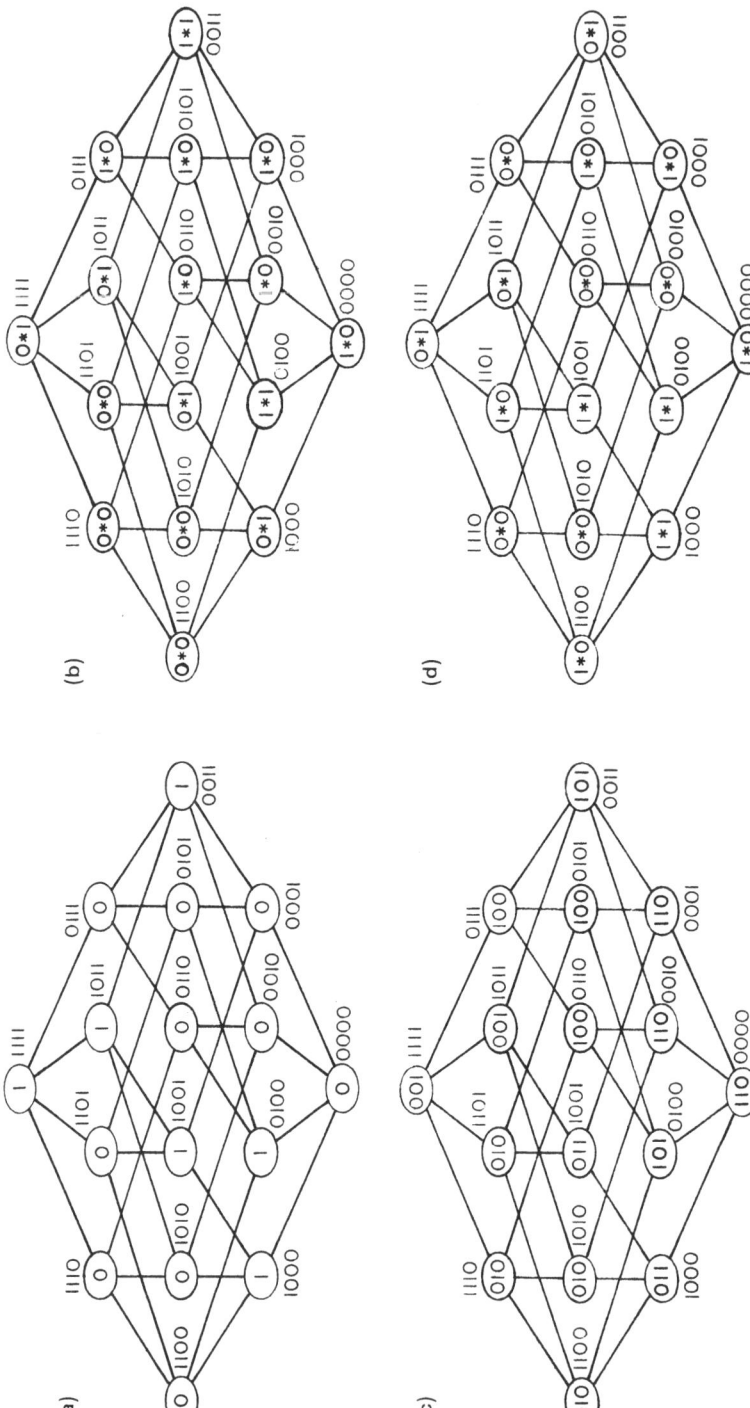

Fig. 13. Example 11. (a) A completely specified function f of four variables. (b) A partially specified feasible $\mathrm{NFS}^1(3,f)$. (c) A completion of $\mathrm{NFS}^1(3,f)$ shown in (b). (d) An infeasible $\mathrm{NFS}^1(3,f) = (x_1 = \bar{x}_2, u_2^*, f)$.

Example 12. Consider the function f discussed in Example 11. The maximum permissible function $\tilde{u}_1$ for $NFS^0(R_f, f)$ is shown in Fig. 14(a) where $\tilde{u}_1(1111) = \tilde{u}_1(1011) = 0$ and $\tilde{u}_1(0010) = \tilde{u}_1(0001) = \tilde{u}_1(0000) = 1$ are the only specified values of $\tilde{u}_1$. If we change any one of these specified values to its complement, the resulting $(\tilde{u}'_1, u^*_2, f)$ will no longer be a feasible $NFS^1(3, f)$. For example, if we set $\tilde{u}'_1(1011) = 1$, we must set $\tilde{u}'_1(1010) = \tilde{u}'_1(1000) = \tilde{u}'_1(0000) = 1$ as shown in Fig. 14(b) (underlined) because $\tilde{u}'_1$ must be a negative function with respect to $x_1, \ldots, x_n$. Then no matter how u^*_2 is specified, there will be an inverse edge along the path $(1011) \rightarrow (1010) \rightarrow (1000) \rightarrow (0000)$ in the resulting labeled 4-lattice. (There are two inverse edges along this path in $C_4(f)$, but only one bit (u_2) is allowed to make the labeled 4-lattice $C_4(f)$ not have inverse edges.) Similarly any of the

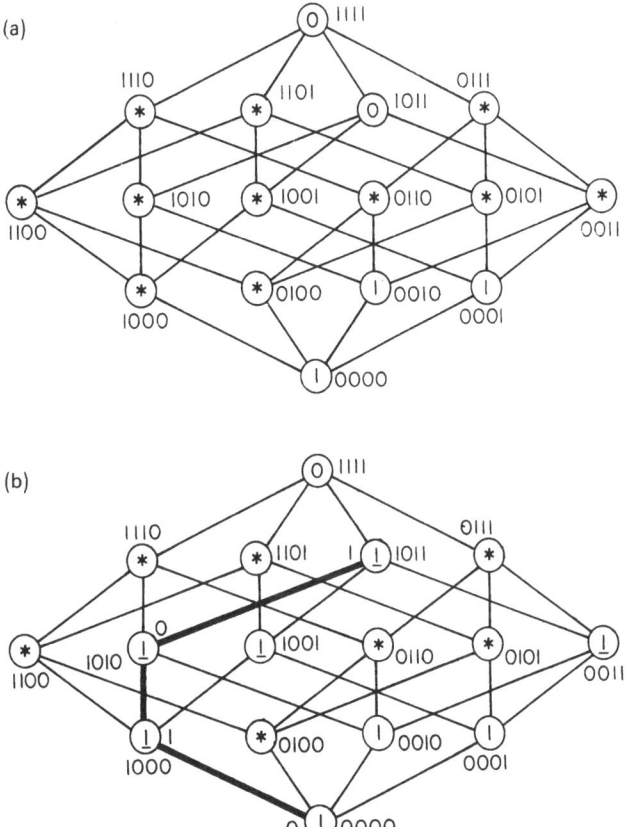

Fig. 14. Example 12. (a) $\tilde{u}_1$ for the f of Fig. 13(a) (Example 11). (b) Changing a specified value $\tilde{u}_1(1011) = 0$ to $\tilde{u}'_1(1011) = 1$ makes $(\tilde{u}'_1, u^*_2, f)$ infeasible. The bold lines show a critical path along which an inverse edge will exist no matter how u^*_2 is assigned.

other four specified values of $\tilde{u}_1$ cannot be changed without causing the resulting $\text{NFS}^1(3, f)$ infeasible. On the other hand, every negative completion u_1 of $\tilde{u}_1$ makes (u_1, u_2^*, f) a feasible $\text{NFS}^1(3, f)$. This can be proved exhaustively, but it is omitted here.

Now we are ready to present an algorithm that obtains $\tilde{u}_i$ based on a given $\text{NFS}^{i-1}(R_f, f) = (u_1, \ldots, u_{i-1}, u_i^*, \ldots, u_{R_f-1}^*, f)$. This algorithm consists of two major steps; an algorithm to obtain conditional minimum labeling (CMNL) and another algorithm to obtain conditional maximum labeling (CMXL), which are similar to algorithms MNL and MXL, respectively.

Algorithm 4. Conditional minimum labeling (*CMNL*).

This algorithm obtains a conditional minimum labeling for a given feasible $\text{NFS}^{i-1}(R_f, f) = (u_1, \ldots, u_{i-1}, u_i^*, \ldots, u_{R_f-1}^*, f)$. The conditional minimum labeling of $\text{NFS}^{i-1}(R_f, f)$ results in a completion $\underline{\text{NFS}}^{i-1}(R_f, f) = (u_1, \ldots, u_{i-1}, \underline{u}_i, \ldots, \underline{u}_{R_f-1}, f)$ of $\text{NFS}^{i-1}(R_f, f)$ such that the label $l(A; u_1, \ldots, u_{i-1}, \underline{u}_i, \ldots, \underline{u}_{R_f-1}, f) \equiv L_{mn}^{i-1}(A)$ for each node A in the corresponding labeled n-lattice $C_n(u_1, \ldots, u_{i-1}, \underline{u}_i, \ldots, \underline{u}_{R_f-1}, f)$ takes the minimum possible value among all feasible completions of $\text{NFS}^{i-1}(R_f, f)$.

Step 1. Assign, as $L_{mn}^{f,i-1}(I)$, the value $\sum_{k=1}^{i-1} 2^{R_f-k} u_k(I) + f(I)$.

Step 2. When $L_{mn}^{f,i-1}(A)$ is assigned to each node A of weight w of C_n, assign, as $L_{mn}^{f,i-1}(B)$ to each node B of weight $w - 1$, the smallest binary integer satisfying the following three conditions: (a) The kth most significant bit of $L_{mn}^{f,i-1}(B)$ is $u_k(B)$ for $k = 1, \ldots, i - 1$; (b) the least significant bit of $L_{mn}^{f,i-1}(B)$ is $f(B)$; and (c) $L_{mn}^{f,i-1}(B) \geq L_{mn}^{f,i-1}(A)$ for every directed edge $\overrightarrow{AB}$ terminating at B. [Notice that each of the ith through $(R_f - 1)$st bits of $L_{mn}^{f,i-1}(B)$ is 0 or 1 depending on what $L_{mn}^{f,i-1}(B)$ is found to be as the smallest binary integer.]

Step 3. Repeat Step 2 until $L_{mn}^{f,i-1}(O)$ is assigned.

Step 4. Denoting the kth most significant bit of $L_{mn}^{f,i-1}(A)$ by $\underline{u}_k(A)$ for $k = i, \ldots, R_f - 1$ and for each $A \in C_n$, we see that $\underline{\text{NFS}}^{i-1}(R_f, f) = (u_1, \ldots, u_{i-1}, \underline{u}_i, \ldots, \underline{u}_{R_f-1}, f)$ has been obtained as the completion of $\text{NFS}^{i-1}(R_f, f)$ by CMNL.

The validity of this algorithm is obvious. Since $\text{NFS}^{i-1}(R_f, f)$ is a feasible partially specified NFS, it must have a feasible completion. The algorithm assigns a minimum possible value as a label to each node, and conditions (a) and (b) of Step 2 guarantee that the resulting labeled n-lattice is a completion of $\text{NFS}^{i-1}(R_f, f)$ while condition (c) of Step 2 guarantees that the labeled n-lattice has no inverse edge, constituting an NFS.

Similarly, algorithm MXL can be modified to obtain a conditional maximum completion of $\text{NFS}^{i-1}(R_f, f)$.

Algorithm 5. Conditional maximum labeling ($CMXL$).

This algorithm obtains a conditional maximum labeling based on a given feasible $\text{NFS}^{i-1}(R_f, f) = (u_1, \ldots, u_{i-1}, u_i^*, \ldots, u_{R_f-1}^*, f)$ for a function f. The conditional maximum labeling of $\text{NFS}^{i-1}(R_f, f)$ results in a completion $\widehat{\text{NFS}}^{i-1}(R_f, f) = (u_1, \ldots, u_{i-1}, \hat{u}_i, \ldots, \hat{u}_{R_f-1}, f)$ of $\text{NFS}^{i-1}(R_f, f)$ such that the label $l(A; u_1, \ldots, u_{i-1}, \hat{u}_i, \ldots, \hat{u}_{R_f-1}, f) \equiv L_{mx}^{f,i-1}(A)$ for each node A in the corresponding labeled n-lattice $C_n(u_1, \ldots, u_{i-1}, \hat{u}_i, \ldots, \hat{u}_{R_f-1}, f)$ takes the maximum possible value among all feasible completions of $\text{NFS}^{i-1}(R_f, f)$.

Step 1. Assign, as $L_{mx}^{f,i-1}(O)$, the value $\sum_{k=1}^{i-1} 2^{R_f-k} u_k(O) + \sum_{k=i}^{R_f-1} 2^{R_f-k} + f(O)$.

Step 2. When $L_{mx}^{f,i-1}(A)$ is assigned to each node A of weight w in C_n, assign, as $L_{mx}^{f,i-1}(B)$ to each node B of weight $w + 1$, the largest binary integer satisfying the following three conditions: (a) The kth most significant bit of $L_{mx}^{f,i-1}(B)$ is $u_k(B)$ for $k = 1, \ldots, i - 1$; (b) the least significant bit of $L_{mx}^{f,i-1}(B)$ is $f(B)$; (c) $L_{mx}^{f,i-1}(B) \le L_{mx}^{f,i-1}(A)$ for every directed edge $\overrightarrow{BA}$ originating from B. [Notice that each of the ith through $(R_f - 1)$st bits of $L_{mx}^{f,i-1}(B)$ is 0 or 1 depending on what $L_{mx}^{f,i-1}(B)$ is found to be as the largest binary integer.]

Step 3. Repeat Step 2 until $L_{mx}^{f,i-1}(O)$ is assigned.

Step 4. Denoting the kth most significant bit of $L_{mx}^{f,i-1}(A)$ by $\hat{u}_k(A)$ for $k = i, \ldots, R_f - 1$ and for each $A \in C_n$, we see that $\widehat{\text{NFS}}^{i-1}(R_f, f) = (u_1, \ldots, u_{i-1}, \hat{u}_i, \ldots, \hat{u}_{R_f-1}, f)$ has been obtained as the completion of $\text{NFS}^{i-1}(R_f, f)$ by CMXL.

The validity of this algorithm is obvious because $\text{NFS}^{i-1}(R_f, f)$ is a feasible partially specified NFS which has at least one $\text{NFS}(R_f, f)$ completion. This algorithm assigns the maximum possible label to each node of the labeled n-lattice, and the conditions in Step 2 guarantee that the labeled n-lattice is an $\text{NFS}(R_f, f)$.

Example 13. Consider the function f shown in Fig. 5(a) for Examples 1 and 4. The $C_3(u_1, u_2, f)$'s based on MNL and MXL are shown in Fig. 5(b) and Fig. 6(a), respectively. These two labeled 3-lattices can also be obtained by CMNL and CMXL from $\text{NFS}^0(R_f, f) = (u_1^*, u_2^*, f)$. Next, for this function f, let us consider an $\text{NFS}^1(R_f, f) = (u_1, u_2^*, f)$ with $u_1 = \overline{x_1 \vee x_2}$ shown in Fig. 15(a) in the form of a partially labeled 3-lattice. According to algorithm CMNL, $\text{NFS}^1(3, f)$ is completed as $\underline{\text{NFS}}^1(3, f)$ as shown in Fig. 15(b). Similarly, $\text{NFS}^1(3, f)$ is completed by algorithm CMXL as $\widehat{\text{NFS}}^1(3, f)$ as shown in Fig. 15(c).

The following algorithm obtains the maximum permissible function $\tilde{u}_i$ for a feasible partially specified $\text{NFS}^{i-1}(R_f, f) = (u_1, \ldots, u_{i-1}, u_i^*, \ldots, u_{R_f-1}^*, f)$.

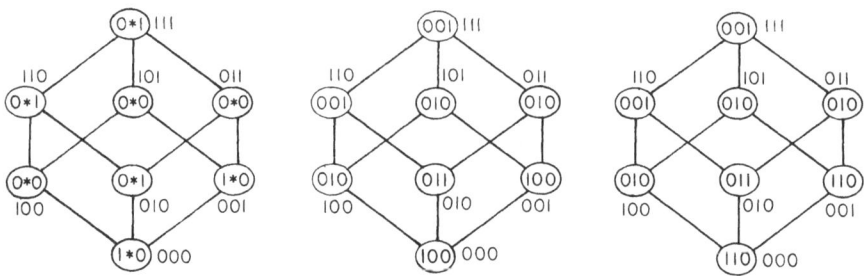

Fig. 15. Example 13 with function f in Fig. 5(a). (a) $NFS^1(3,f) = (u_1 = \overline{x_1 \vee x_2}, u_2^*, u_3 = f)$. (b) $\underline{NFS}^1(3,f) = (u_1, u_2, f)$ obtained from $NFS^1(3,f)$ by algorithm CMNL. (c) $\widehat{NFS}^1(3,f) = (u_1, \hat{u}_2, f)$ obtained from $NFS^1(3,f)$ by algorithm CMXL.

Algorithm 6. Derivation of the maximum permissible function $\tilde{u}_i$ for a given $NFS^{i-1}(R_f, f) = (u_1, \ldots, u_{i-1}, u_i^*, \ldots, u_{R_f-1}^*, f)$ (*MPF*).

Step 1. First, we must obtain a completion $\underline{NFS}^{i-1}(R_f, f) = (u_1, \ldots, u_{i-1}, \underline{u}_i, \underline{u}_{i+1}, \ldots, \underline{u}_{R_f-1}, f)$ of $NFS^{i-1}(R_f, f)$ according to algorithm CMNL.

Step 2. Next, we must obtain another completion $\widehat{NFS}^{i-1}(R_f, f) = (u_1, \ldots, u_{i-1}, \hat{u}_i, \hat{u}_{i+1}, \ldots, \hat{u}_{R_f-1}, f)$ according to algorithm CMXL.

Step 3. For each node A of C_n, do the following:

    (i) assign $\tilde{u}_i(A) = 0$ if $\underline{u}_i(A) = 0$ and $\hat{u}_i(A) = 0$,

    (ii) assign $\tilde{u}_i(A) = 1$ if $\underline{u}_i(A) = 1$ and $\hat{u}_i(A) = 1$,

    (iii) assign $\tilde{u}_i(A) = *$ (unspecified) if $\underline{u}_i(A) = 0$ and $\hat{u}_i(A) = 1$.

Theorem 7. The function obtained by algorithm MPF is the maximum permissible function for the feasible partially specified $NFS^{i-1}(R_f, f) = (u_1, \ldots, u_{i-1}, u_i^*, \ldots, u_{R_f-1}^*, f)$.

Proof. To prove that $\tilde{u}_i$ is the maximum permissible function for $NFS^{i-1}(R_f, f)$, we have to prove: (i) there is always a solution $\tilde{u}_i$ that is negative with respect to $x_1, \ldots, x_n, u_1, \ldots, u_{i-1}$ if $NFS^{i-1}(R_f, f)$ is a feasible partially specified NFS; (ii) changing any specified component of $\tilde{u}_i$, i.e., changing $\tilde{u}_i(A) = 0$ to $\tilde{u}_i'(A) = 1$ or $\tilde{u}_i(A) = 1$ to $\tilde{u}_i'(A) = 0$ will make the corresponding $\widehat{NFS}^{i-1}(R_f, f)$ infeasible; and (iii) any negative completion u_i of $\tilde{u}_i$ (with respect to $x_1, \ldots, x_n, u_1, \ldots, u_{i-1}$) will make the corresponding $(u_1, \ldots, u_i, u_{i+1}^*, \ldots, u_{R_f-1}^*, f)$ a feasible partially specified NFS of length R_f and degree i for function f.

(i) Since the partially specified NFS given is feasible, there must exist at least one completion $(u_1, \ldots, u_{i-1}, u_i, \ldots, u_{R_f-1}, f)$ of $(u_1, \ldots, u_{i-1}, u_i^*, \ldots, u_{R_f-1}^*, f)$ such that $C_n(u_1, \ldots, u_{R_f-1}, f)$ is a labeled n-lattice without any inverse edge. Algorithm CMNL assigns the minimum possible value to each node of C_n so that the resulting labeled n-lattice has no inverse edge. Therefore, Step 1 of algorithm MPF can always be successfully executed without any problem (e.g., the conditions in Step 2 of CMNL may not be simultaneously satisfied without additional bits). Similarly, Step 2 of algorithm MPF can be successfully executed. Besides, for every node A in C_n, $L_{mn}^{f,i-1}(A) \leq L_{mx}^{f,i-1}(A)$, and therefore $\underline{u}_i(A) \leq \hat{u}_i(A)$. The three cases in Step 3 of algorithm MPF exhaust all possible combinations of $\underline{u}_i(A)$ and $\hat{u}_i(A)$, so that $\tilde{u}_i$ can always be determined by algorithm MPF for the given $\text{NFS}^{i-1}(R_f, f)$. Furthermore, there must be some node A such that $\tilde{u}_i(A) = 0$ because otherwise (i.e., if $\tilde{u}_i = 1$ or $*$ for each node A) $\hat{u}_i = 1$ for every A results and $(u_1, u_2, \ldots, u_{i-1}, \hat{u}_{i+1}, \ldots, \hat{u}_{R_f-1}, f)$ without $\hat{u}_i = 1$ would be an NFS of length $R_f - 1$ for f which contradicts the assumption of the NFS having a minimum length R_f. Similarly, there must be some node B such that $\tilde{u}_i(B) = 1$ because otherwise $(u_1, u_2, \ldots, u_{i-1}, \underline{u}_{i+1}, \ldots, \underline{u}_{R_f-1}, f)$ would be an NFS that results in the same contradiction. This proves that algorithm MPF can always be successfully executed.

Now we have to show that $\tilde{u}_i$ is negative with respect to $x_1, \ldots, x_n$, $u_1, \ldots, u_{i-1}$. According to the definition of $\text{NFS}^{i-1}(R_f, f)$, $(u_1, \ldots, u_{i-1})$ is an NFS of length $i - 1$, and therefore $C_n(u_1, \ldots, u_{i-1})$ has no inverse edge. Assume $\tilde{u}_i$ is not negative with respect to $x_1, \ldots, x_n, u_1, \ldots, u_{i-1}$. Then by Theorem 3 there must exist two nodes A and B in C_n such that (a) $(a_1, \ldots, a_n, u_1(A), \ldots, u_{i-1}(A)) > (b_1, \ldots, b_n, u_1(B), \ldots, u_{i-1}(B))$, and (b) $\tilde{u}_i(A) = 1$ and $\tilde{u}_i(B) = 0$. From condition (a), $A > B$ must hold. Also $u_k(A) = u_k(B)$ for $k = 1, \ldots, i - 1$ must hold because $(u_1, \ldots, u_{i-1})$ is an $\text{NFS}(i - 1, u_{i-1})$ by Definition 19, and therefore $l(A; u_1, \ldots, u_{i-1}) = l(B; u_1, \ldots, u_{i-1})$ for $A > B$. However, this can never occur because $\tilde{u}_i(A) = 1$ and $\tilde{u}_i(B) = 0$ mean that $\hat{u}_i(A) = 1$ and $\hat{u}_i(B) = 0$, respectively, according to Step 3 of algorithm MPF, contradicting the fact that $\hat{u}_i(A)$ and $\hat{u}_i(B)$ are obtained by algorithm CMXL that produces a labeled n-lattice $C_n(u_1, \ldots, u_{i-1}, \hat{u}_i, \ldots, \hat{u}_{R_f-1}, f)$ without an inverse edge. Thus, $\tilde{u}_i$ must be negative with respect to $x_1, \ldots, x_n, u_1, \ldots, u_{i-1}$.

(ii) Now let us prove that if any specified value of $\tilde{u}_i(A)$ is changed from $\tilde{u}_i(A) = 1$ to $\tilde{u}_i'(A) = 0$, or from $\tilde{u}_i(A) = 0$ to $\tilde{u}_i'(A) = 1$, then the resulting $(u_1, \ldots, u_{i-1}, \tilde{u}_i', u_{i+1}^*, \ldots, u_{R_f-1}^*, f)$ will not be feasible, i.e., no completion of $(u_1, \ldots, u_{i-1}, \tilde{u}_i', u_{i+1}^*, \ldots, u_{R_f-1}^*, f)$ can be an $\text{NFS}(R_f, f)$. This can be proved easily based on the properties of the labels obtained by CMNL and CMXL. Obviously, $L_{mn}^{f,i-1}(A)$ is the minimum possible label for A among all possible labelings corresponding to feasible completions of $\text{NFS}^{i-1}(R_f, f)$. Similarly, $L_{mx}^{f,i-1}(A)$ is the maximum possible label for A. On the other hand, $\tilde{u}_i(A) = 0$ means both $\hat{u}_i(A) = 0$ and $\underline{u}_i(A) = 0$ which implies

$$\sum_{k=1}^{i-1} 2^{R_f-k} u_k(A) \leq L_{mn}^{f,i-1}(A) \leq L_{mx}^{f,i-1}(A) < \sum_{k=1}^{i-1} 2^{R_f-k} u_k(A) + 2^{R_f-i}$$

However, if $\tilde{u}_i(A) = 0$ is changed to $\tilde{u}_i' = 1$, then any completion of $(u_1, \ldots, u_{i-1}, \tilde{u}_i', u_{i+1}^*, \ldots, u_{R_f-1}^*, f)$ will assign a label $L(A) \geq \sum_{k=1}^{i-1} 2^{R_f-k} u_k(A) + 2^{R_f-1} > L_{mx}^{f,i-1}(A)$, which contradicts the property that $L_{mx}^{f,i-1}(A)$ is the maximum possible label attached to A for any feasible completion of $(u_1, \ldots, u_{i-1}, u_i^*, \ldots, u_{R_f-1}^*)$. Consequently, $\tilde{u}_i(A)$ can not be changed from 0 to 1 without destroying the feasibility. Similarly, no $\tilde{u}_i(A) = 1$ can be changed to $\tilde{u}_i'(A) = 0$ because otherwise every completion of $(u_1, \ldots, u_{i-1}, \tilde{u}_i', u_{i+1}^*, \ldots, u_{R_f-1}^*, f)$ will assign a label to A which is less than $L_{mn}^{f,i-1}(A)$, and thus make this sequence of functions infeasible. This completes the proof for (ii).

(iii) To prove that $\tilde{u}_i$ is indeed the maximum permissible function for $\text{NFS}^{i-1}(R_f, f)$, we have to show that every negative completion u_i (with respect to $x_1, \ldots, x_n, u_1, \ldots, u_{i-1}$) of $\tilde{u}_i$ produces a feasible $\text{NFS}^i(R_f, f)$. In other words, we have to prove that $(u_1, \ldots, u_i, u_{i+1}^*, \ldots, u_{R_f-1}^*, f)$ has at least one completion which is an $\text{NFS}(R_f, f)$. Let us consider a labeled n-lattice $C_n(u_1, u_2, \ldots, u_i, v_{i+1}, \ldots, v_{R_f-1}, f)$ such that

$$v_j(A) = \underline{u}_j(A) \text{ for } j = i + 1, \ldots, R_f - 1 \text{ if } u_i(A) = 0; \text{ and}$$

$$v_j(A) = \hat{u}_j(A) \text{ for } j = i + 1, \ldots, R_f - 1 \text{ if } u_i(A) = 1$$

Because u_i is a completion of $\tilde{u}_i$, $u_i(A) = 0$ means either $\tilde{u}_i(A) = 0$ [i.e., both $\underline{u}_i(A) = \hat{u}_i(A) = 0$] or $\tilde{u}_i(A) = *$ [i.e., $\underline{u}_i(A) = 0$ and $\hat{u}_i(A) = 1$]. Similarly, $u_i(A) = 1$ means either $\tilde{u}_i(A) = 1$ (i.e., both $\underline{u}_i(A) = 1$ and $\hat{u}_i(A) = 1$) or $\tilde{u}_i(A) = *$ (i.e., $\underline{u}_i(A) = 0$ and $\hat{u}_i(A) = 1$). Therefore, the above labeled n-lattice has the following labels:

$$L(A) = L_{mn}^{f,i-1}(A), \text{ if } u_i(A) = 0$$

$$L(A) = L_{mx}^{f,i-1}(A), \text{ if } u_i(A) = 1$$

Next we shall prove that $C_n(u_1, u_2, \ldots, u_i, v_{i+1}, \ldots, v_{R_f-1}, f)$ is an $\text{NFS}(R_f, f)$. This will, in turn, prove that any negative completion of $\tilde{u}_i$ with respect to $x_1, \ldots, x_n, u_1, \ldots, u_{i-1}$ produces a feasible $\text{NFS}^i(R_f, f)$. Suppose there is an inverse edge $\overrightarrow{AB}$ in $C_n(u_1, u_2, \ldots, u_i, v_{i+1}, \ldots, v_{R_f-1}, f)$. Since $(u_1, \ldots, u_{i-1})$ is an $\text{NFS}(i - 1, u_{i-1})$ which has no inverse edge, $u_j(A) = u_j(B)$ must hold for $j = 1, \ldots, i - 1$. Therefore, the following three cases must be considered:

(a) $u_i(A) = u_i(B) = 0$, but $L(A) > L(B)$

This can never occur because from the above conclusion we have $L(A) = L_{mn}^{f,i-1}(A)$ and $L(B) = L_{mn}^{f,i-1}(B)$ which are produced by algorithm

CMNL which guarantees the produced labeled n-lattice have no inverse edge.

    (b) $u_i(A) = u_i(B) = 1$, but $L(A) > L(B)$

This can not occur because we have $L(A) = L_{mx}^{f,i-1}(A)$ and $L(B) = L_{mx}^{f,i-1}(B)$ which are produced by algorithm CMXL which guarantees the produced labeled n-lattice have no inverse edge.

    (c) $u_i(A) = 1, u_i(B) = 0$

Because u_i is a negative completion of $\tilde{u}_i$ with respect to $x_1, \ldots, x_n$, $u_1, \ldots, u_{i-1}$, there can be no inverse edges in $C_{n+i-1}(u_i)$. However, $(a_1, \ldots, a_n, u_1(A), \ldots, u_{i-1}(A))$ and $(b_1, \ldots, b_n, u_1(B), \ldots, u_{i-1}(B))$ form a directed edge in $C_{n+i-1}(u_i)$ with $u_i(A) = 1$ and $u_i(B) = 0$. This contradicts the fact that $C_{n+i-1}(u_i)$ has no inverse edge. Therefore, $u_i(A) = 1$ and $u_i(B) = 0$ do not occur.

Summarizing (a), (b), and (c), any negative completion u_i of $\tilde{u}_i$ will produce a feasible partially specified negative-function sequence, $\text{NFS}^i(R_f, f) = (u_1, \ldots, u_i, u_{i+1}^*, \ldots, u_{R_f-1}^*, f)$.

Thus, the theorem statement is proved.   □

5.4. Design Algorithm of Irredundant MOS Networks

Based on the algorithm for obtaining maximum permissible functions, we present our algorithm for the design of irredundant MOS networks as follows.

Algorithm 7. Design of irredundant MOS networks with a minimum number of MOS cells for a given function f (*DIMN*).

    Step 1. Let $\text{NFS}^0(R_f, f) = (u_1^*, \ldots, u_{R_f-1}^*, f)$ and set $i = 1$. [If R_f is not known at this step, it will be obtained after $\underline{\text{NFS}}^0(R_f, f)$ is obtained by applying CMNL in Step 2.]

    Step 2. Use the algorithm CMNL to obtain $\underline{\text{NFS}}^{i-1}(R_f, f) = (u_1, \ldots, u_{i-1}, \underline{u}_i, \ldots, \underline{u}_{R_f-1}, f)$.

    Step 3. Use the algorithm CMXL to obtain $\widehat{\text{NFS}}^{i-1}(R_f, f) = (u_1, \ldots, u_{i-1}, \hat{u}_i, \ldots, \hat{u}_{R_f-1}, f)$.

    Step 4. Obtain function $\tilde{u}_i$ by setting:

$$\tilde{u}_i(A) = 0, \text{ if } \underline{u}_i(A) = \hat{u}_i(A) = 0;$$

$$\tilde{u}_i(A) = 1, \text{ if } \underline{u}_i(A) = \hat{u}_i(A) = 1; \text{ and}$$

$$\tilde{u}_i(A) = *, \text{ if } \underline{u}_i(A) = 0 \text{ and } \hat{u}_i(A) = 1$$

Step 5. Obtain an irredundant MOS cell configuration for $\tilde{u}_i$ with respect to $x_1, \ldots, x_n, u_1, \ldots, u_{i-1}$ by an appropriate algorithm (e.g., the approaches in Section 4). Let u_i denote the function realized by this cell (u_i is now a completion of $\tilde{u}_i$ with respect to $x_1, \ldots, x_n$).

Step 6. If $i = R_f - 1$, design an irredundant MOS cell configuration for f with respect to $x_1, \ldots, x_n, u_1, \ldots, u_{R_f-1}$ and terminate this algorithm; otherwise set i to $i + 1$ and go to Step 2.

Theorem 8. An MOS network designed by algorithm DIMN (Algorithm 7) for function f is irredundant.

Proof. Let the network designed by algorithm DIMN for function f realize the following NFS:

$$\text{NFS}(R_f, f) = (u_1, \ldots, u_{R_f-1}, f)$$

Suppose that there are redundant FETs in the above network. Let g_i denote a gate (MOS cell) such that g_i has at least one redundant FET but every g_j, for $j = 1, \ldots, i - 1$, has no redundant FETs. Let $\text{N}\overset{\circ}{\text{F}}\text{S}(R_f, f)$ be the NFS realized by the MOS network after multiple extraction of these redundant FETs. Then

$$\text{N}\overset{\circ}{\text{F}}\text{S}(R_f, f) = (u_1, \ldots, u_{i-1}, \overset{\circ}{u}_i, \ldots, \overset{\circ}{u}_{R_f-1}, f)$$

where $u_1, \ldots, u_{i-1}$ are unchanged because no FETs have been extracted from gates $g_1, \ldots, g_{i-1}$ of the network. Let $\tilde{u}_i$ be the function obtained by Step 4 of Algorithm 7 (DIMN) in the ith iteration. Clearly, $\overset{\circ}{u}_i$ is not a completion of $\tilde{u}_i$ because u_i was obtained by Step 5 which designs an irredundant MOS cell configuration for $\tilde{u}_i$ (that means that g_i will not realize a completion of $\tilde{u}_i$ if any FET extracted from g_i). Since $\tilde{u}_i$ is the maximum permissible function based on $\text{NFS}^{i-1}(u_1, \ldots, u_{i-1}, u_i^*, \ldots, u_{R_f-1}^*, f)$ (Theorem 7), $(u_1, \ldots, u_{i-1}, \overset{\circ}{u}_i, u_{i+1}^*, \ldots, u_{R_f-1}^*, f)$ can not be a feasible partially specified NFS for f (Definition 19), contradicting the assumption that $\text{N}\overset{\circ}{\text{F}}\text{S}(R_f, f) = (u_1, \ldots, u_{i-1}, \overset{\circ}{u}_i, \ldots, \overset{\circ}{u}_{R_f-1}, f)$ is an $\text{NFS}(R_f, f)$. Consequently, the MOS network designed by algorithm DIMN must be irredundant. □

For better understanding, the steps of algorithm MPF were explicitly repeated as Steps 2, 3, and 4 of algorithm DIMN. Steps 1, 2, 3, 4, and 6 of algorithm DIMN involve only simple labeling and comparisons. Step 5 requires an irredundant MOS cell configuration for an incompletely specified function. This can be obtained by using the approaches discussed in Section 4. As explained in Section 4, these approaches are relatively simple compared to algorithms for obtaining irredundant disjunctive or conjunctive forms for an arbitrary function because these approaches are especially tailored for negative functions.

5.5. Examples

Two examples with step-by-step applications of Algorithm 7 are shown below.

Example 14. Consider the function f of Example 1. The 3-lattice with respect to f, i.e., $C_3(f)$, is shown in Fig. 16(a). Step 2 of Algorithm 7 obtains $\underline{NFS}^0(3, f)$ shown in (b) which is identical to the labeled 3-lattice obtained by MNL shown in Fig. 5(b). Similarly, Step 3 obtains $\widehat{NFS}^0(3, f)$ shown in (c). Step 4 then compares $\underline{u}_1$ and $\hat{u}_1$ and obtains $\tilde{u}_1$ and $\widetilde{NFS}^0(3, f)$ shown in (d). The $NFS^1(3, f)_1 = (\bar{x}_1, u_2^*, f)$ in (e) is obtained by Step 5. Step 5 also obtains two other irredundant MOS cell configurations for u_1 and their corresponding $NFS^1(3, f)_2$ and $NFS^1(3, f)_3$ which will be discussed later. After Step 6, the algorithm returns to Step 2 and obtains $\underline{NFS}^1(3, f)_1$, $\widehat{NFS}^1(3, f)_1$, $\widetilde{NFS}^1(3, f)_1$, and $NFS^2(3, f)_1$ shown in (f), (g), (h), and (i), respectively. Since $R_f = 3$, $NFS^2(3, f)_1$ is completely specified negative-function sequence with respect to x_1, x_2, and x_3. Step 6 of the algorithm obtains an irredundant MOS cell configuration for f. The completed design is shown in (s). As proved before, this MOS network has no redundant FETs. Furthermore, this network happens to consist of a minimum number of FETs because three load FETs and five driver FETs are the minimum number of FETs required by function f which can be proved as follows. Based on algorithm MNL, we know that function f requires three MOS cells which means that there are three load FETs and at least two interconnections between cells in any minimum MOS network for f. Since f is a function of exactly three variables, there are at least three interconnections from external variables (x_1, x_2, and x_3) to the three MOS cells. Therefore, in a minimum MOS network for f, there are at least three MOS cells and five interconnections which means that f requires at least three load FETs and five driver FETs.

As mentioned above, Step 5 of the algorithm can also obtain $NFS^1(3, f)_2 = (\bar{x}_2, u_2^*, f)$ and $NFS^1(3, f)_3 = (\bar{x}_3, u_2^*, f)$, shown in Figs. 16(j) and 16(o), respectively. From Fig. 16(j), the algorithm obtains $\underline{NFS}^1(3, f)_2$, $\widehat{NFS}^1(3, f)_2$, $\widetilde{NFS}^1(3, f)_2$, and $NFS^2(3, f)_2$, shown in (k), (l), (m), and (n), respectively. $NFS(3, f)_2$ and $NFS(3, f)_1$ are indistinguishable, because the permutation of u_1 and u_2 in $NFS(3, f)_2$ results in $NFS(3, f)_1$. The corresponding MOS network for both $NFS(3, f)$'s is shown in Fig. 16(s). Similarly, from (o), the algorithm obtains $\underline{NFS}^1(3, f)_3$, $\widehat{NFS}^1(3, f)_3$, and $\widetilde{NFS}^1(3, f)_3$, shown in (p), (q), and (r), respectively. Since $\tilde{u}_2$ in $\widetilde{NFS}^1(3, f)_3$

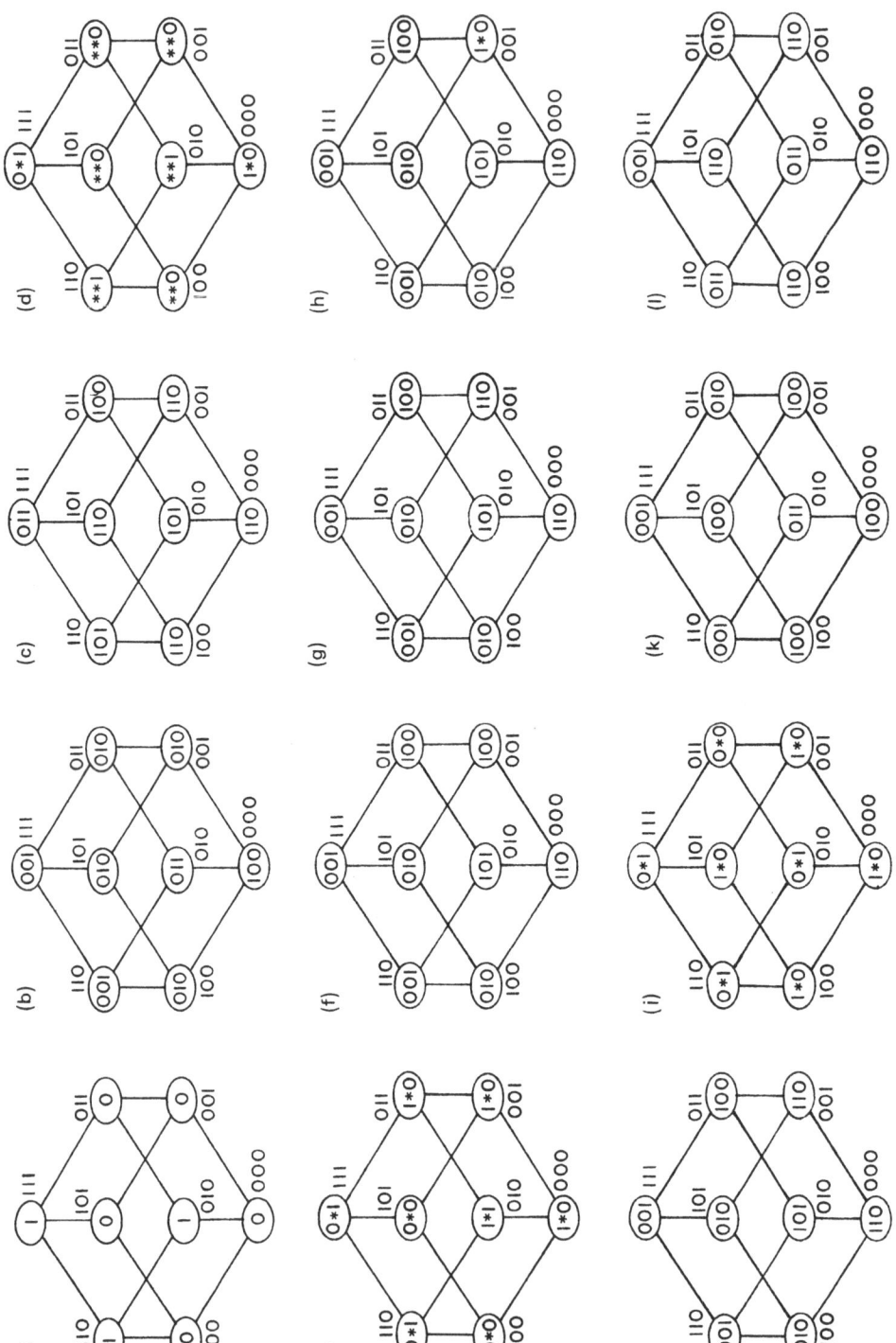

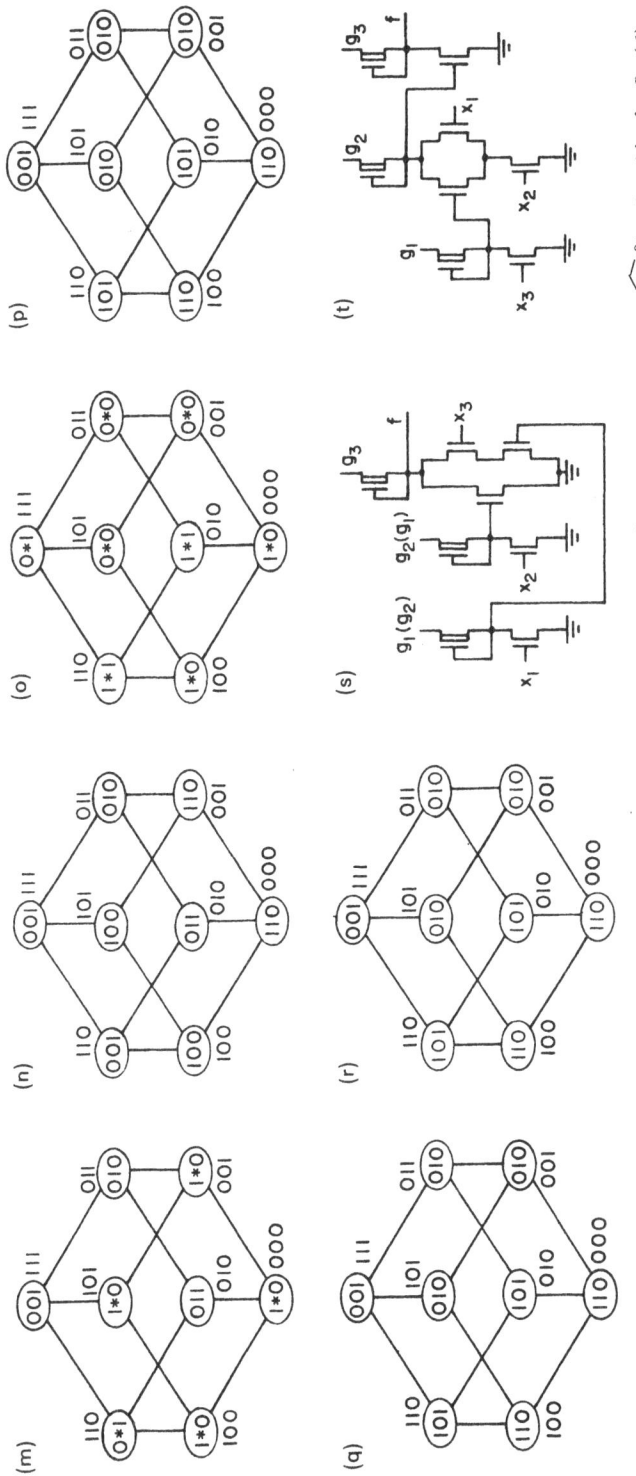

Fig. 16. Example 15 with function f of Fig. 5(a). (a) $C_3(f)$ for $f = x_1x_2 \vee x_2\bar{x}_3$. (b) $\overline{\text{NFS}}^0(3, f) = (\hat{u}_1, \hat{u}_2, f)$. (c) $\widehat{\text{NFS}}^0(3, f) = (\hat{u}_1, \hat{u}_2, f)$. (d) $\overline{\text{NFS}}^0(3, f) = (u_1, u_2, f)$. (e) $\text{NFS}^1(3, f)_1 = (\bar{x}_1, u_2^*, f)$. (f) $\underline{\text{NFS}}^1(3, f)_1 = (\bar{x}_1, u_2^*, f)$. (g) $\text{NFS}^1(3, f)_1 = (\bar{x}_1, \hat{u}_2, f)$. (h) $\widehat{\text{NFS}}^1(3, f)_1 = (\bar{x}_1, \hat{u}_2, f)$. (i) $\overline{\text{NFS}}^1(3, f)_1 = (\bar{x}_1, u_2^*, f)$. (j) $\text{NFS}^1(3, f)_2 = (\bar{x}_2, u_2^*, f)$ obtained from (d). (k) $\underline{\text{NFS}}^1(3, f)_2 = (\bar{x}_2, u_2^*, f)$. (l) $\text{NFS}^1(3, f)_2 = (\bar{x}_2, \hat{u}_2, f)$. (m) $\text{NFS}^1(3, f)_1 = (\bar{x}_1\bar{x}_2, f)$. (n) $\text{NFS}^2(3, f)_2 = (\bar{x}_2, \bar{x}_1, f)$. (o) $\text{NFS}^1(3, f)_3 = (\bar{x}_3, u_2, f)$ obtained from (d). (p) $\underline{\text{NFS}}^1(3, f)_3 = (\bar{x}_3, u_2, f)$. (q) $\overline{\text{NFS}}^1(3, f)_3 = (\bar{x}_3, \hat{u}_2, f)$. (r) $\text{NFS}^1(3, f)_3 = \text{NFS}(3, f) = (\bar{x}_3, f, f)$. (s) Irredundant MOS network corresponding to NFS(3, f)'s in (i) and (n). (t) Irredundant MOS network corresponding to NFS(3, f)₃ in (r).

has no unspecified value with respect to x_1, x_2, and x_3, $\widehat{\text{NFS}}^1(3,f)_3 =$ NFS$(3,f)_3$. The MOS network corresponding to NFS$(3,f)_3$ is shown in (t), which also consists of a minimum number of FETs for function f as we can prove in the same manner as before.

As evident from Example 14, Steps 2, 3, and 4 are deterministic. By this we mean that given a NFS$^{i-1}(R_f,f)$, subsequent $\underline{\text{NFS}}^{i-1}(R_f,f)$, $\widehat{\text{NFS}}^{i-1}(R_f,f)$ and $\widetilde{\text{NFS}}^{i-1}(R_f,f)$ are uniquely determined. On the other hand, Step 5 is generally nondeterministic because we may obtain more than one irredundant MOS cell configuration for a given $\tilde{u}_i$. In this simple example, when Step 5 of the algorithm is reached for the first time, three irredundant MOS cell configurations for $\tilde{u}_1$ can be found. If we are only interested in one irredundant MOS network design for f, any one of the three can be used. No matter which particular irredundant MOS cell configuration is chosen, the designed MOS network will be irredundant.

It should be noted that this algorithm usually requires $R_f - 1$ iterations, deriving NFS$^{i-1}(R_f,f)$, $\underline{\text{NFS}}^{i-1}(R_f,f)$, $\widehat{\text{NFS}}^{i-1}(R_f,f)$, $\widetilde{\text{NFS}}^{i-1}(R_f,f)$ and NFS$^i(R_f,f)$ in each iteration for $i = 1,\ldots, R_f - 1$. However, if $\widetilde{\text{NFS}}^{i-1}(R_f,f)$ becomes a completely specified function with respect to $x_1,\ldots, x_n$, for some $i < R_f$ [i.e., $\underline{\text{NFS}}^{i-1}(R_f,f) = \widehat{\text{NFS}}^{i-1}(R_f,f)$ holds], then $\widetilde{\text{NFS}}^{i-1}(R_f,f) = \text{NFS}^i(R_f,f) = \text{NFS}(R_f,f)$ must hold. In this case, the algorithm only requires i iterations. Even in this case, however, Step 5 of the algorithm must be executed $R_f - i - 1$ additional times in order to design the irredundant MOS cells for $u_{i+1},\ldots, u_{R_f-1}$ (the cell design for f is taken care of by Step 6). In Example 14, when we choose $u_1 = \bar{x}_3$ as the irredundant MOS cell configuration of $\tilde{u}_1$, $\underline{\text{NFS}}^1(3,f)_3$ and $\widehat{\text{NFS}}^1(3,f)_3$ become the same. Therefore in this case, $\underline{\text{NFS}}^1(3,f)_3 = \widehat{\text{NFS}}^1(3,f)_3 = \text{NFS}(3,f)_3$.

Another point to be noted is that the exhaustion of all alternatives in Step 5 may not give all irredundant MOS networks for the given function for the following reasons. First, the algorithm does not give a solution which is irredundant but consists of more cells than the minimum number required. Next, some irredundant MOS network with a minimal number of MOS cells may not be produced by this algorithm. The following example demonstrates this fact.

Example 15. Consider the odd-parity function of three variables, $f = x_1 \oplus x_2 \oplus x_3$. According to Algorithm 7, $\underline{\text{NFS}}^0(3,f)$, $\widehat{\text{NFS}}^0(3,f)$, and $\widetilde{\text{NFS}}^0(3,f)$ are obtained as shown in Fig. 17(a), (b), and (c), respectively. From $\tilde{u}_1$ in $\widetilde{\text{NFS}}^0(3,f)$, $u_1 = \bar{x}_1$, $\bar{x}_2$, or $\bar{x}_3$ are obtained as the only irredundant MOS cell configurations for $\tilde{u}_1$. This means that every solution obtained by Algorithm 7 will contain an MOS cell which works as an inverter for one of the input variables. However, the MOS network, shown in Fig. 17(d),

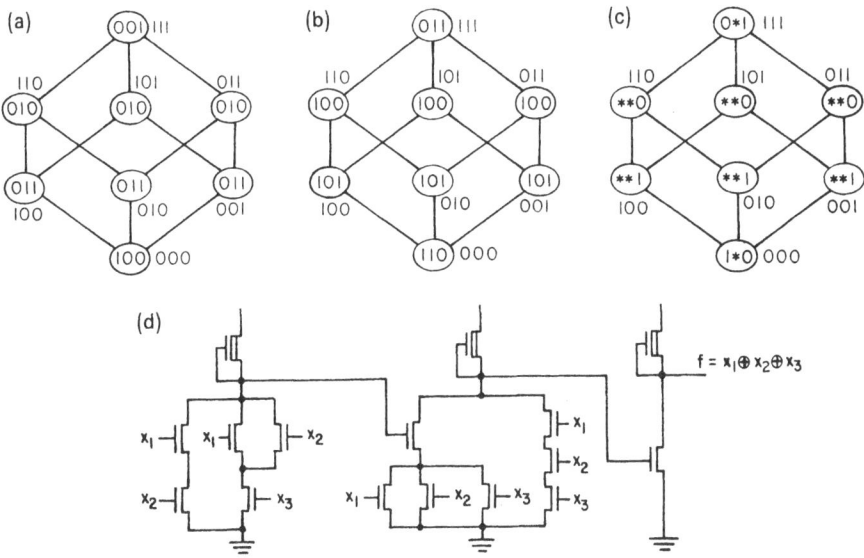

Fig. 17. Example 15 with $f = x_1 \oplus x_2 \oplus x_3$. (a) $\underline{\text{NFS}}^0(3, f) = (\underline{u}_1, \underline{u}_2, f)$ for $f = x_1 \oplus x_2 \oplus x_3$. (b) $\widehat{\text{NFS}}^0(3, f) = (\hat{u}_1, \hat{u}_2, f)$. (c) $\widetilde{\text{NFS}}^0(3, f) = (\tilde{u}_1, u_2^*, f)$. (d) Irredundant MOS network for f that cannot be produced by Algorithm 7.

which realizes f is irredundant but contains no such MOS cell. Therefore, some irredundant MOS networks with a minimum number of cells can not be designed by Algorithm 7.

6. INTERACTIVE DESIGN

The algorithms discussed in Section 5 are easily extended to the case of incompletely specified functions and the case of multioutput networks.[8] Also, they are extended to MOS networks of exactly two levels.[15] All these algorithms, which will be published elsewhere, yield networks with excessively complex cells for some functions, though the number of cells in the networks is minimum and FETs and consequently interconnections are irredundant. Interactive design is discussed in the following in order to solve this problem.

6.1. Advantages and Disadvantages of Algorithm DIMN

MOS networks for many sample functions have been designed by the algorithms discussed in the previous sections. (Computer programs for algorithm DIMN and the extensions for completely or incompletely specified and single- or multi-output functions were developed by Yamamoto[16] and then extended by Yeh[17] to include the design of multi-output networks where all outputs are in the last level. Computer programs for the algorithms of Liu[6] were developed by Shinozaki.[18] Algorithm DIMN and its extension yield MOS networks that are not worse and usually substantially better than networks by the previous algorithms, as exemplified by the following example.

Example 16. Let us design MOS networks for function $f = x_1(x_2 \oplus x_3 \oplus x_4)$. Applying the algorithm of Nakamura *et al.*[5], the labeled lattice in Fig. 18(a) is obtained and in (b) we derive the corresponding MOS network with the minimum number of MOS cells, 3, which has 20 driver MOSFETs. Applying algorithm DIMN, the labeled lattice in (c) and the corresponding MOS network in (d) are obtained. The irredundant MOS network in (d) has the same number of cells as (b) but the number of driver MOSFETs is reduced to only 12.

Although algorithm DIMN usually yield much simpler MOS networks with a minimum number of MOS cells than other design algorithms (as seen in Example 16), the algorithm yields MOS networks with some very complex cells for some functions. For example, the MOS network for a 5-variable function designed by algorithm DIMN contains a cell where 4 MOSFETs are in series and 16 MOSFETs are in parallel.

6.2. Interactive Design

As discussed in Muroga,[1] complex cells are not desirable in terms of speed or chip area: roughly speaking, at most two MOSFETs can be connected in series for high-speed MOS networks; more (but at most several) MOSFETs can be connected in series for slower networks; and at most several MOSFETs can be connected in parallel for any speed. Thus, we need to design MOS networks, complying with the above circuit restrictions (i.e., the permissible number of MOSFETs connected in series or parallel, depending on the speed requirement). Of course we may have to give up the minimization of the number of MOS cells in a network to be designed.

In order to solve this problem, interactive methods have been developed. In other words, MOS networks designed by the algorithms described in Sections 3–5, displayed on a CRT screen, are interactively modified by the designer into those complying with the circuit restrictions, by breaking complex cells into simpler cells. The following interactive design approach has been developed.

Interactive Design Approach. The approach consists of three phases.

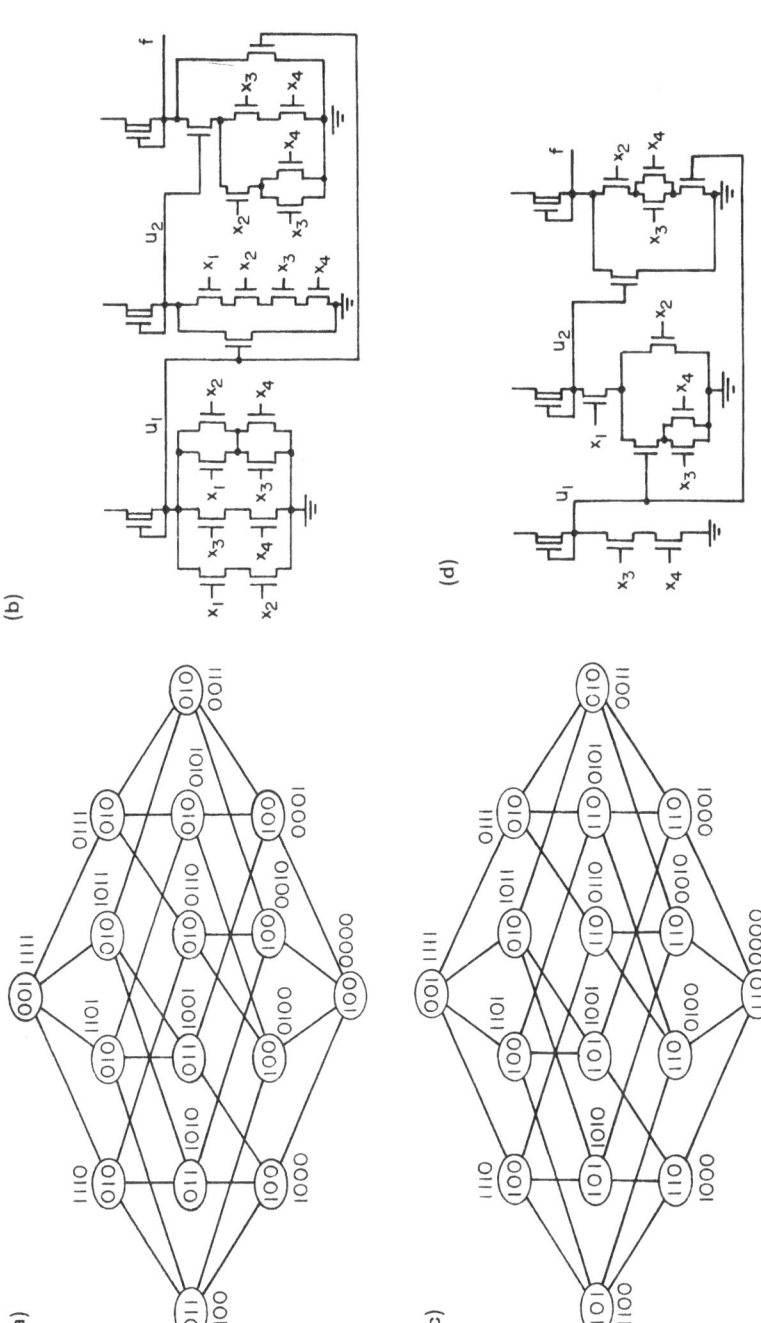

Fig. 18. Example 16 with $f = x_1(x_2 \oplus x_3 \oplus x_4)$. (a) NFS(3, f). (b) MOS network corresponding to (a). (c) NFS(3, f) by algorithm DIMN. (d) Irredundant MOS network corresponding to (c).

Phase 1. Design a network by algorithm DIMN (using the program of Yamamoto[16] or Yeh[17]). If any cell of the designed MOS network violates the circuit restrictions, go to Phase 2.

Phase 2. If we assign appropriate values to $\tilde{u}_i(A) = *$ instead of keeping $*$'s like the program of Yamamoto, then cells in later levels (corresponding to u_j's where $j > i$) may be simplified, complying with the circuit restrictions. There are many possibilities in assigning values to $\tilde{u}_i(A) = *$ for different A's in Step 5 of algorithm 7, and it is not easy to find efficient algorithms for assigning appropriate values. So we try to interactively assign appropriate values to $\tilde{u}_i(A)$'s for all i's and A's when $\tilde{u}_i(A) = *$, such that every cell satisfies the circuit restrictions.[19,20] If we succeed, we have obtained an MOS network which still has a minimum number of cells but not necessarily irredundant FETs, complying the circuit restrictions. If not, go to Phase 3.

Phase 3. We interactively further modify the MOS network by using additional MOS cells such that each cell complies with the circuit restrictions. One or more cells at a time in the MOS network which is displayed on a CRT screen is converted into simpler cells which comply with the circuit restrictions. The conversion can be done in either of the following two manners:

(i) One or more MOS cells is directly converted into simpler MOS cells.[19-21]

(ii) Each MOS cell in the network is converted into a subnetwork of AND, OR, NAND, and NOR gates (the NAND or NOR gate is used only as the output gate of the subnetwork). The new network consisting of these subnetworks are modified interactively, and then the final network is converted back into an MOS network.[19,22]

The AND, OR, NAND, and NOR gates in (ii) may be easier to manipulate than the MOS cells in (i), though MOS networks must be converted into and from those of these gate types.

7. CONCLUSION

In this chapter, design procedures of MOS networks with a minimum number of cells have been discussed. Especially those with irredundant MOSFETs in each cell and consequently with irredundant interconnections among cells (algorithm DIMN and its extensions) have been discussed in detail, along with their extensions in interactive design approaches. The interactive design approaches look promising since, generally, interactive design approaches yield logic networks of better quality than complete automation of logic design, as exemplified in Darringer *et al.*[23]

There are some other design procedures that are not along the lines of those outlined in this chapter, i.e., heuristic procedures without guaranteeing the minimality of the number of MOS cells (even in the beginning of design).[24,25] It is not known at this stage what advantages and disadvantages (e.g., in terms of design time, ease of use, or network qualities) these procedures have.

Logic design is still a time-consuming part of LSI or VLSI chip design, not to mention layout. (Automated layout is discussed by Shirakawa *et al.*,[26] for example, for a semi-regular-structured layout.) Its automation even in an interactive approach is strongly desired particularly for logic design of MOS networks. This is because if the capability of the MOS cell in representing a negative function that is much more complex than NOR or NAND gates is utilized to its fullest extent, compact networks can be designed, reducing chip-size—but it is time-consuming without the use of a computer.

REFERENCES

1. S. Muroga, *VLSI System Design*, Wiley, New York (1982).
2. S. Muroga, *Logic Design and Switching Theory*, Wiley, New York (1979).
3. T. Ibaraki, and S. Muroga, Synthesis of networks with a minimum number of negative gates, *IEEE Trans. Comput.* **C-20**(1), 49–58 (1971).
4. T. Ibaraki, Gate-interconnection minimization of switching networks using negative gates, *IEEE Trans. Comput.* **C-20**(6), 698–706 (1971).
5. K. Nakamura, N. Tokura, and T. Kasami, Minimal negative-gate networks, *IEEE Trans. Comput.* **C-21**(1), 5–11 (1972).
6. T. K. Liu, Synthesis of logic networks with MOS complex cells, Report UIUCDCS-R-72-517, Department of Computer Science, University of Illinois, Urbana, Ph.D. Dissertation (1972). Also *IEEE Trans. Comput.* **C-24**(1), 72–79 (1975); **C-26**(6), 581–588 (1977); **C-26**(8), 826–831 (1977).
7. K. Nakamura, Synthesis of gate minimum multioutput two-level negative-gate networks, *IEEE Trans. Comput.* **C-28**(10), 768–772 (1979).
8. H. C. Lai, A study of current logic design problems, Department of Computer Science, University of Illinois, Urbana, Ph.D. Dissertation (1976).
9. S. Muroga, *Threshold Logic and Its Applications*, Wiley, New York (1971).
10. E. N. Gilbert, Lattice theoretic properties of frontal switching functions, *J. Math. Phys.* **33**, 57–67 (1954).
11. A. A. Markov, On the inversion complexity of a system of functions, *J. ACM* **5**(4), 331–334 (1958).
12. D. E. Muller, Minimizing the number of NOT elements in combinational circuits, Memorandum, Bell Telephone Laboratories (1958).
13. E. L. Lawler, An approach to multilevel Boolean minimization, *J. ACM* **11**(3), 283–295 (1964).
14. Y. Moriwaki, Synthesis of minimum contact networks based on Boolean polynomials and its programming on a digital computer, *Rep. Inst. Ind. Sci., Univ. Tokyo* **21**(6) (1972).
15. K.-C. Hu, Logic design methods for irredundant MOS networks, Report No. UIUCDCS-R-80-1053, Department of Computer Science, University of Illinois, Urbana, Ph.D. Dissertation (1980).

16. K. Yamamoto, Design of irredundant MOS networks: A program manual for the design algorithm DIMN, Report No. UIUCDCS-R-76-784, Department of Computer Science, University of Illinois, Urbana (1976).

17. C.-C. Yeh, Design of irredundant multiple-level MOS networks for multiple-output and incompletely specified functions, Report No. UIUCDCS-R-77-896, Department of Computer Science, University of Illinois, Urbana (1977).

18. T. Shinozaki, Computer program for designing optimal networks with MOS gates, Report No. UIUCDCS-R-72-502, Department of Computer Science, University of Illinois, Urbana (1972).

19. K. Shimizu, and S. Muroga, Interactive logic design of MOS networks, Department of Computer Science, University of Illinois, Urbana, Preliminary Memo (1981).

20. N. S. Fiduccia, Logic design of MOS networks under complexity restrictions, Report No. UIUCDCS-R-82-1100, Department of Electrical Engineering, University of Illinois, Urbana, M.Sc. Thesis (1982).

21. J. N. Culliney, Topics in MOSFET network design, Report No. UIUCDCS-R-77-851, Department of Computer Science, University of Illinois, Urbana, Ph.D. Dissertation (1977).

22. K. Won, Interactive design of MOS networks by algorithm DIMN, Department of Computer Science, University of Illinois, Urbana, M.Sc. Thesis (1982).

23. J. A. Darringer, W. H. Joyner, Jr., C. L. Berman, and L. Trevillyan, Logic synthesis through local transformation, *IBM J. Res. Dev.* **25**(4), 272–280 (1981).

24. Y. M. El-Ziq, Logic design automation of MOS combinational networks with fan-in, fan-out constraints, *Proc. 15th DA Conf.*, 240–249 (1978).

25. Y. M. El-Ziq, and S. Y. C. Su, Computer-aided logic design of two-level MOS combinational networks with statistical results, *IEEE Trans. Comput.* **C-27**(10), 911–923 (1978).

26. I. Shirakawa, *et al.*, A layout system for the random logic portion of MOS LSI, *Proc. 17th DA Conf.*, 92–99 (1980); also, *IEEE Trans. Comput.* **C-30**(8), 572–581 (1981).

Index

A

Acceptor automaton, generation of, 284–285
Actions, MAP, SET, SYNTH, 266
After-image logging, 153
Algorithm CMNL, 320
Algorithm CMXL, 321
Algorithm complexity, 17
Algorithm DIMN, 325
Algorithm MNL, 294
Algorithm MPF, 322
Algorithm MXL, 299
Apex, 130
Arc categories, ACT, JUMP, POP, PUSH, 265
Array, 6
Automated logic design of MOS network, 287
Automaton construction, 274–276

B

Bachman's diagram, 106
Backus–Naur form of ITN, 264
Balanced tree, 159
Before-image logging, 153
Binding function, 186
Block buffering techniques, 169

C

Cluster, 298
Cluster based on MNL, 298

Clustered n-lattice, 298
Common descriptors, 231
Common pattern subsets, 232–233
Common values, 231
Complemented irredundant conjunctive form, 305
Complemented irredundant disjunctive form, 305
Complemented minimum products-of-sums form, 305
Complemented minimum sum-of-products form, 305
Concurrency, 150, 201
Constraints
  aggregate, 105
  domain, 67
  existential, 104
  interdomain, 69
  interrelation, 87
  into, 88
  intrarelation, 87
  onto, 88
  relationship, 89
  semantic, 63, 110

D

Data definition processor, 172
Data structure, 3
Database, 3, 20–23
  administrators, 187
  conceptual, 22
  directors, 171
  distribution, 154